Colin Bamford and Susan Grant

Cambridge International AS and A Level

Economics

Second edition

CAMBRIDGE
UNIVERSITY PRESS

CAMBRIDGE
UNIVERSITY PRESS

University Printing House, Cambridge CB2 8BS, United Kingdom

Cambridge University Press is part of the University of Cambridge.

It furthers the University's mission by disseminating knowledge in the pursuit of education, learning and research at the highest international levels of excellence.

www.cambridge.org
Information on this title: www.cambridge.org/9780521126656

© Cambridge University Press 2002, 2010

The authors and publishers are grateful to Keith Brunskill, Gordon Cain, Stephen Munday and Steve Tidball for permission to reproduce material from the first edition of Cambridge AS and A Level Economics.

First published 2002
Second edition 2010
9th printing 2014

Printed in Poland by Opolgraf

A catalogue record for this publication is available from the British Library

ISBN 978-0-521-12665-6 Paperback with CD-ROM for Windows and Mac

Contents

Preface

This second edition of *Cambridge International AS and A Level Economics* has been specifically produced for the Cambridge International Examinations (CIE) AS and A Level Economics syllabus (code 9708).

The text is divided into two clearly identified components, Core (AS Level) and Supplement (A Level), both of which are self-contained programmes of study. The Core component also serves as underpinning for students taking the A Level course.

This Coursebook and accompanying Student's CD-ROM have been written by two experienced teachers and authors who hold senior examining positions with Cambridge Assessment. The Coursebook and CD-ROM are the only ones that are officially endorsed by CIE in support of their examinations in Economics at this level. The course has the following important features:

- Each of the components explicitly follows the new CIE syllabus.
- There is an introductory chapter on the skills students need to study Economics in an effective way and a final chapter that gives valuable advice on how to succeed in examinations.
- Specimen questions from recent CIE examinations are reproduced at the end of each chapter.
- A large number of self-assessment tasks are included in the text. Most are new to this edition and are based on countries where students are taking the CIE examinations.
- Detailed answers to all the self-assessment tasks and exam practice questions are provided on the Student's CD-ROM.
- Each chapter contains key terms, including those specified in Section 4 of the CIE syllabus; these key terms and many others are defined in the glossary at the end of the book.
- A Teacher's Resource CD-ROM (ISBN 978-0-521-12664-9) is also available to accompany the course. It provides a wealth of additional practice materials including short-answer, multiple-choice, data response and essay questions (all with answers) as well as homework suggestions and schemes of work.

Although the book has been specifically produced for the CIE examinations, it will also be of value to students and teachers of other Economics examinations at these levels. It should particularly appeal to international students, given the emphasis on developing and newly emerging economies.

Finally, I would like to record some thanks. First, to my co-author, Susan Grant, for her comments on the draft text and for the production of the excellent CD-ROMs that accompany this edition. Secondly, to my colleagues who contributed to the first edition and who have allowed us to use some of the text they wrote. I should also like to thank my daughter Alice for help with word processing the text; my eldest daughter Emily, whose work in Africa gave me an excuse to get a first-hand insight into some of the problems facing this continent; and, finally, to my wife Elisabeth for her understanding and patience during the many hours I have spent on the computer.

Susan Grant and I hope that you find the course that we have produced useful and that it helps you achieve success in CIE Economics.

Colin G. Bamford
June 2010

Authors

Colin Bamford (Coursebook author)

Professor Colin Bamford is Associate Dean and Head of the Department of Logistics and Hospitality Management at the University of Huddersfield, UK. He has written various applied Economics textbooks and published widely in his specialist field of Transport Economics. He is currently Chief Examiner in Economics with OCR and has over 30 years' experience of examining CIE and UK AS and A Levels. He is the current President of the Economics and Business Enterprise Association.

Susan Grant (CD-ROM author)

Susan Grant is a Lecturer in Economics at Abingdon and Witney College. She has written more than 20 Economics books and is a Principal Examiner with CIE and OCR.

Introduction: the economist's toolkit and the CIE examinations

On completion of this introduction you should:

- have a broad idea of what is meant by Economics
- know how economists seek to explain economic phenomena
- be aware of the 'toolkit' of skills required for a study of Economics
- be aware of the requirements of the CIE Economics syllabus

What is Economics?

There are almost as many definitions of Economics as there are economists! Although a definition of the subject is to be expected, it is probably more useful at this stage to set out a few examples of the sort of issues which concern professional economists. These topics occur in an introductory form in the CIE Economics syllabus.

Let us take you first of all. Most people find that they want to lead an exciting and full life but unfortunately do not always have the money necessary to buy or to do all they want. So, choices have to be made, or as an economist would say, individuals have to decide:

- how to allocate their scarce resources in the most efficient way.

A body of economic principles and concepts has been developed to explain how people, and also businesses, behave in this situation. This is a typical example of what an economist would refer to as **microeconomics**.

It is not only individuals and firms who are faced with having to make choices. Governments face many such problems. For example, how does a country's government decide how much to spend on health or social security and how much should go into providing new roads and infrastructure for, say, tourism? This is the same type of problem facing all of us in our daily lives but on a different scale.

Governments also have extensive responsibilities in looking after the well-being of their national economies. The finance ministers, for example, prepare an annual budget for their economies, in which taxation and government expenditure plans are reviewed. It is also an opportunity to 'manage the economy' by seeking to ensure that policy objectives are being met. An economist would say that the finance ministers have to decide:

- how to keep the rate of change of prices (inflation) under control, or
- how to reflate the economy to increase the number of jobs that are available.

These are typical topics which come under the broad heading of **macroeconomics** since they relate to the economy as a whole.

As you read through this text you will come across many other economic problems and issues of both a micro and macro nature. You may now find it useful to complete self-assessment task 1 below.

SELF-ASSESSMENT TASK 1

1 Make a list, in your own words, of some of the economic decisions that:
   - you are facing
   - your family has to take
   - your country has to take.
2 Pick up any quality newspaper. Look through it systematically and make a note of the various
   - microeconomic
   - macroeconomic
   problems and issues you find.
   Did you find it easy to classify problems in this way?

The last part of the above task was designed to help you to appreciate that many economic problems and issues cannot be satisfactorily classified as micro or macro. In other words, such problems encompass both of the main branches of Economics. For example, an increase in taxation on petrol may reduce the demand for petrol. Depending on the extent of this, there is an effect on the income of individuals and the government and, in turn, this affects the economy as a whole. So, there can be complex interrelationships coming into play. This is one of the reasons that Economics is such an interesting subject to study.

As you read through this text, you will be introduced to concepts, theories and simple models which are used by economists to explain the many economic problems and issues that come within the scope of Economics. In time, you will build up a portfolio of such techniques, from a micro and macroeconomic perspective. Virtually all have their origin in some sort of practical investigation, i.e. a study of real economic phenomena. Some concepts have their origin centuries ago; others are much more contemporary or may have been refined and revised in the light of the growing complexity of the present-day global economy. Again, this serves to enhance the interesting nature of the study of Economics.

It is appropriate from the outset to attempt to give a clear definition of Economics. For a start, Economics is a social science – it adopts a scientific framework but is particularly concerned with studying the behaviour of humans as consumers, in business or in taking decisions about the economy as a whole. More specifically:

'Economics is the study of how scarce resources are or should be allocated.'

All of the problems and issues you will come across fit into this broad definition.

Regardless of what you may think about Economics and economists at this stage of your CIE studies, few would deny that Economics is a logical subject and that the advice provided by economists is derived from a set of well-established principles relating to the operation of the market economy. Figure 1 shows in simple terms how economists think and how they seek to explain real problems and issues like those you will have come across in the first self-assessment task.

At this stage, bear this process in mind and return to it whenever you are learning new concepts as it will help you understand how economists think and operate.

Economists cannot always be certain that what they say is completely accurate or how the advice they provide will affect an economy. Much of the content of this book consists of **positive statements** which are factual and usually acceptable to all economists. For example:

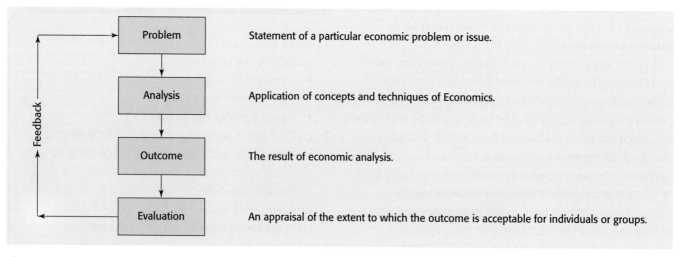

Figure 1 *The road to economic explanation*

- the inflation rate in 2009 was 2.5%
- the inflation rate of 2.5% in 2009 had little impact on business confidence at a time of global recession.

On other occasions, economists make **normative statements** involving value judgements. For example:

- the government should cut fuel tax to reduce the rate of inflation
- public sector workers should reduce their demands for higher wages.

These latter statements express an opinion about what ought to happen. Unlike positive statements, where economists can use data and practical evidence, normative statements involve value judgements which are often drawn from the economist's personal views, political beliefs and ethics. As you study the content of the chapters, keep this important distinction in mind. You will also need to think about it when answering some of the more demanding CIE A Level examination questions.

It is now appropriate to give a fuller definition of Economics. We have established that Economics is a social science. More specifically, it is the study of how society provides for itself by making the most efficient use of scare resources so that both private and social welfare may be improved. Economics provides a framework for studying how individuals, households, firms, governments and global organisations behave and take a wide range of decisions.

Interest in Economics has never been stronger than it is at present. From mid 2008, the global economy was thrown into the most serious recession in modern times. The effects of the downturn have been worldwide. Rich, poor and emerging economies have all been affected. In turn, there has been a profound impact on the lives and economic well-being of people throughout the world. Billionaires such as Warren Buffet and Bill Gates through to families surviving on subsistence incomes in the poorest parts of Africa have experienced some sort of effect.

The following article from *The Economist* looks at one fundamental effect of global recession, the collapse of manufacturing. It is very clear when you read this article that manufacturing industries across the world have suffered badly. In some cases they are unlikely ever to recover. When you have read and thought about the article, see if you can answer some of the self-assessment task that follows. If not, you will find it useful to refer back to it once you have acquired a better knowledge of the subject.

SELF-ASSESSMENT TASK 2

Read the feature below and answer the questions that follow.

The collapse of manufacturing

The financial crisis has created an industrial crisis. What should governments do about it?

$0.00, not counting fuel and handling: that is the cheapest quote right now if you want to ship a container from southern China to Europe. Back in the summer of 2007 the shipper would have charged $1400. Half-empty freighters are just one sign of a worldwide collapse in manufacturing. In Germany, December's machine-tool orders were 40% lower than a year earlier. Half of China's 9000 or so toy exporters have gone bust. Taiwan's shipments of notebook computers fell by a third in the month of January. The number of cars being assembled in America was 60% below January 2008.

The destructive global power of the financial crisis became clear last year. The immensity of the manufacturing crisis is still sinking in, largely because it is seen in national terms – indeed, often nationalistic ones. In fact manufacturing is also caught up in a global whirlwind.

Industrial production fell in the latest three months by 3.6% and 4.4% respectively in America and Britain (equivalent to annual declines of 13.8% and 16.4%). Some locals blame that on Wall Street and the City. But the collapse is much worse in countries more dependent on manufacturing exports, which have come to rely on consumers in debtor countries. Germany's industrial production in the fourth quarter fell by 6.8%; Taiwan's by 21.7%; Japan's by 12% – which helps to explain why GDP is falling even faster there than it did in the early 1990s. Industrial production is volatile, but the world has not seen a contraction like this since the first oil shock in the 1970s – and even that was not so widespread. Industry is collapsing in eastern Europe, as it is in Brazil, Malaysia and Turkey. Thousands of factories in southern China are now abandoned. Their workers went home to the countryside for the new year in January. Millions never came back.

Factories floored

Having bailed out the financial system, governments are now being called on to save industry, too. Next to scheming bankers, factory workers look positively deserving. Manufacturing is still a big employer and it tends to be a very visible one, concentrated in places like Detroit, Stuttgart and Guangzhou. The failure of a famous manufacturer like General Motors (GM) would be a severe blow to people's faith in their own prospects when a lack of confidence is already dragging down the economy. So surely it is right to give industry special support?

Despite manufacturing's woes, the answer is no. There are no painless choices, but industrial aid suffers from two big drawbacks. One is that government programmes, which are slow to design and amend, are too cumbersome to deal with the varied, constantly changing difficulties of the world's manufacturing industries. Part of the problem has been a drying-up of trade finance. Nobody knows how long that will last. Another part has come as firms have run down their inventories (in China some of these were stockpiles amassed before the Beijing Olympics). The inventory effect should be temporary, but, again nobody knows how big or lasting it will be.

The other drawback is that sectoral aid does not address the underlying cause of the crisis – a fall in demand, not just for manufactured goods, but for everything, because there is too much capacity (far too much in the car industry), some businesses must close however much aid the government pumps in. How can governments know which firms to save or the 'right' size of industry? That is for consumers to decide. Giving money to the industries with the loudest voices and cleverest lobbyists would be unjust and wasteful. Shifting demand to the fortunate sector that has won aid from the unfortunate one that has not will only exacerbate the upheaval. One country's preference for a given industry risks provoking a protectionist backlash abroad and will slow the long-run growth rate at home by locking up resources in inefficient firms.

Nothing to lose but their supply chains

Some say that manufacturing is special, because the rest of the economy depends on it. In fact, the economy is more like a network in which everything is connected to everything else, in which every producer is also a consumer. The important distinction is not between manufacturing and services, but between productive and unproductive jobs.

Some manufacturers accept that, but proceed immediately to another argument: that the current crisis is needlessly endangering productive, highly skilled manufacturing jobs. Nowadays each link in the supply chain depends on all the others. Carmakers cite GM's new Camaro, threatened after a firm that makes moulded-plastic parts went bankrupt. The car industry argues that the loss of GM itself would permanently wreck the North American supply chain. Aid, they say, can save good firms to fight another day.

Although some supply chains have choke points, that is a weak general argument for sectoral aid. As a rule, suppliers with several customers, and customers with several suppliers, should be more resilient than if they were a dependent captive of a large group. The evidence from China is that today's lack of demand creates the spare capacity that allows customers to find a new supplier quickly if theirs goes out of business. When that is hard, because a parts supplier is highly specialised, say, good management is likely to be more effective than state aid. The best firms monitor their vital suppliers closely and buy parts from more than one source, even if it costs money. In the extreme, firms can support vulnerable suppliers by helping them raise cash or by investing in them.

If sectoral aid is wasteful, why then save the banking system? Not for the sake of the bankers, certainly; nor because state aid will create an efficient financial industry. Even flawed bank rescues and stimulus plans, like the one Barack Obama signed into law this week, are aimed at the roots of the economy's problems: saving the banks, no matter how undeserving they are, is supposed to keep finance flowing to all firms; fiscal stimulus is supposed to lift demand across the board. As manufacturing collapses, governments should not fiddle with sectoral plans. Their proper task is broader but no less urgent: to get on with spending and with freeing up finance.

Source: The Economist, *21 February 2009*

1 What have been the causes of the collapse in global manufacturing?

2 Why might governments wish to support their manufacturing sectors?

3 Why does *The Economist* argue against such intervention?

The economist's toolkit

The economist has a varied toolkit, a term that can be used to describe the skills and techniques available for the analysis of economic problems. Two skills which are of particular relevance for the CIE examinations are:

- the ability to interpret and use data
- the ability to write in a clear and effective way.

Note: you may find it helpful to refer back to this section of the book intermittently when you are undertaking some of the self-assessment tasks. You should also refer back to this section before you take any of the CIE examinations.

Data skills

Five main skills are required in the CIE examinations. These skills are:

- the ability to pick out the main features in a data set
- how to calculate a simple average and know what it means
- a knowledge of trends and the rate of change in a set of time series data
- a working knowledge of index numbers

- how to interpret economic information produced in visual form.

In addition, you will find it useful to know how and why economists make forecasts.

It is important that you feel confident in handling data – these simple skills will help you. You will also gain confidence as you become more familiar with economic data and complete the various self-assessment tasks in each chapter.

Economic data are of two main types.

- **Time series data** As the name suggests, the same information is recorded over a period of time, namely a period of years, for months in a year, days in a week and so on.
- **Cross-sectional data** The easiest way to imagine this type of data is in terms of a 'snapshot', i.e. a picture taken at a given time.

Another important introductory point concerns the nature of the data itself. Again, two types can be recognised:

- **Discrete data** The simplest way to imagine this is in terms of values which are shown as whole numbers, e.g. number of people or number of cars.

- **Continuous data** Such values can usually be measured in a precise way and are not confined to whole numbers, e.g. income, inflation or economic growth.

So, when you are confronted with economic data for the first time, ask yourself:

- Is the data shown a time series or cross-sectional data?
- Are the values of the data discrete or continuous?

Below are three further matters to consider; these are also important when you come across a data set for the first time, particularly in the time-constrained examination situation.

- **Title and source of data** The title should give you a clear guide as to what the data is about. A lot of economic data is from governmental or other official sources such as the World Bank. This should mean that it is accurate, although this may not necessarily be so. If the data has come from other sources, be wary about what it shows – it may have been produced in such a way as to make a particular viewpoint.
- **Estimates** Some data will be an estimate that has been made by the organisation responsible for collecting the data. This is often necessary as there is invariably a time lag in producing more accurate information. In other instances if no data has been collected or it is difficult to collect data then the organisation will produce an estimate.
- **Forecast** Economists rely heavily on forecasts in order to take policy decisions (see page 9). Therefore, key economic variables are often forecasted in order to assist this process. Such data is likely to be reasonably accurate but should never be taken to be precise.

Data skill 1 – How to pick out the main features in a data set

Look at the data in Table 1. This gives the average unemployment rates for 14 euro area members.

Country	Percentage
Austria	4.0
Belgium	7.2
Czech Republic	6.8
Finland	6.6
France	8.3
Germany	7.8
Greece	7.8
Ireland	9.6
Italy	6.7
Luxembourg	5.1
Netherlands	3.9
Portugal	7.8
Slovenia	7.8
Spain	14.8
Average euro area	8.2

Table 1 *Euro area unemployment rates in January 2009*
Source: Eurostat, *2009*

The first skill you need to develop is what is known as 'eyeballing'. All this means is looking at a data set and going down the columns (or across the rows) very quickly to pick out the main features. This is a very useful thing to do, particularly in examinations when it could give you a clue as to what questions might follow.

Looking at Table 1, you can quickly see that there is a wide variation in average unemployment rates for euro area members in January 2009. Spain has the highest rate at around 15%, whereas unemployment was lowest in the Netherlands at less than 4%. For the two largest members, Germany and France, the average unemployment rate was just below and just above the euro area average.

The average of 8.2% shown is often used to summarise a particular set of data. In this case, it is what is known as a 'weighted average', the weights being the actual numbers of unemployed people in each of the 14 countries listed in Table 1. The weights are necessary since the populations of the countries are different. If they were all equal, the average would be the sum of all the percentages divided by 14.

The average, or mean, can be affected by extreme values. To some extent the use of weighting reduces this problem compared to a situation where all values have an equal weight.

Data skill 2 – How to pick out trends and the rate of change in a data set

Now look at the data in Table 2. This shows the annual percentage change in consumer prices and food and drink prices in Pakistan from 2000 to 2006. (As you will learn later the former is a good measure of inflation in an economy.)

This data set is a time series. You can get an overview of the data by looking at how it has changed on a year-to-year basis over the period.

	All items	Annual change	Food & drink	Annual change
2001	3.0		2.6	
		+		+
2002	3.7		3.2	
		+		+
2003	4.3		5.7	
		+		+
2004	9.8		12.2	
		−		−
2005	8.3		6.9	
		−		+
2006	7.4		10.5	

Table 2 *Average annual percentage change in consumer prices for high-income earners in Pakistan, 2001–2006*

Source: Pakistan Statistical Yearbook, *2008 (adapted)*

A closer look at Table 2 shows that:

- the annual percentage change in consumer prices is positive from 2001 to 2006
- it peaks in 2004
- food and drink prices are also rising on an annual basis, again with a peak in 2004
- there does not appear to be a clear relationship between the two sets of data.

For time series data like that in Table 2, you may find it useful to write a '+' or a '−' sign between each year, so that you can see how the rate of change varies over time. It is conventional to put these signs between the years in question. When you do this, you can see that the rate of change for 'all items' increased for the first three annual periods but then fell. The increase from 2003 to 2004 was particularly steep. The annual rate of change for food and drink prices followed a similar pattern except for 2005 to 2006 when it was positive.

A final word of warning. Consumer prices and food and drink prices have increased consistently since 2001. Inflation therefore has persisted, although in some years such as 2005 and 2006 the annual rate of change has fallen. This does not mean prices have fallen. It simply means that the annual rate of increase has slowed down. A common mistake that many students make when considering data like that in Table 2 is to wrongly assume that prices have fallen. This is not so.

Data skill 3 – A working knowledge of index numbers

With time series data especially, it is often helpful to show the data in index form, with a base year of 100. Thereafter, data for subsequent years is shown in the form of an index. This avoids some of the difficulties mentioned above when considering the rate of change in time series data.

To construct an index number:

- Identify a base year. This should be typical and is given an index of 100.
- Divide the base year data by 100. Use this figure to calculate an index number for each year of the data. For example, if a selection of goods bought in Pakistan cost 50 rupees in 2000 and 51.5 rupees in 2001, the respective indices will be as shown in Table 3.

When you do this, the data is transformed into what is shown in Table 3.

	All items	Food & drink
2000	100	100
2001	103.0	102.6
2002	106.8	105.9
2003	111.4	111.9
2004	121.4	125.5
2005	131.5	134.2
2006	141.2	148.3

Table 3 *Index of consumer prices for high-income earners in Pakistan, 2001–2006 (2000 = 100)*

An effective way of considering this form of data is to use a level and trend approach. Level is concerned with the difference between the start year and the final year. Trend refers to the year-to-year changes shown in Table 2 above.

So, the following additional points can now be made:

- Consumer prices rose by 41.2% over the period 2000 to 2006.
- Food and drink prices rose at above this rate for the period as a whole.
- Food and drink prices rose faster than the rate of inflation towards the end of the period, with the exception of 2005.

It could also be tentatively concluded that the effects of increasing food prices have not had too big an impact on high-income earners.

Data skill 4 – How to interpret economic information produced in a visual form

Increasingly, economic information is produced in a visual form in the media. Figure 2 contains two examples of bar charts. Such representations are particularly effective for mapping out time series data. The basic principle is that the height of each bar represents the data shown on the vertical scale, in this case, tourist arrivals in Mauritius.

The value of bar charts is that it is possible to see at a glance changes in the level and trend. Figure 2a shows the annual numbers of tourist arrivals over a ten-year period from 1998 to 2007. What is quite clear is that the level of tourist arrivals has steadily increased over this period. A closer examination shows that the annual change was greatest from 1999 to 2000 and from 2006 to 2007. Between these two periods, the annual change was reasonably consistent.

Figure 2b adds a further dimension, namely that for one year, 2007, it shows that there have been monthly variations in tourist arrivals, a point not immediately obvious from the annual data alone. Tourist arrivals peaked in December and were lowest in June. The actual arrivals can easily be read off the vertical scale.

Figure 3 is an example of a pie chart. The basic principle behind its construction is that the respective shares are shown by the relative sizes of the slices of the pie. These shares are determined by allocating 360° for the overall total – the share of each segment is then determined by the following formula:

$$\text{size of each segment} = \frac{\text{number in a given segment}}{\text{overall total}} \times 360°$$

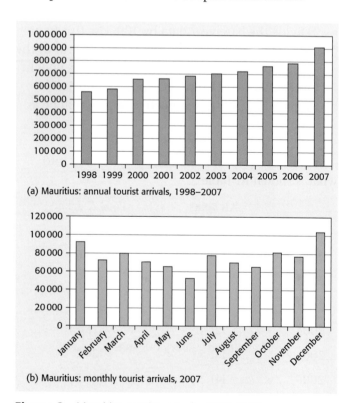

(a) Mauritius: annual tourist arrivals, 1998–2007

(b) Mauritius: monthly tourist arrivals, 2007

Figure 2   *Mauritius: tourist arrivals, 1998–2007*

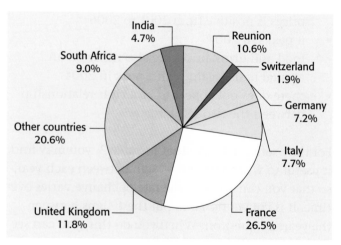

Figure 3   *Percentage distribution of tourist arrivals in Mauritius by country of residence, 2007*

So, for a total frequency of 200, a segment which has 50 observations in it will be represented by a 90° slice of pie.

Figure 3 shows the country of residence for tourist arrivals in Mauritius in 2007. As this shows, the largest percentage of tourists come from France. This percentage is over twice as large as arrivals for the second largest group by country, tourists from the UK. Very conveniently, Figure 3 shows the actual percentages in each segment. This is not always the case, but it is possible to make estimates from the relative sizes of each slice of the pie.

Students with access to Microsoft Excel will be able to produce a wide range of bar charts and pie charts with this software.

Newspapers and magazines such as *The Economist* increasingly represent economic information in highly attractive ways, combining various forms of representation. Figure 4 is a typical example.

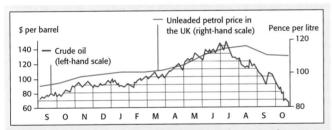

In October 2008 the Organization of the Petroleum Exporting Countries (OPEC) share of crude oil reserves was 78 per cent. On 24 October OPEC agreed to a cut in production of up to 3 million barrels of oil per day in a bid to halt the falling oil price.

Figure 4 *Oil – the crude facts: September 2007–October 2008*

Source: The Economist, *24 October 2008*

How and why economists make forecasts

One of the most important tasks of the professional economist, whether in government or private sector employment, is to be able to forecast future economic phenomena. Many economic variables are heavily dependent upon the state of the economy. For example, forecasts of economic growth are widely used by economists for all sorts of reasons related to economic policy and business well-being.

Study the information in Figure 4 and then answer the following questions.

1 a For the period September 2007 to October 2008 describe the trend in:
  - world crude oil prices
  - the price of unleaded petrol in the UK.

b What relationship (if any) can you see between these two variables?

c How is a 3 million barrels a day cut in OPEC's crude oil production likely to affect the world price?

d What might you deduce from Figure 4 about OPEC's success in determining the world price of fuel?

2 Study the information in Figure 5 and then answer the questions that follow.

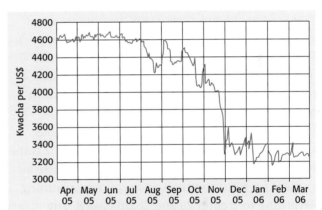

Figure 5 *Zambian exchange rate (kwacha per US$), April 2005–March 2006*

Source: Adapted from *CIE Economics 9708 paper 2, May/June 2008*

a Describe how the Zambian exchange rate has changed against the US dollar between April 2005 and March 2006.

b In which month did the greatest change take place?

c Over the period shown in Figure 5 (April 2005–March 2006), the Zambian exchange rate has appreciated against the US dollar. This means that people in Zambia needed to spend less of their own currency for each US dollar. How might this appreciation affect the economies of Zambia and the USA? (You may wish to return to this question later.)

Types of forecast

Economists use various types of forecasting method. These are the three main ones are:

- Statistical forecasts based on simple or complex future extrapolation techniques.
- Using models to produce a range of forecasts – this is particularly true of models of the economy involving complex interrelationships.
- Forecasts based on intuition, experience or even guesswork, i.e. not involving statistical methods.

Macro- and microeconomic forecasts

Finance ministers and other government officials find it essential to have estimates of projected variables such as the unemployment rate, inflation rate, balance of payments position and economic growth rate. These macroeconomic forecasts are required on a short-term basis (one year or less) or over a longer period of time. In the case of the unemployment rate, the importance of forecasting is shown in Figure 6.

This seems quite simple. In practice though the process is much more difficult and at stages 3 and 4 further assumptions are to be made with regard to other sources of revenue and taxation.

Microeconomic forecasts are not quite as obvious, but one example which develops out of Chapter 2 is the need to be able to make forecasts of demand. These are important for future business and economic planning.

Returning to Figures 2a and 2b on page 8, any business in the tourism sector has a need for a forecast of future numbers of tourists. This is by no means easy because of the many factors involved. We can get an idea of some of these from the general determinants of demand that are analysed in Chapter 2. They include:

- the average price of tourism in Mauritius
- the income of tourists
- the price of substitute destinations and the price of complements such as air travel

- a range of non-price factors that might determine whether tourists are attracted to Mauritius.

Looking at each of these factors, it is clear that a whole series of separate forecasts has to be made before an aggregate forecast can be made. These include:

- forecast inflation rates in Mauritius
- forecast economic growth rates in countries generating tourists for Mauritius
- forecasts of the costs of tourism in competing destinations and forecasts of the future cost of air travel
- alternative tourism destination and leisure options in the tourists' home market
- safety and security issues, health issues and so on, globally as well as in Mauritius.

As you can see, some of these are macroeconomic forecasts. So, in order to obtain what might appear to be a simple future estimate, access to a mass of other statistical information is required. It is for this reason that forecasts may not always be close to what actually occurs.

Forecasting over a longer time period is even more problematic due to the many uncertainties that are involved. An example of this is the forecast made in 2006, which is shown in Figure 7. Global recession in 2008–09, for example, could not have been foreseen. Revised forecasts would seem necessary. At best Figure 7 should be seen as providing a very broad indication of what might be the case in 2026.

How to write in a clear and effective way

It is beyond the scope of this book to include a lot of material in this part of the toolkit. However, much of the work of economists is communicated in a written manner, in books and newspaper articles in particular. For students, examinations in Economics

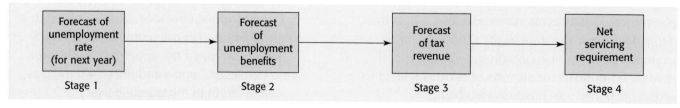

Figure 6 *Use of unemployment forecasts*

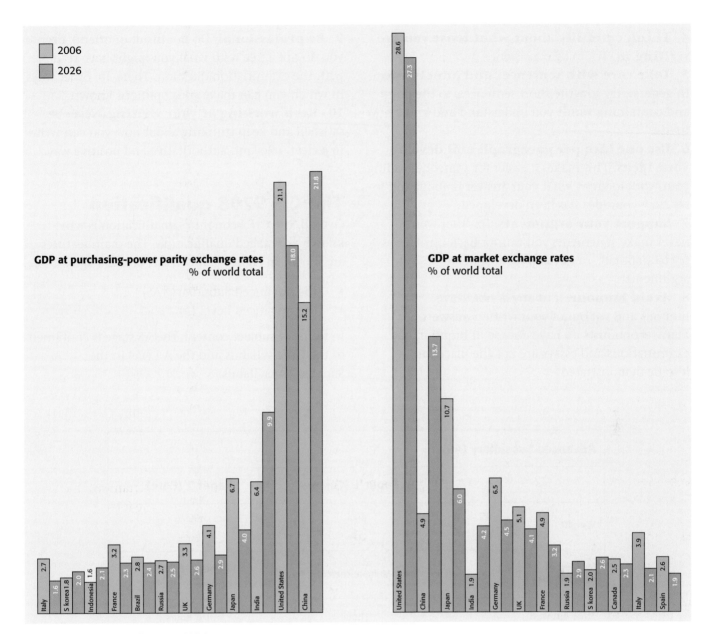

Figure 7 *Forecasts of GDP in 2026*

Source: Economist Intelligence Unit, 2005

require ideas to be communicated in a written form. The section on examination skills in Chapter 8 gives you very specific advice on how to impress examiners.

From a more general standpoint, you must always think about what you are writing and how you might improve your writing skills. You can enhance these skills by reading good newspapers, particularly if you read material which supports your A Level studies.

For the time being, you might like to think about the following Ten Tips for Budding Writers:

1 Be clear and precise in your writing. Use words you understand and when using technical terms, be specific. This is important because Economics has many terms which are very similar.

2 Remember to match your writing to your audience. In most cases this will be your teacher or a CIE examiner. They are likely to be older than you and will be looking to read material which is written in a relevant way and uses appropriate economic terms and concepts.

3 Write impersonally. In other words, do not use 'I' or 'we' in your written essays and examination answers. This applies particularly when you are asked to make an evaluation of an economic issue or argument.

4 Think carefully about what tense you are writing in. Try to be consistent.

5 Take care with sentences and punctuation. In general, try to write short sentences, to the point and containing words you understand and know how to use.

6 Use one idea per paragraph and develop your ideas. This makes it easier for someone reading your work to know what your answer is about and to see how your idea has been developed.

7 Support your arguments. In other words, never make statements you cannot back up. Always try to elaborate, or develop, your statements and arguments.

8 Avoid humour. If in any doubt, leave humour and wit out of your written answers. Many economists do have a sense of humour, but examinations and essays are not the place for it to be demonstrated.

9 Be professional. Do not insult or offend, even if you do not agree with what you might have read or with the examination question. There are other ways in which you can make your opinions known.

10 Keep working at your writing. Never be satisfied and keep thinking about how you can write in a clear, relevant, authoritative and positive way.

The CIE 9708 qualification

Overall, the CIE Economics qualification is what is known as a staged qualification. The main features are shown in Figure 8. It consists of two stages:

- the Advanced Subsidiary (AS)
- the Advanced Level (A).

In terms of subject content, the AS stage is contained in the Core syllabus and the A Level in the Supplement syllabus.

Advanced Subsidiary (AS)		Paper 1 (Core)	Paper 2 (Core)
Weight	AS	40%	60%
	A level	20%	30%
Method of assessment		Multiple-choice	Data response Structured essay
Time allowed		1 hour	1½ hours

Advanced Level (A)		Paper 3 (Supplement)	Paper 4 (Supplement)
Weight	A level	15%	35%
Method of assessment		Multiple-choice	Data response Essay
Time allowed		1 hour	2¼ hours

All of the question papers will be available in both June and November.

Figure 8 *CIE's Economics syllabus*

The AS is a recognised international qualification. Some students may decide that this is what they wish to study and finish their studies at the end of this stage. To complete the full A Level, you will have to take the two Supplement examinations in addition to the two AS examinations.

Chapter 8 provides important advice on examination skills and how to prepare for examinations. Do study this carefully before you take any of the examination papers.

As you work systematically through the Core and Supplement chapters, try to tackle all the self-assessment tasks. In this way you will become increasingly familiar with the content of Economics and the sort of assessments used by CIE.

So, good luck and welcome to CIE Economics!

Basic economic ideas
Core

On completion of this core section you should know:

- what is meant by scarcity and the inevitability of choices that have to be made by individuals, firms and governments
- what is meant by opportunity cost
- why the basic questions of what, how and for whom production takes place have to be addressed in all economies
- what is meant by factors of production, namely land, labour, capital and enterprise
- what is meant by the division of labour
- the characteristics of a production possibility curve
- how resources are allocated in market, planned and mixed economies
- problems of transition when central planning in an economy is reduced
- the difference between positive and normative statements in Economics
- the functions and characteristics of money.

One economic problem or many?

Economists have to deal with a whole range of economic problems. You may have seen TV programmes about the misery of unemployment and poverty; you may have read about the difficulties caused by inflation or heard politicians discuss exchange rate crises on the evening news. You may also be aware of debates surrounding issues such as the acute shortage of skilled labour, the benefits of greater liberalisation of international trade, the problems of global warming and the population explosion in many developing economies. Despite this extensive range of issues, which economists are trained to consider, they often talk about 'the economic problem'. This is the fundamental problem from which all others arise. This is the fact that we have scarce **resources** to satisfy our unlimited **wants**. As a result of this problem, which is sometimes called the problem of **scarcity**, we have to make a **choice**, and it is the task of the economist to explain and analyse the nature of choice facing economic agents, such as consumers, producers and governments.

The **economic problem** is: 'scarce resources in relation to unlimited wants'. This problem is summarised in Figure 1.1 (page 16). Because the basic

economic problem exists, societies need to confront the following three interrelated questions:

1 What to produce?

Because we cannot produce everything, we need to decide what to produce and in what quantities. We have to choose, for example, whether to produce lots of goods and services, such as food, clothing and vehicles, to improve our standard of living, or whether we need to produce lots of military hardware to improve our defences.

2 How to produce?

This question arises from the basic economic problem that, since resources are scarce in relation to unlimited wants, we need to consider how resources are used so that the best outcome arises. We need to consider how we can get the maximum use out of the resources available to us. It should be noted, however, that other issues besides purely economic concerns should be considered when deciding how to produce. It may be true, for example, that through slavery or forced labour we could produce more goods and services in an economy, but there is a moral objection to such arrangements. Similarly, crop yields could well be

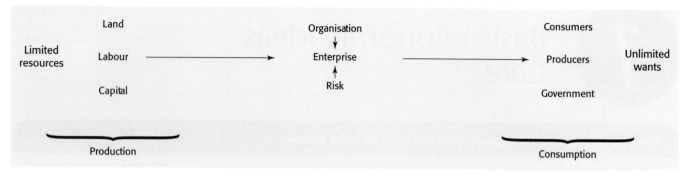

Figure 1.1 *Elements of the economic problem*

increased through the introduction of genetically modified plants but this may lead to damage to the ecosystem. The decision to maximise output and satisfy more wants would need to consider the full impact on the environment and any potential long-term health risks.

3 For whom to produce?

Because we cannot satisfy all the wants of all the population, decisions have to be taken concerning how many of each person's wants are to be satisfied. On a broad level we need to decide whether everyone is going to have a more or less equal share of what is produced or whether some will have more than others. In some economies there are deliberate attempts to create a more egalitarian society through policies that redistribute wealth and income from the rich to the poor. This could be achieved through

SELF-ASSESSMENT TASK 1.1

Read the feature below and then answer the questions that follow.

Survey on the economics of ageing: the luxury of longer life

In the world's rich countries, when you retire at 65 you can expect to live, on average, for another 15 or 20 years. A hundred years ago you would, on average, have been already dead. The late 20th century has brought to many the ultimate gift: the luxury of ageing. But like any luxury, ageing is expensive. Governments are fretting about the cost already, but they also know that far worse is to come. Over the next 30 or 40 years, the demographic changes of longer lives and fewer births will force most countries to rethink in fundamental ways their arrangements for paying for and looking after older people.

Thanks to state transfers, being old in many developed countries no longer means being poor. Old people expect decent pensions to live on; they will make heavier demands on medical

services; some will need expensive nursing care since younger relatives will be concerned about making the most of their own lives. At the same time, the number of people in work – who will have to foot the bill – will stay much the same. Consequently each worker will have to carry a much heavier burden.

Mass survival to a ripe old age will not be confined to rich countries. Most developing countries, whose populations are now much younger than the developed world's, are starting to age fast. This is particularly true for Caribbean economies such as Barbados as the population pyramids below indicate. The new combination of age and relative poverty will create many problems for such countries. These problems are already familiar to industrialised European countries and the USA. The problem for poorer countries is that they have fewer resources to draw on to tackle these pressures. In addition, ethical problems over the use of scarce resources will be magnified.

Source: The Economist, *27 January 1996 (adapted) and the* US Census Bureau, *2006*

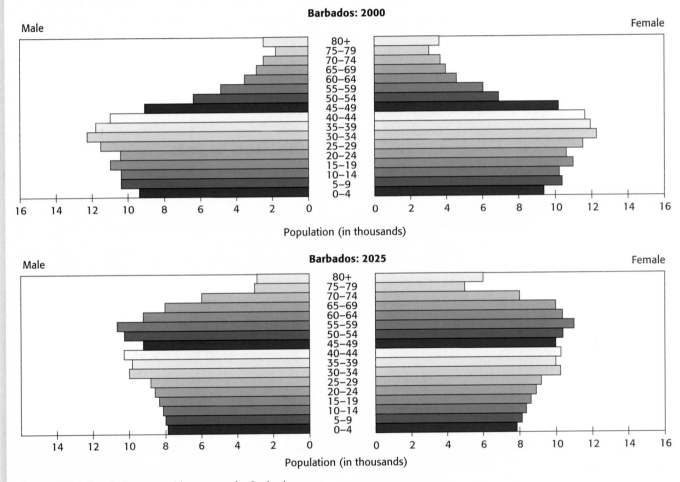

Figure 1.2 *Population pyramid summary for Barbados*

1 Summarise the projected changes in the population of Barbados from 2000 to 2025.
2 Discuss the likely effects of these changes on decisions concerning:
   a what to produce
   b how to produce
   c for whom to produce.
3 Comment on 'ethical problems over the use of scarce resources' facing the government of Barbados in meeting the needs of its changing population.

progressive taxation systems. In other economies there are no such policies and inequalities of wealth and income, usually based upon inheritance, remain extreme. In answering this question, moral aspects of decision making are again important.

Limited resources

In Economics we categorise the resources available to us into four types. These are known as **factors of production**:

1 **Land**   This factor is the natural resource. It includes the surface of the earth, lakes, rivers and forests. It also includes mineral deposits below the earth and the climate above.
2 **Labour**   This factor is the human resource, the basic determinant of which is the nation's population. Not all of the population are available to work, because some are above or below the working population age and some choose not to work.
3 **Capital**   This factor is any man-made aid to production. In this category we would include a simple spade and a complex car-assembly plant. **Capital** goods help **land** and **labour** produce more units of output – they improve the output from land and labour.

   These three factors are organised into units of production by firms.
4 **Enterprise (or entrepreneurship)**   This factor carries out two functions. Firstly, the **enterprise** factor organises the other three factors of production. Secondly, enterprise involves taking the **risk** of production, which exists in a free enterprise economy. Some firms are small with few resources. The functions of enterprise are undertaken by a single individual, the **entrepreneur**. In larger, more complex firms the functions are divided, with salaried managers organising the other factors and shareholders taking the risk.

Some economies have a large quantity of high-quality factors of production at their disposal. They can create lots of goods and services to satisfy the wants of their population. They are said to have a good **factor endowment**. Some economies lack sufficient quantities of one or more of the factors. Developing countries, for example, might have large quantities of land and labour but lack sufficient capital and enterprise. The former planned economies of Eastern Europe, such as Poland, have found it difficult to develop because they have few people with entrepreneurial experience.

Production and consumption

Resources are combined in the process of **production** to create goods and services. Goods and services have the capacity to satisfy wants. The process through which individuals use up goods and services to satisfy wants is known as **consumption**. Some goods, such as a chocolate bar, are quickly used up to satisfy our wants. Other things satisfy wants over a longer period. These are called consumer durables. Examples of consumer durables include television sets, refrigerators and vehicles.

Unlimited wants

We can all identify certain basic wants which must be satisfied if we are to stay alive. These include the obvious essentials of food, shelter and clothing. We might also identify those wants which are clearly less essential but which we think improve our quality of life. Some might include television sets, cars, trips to the cinema and so on. These are sometimes called luxuries, but it is important to remember that what might be a luxury for one individual may be considered an essential for others. This is because we all have a **scale of preference** with our more urgent wants at the top and the less urgent ones at the bottom. Each individual's scale of preference is a product of a complex set of influences, involving culture, upbringing and life experiences. These together influence our likes and dislikes. Unsurprisingly, since we all have different experiences, there is bound to be great variation between any two individuals' scales of preferences. You may find it interesting to conduct a class exercise in which everyone makes a list of ten wants in descending order of priority. When you compare results you may be surprised to find that, although there may be broad agreement on the first few choices, there is likely to be considerable variation as you compare people's choices over the full list. You may also consider how your list would compare to lists compiled by others with very different life experiences, such as your teacher, your grandparents or even a student of Economics in another country. A further point to consider is whether you could imagine any end to your list if you were not limited to ten choices. It is important to remember that our wants are continually expanding, developing and changing.

Some wants expand as we grow up, marry and raise a family. Imagine how our housing **needs** change as we go through this process or how we change from wanting a small car with two doors to wanting a large, family saloon with four doors. Some of our wants develop and expand when we see others around us enjoying goods and services and we feel the need to keep up. Sometimes our wants change as we have new experiences, for example we might decide to go on a diet because we have seen a TV programme about obesity.

All of this points to the fact that we can never imagine a time when all our wants are satisfied. Our wants are continually expanding and changing. Despite the fact that we are continually finding new, more efficient ways to produce more and more goods and services with the resources available to us, we are still faced with the basic economic problem that we have limited resources and unlimited wants. This is sometimes called the problem of scarcity. As a result we have to make choices.

The economic problem described above only occurs when we are dealing with what are known as **economic goods**. These are goods which have a cost in terms of the real resources used. They are therefore scarce in nature. The opposite are **free goods**, which have no price attached to them and which require no factors of production for their enjoyment by consumers. Consequently there are few examples, other than say wild berries, fruit and some animals that can be hunted for their meat by anyone who seeks to do so.

Specialisation and exchange

One of the ways in which more goods and services can be produced in the economy is through the process of **specialisation**. This refers to a situation where individuals and firms, regions and nations concentrate upon producing some goods and services rather than others. This can be clearly illustrated at the individual level. Within the family there may be some specialisation in the performance of household tasks, with one person doing the ironing and gardening while another does the shopping and cooking. At the workplace, of course, the fact that some people are labourers or lorry drivers while others have office jobs is also a reflection of specialisation. At this level, specialisation allows individuals to concentrate upon what they are best at and thus more goods and services will be produced. With specialisation, however, although more is produced, no one is self-sufficient. It becomes necessary to exchange goods and services. As an individual specialises they will produce a surplus beyond their needs, which they can exchange for the surpluses of others.

With the expansion of trade and the development of **markets**, the benefits of regional and national specialisation became apparent. Surpluses produced by regions and countries were bought and sold, allowing world living standards to rise. Just as individuals concentrated on what they were best at, so did regions and countries.

Specialisation has clearly resulted in a massive expansion in world living standards, but there are dangers too. Given the pace of technological change in modern society, there is always the possibility that the specialist skills and accumulated experience, which any individual has acquired, may become redundant as the economy develops. Individuals need to be flexible and multi-skilled and to be able to move between occupations. At regional and national levels, changes in consumers' wants can sometimes mean that the goods and services produced in a region or country are no longer required in the same quantity and unemployment can result. Policies then have to be adopted to deal with the economic and social problems that will arise. This issue will be looked at in depth in Chapter 7 Supplement.

The division of labour

With the technical advances of the last few hundred years, production of goods and services has happened on a much bigger scale. The concentration of large numbers of workers within very large production units allowed the process of production to be broken down into a series of tasks. This is called the **division of labour**. For example, **Adam Smith**, writing at the end of the eighteenth century, showed how the production of pins would benefit from the application

Read the feature below and answer the questions that follow.

Rich and miserable … or poor and happy?

It is often said that those who say that money can't buy you happiness simply don't know where to shop.

After all, spending money makes you happy, right? Wrong. According to economists it's a myth that the more we spend, the better we feel. The link between happiness and income/consumption is tenuous.

The West is much richer than it was 50 years ago, but:

- in the USA, reported 'happiness' has gone up only fractionally over this period
- in Europe, 'satisfaction with life' is actually lower than it was 20 years ago.

This is evidenced in a number of ways. For example:

- in rich countries, male suicide rates have gone up
- unemployment rates have increased – unhappiness is far more prevalent amongst the jobless.

According to Professor Andrew Oswald of Warwick University, money is to blame for this state of affairs. He argues that it buys very little well-being, yet everyone wants more of it. He says it is akin to the spectator who stands up at a football match to get a better view; by the time all of his neighbours are standing up, everybody is no better off than before.

Other economists agree:

- Yew Kwang Ng, a Chinese economist, has argued that the environmental costs of the additional production and consumption, 'to keep up with the Joneses', may make people worse off.
- Robert Frank, an American economist, argues that we would all be better off if we agreed to consume less. We could work less, meet other people more regularly and cut down on workplace commuting.

These arguments are unlikely to go down well in emerging economies. It is through growth that people become materially better off. It is surely wrong to deny these benefits to the populations of China, Malaysia, Mauritius, Pakistan, South Africa and so on … or is it better to learn from the mistakes made by countries such as the USA and many EU member states. If 'yes', then these economies and others should transfer more resources into things that make people happy such as better education, good health and a decent environment.

Source: The Guardian, *22 November 1997 (adapted)*

The article expresses the view that, through economic growth, people may actually be worse off.

1 What other examples can you think of which might support the views of these economists?

2 Do you see any conflict between these views and your understanding of the 'economic problem'?

of the division of labour in a factory. He suggested that pin making could be divided into 18 distinct operations and that, if each employee undertook only one of the operations, production would rise to 5000 pins per employee per day. This was compared to his estimate that each employee would be able to produce only a few dozen each day if they produced pins individually.

Although the division of labour raised output, it often created dissatisfaction in the workforce, who became bored with the monotonous nature of their task. In the United States the process was taken a stage further in the 1920s when Henry Ford introduced conveyor belt production into the car industry. Ford's method of car production provided the model for much of manufacturing production in the twentieth century. In more recent times the de-humanising impact of production techniques, such as those using a conveyor belt, have been recognised and alternative methods of production have been introduced.

Choice and opportunity cost

Given limited resources and unlimited wants we have to choose which wants to satisfy. The true cost of any choice we make between alternatives is expressed by economists through the notion of **opportunity cost**. This looks at the cost of our choice in terms of the next best alternative forgone. For example, suppose you were given a $15.00 gift voucher for your birthday. You could either buy a new compact disc which costs $15.00 or two paperback books for $7.50 each. It is clear that you could not have the CD and the books. The opportunity cost of the CD, therefore, is the two paperback books. The value of the concept of opportunity cost is that it brings home to us the real cost of our choices. It can be applied in a variety of contexts in Economics and is helpful for economic decision-makers, such as households, firms and governments.

Production possibility curves

How many goods and services an economy is capable of producing is determined by the quantity and quality of resources available to it, together with the state of technical knowledge. These factors determine an economy's production possibilities.

Example: an imaginary economy, given its available resources, can produce either military goods or consumer goods or a combination of each. The various possibilities are shown in Table 1.1.

Military goods	Consumer goods
10 000	0
8 000	4 000
6 000	8 000
4 000	12 000
2 000	16 000
0	20 000

Table 1.1 *Production possibility schedule 1*

It is sometimes useful to illustrate the choices open to an economy by considering the **production possibility curve**. From the schedule in Table 1.1 we can produce a production possibility curve with military goods plotted on the vertical axis and consumer goods on the horizontal axis.

Figure 1.3 shows all possible combinations of military goods and consumer goods which could be produced given the existing quantity and quality of resources in our imaginary economy and the existing state of technical knowledge. At point *a*, only military goods are produced, and, at point *d*, only consumer goods are produced, but between these two extremes lie all the other possibilities. The term production possibility curve emphasises that this shows what levels of output an economy can achieve with its existing resources. It can also be used to show what the economy is not able to achieve. Point *Y* on the graph represents a combination of military and consumer goods which it is not possible to achieve. It is beyond our production possibilities. Sometimes

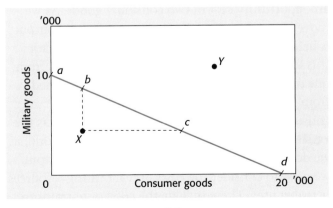

Figure 1.3 *A production possibility curve*

21

the curve is called a **production frontier** because it draws the boundary between what can and cannot be achieved.

Figure 1.3 is also useful in illustrating the real cost to society of unemployed resources. The point *X* on the diagram represents a production of 4000 military goods and 3000 consumer goods. This is possible to achieve because it is within the production frontier, but it represents a point where some resources are unemployed or not employed effectively. The economy is capable of moving to point *b* with more military goods and the same number of consumer goods or to point *c*, which would bring more consumer goods and the same quantity of military goods. Alternatively, at a point between *b* and *c*, the economy can have more of both types of goods. Looking at the diagram in this way illustrates the waste from unemployed resources. We are not satisfying as many of our wants as possible.

A further alternative name for the production possibility curve is the **product transformation curve**. This emphasises a further use for the concept in introductory Economics. In Figure 1.3 as the economy moves along the curve from point *a* through to point *d* then a different combination of goods is being chosen. More consumer goods are being produced and fewer military goods. This emphasises that the cost of producing more consumer goods is the military goods which have to be sacrificed. Given the figures, we can calculate the opportunity cost of consumer goods in terms of military goods. A move from *b* to *c* on the graph leads to a gain of 8000 consumer goods but we sacrifice 4000 military goods. The opportunity cost of one consumer good is therefore half of a military good. This is equivalent to one military good having an opportunity cost of two consumer goods. As we move along the curve the composition of our output is being transformed. We should also note that for this to happen we need to switch our resources from one use to another. Resources have to be switched from producing military goods to producing consumer goods and vice versa. This is known as the **reallocation of resources** and in the real world, as we decide to change the composition of our output, we need to consider the costs of reallocating resources between uses. These include the costs of re-training the workforce in the skills required to produce

different types of goods and services. This might take a long time and might only be possible as new entrants to the labour force are trained in new skills. The extent to which resources can be reallocated from one line of production to another is known as **factor mobility** and, if we want resources to be swiftly allocated to the new use, we have to ensure that factors are as mobile as possible.

It should be noted, in our example, that the opportunity cost of military goods in terms of consumer goods has not changed because we have chosen different combinations of the two goods. This is in fact quite unrealistic. A more likely outcome is that the production possibility curve will illustrate increasing costs. Consider the production possibility schedule in Table 1.2, which shows the quantities of agricultural goods and manufactured goods that can be produced in an economy given existing resources and state of technology.

Agricultural products	Manufactured products
700	0
660	100
600	200
500	300
300	400
0	500

Table 1.2 *Production possibility schedule 2*

Assume that initially the economy is producing at point *p* with 660 agricultural products and 100 manufactured products (see Figure 1.4). Then assume that it is decided to move to point *q* to gain an extra 100 units of manufactured products. Clearly, resources need to be reallocated from agricultural use to manufacturing. At first the least fertile land will be reallocated and only 60 units of agricultural produce will be sacrificed. This means that each extra consumer good has cost 0.6 of an agricultural good. Now compare this with a movement from *r* to *s*, to gain an extra 100 manufactured goods we have to sacrifice 200 agricultural goods. This means that one extra manufactured good has cost two agricultural goods. The cost has increased as we have reallocated our resources. This is because at this stage we are

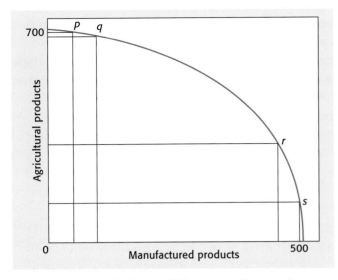

Figure 1.4 *A production possibility curve with increasing costs*

switching the more fertile land into manufactured good production so that agricultural output is going to be affected to a much greater extent. This diagram illustrates a production possibility curve with increasing costs.

Shifts in production possibility curves

A production possibility curve is drawn on the assumption that the quantity and quality of resources and the state of technology are fixed. Through time, of course, economies can gain or lose resources; the quality of resources and the state of technical knowledge can change. Such changes will shift the production possibility curve to a new position. Figure 1.5 illustrates the outcomes of changes in the quantity and quality of resources and changes in technology.

Figure 1.5a shows a situation in which the production possibilities available to an economy have expanded. This is known as **economic growth**. This could be due to an increase in the quantity and/ or the quality of resources available to the economy or an improvement in the state of technology. Here the changes have improved the economy's ability to produce both agricultural and manufactured products. In Figure 1.5b, however, only the ability to produce agricultural products has been improved. This could perhaps be because there has been a technological breakthrough in producing agricultural products, which does not apply to the production of manufactured products. Nevertheless, this economy's production possibilities have improved and the curve has shifted outwards from the origin.

The production possibilities could also have declined. This could be because in some way the resources available to the economy have declined. Perhaps some of the economy's natural resources have become exhausted or the working population is falling. It might also be because the available technology has changed. An example might be the impact of controls on global emissions, which will affect production possibilities as controls become more rigorous.

Making use of production possibility curves

We can use production possibility curves to illustrate some of the issues facing economic decision makers in the real world.

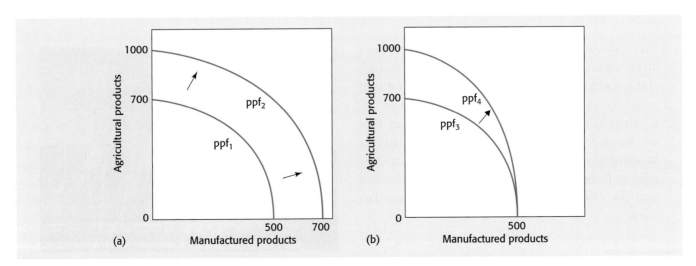

Figure 1.5 *Shifts in production possibility curves*

23

Jam today or more jam tomorrow?

As stated previously, the production possibilities open to an economy are determined by the quantity and quality of resources available. In the process of production, resources are used up and they need to be replaced if production possibilities are to be maintained. The terms **capital consumption** or depreciation describe the using up of capital goods during the process of production. Some resources need to be devoted to the production of capital goods if production possibilities are to be maintained. The creation of capital goods in the process of production is known as **investment**.

This can be defined as 'any production not for current consumption'. A choice has to be made therefore between producing consumer goods and services or producing capital goods through the process of investment. The more consumer goods and services produced, the higher the current standard of living, but the standard of living might fall in the future if there is a failure to produce sufficient capital goods to replace those worn out in the process of production. In addition, the quality of an economy's capital goods will not be improved and the full benefits of new technology will not be enjoyed if there is a failure to devote sufficient resources to investment.

Figure 1.6 shows the production possibilities between capital goods and consumer goods.

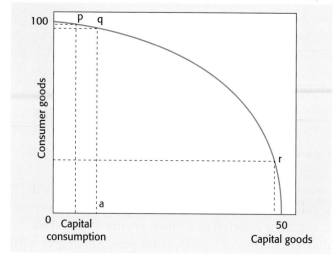

Figure 1.6 *The choice between consumer goods and capital goods*

SELF-ASSESSMENT TASK 1.3

Read the feature below and then answer the questions that follow.

Sweet dreams: high oil prices means sugar could be used as a fuel source

The Caribbean sugar industry is suddenly looking sweet again after years of decline. That's because it is a source of ethanol, the alternative fuel that some see as an answer to rocketing oil prices.

Ethanol, a cleaner-burning alternative fuel that can be made from corn or sugar cane, is also drawing renewed government interest and was a key topic for leaders from Central America, Mexico, Colombia and the Dominican Republic when they met last week.

Markets for ethanol are growing due to the insatiable demand for fuel and increasing demand for alternative energy sources. However, Caribbean sugar is particularly attractive because of the region's preferential trade access to the US market.

In the Dominican province of Monte Plata, a consortium led by the Belgium based Alcogroup has announced plans to build an ethanol plant, while the Dominican sugar co-operative says it is in talks with other partners to convert at least one sugar mill into an ethanol distillery.

'People are sort of tripping over one another to put up the mills,' said Lester Lave, an economics professor at Carnegie Mellon University in Pittsburgh, Pennsylvania, who studies alternative fuels. In Jamaica, Aracatu, a company based in Brazil, one of the world's leading ethanol producers, sought to buy out the struggling state-owned Sugar Corporation of Jamaica so it could enter the UK market without paying tariffs under a regional free-trade agreement.

Brazil has also announced plans to advise other countries, including Haiti and Guatemala, on producing the fuel.

'In the next ten to 15 years, ethanol will be the king of fuels,' said Juan Antonio Japa, general manager of the Dominican Republic's national sugar cooperative.

This wave of interest comes just as sugar production was fading fast throughout the Caribbean, with growers turning to other crops and sending fewer machete-wielding workers into the cane fields. The industry has fallen on hard times because of free trade deals and competition from cheaper sources of sugar such as Brazil.

Source: Caribbean Times, *23 June 2006 (adapted)*

1 Sketch a production possibility curve (PPC) to show the choices that are now facing Caribbean sugar farmers.
2 On your diagram show how a reduction in sugar cane production for food and rum products from 80% to 50% of total production affects the amount that is going to produce ethanol. Use the concept of opportunity cost to explain this trade-off.
3 Modify your diagram to show how the PPC changes due to:
 • better cultivation methods that result in more sugar cane being produced
 • the damaging effects of a tornado that result in less sugar cane being produced.
4 On your diagram, show and explain points where production is efficient and inefficient.

These possibilities are determined by the quantity and quality of resources in the economy, which include the capital goods that have been produced in the past. If we assume that the quantity of capital goods which are wearing out in each time period is shown at *a*, then we can see the consequences of our choices. If we fail to produce the quantity at *a* then our capital stock will decline. Production possibilities will diminish and the curve will shift to the left.

Hard choices for developing economies
Developing economies are characterised by low standards of living. If they are to grow then they need to increase their capital stock. Like all economies they need to divert resources from current consumption to investment. Some resources must be devoted to consumption, however, to keep their expanding populations alive.

We refer to this as the subsistence level of consumption. The difficulty is that in the poorest developing economies almost all their production possibilities need to be devoted to subsistence.

In Figure 1.7, *0–a* represents the capital consumption in a **developing economy** and *0–b* represents the consumer goods required for the subsistence of the population.

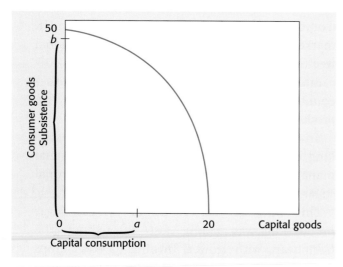

Figure 1.7 *Capital consumption in a developing economy*

SELF-ASSESSMENT TASK 1.4

Explain the choices facing decision-makers in the developing economy shown in Figure 1.7. Discuss the difficulties they face and suggest possible solutions to their problems.

A hydroelectric power station in Africa

Economic structure

The term **economic structure** refers to the way in which an economy consists of various sectors. It is used to show the balance of economic activity, usually measured in terms of the value of total output, between these sectors. The following sectors are recognised:

• **Primary sector** This consists of agriculture, fishing and activities such as mining and oil extraction.

• **Secondary sector** This term is used to describe the wide range of manufacturing activities that are found in an economy. Typical examples are: food processing, textiles and clothing, iron and steel production, vehicle manufacturing, and electronics.

• **Tertiary sector** This is the service sector and covers a range of diverse activities such as retailing, transport, financial services, education, call centre services and information technology.

As economies develop, their economic structure changes – there is a progression from primary to secondary to tertiary activities. In developed economies, the tertiary sector tends to be the principal employer. In the UK, for example, in 2008 around four out of every five people in employment were employed in the tertiary sector. This is not the case in less developed economies. In Tanzania and Kenya, by way of contrast, similar proportions of workers are employed in the primary sector alone.

Different allocative mechanisms

The problem of scarcity, which in turn requires choices to be made, is one that is common to all economies, rich and poor. The choices that are made and which can realistically be made in turn are determined by the **economic system** of a particular country. This term is used to describe the means or allocative mechanism by which its people, businesses and government make choices. Traditionally, economists have recognised three distinct types of economic system – these are the **market economy**, the **command** or **planned economy** and the **mixed economy**. Let us briefly consider each in turn.

The market economy

In a market economy decisions on how resources are to be allocated are usually taken by millions of households and thousands of firms – the exact number will of course depend on the size of economy. The key point is that they interact as buyers and sellers in the market for goods and services. Prices and the operation of the price system underpin this interaction; in turn, prices act to indicate the likely market value of particular resources. For example, a commodity in short supply but which has a high demand attached to it will have a high price.

SELF-ASSESSMENT TASK 1.5

	India		Pakistan	
	Total output (%)	Labour force (%)	Total output (%)	Labour force (%)
Agriculture	17.2	60	20.4	43.0
Industry	29.1	12	26.6	20.3
Services	53.7	28	53.0	36.6

Table 1.3 *The economic structures of India and Pakistan in 2008*

1 Using the information in Table 1.3 compare the economic structure of Pakistan with that of India.

2 In which country:

   a is agriculture more efficient?

   b are services more efficient?

3 Explain how you have arrived at your answers.

4 Discuss whether countries such as Pakistan and India might be concerned if a large proportion of the labour force got new employment in industry or in the service sector (such as call centres).

A call centre in India

Alternatively, one which has a high supply and low demand will have a much lower price attached to it. Prices and the self-interest of people and businesses therefore act as a guide to the decisions that have to be taken.

Economics as a subject has its origin in the notion that prices and the **market mechanism** are the 'best' way of handling economic problems. This notion can be particularly attributed to the Scottish economist Adam Smith, who is remembered for his reference to an 'invisible hand' (the price system) that brings together private and social interests in an harmonious way. This is the fundamental philosophy underpinning the workings of the market economy.

The government has a very restricted part to play in a market economy. For example, in Smith's view, it should control national defence, act against monopolies, issue money, raise taxes and so on whilst protecting the rights of the private sector. It certainly should not try to influence the dealings of individuals in the market or to regulate the workings of that market. Figure 1.8 is a simple representation of these functions.

Before moving on, it must be made clear that the market economy is an ideal which does not exist in today's complex, globalised economy. Arguably, its most important representation is the United States

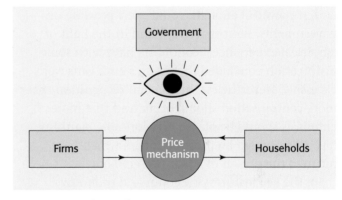

Figure 1.8 *The market economy*

of America (USA), and it should be stressed that here federal and state governments play important roles in the economy and society, as well as in providing defence, law and order and other public services.

The command economy

Like the market economy, the command or centrally planned economy in its purest form exists only in theory. In this second type of economy, the government has a central role in all decisions that are made and, unlike the market economy, the emphasis is on centralisation. Central planning boards and organisations make decisions in enterprises that are state-owned or under state regulation and control. Whereas in a market economy consumer sovereignty influences resource allocation, in a command economy, it is central planners who determine the collective preferences of consumers and manufacturing enterprises.

The planned economies of the last 50 years or so have their economic logic in the Marxian criticism of the market economy. This particular objection was essentially one of class conflict between the wealthy owners of capital and the poor working classes who provided this wealth through the production process. Marx was also critical of the built-in unemployment arising out of the market system. For example, he had observed the trend to replace labour with machines (capital) and the inability of labour to secure higher wages. Under a command economy, unemployment is not an issue. Marx was also very concerned about the way in which the market economy fostered the concentration of productive resources in the hands of large monopolistic industrial and commercial organisations. As such he maintained that they corrupted the workings of demand and supply and, if powerful enough, could exert pressure on governments. Retrospectively, and in the light of empirical experience, economists have with some justification concluded that Marx's criticisms were excessive. Nevertheless, his general recognition that more centralisation should occur and that more emphasis should be placed on economic planning has been applied by those countries which have pursued the notion of a planned economy.

So, the key features of a command economy are that central government and its constituent organisations take responsibility for:

- the allocation of resources
- the determination of production targets for all sectors of the economy
- the distribution of income and the determination of wages
- the ownership of most productive resources and property
- planning the long-term growth of the economy.

From a practical standpoint, some of these decisions have to be decentralised, either geographically or by sector, to other government organisations. In certain cases, these bodies have control over the workings of a limited market mechanism. A good example of this is where basic foodstuffs such as bread and meat are heavily subsidised to keep prices at a fixed level and so exempt consumers from the price fluctuations which are so commonplace in the market economy. Artificially low prices result in excess demand relative to supply – queuing becomes a way of life. Also from a practical standpoint it is very difficult for all enterprise to be state-owned – there has to be a limited opportunity for the private ownership of small businesses such as shops, restaurants and personal services like hairdressing and cleaning. For more substantive businesses, ownership is often on a shared basis between the state and the private sector. This often involves foreign investors who are keen to exploit the opportunities of an emerging market economy.

Queuing for bread

The outcome of the command economy is that central planning tends to set goals for the economy that differ from those of the market economy. In particular they have a clear objective of achieving as high a rate of economic growth as possible in order to 'catch up' on the progress being made by much more advanced market economies. The command economy is more correctly described as one of sacrificing current consumption and standards of living in order to achieve enhanced future well-being. This is the sacrifice that has to be made by the present generation for the benefit of future generations.

The last point can be illustrated by returning to the production possibility curve. Figure 1.9 indicates that the economy can choose between capital goods or consumer goods. The former represent an investment in machinery, equipment, infrastructure, technology and so on which will in time increase the

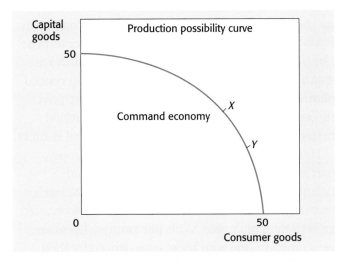

Figure 1.9 *Command economies' production possibilities*

productive capacity in the economy. Consumer goods like cars, refrigerators and televisions are for current consumption. In making this choice, command economies have chosen to produce at point *X* on their production possibility curve rather than at point *Y*, where consumer needs are satisfied in full.

This is, of course, a highly simplified representation of what in reality is a very complex process of centralised decision making. The extent to which economies choose *X* rather than *Y* also varies, depending on the degree to which the economy sees growth as its first and only economic objective.

The mixed economy

It is clear from the brief analysis of market and command economies that, in the 'pure' sense, these types of economic systems occur in theory and not in reality. In contrast, the mixed economy is undoubtedly the characteristic form of economic organisation within the global economy. As its name indicates, it involves both private and public sectors in the process of resource allocation. Consequently, decisions on most important economic issues involve some form of planning (by private as well as public enterprises) and interaction between government, businesses and labour through the market mechanism. Private ownership of productive resources operates alongside public ownership in many mixed economies, although, increasingly, the trend is towards the privatisation of certain activities that were once in public sector hands.

The best example of this is undoubtedly the UK economy in the mid-1970s when the public and private sectors were of broadly equal importance. At this time the government was responsible for:

- substantial areas of public expenditure such as health care, social services, education and defence
- the direct operation of nationalised industries, such as coal, iron and steel, railways, gas, water, telephones and electricity
- providing support for large areas of manufacturing, such as vehicle production, aerospace and electronics, in partnership with the private sector.

Over the past 30 years, the strength of the public sector in the UK has been substantially reduced, not only through privatisation but also through a policy of non-intervention when private companies experience financial difficulties in their markets. Controversially, in the last few years, governments have made little or no attempt to stem the demise of car manufacturing in the UK as, one by one, former British-owned companies have been rationalised by their non-UK owners.

The modern view of recent UK governments, both Conservative and Labour, is that their responsibilities are for the overall management of the macroeconomy and for the funding of particular public and **merit goods** which overall would be underconsumed if left to the private sector alone to provide. Merit goods are goods, such as health care and education, which have positive externalities associated with them and where there is likely to be underconsumption without government intervention. It is also the case that new forms of regulation and control have had to be introduced in order to protect consumers from possible exploitation by the private sector providers of essential services. A very popular outcome of the UK experience is that millions more people now hold shares in such businesses.

Elsewhere, there have been similar trends. One of the most dramatic has been the restructuring of the economy of the former Soviet Union (*perestroika* as it is sometimes called). Under President Gorbachev's reforms, small private businesses could be set up in the service sector (for example cafés, retail shops, garages and taxi hire) and workers could form their own co-operatives to market and sell surplus production from monolithic state manufacturing companies.

The US economy is also an example of a mixed economy, somewhat contrary to common perception. For example:

- the government at all levels is an important employer and provides basic services, such as education and various types of medical care
- government agencies regulate and control the provision of some essential services, such as energy, telecommunications and transportation
- indirect support is given to various strategically important companies.

These are over and above the expected provision of external defence and internal security services.

It is not easy to explain the importance of a government's role in any particular mixed economy. In most cases the only real explanation is that it is usually a case of differing political philosophies. Figure 1.10 provides a largely normative assessment of where particular economies fall in terms of the relative strengths of market and planned systems of resource allocation. In all cases, except arguably for North Korea, countries are moving towards giving the market mechanism an ever-increasing role in their economic structures.

In more recent times, the experience of the newly industrialising countries (NICs) is interesting. In terms of allocative mechanisms, some, such as Singapore and Hong Kong, opted for a strong focus on the market to allocate resources and through this have created an economic situation where enterprise can be encouraged and rewarded. Other South East Asian 'Tigers' have placed more emphasis on central planning, whilst China's phenomenal growth over the last decade has been based on the controlled management of the economy within a global context.

The new **Tiger economies** of central Europe, particularly the Czech Republic, Hungary and Poland, have re-orientated their economies to foreign investors. In this way, they hope to achieve forecasted growth rates of around 5–7% per annum. These are very much in line with those experienced by their Asian counterparts, yet significantly higher than those experienced in the past by more developed economies.

Central Hong Kong

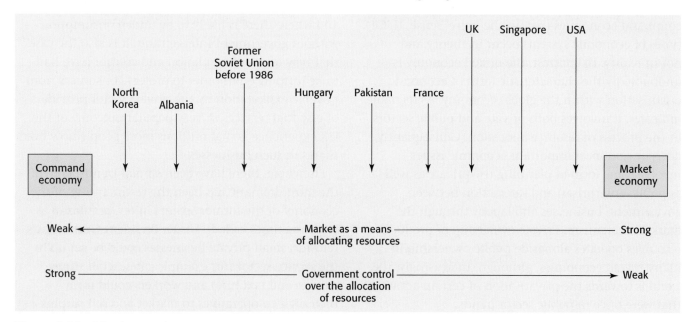

Figure 1.10 *Mixed economic systems*

1 Think carefully about the ways in which your own economy allocates resources. Make a few notes on the ways in which:
- the government
- the market mechanism

are responsible for decision making.

2 Use the above information to insert your own economy into the scale shown in Figure 1.10. How has its relative position changed in recent years?

3 What information might an economist use to quantify the relative importance of the government and the market mechanism within an economy?

Problems of transition when central planning in an economy is reduced

Basic principles

As explained above, most developing economies have a strong foundation based on the model of a centrally planned economy. Over the past 20 years most have recognised the benefits for the economy when less activity is controlled by the government and when competitive markets and the private sector have an increasing role to play. Internationally, this approach is consistent with that of the World Bank which, as part of its policy to promote development, encourages such economic reforms.

Figure 1.11 (page 32) shows two diagrams which represent the general position of a centrally planned economy before reform and the situation once changes have been introduced. The labels at the bottom of each diagram generally summarise the state of affairs. The direction and relative size of the arrows are important – these show the relationships between the different sectors and the strength of their importance. In promoting economic development and in the allocation of funding, the World Bank seeks to ensure that recipient countries are implementing the processes of economic reform shown in this figure.

Positive and normative economics

It is useful now to make a distinction between **positive** and **normative economics**. Economics is a social science. As such it has developed through using positive analysis that is devoid of any **value judgements.** Typical positive statements include the following:

- A fall in supply of petrol will lead to an increase in its price …
- An increase in tourist numbers in the Maldives will create more employment …
- An increase in taxation on cigarettes will result in fewer cigarettes being sold …

These are statements of what will happen. No value judgements are involved. When values come into the analysis, then this is normative economics. Here an opinion or value judgement is being made. The above statements can become normative, for example, by adding:

- … and this should be positive for the environment.
- … and therefore the government of the Republic of Maldives should do everything it can to help.
- … and this should improve the nation's health.

1 Assume that an economy undergoes the process of reform shown in Figure 1.11.
  a Give an example of an organisation which will disappear with a move to competitive markets.
  b Give an additional source of revenue for the government.
  c Give a source of expenditure for the government which is no longer appropriate.

2 Briefly describe how the roles of government and the private sector will change after the implementation of economic reforms.

3 Discuss the extent to which it is appropriate for your country to adopt the market-based system shown in the lower part of the diagram.

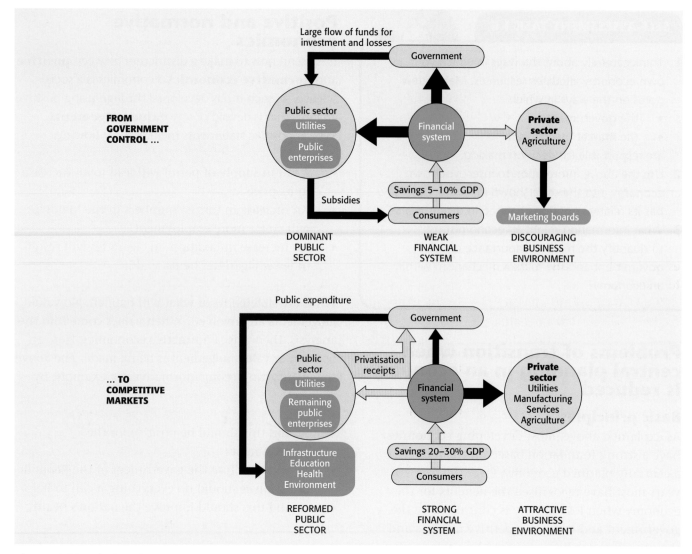

Figure 1.11 *The broad process of economic reform*

Source: World Bank, 1995 (adapted)

Money: its functions and characteristics

In some respects money is something that virtually all of us take for granted. We need it in order to carry out our daily lives, to pay for things such as riding on a bus, purchasing a bottle of water or soft drink, buying lunch and so on. Handing over a few coins or a note is essential if we are to be able to buy what we want to satisfy our day-to-day needs. Larger sums, of course, are required for things such as clothes, shoes, cars and even school fees.

The money which we use for purchases is usually a national currency such as dollars, pounds or rupees (in Mauritius and Pakistan for example). For 16 EU member states the supranational euro has been in general use since 2002. The coins and notes have little or no intrinsic value – their value stems directly from the fact that sellers have complete confidence in the money given to them that prompts them to exchange it for the products we want to buy.

So what is money? A simple definition is that it is anything that is regularly used to buy goods and services. Normally, this is coins and notes but the definition also includes **cheques**, debit cards and credit cards. To be acceptable from a day-to-day practical standpoint, money must also be portable and durable. However, money can also be in the form of a valuable commodity such as gold or platinum. In Russia, for example, oil has been widely exchanged for imports such as buses and trucks from Hungary or agricultural goods from Poland.

Where there is hyperinflation, as in Zimbabwe in recent years, people lose confidence in money. Many farm workers, for instance, have preferred to be paid in produce as this will keep its value and can be easily swapped for other things such as cooking oil, sugar or bread. The direct exchange of one good or service for another in this way is known as **barter**. Where this is the only way of exchange, then the process of trade and exchange becomes lengthy and difficult. It is also very impractical since there must be a **coincidence of wants**, whereby both parties in a transaction actually have the goods or services that the other wants. Money is therefore essential if the processes of exchange and trade are to take place.

Zimbabwe's descent into economic catastrophe has been a long drawn-out affair. Following a drop in agricultural production after controversial land seizures, exports fell and foreign investors went elsewhere. The government sought to solve its **liquidity** problems by borrowing from foreign banks, knowing that it could not meet its loan repayments. The government made the situation worse by printing more money, much of which was used to pay the army, police and civil servants. Eventually, inflation reached more than one million per cent and local people lost all confidence in the Zimbabwean dollar.

Ten million dollar note from Zimbabwe

Bearing the above in mind, economists recognise the following four essential functions of money:

- A **medium of exchange** Money is the 'medium', or form, that buyers use for purchases; sellers are willing to accept this medium in exchange for these purchases. By handing over money physically, or by transferring money electronically through the banking system, this is a common, automatic acceptance of money fulfilling this function.

- A **unit of account** Prices are quoted in terms of common monetary units. For instance, in the USA dollars and cents are used, while in Pakistan rupees and paise are used. This function is of relevance for current and future transactions since it is quite clear just how much money is required for a particular transaction. It also allows different values to be added, measured and compared. Where money is borrowed, then the lender usually requires **interest** to be paid for this privilege. The 'account' aspect allows the sum of money to be recorded and for different values to be added or compared.

- A **standard for deferred payment** Not all payments we make are immediate. Some household bills are paid monthly, others may be paid annually. Following on from money as a unit of account, payments can be made in the future once terms have been agreed between the parties involved.

- A **store of wealth** Money can be held or 'stored' for a period of time, usually with a bank or other financial institution, before it is used. This important function means that money is a **measure of value** over time. Where this value is accumulated, then it represents a source of wealth to its owner. In 2008, the two richest people in the world were both from the USA: Warren Buffet and Bill Gates. Their personal wealth was in a wide range of assets, not just in bank accounts. Money was the common basis on which their wealth was estimated.

These functions of money are vital for the smooth operation of all economies. If any of the functions breaks down, as in the case of Zimbabwe where money lost all meaning as a store of value or wealth, economic collapse is the inevitable outcome. It is therefore essential that a prudent government puts economic policies in place to ensure that this does not happen.

PRACTICE QUESTIONS

On completion of this chapter you should be able to attempt the following short-answer questions.

1 a Define the following terms:

    i scarcity   [2]

    ii opportunity cost.   [2]

b Draw a 'production possibility frontier' diagram to illustrate increasing opportunity cost.   [2]

[6 marks]

2 a Copy the production possibility frontier diagram shown in Figure 1.12 and indicate the following:

    • an inefficient production point   [2]

    • a production point that is unattainable.   [2]

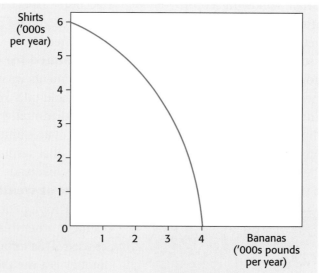

Figure 1.12 *Production possibility frontier*

b What is the additional cost, in shirts, of increasing the production of bananas from **1000** pounds per year to **2000** pounds per year?   [2]

[6 marks]

3 a State **one** reason why it is necessary to make economic choices.   [1]

b State **three** major questions that must be asked when deciding what goods and services should be produced.   [3]

c Susan uses the two hours available to her to answer her email rather than study for her Economics examination. What is the cost to her of choosing to read her emails rather than study for her Economics examination? Briefly explain your answer.   [2]

[6 marks]

4 a Use the information in the following table to construct a production possibility frontier (PPF). [3]

Pineapples	Mangoes
0	500
200	450
350	350
425	275
475	125
500	0

b Mark the point (300,300) on your diagram. [1]

c State why this point does not represent an efficient use of resources. [1]

d What does the shape of the PPF you have drawn say about the opportunity costs of producing **one** more unit of pineapples or mangoes? [1]

[6 marks]

SUMMARY

In this core section it has been shown that:

- All economies face the so-called economic problem of limited resources and unlimited wants.
- Choice is necessary in order to decide what to produce, how to produce and for whom to produce.
- Factors of production (land, labour, capital and enterprise) are essential for the production process.
- Specialisation allows more goods and services to be produced. Money facilitates specialisation and exchange.
- The true cost of choices we have to make is known as opportunity cost.
- A production possibility curve is a representation of what can be produced in an economy and the trade-offs involved in making choices.
- There are various types of economic system for the allocation of resources; the mixed economy is typical.
- There are problems of transition when former centrally planned economics move to mixed economies.
- Money has four functions that are essential for the smooth operation of any economy.

1 Basic economic ideas
Supplement

On completion of this supplement section you should know:

- what economists mean by an efficient or optimum allocation of resources
- what is meant by economic efficiency and how this can be looked at in terms of productive and allocative efficiency
- the relationship between competition and economic efficiency.

Introduction

The fundamental economic problem was considered earlier in the core section. In essence, this was explained as the difficulty of having limited or scarce resources with which we wish to do an infinite number of things. In turn, this leads us to having to make economic choices.

The basic concept of **economic efficiency** stems from this fundamental economic problem. Economic efficiency is said to exist when it could be judged that all of our scarce resources were being used in the 'best' possible way. This means that the greatest possible level of infinite wants is being met with those scarce resources. Economic efficiency is therefore an important basic concept in Economics. It is something that is always judged to be desirable. It represents the best possible solution to the economic problem. As you will see, it pervades many of the topics that follow, both microeconomic and macroeconomic.

The purpose of this short section is to develop this important concept. In particular, it will introduce the two different parts of economic efficiency.

The two parts of economic efficiency

Two things are required if economic efficiency can be said to exist:

- **Productive efficiency** Products must be made with the least possible use of scarce resources. To put it another way, goods and services must be produced with the least-cost methods available.

- **Allocative efficiency** The products that are most wanted must be produced. Those goods and services that lead to the greatest possible satisfaction of our infinite wants are those that should be made.

Only when both these parts of efficiency co-exist can it be judged that the best possible use is being made of our scarce resources. This, therefore, constitutes a situation of **optimum allocation of resources**.

This idea of economic efficiency can be looked at from a global perspective. Economic efficiency is achieved when economies are using all of the world's resources in the best possible way. We frequently hear concerns that, as a global society, we are failing to do this. This point is very clearly made in Chapter 4 where the use of protectionist trade policies by the US, and to a lesser extent the EU, are considered. We have to conclude that global economic efficiency is not being achieved.

A few simple examples will help to explain the concept of global economic efficiency:

- **Oil** The global supply of oil will one day run out, although just when this will happen is not clear. Consumption continues to increase not only in developed economies but increasingly in developing and emerging economies such as China, India and Pakistan. Growing populations, rising living standards and rocketing car ownership levels are just three reasons behind this increase in demand. Here and elsewhere though the use of oil is invariably inefficient; much is wasted through traffic congestion, the use of gas-guzzling vehicles and the inefficient use of oil and oil products in manufacturing.

- **Timber**   The world demand for timber and timber products such as paper and cardboard shows little sign of abating. By the start of this century, only about one-fifth of the world's forests remained intact, with the worst destruction being that of the Amazonian rain forests and other forests in the Congo Basin, Canada and South East Asia. The negative externalities (external costs associated with the consumption of goods) of this destruction are overlooked by the large, powerful global companies who control the sale of timber and pulp on the world market.

- **Water**   As the global population grows and the effects of climate change become reality, water as a resource will get scarcer and be a major political issue. This is already beginning to occur in those countries that share natural water resources. Scant attention is often paid in developed countries as to how a more efficient use can be made of this essential resource.

Productive efficiency

We now know that for productive efficiency to exist products must be made using the least possible resources or incurring the lowest possible cost of production. Productive efficiency can be shown through a firm's cost curves. This is illustrated in Figure 1.13.

Here, we can see that there are two parts to lowest cost production. First, production must take place on the lowest possible average cost curve (AC^3). Secondly, production needs to occur at the lowest point on that lowest cost curve (point X on the diagram). This second condition is known as 'technical' efficiency. The lowest point on a firm's average cost curve is, therefore, a point of technical efficiency.

The production possibility curve, which was introduced in the core section of this chapter, may help to clarify productive efficiency. This curve shows the maximum production points for combinations of any two products (e.g. capital goods and consumer goods produced in an economy). Given this, it must be true that productive efficiency can only

exist when an economy is producing right on the boundary of its production possibility frontier as in Figure 1.14.

The problem with point X is that more products could be made with the resources available. In other words, the goods are not being produced using the least possible resources: this is productive inefficiency. At point Y, it is not possible to produce any more because of the scarce resources that are available to an economy. The minimum possible resources are being used to make the products. This is thus a point of productive efficiency.

Competition can be seen to lead to productive efficiency. In general terms, this is the case as firms are constrained to produce at the lowest possible cost

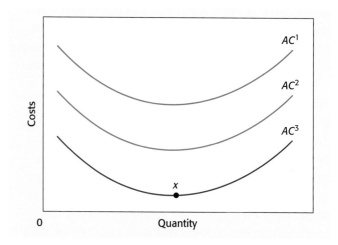

Figure 1.13   *Productive efficiency*

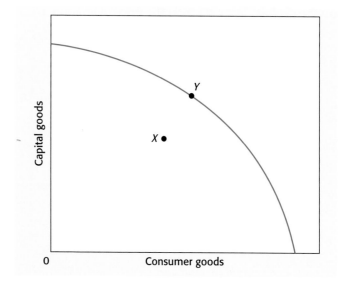

Figure 1.14   *Productive efficiency in an economy*

in a competitive market. Firms have the incentive of profit to make their products at the lowest possible cost: the lower the cost, the greater the possible profit. Alternatively, a failure to produce at the lowest possible cost in a competitive market may lead to bankruptcy for a firm. As rivals will produce at lowest cost, the price for the firm that has failed to minimise costs will be too high and thus there will be low demand.

More specifically, it can be seen that perfect competition leads to the necessary conditions for productive efficiency (see Chapter 2 for details of perfect competition), as shown in Figure 1.15.

The point of long run equilibrium for a perfectly competitive firm is given by price p and output q. At this point, it can be seen that the firm is producing at the lowest point on its average cost curve. This implies that there is technical efficiency. Given that the competition in this market will also constrain firms to be producing on their lowest possible average cost curve, then this point is productively efficient.

Allocative efficiency

It is not enough for products to be produced at the lowest possible cost. The right products must also be produced if there is to be economic efficiency. Allocative efficiency is all to do with allocating the right amount of scarce resources to the production of the right products. This means producing the combination of products that will yield the greatest possible level of satisfaction of consumer wants.

As stated earlier, the point of allocative efficiency can be deemed to exist when the price of a product is equal to its marginal cost of production. In this situation, the price paid by the consumer will represent the true economic cost of producing the last unit of the product. This should ensure that precisely the right amount of the product is produced. This idea can be illustrated through the following simple example:

Quantity	1	2	3	4	5	6	7
Price ($)		5	5	5	5	5	5	5
Marginal cost ($)		2	3	4	5	6	7	8

For this product, an output of one unit would not be productively efficient. Here, the cost of producing the product is less than the value put on it by the consumer (as represented by the price that the consumer is willing to pay for that product). The product should certainly be produced, but there is scope for further worthwhile production from this point. This is also true when two or three units of the product are made. On the other hand, an output of seven units of the product should not be produced. Here, the seventh unit costs $8 to produce but is only valued at $5 by the consumer. The same problem exists with output levels of five and six. Thus, there is only one ideal output level (that is, one output level that will yield allocative efficiency) and that is an output of four units where price is equal to the marginal cost.

It should be noted that, unlike productive efficiency, it is not possible to illustrate allocative efficiency on the production possibility frontier. Any point on the frontier could potentially be such a point. The exact location will depend upon consumer preferences and these are not indicated on this model.

A competitive market can lead to allocative efficiency. In such a market, firms are constrained to produce those products that consumers most desire relative to their cost of production. As with productive efficiency, there are two motivations. First, the desire to make the greatest possible profit will drive firms to produce such products and will lead to the highest possible demand and hence the greatest revenue and profits. Secondly, firms in competitive markets will be forced to produce those products most demanded by consumers as other firms will certainly also do so. A failure to produce such products in this sort of market will force firms to close.

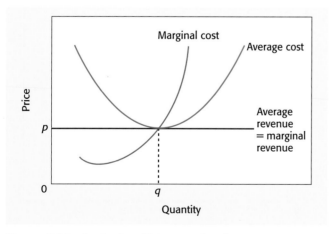

Figure 1.15 *Productive efficiency and perfect competition*

An alternative way to consider how a competitive market will achieve allocative efficiency is through the perfectly competitive diagram as shown in Figure 1.15. It can be seen that the point of equilibrium in this diagram (price p and output q) is a position at which price is equal to marginal cost. This is the technical requirement to give allocative efficiency as explained above.

The suggestion is thus made that in fully (or perfectly) competitive markets there will be economic efficiency. Both productive and allocative efficiency will exist.

SPECIMEN EXAM QUESTIONS

1 Explain what type of efficiency each of the following might lead towards.
   a A firm uses a new machine that costs less than the old one but produces more.
   b A company swaps production to a different product that sells at the same price but is in greater demand.
   c A car plant makes 1000 workers redundant because their jobs can now be done by robots that cost less over a period of time than paying workers' wages.
   d Following privatisation, firms in an industry have to change what they produce in order to make a profit.

2 The use of the internet has allowed consumers to purchase products from all over the world in a way that was not previously possible. It has been seen that this has greatly increased the level of competition faced by firms in different markets as they now have to compete directly in a global market. Discuss the ways in which this development could lead to greater economic efficiency in world markets.

SUMMARY

In this supplement section it has been shown that:

- Efficiency is a fundamental concept in Economics relating to how well scarce resources are allocated.
- There are two parts to economic efficiency. Productive efficiency is achieved when firms produce at the lowest possible point on their lowest cost curve. Allocative efficiency is when the price of a product is equal to its marginal cost of production. Both these forms of efficiency must exist if there is to be economic efficiency.
- Competition can lead to both productive and allocative efficiency. A perfectly competitive market is the only one where this is achieved.

2 The price system
Core

Introduction

Consider these newspaper headlines:

'Price hike sends gold demand to 6 year low' (*Daily Telegraph*, UK, 20 August 2009)

'Fear of food riots as surge in demand hits nations across the Far East' (*The Times*, UK, 8 April 2009)

'Abdullah to flood market with cooking oil to allay shortage fears' (*South China Morning Post*, 9 January 2008)

'Crash of tea market takes fortunes with it' (*International Herald Tribune*, 10–11 January 2009)

The **price mechanism** underpins each of these particular events. It does so within the context of a **market**. In terms of the above headlines, the markets involved are:

- the global market for gold
- the market for rice in many countries in South East Asia
- the market for cooking oil in Malaysia
- a specialist tea market in a region of China.

These are just a few examples of markets. We will look at some of these examples later once you have learned about how markets work.

To many people a market is something that happens in the town or city centre once or twice a week. It is characterised by a large number of traders setting up stalls to sell a whole range of products: food – such as fruit, vegetables, fish; clothing; and a wide selection of other items. Economists, however, take a broader view of the word 'market'. The essence of any market is trade – somebody has something to sell and somebody else wants to buy the product that is offered. So, whenever people come together for the purposes of exchange or trade, we have a market.

For example, economists talk about the housing market, where people buy and sell houses. Look in the newspapers or in the windows of property agents' offices and you will see evidence of this market. They also refer to the labour market, where individuals' labour power is 'bought and sold' – if any of you have part-time or full-time jobs, you have participated in the labour market as a seller of labour.

The television newsreaders often refer to the stock market, where shares are bought and sold, and the foreign exchange market, where currencies are bought and sold.

These examples indicate that to an economist a market does not have to have a clearly defined physical presence as the typical town or street market might have. It is simply a term used to describe the process through which products that are similar are bought and sold.

SELF-ASSESSMENT TASK 2.1

How do you participate in the following markets?

1 The fast food market.
2 The telecommunications market.
3 The transport market.

Demand

To an economist:

> **demand** refers to the *quantities of a product that purchasers are willing and able to buy at various prices per period of time, all other things being equal.*

Definitions are of critical importance in Economics, so let us break this definition down to understand in some depth what it means.

- **Quantities**   Economists often deal with numerical values and very often try to represent information in a quantitative way. This point is reinforced by using the term 'prices'.
- **Product**   This is a general term that simply refers to the item that is being traded. It can be used for goods or services. We could also stretch this to include tradable items like money or other financial assets such as shares.
- **Purchasers**   These are the buyers of the product and are often referred to as 'consumers', although they may simply be intermediaries in the production–consumption chain, e.g. Nestlé purchasing large amounts of cocoa to be used in the production of chocolate for sale to the

final consumer. We could look at an individual purchaser's demand for a product or, more usefully, we can aggregate this to look at the demand of an overall market.

- **Willing to buy**   Clearly purchasers must want a product if they are going to enter into the market to buy it.
- **Able to buy**   To an economist, the notional demand for a product, which emerges from wanting it, must be backed by purchasing power if the demand is to become **effective demand**. Companies are only willing to sell a product if the purchaser has monetary ability to pay for the product – the world is full of wishful thinkers who would love to own something they just cannot afford. It is, however, effective demand that is of real importance for economists.
- **Various prices**   Prices are crucial to the functioning of a market. Although many things influence demand for a product, it is at the moment of purchase, when we have to hand over our money and pay the price, that we really judge whether the product is value for money – in other words, whether we really are willing and able to buy it. As the price goes up, and provided no other changes have occurred, more and more people will judge the product to be less worthwhile.
- **Per period of time**   Demand must be time related. It is of no use to say that the local McDonalds sold 20 Big Macs to consumers unless you specify the time period over which the sales occurred. If that was per minute then demand is probably quite high, but if that was per week then clearly there is little demand for Big Macs in this particular market.
- **Other things being equal**   We will see shortly that there are numerous potential influences on the demand for a product. Analysing the connections between the various elements is very difficult if many of these elements are changing simultaneously. So, for simplicity, we start with the assumption that all the other factors influencing demand are constant and analyse the response of purchasers on the basis that price alone changes. This is sometimes referred to as the *ceteris paribus* assumption.

The demand curve

Let us now take the definition of demand and represent it diagrammatically to construct a **demand curve**. We will make up an example based on the overall **market demand** for computers (PCs) to illustrate the point. Let us assume that we can identify a typical PC, i.e. one with a set of standard specifications. Let us also assume that we have collected statistical data about people's preferences and that the quantity of PCs that people are willing and able to buy at various prices per period of time, other things being equal, can be represented by the data in Table 2.1. This is known as a **demand schedule**. We can now plot the market demand schedule on a graph to see how the quantity demanded of PCs relates to variations in price. This demand curve therefore represents the aggregation of many individual demand curves. Figure 2.1 shows the market demand curve for the data in Table 2.1.

PCs have a consistent market demand

Price of a 'standard' PC ($)	Quantity demanded per week – demand curve D_0
2000	1000
1800	2000
1600	3000
1400	4000
1200	5000
1000	6000
800	7000

Table 2.1   *Market demand schedule*

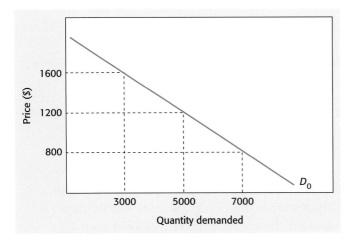

Figure 2.1   *The market demand curve for PCs*

What the demand curve in Figure 2.1 shows us:

- An inverse or negative quantitative relationship between price and quantity demanded. The **law of demand** is:
  - when price goes up, there is a *decrease* in *quantity demanded*
  - when price goes down, there is an *increase* in *quantity demanded*.

  Notice the language that is being used here – changes in price cause a **change in quantity demanded** and we illustrate this by movements up and down the demand curve.

- A causal relationship – changes in price cause changes in the quantity demanded.
- A linear relationship – this demand curve has been drawn, again for simplicity, as a straight line. However, it is perfectly acceptable for price and quantity demanded to be related in a non-linear manner.
- A continuous relationship – we could look at the diagram and find out at what price consumers would be willing and able to buy, say, 1259 PCs.
- A time-based relationship – the time period here is weekly.
- Other things being equal.

Figure 2.1 is a very useful diagram since it allows us to visualise a quite complex relationship – simple pictures are usually easier to understand and remember than a large number of words. It also allows us to estimate how much consumers may spend when buying PCs or, conversely, how much revenue companies may receive from selling PCs. If the price of each PC is $1800 and the above information is accurate, then consumers will buy 2000 units and their total spending will be equal to $3 600 000, which, of course, will be the revenue that companies receive from selling this quantity of the product. (Note that, since we do not know the firm's production and distribution costs, we are as yet unable to say anything about profit.)

Shifts in the demand curve

Whilst the above analysis is useful, it is clearly limited because the price of a PC is not the only nor, in many cases, the most important factor influencing demand for it – other things play a part and are not always constant. Changes in these 'other things being equal' factors are shown by shifts in the demand curve. A rightward shift indicates an increase in demand; a leftward shift indicates a decrease in demand. Notice how the language changes here when we are talking about a shift in the whole curve rather than simply a movement along it – a **change in demand** rather than a change in the quantity demanded (see Table 2.2 and Figure 2.2). What the horizontal and vertical shifts in Figure 2.2 show:

- Horizontal shift – consumers are now willing and able to buy more PCs at each and every price. So, whereas previously they had only been prepared to buy 3000 units per week at $1600 each, now they are prepared to buy 4000.
- Vertical shift – consumers previously were prepared to pay $1600 for 3000 PCs, now they are prepared to pay $1800 each for that quantity.

Price of a 'standard' PC ($)	Quantity demanded per week – demand curve D_2
2000	2000
1800	3000
1600	4000
1400	5000
1200	6000
1000	7000
800	8000

Table 2.2 *Shifts in the demand curve*

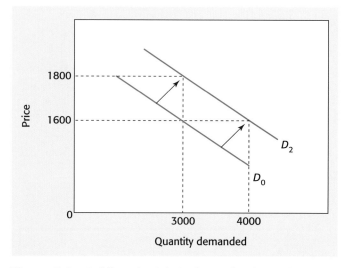

Figure 2.2 *A shift to the right in the market demand curve for PCs*

Causes of shifts in the demand curve

Individuals may differ widely in their attitudes towards products. We could therefore spend a lot of time constructing a very long list of non-price influences. This might be useful in certain circumstances but not in all cases. Fortunately, economists have identified three key non-price categories that can be used to describe and analyse

Use the information in Table 2.3 to draw a demand curve and explain what has happened to that demand curve – you are showing a decrease in demand. Draw in demand curve D_0 from Figure 2.2 as well so that you can use it as the basis for your comparison.

Price of a 'standard' PC ($)	Quantity demanded per week – demand curve D_1
2000	0
1800	1000
1600	2000
1400	3000
1200	4000
1000	5000
800	6000

Table 2.3

the factors that influence the demand for most products. They are:

- the financial ability to pay for the product
- our attitudes towards the product itself
- the price, availability and attractiveness of related products.

Let us look at each in turn.

The financial ability to pay

We have already noted the importance of effective demand. So what influences someone's ability to pay for a product? The key factors are:

- an individual's income or more specifically, the purchasing power of their income after taxation
- the availability of loans/credit and the interest rate that must be paid on loans or credit card balances.

In general we would expect a positive relationship between the financial ability to pay and the demand for a product. So an increase in the purchaser's

financial ability to pay generally leads to an increase in demand. This is represented by a rightward shift in the demand curve from D_0 to D_2 in Figure 2.2. A decrease in the ability to pay would lead to a decrease in demand, and this would be represented by a leftward shift in the demand curve from D_2 to D_0.

There is an important qualification to this general rule. The single most important influence on people's financial ability to pay for goods and services is generally considered to be income. In most cases there is a positive relationship between income and product demand – this means that as income rises, the demand for the majority of goods and services also increases; as income falls, so does the demand for most products. Products that are characterised by such a relationship are labelled **normal goods**.

However, there are some products that are characterised by a negative relationship between income and demand. In Asia, for example, as incomes rise, the demand for staple foodstuffs such as rice and vegetables falls. Consumers are able to purchase more meat and fish with their increased spending power. The demand for better clothing and eating out in restaurants will also increase, whilst the demand for second-hand clothing and meals taken at street stalls will fall. Products for which demand decreases as income increases are called **inferior goods**.

Draw diagrams and briefly explain how you expect changes in the following to influence the position of the demand curve for PCs:

a   an increase in interest rates
b   a large increase in unemployment
c   a sustained rise in earnings from work
d   a reduction in income tax.

Attitudes towards the products

We all buy products for a reason: our behaviour is purposefully motivated, at least at the time of purchase! Economists usually consider our behaviour to be a reflection of our tastes and preferences towards different types of goods and services. You may buy a particular type or brand of PC because of its reputation for reliability. You may buy a pair of brand-name trainers because you want to play sport and you genuinely believe them to be of better quality or you may buy them simply because they are fashionable and you want to look cool.

Detailed understanding of the psychological motives that determine our behaviour are beyond our scope here, but clearly we are influenced by our own individual likes and dislikes, by peer pressure, and by various forms of advertising and the marketing images that surround us. Nowhere is this more evident than in markets for designer clothing and accessories, where tastes and preferences can be extremely volatile.

SELF-ASSESSMENT TASK 2.6

Would you classify the following products as normal goods or inferior goods? In each case draw a diagram to explain how a decrease in income will shift the demand curve. Explain your reasoning. What difficulties did you have in deciding? What information would you need to resolve these difficulties?

a Premium brand orange juice	**d** Orange cordial
b Hotel accommodation	**e** Guest house accommodation
c Standard TV sets	**f** HD flat screen TVs

The price, availability and attractiveness of related products

Economists classify types of related products into the following two categories:

- **Substitute goods** are alternatives that satisfy essentially the same wants or needs. The range of substitutability can be fairly narrow, e.g. in terms of different product brands: Acer and Dell computers; Sony and Samsung mobile phones; and Nissan and Toyota cars. The range of substitutability can also be broad e.g. in terms of product groups, such as different types of transport – rail, buses taxis and cars; different types of soft drinks – Sprite, Pepsi Cola or Lipton lemon tea. Changes in the price or attractiveness

---

SELF-ASSESSMENT TASK 2.7

1 What, at present, is the dominant brand of sports clothing? Why do you think it is dominant? Is it because it is of genuinely superior quality or is there another explanation?

2 Think of a successful advertising campaign that is running on TV at present. Why is it successful and what impact would you expect it to have on sales over the next six months?

Nike trainers – a fashionable designer brand

---

of one of these products will have an impact on the demand for all substitutes.

- **Complementary goods** are products that enhance the satisfaction we derive from another product. Common examples are toothbrushes and toothpaste, tennis balls and racquets, laptops and dongles. In some cases, without the complement the main product would be useless. Examples here include: cars and fuel; DVDs and DVD players; and mobile phones and top-up cards. Once again changes in price or attractiveness of one of these products will have an impact on the demand for the complementary good. In such cases this is known as **joint demand**.

Other demand-influencing factors

Clearly, this is not an exhaustive list of the factors that influence demand. Each product will have some factors that are peculiar to it, for instance, the weather may influence the demand for ice cream.

1 What would you expect to happen to the demand for Dell PCs if Acer cut its prices?

2 What would you expect to happen to the demand for all PCs if the price of software and printers came down sharply?

Use a diagram to help explain your answers.

Expectations of the future can be important in determining the demand for certain products. If food prices or share prices are expected to rise, this can be a major influence in boosting demand. If unemployment or interest rates are expected to go up, this can have a dampening effect on the demand for some products.

Another factor may be **composite demand**. This occurs where products are used for more than one purpose, for example, where an increase in demand for sugar cane for biofuel purposes is likely to increase the price and availability of sugar cane for refining.

The skill of the economist is to use the categories above and knowledge or intuition to identify the key influences on demand, in any particular market, to explain past behaviour or to try to predict future behaviour. This is by no means easy.

The concept of elasticity

In our analysis of demand, the focus up to this point has been on understanding the general direction of any change in price or any change in the other factors that influence demand. To add greater meaning to this explanation, it is necessary to look at the extent of any change in price or change in another influencing factor on the equilibrium position.

A few simple examples will show why this is necessary. For some products, e.g. rice, a small change in price is likely to have only a modest impact on the quantity demanded. For other food products, particularly where there are close substitutes, a small change in price may have a much larger change on the quantity demanded. Similarly, if there is a change in income, there may be little effect on the demand for some products and a much greater effect on demand for others. For example, an increase in income may lead to an increase in demand for restaurant meals yet result in little or no change in demand for eating at local cafés or street stalls.

The concept that explains these variations is referred to in Economics as elasticity. As we shall explain later, this term can be applied to the supply side as well as the demand side of the market. It is defined as 'a numerical measure of responsiveness of one variable following a change in another variable, other things being equal'.

The extent of any change is important, particularly from a business standpoint. Where a small change in price, for example, produces a bigger change in the quantity demanded, then the relationship is said to be **elastic**. Alternatively, if a large change in the price produces only a small change in the quantity demanded, then the relationship is **inelastic**. The distinction is important as you will now see.

Price elasticity of demand (PED)

Price elasticity of demand is a numerical measure of the responsiveness of demand for a product following a change in the price of that product. If demand is elastic, then a small change in price will result in a relatively large change in quantity demanded. On the other hand, if there is a large change in price and a far lesser change in quantity demanded, then demand is price inelastic. A numerical example will help clarify this. First, however, we need a way of expressing PED in a numerical form – the formula we will use at this stage is:

$$PED = \frac{\% \text{ change in quantity demanded of a product}}{\% \text{ change in price of that product}}$$

Let us take two specific examples of price changes for two general products that we will call product A and product B (see Figure 2.3). Assume that both of these unrelated products are currently priced at $100 and demand for them is 1000 units per month. Consider what might happen to the demand for A and B if the price rises to $105. The quantity demanded of product A only falls from 1000 to 990, whereas the quantity demanded of product B falls from 1000 to 900. Now let us put these values into the PED equation to calculate the elasticity.

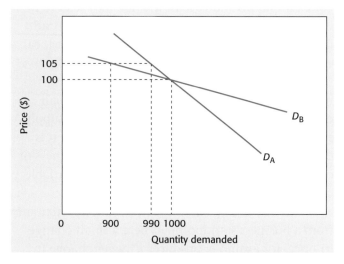

Figure 2.3 *Price inelastic and price elastic demand curves*

Product A $\dfrac{\%\text{ change in quantity demanded of A}}{\%\text{ change in price of A}}$

$= \dfrac{-1\%\text{ fall}}{+5\%\text{ increase}} = (-)\,0.2$

Product B $\dfrac{\%\text{ change in quantity demanded of B}}{\%\text{ change in price of B}}$

$= \dfrac{-10\%\text{ fall}}{+5\%\text{ increase}} = (-)\,2.0$

Notice that in both cases a negative figure is given. This is because of the negative (or inverse) relationship between price and quantity demanded; in other words, as the price goes up, the quantity demanded goes down. Economists conventionally refer to PED in absolute terms by ignoring the negative sign.

In the case of product A, because the numerical value (0.2) is less than 1, we say that the demand for

this product is relatively inelastic or unresponsive to price changes. Over this particular range of prices, the 5% increase has resulted in a much smaller change in quantity demanded.

In the case of product B, because the numerical value (2.0) is greater than 1, we say that the demand for this product is relatively elastic or responsive to price changes. Over this particular range of prices, the same 5% price change has caused a much bigger change in quantity demanded.

Some special PED values

It is important to realise that mathematically PED values can range from 0 to infinity. These values need explanation. Consider, for example the demand curve shown in Figure 2.4. Irrespective of the price charged, consumers are willing and able to buy the same amount – in this case demand would be said to be **perfectly inelastic**. Let us look at the PED calculation for an increase in price from $10 to $11.

$$\text{PED} = \frac{\%\text{ change in quantity demanded}}{\%\text{ change in price}} = \frac{0\%}{+10\%} = 0$$

Hence, when the PED = 0, demand is perfectly inelastic, completely unresponsive to price changes.

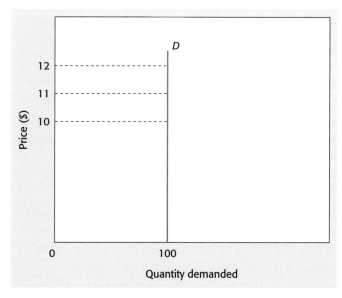

Figure 2.4 *A perfectly inelastic demand curve*

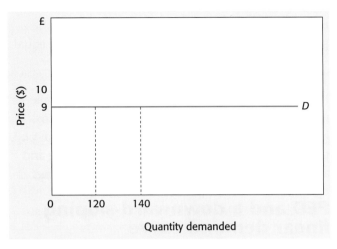

Figure 2.5 *A perfectly elastic demand curve*

Consider the demand curve in Figure 2.5. At a price of $10 per unit consumers are not prepared to buy any of this product; however, if price falls to $9, they will buy all that is available. The relative change in quantity demanded here, of course, is infinite, since the original demand was zero. So:

$$PED = \frac{\% \text{ change in quantity demanded}}{\% \text{ change in price}} = \frac{\infty}{-10\%} = (-)\infty$$

In this case, demand is **perfectly elastic**.

Unitary elasticity

If the relative increase in price is exactly matched by the relative fall in quantity demanded, then the PED value will equal (–)1 and demand will be said to have **unitary elasticity** over that particular price range. So if, for example, the price of the product goes from $1000 to $1050 and the quantity demanded decreases from 10 000 to 9500, then the PED will equal (–)1 over this particular range of prices.

Factors affecting price elasticity of demand

There are three key factors that influence whether, over a particular price range, demand for a product is likely to be price elastic or inelastic. These are discussed below.

The range and attractiveness of substitutes

The greater the number of substitute (alternative) products and the more closely substitutable those

1 Calculate the PEDs in each of the following cases shown in Table 2.4 and explain whether demand would be considered price elastic or price inelastic.

Original price	New price	Original quantity demanded	New quantity demanded
a $100	$102	2000 units per week	1950 units per week
b $55.50	$54.95	5000 units per week	6000 units per week

Table 2.4

2 With the aid of a numerical example of your choice explain the meaning of these PED values:
  a PED = (–) 1.5
  b PED = (–) 0.6.

products are, the more we would expect consumers to switch away from a particular product when its price goes up (or towards that product if its price falls).

It is important, however, to distinguish between the substitutability of products within the same group of products and substitutability with goods from other product groupings. For example, different types of orange juice are a group of products in their own right; they are also part of a larger group of fruit juices and part of the even bigger category of products that we could label as 'drinks'. If we are concerned with the price elasticity of demand for a particular type of orange juice produced by a specific manufacturer, then it will probably have a fairly high PED (probably) because of the range of substitutes. As we aggregate products into groupings, such as 'fruit juices', or 'all soft drinks', demand will start to become more price inelastic.

Other substitutability issues to consider include:

- the quality and accessibility of information that consumers have about products that are available to satisfy particular wants and needs
- the degree to which people consider the product to be a necessity

- the addictive properties of the product, i.e. whether the product is habit forming
- the brand image of the product.

The relative expense of the product

A rise in price will reduce the purchasing power of a person's income (real income). The larger the proportion of income that the price represents, the larger will be the impact on the consumer's real income level of a change in the product's price. For example, a 10% increase in the price of a flight to Malaysia will have a bigger impact than a 10% rise in the price of a bus trip into town. The greater the relative proportion of income accounted for by the product, the higher the PED, other things being equal.

Time

In the short-term, perhaps weeks or months, people may find it hard to change their spending patterns. However, if the price of a product goes up and stays up, then over time people will find ways of adapting and adjusting, so the PED is likely to increase over time.

PED and a downward-sloping linear demand curve

So far PED and the slope of a demand curve may appear to be the same – this, however, is incorrect. Table 2.6 and the associated self-assessment task will help you see the difference.

SELF-ASSESSMENT TASK 2.10

1 Classify the following products into whether, in your opinion, the PED is likely to be relatively high (elastic) or relatively low (inelastic). Justify your classification.

- Coca Cola
- Nike trainers
- a particular brand of petrol
- fresh vegetables
- Cadbury chocolate
- all forms of car fuel
- soft drinks in general
- all sweet products
- wheat flour.

2 A manufacturer has received a market research estimate of PED values for its shirts currently sold in three markets: independent retailers, prestige fashion stores and via mail order. Explain and comment upon the PED values shown in Table 2.5.

Market	Current price	Current sales	PED value
Independent retailers	$8	40 000 p.a.	−1.0
Fashion stores	$15	10 000 p.a.	−0.2
Mail order	$10	3 000 p.a.	−3.0

Table 2.5 *PED values*

Price of product R ($/unit)	Quantity demanded of product R (units per week)
10	0
9	1 000
8	2 000
7	3 000
6	4 000
5	5 000
4	6 000
3	7 000
2	8 000
1	9 000
0	10 000

Table 2.6 *Demand schedule for product R*

Income elasticity of demand

Income elasticity of demand (YED) is defined as a numerical measure of the responsiveness of demand following a change in income alone. Once again if demand is responsive, then it is classified as elastic; if unresponsive, it is inelastic.

The formula used in this case is:

$$YED = \frac{\% \text{ change in quantity demanded}}{\% \text{ change in income}}$$

SELF-ASSESSMENT TASK 2.11

Use the information in Table 2.6 to calculate the PED values as prices fall from $10 to $9, from $9 to $8, from $8 to $7 and so on. You should see that the PED value falls as you move down the demand curve. In the top half of the demand curve, PED > 1; in the bottom half of the demand curve, PED < 1. We could show that for very small changes in price, PED = 1 at the mid-point of the demand curve. That is why, in theory, a demand curve with unitary price elasticity throughout can be drawn. Total expenditure (the area beneath this curve) for any price quantity combination is constant.

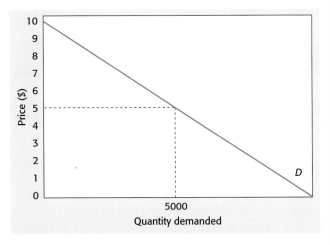

Figure 2.6   *The demand curve for product R*

It is important to recognise that the relationship between income and demand changes may not always be positive. If an increase in income leads to an increase in demand (or a decrease in income leads to a decrease in demand), then there is a positive relationship and the product is classified as normal, and the YED has a positive value. However, there are some products (inferior goods) that exhibit a negative relationship between income and demand. Here an increase in income would cause a decrease in demand (a decrease in income would cause an increase in demand) and the YED has a negative value. So the sign that precedes the YED tells you the nature of the relationship between income and demand; the numerical value tells you the strength of that relationship.

For example, there has been a 2% increase in consumer income and that has led to the changes in demand shown in Table 2.7.

	Original demand (per period of time)	New demand
Product A	100 units at the current price ($10)	103 units at the same price ($10)
Product B	100 units at the current price ($10)	99 units at the same price ($10)
Product C	100 units at the current price ($10)	101 units at thesame price ($10)

Table 2.7   *Change in demand*

$$\text{YED of A} = \frac{3\% \text{ increase in demand}}{2\% \text{ increase in income}}$$

$$= +1.5 \text{ (normal good – elastic response)}$$

$$\text{YED of B} = \frac{1\% \text{ decrease in demand}}{2\% \text{ increase in income}}$$

$$= -0.5 \text{ (inferior good – inelastic response)}$$

$$\text{YED of C} = \frac{1\% \text{ increase in demand}}{2\% \text{ increase in income}}$$

$$= +0.5 \text{ (normal good – inelastic response)}$$

Cross elasticity of demand

Cross elasticity of demand (XED) is a numerical measure of the responsiveness of demand for one product following a change in the price of another related product alone.

The formula used is:

$$\text{XED} = \frac{\% \text{ change in quantity demanded of product A}}{\% \text{ change in the price of product B}}$$

Products that are substitutes for each other (e.g. different types of laptop computer) will have positive values for the XED. If the price of B goes up, then people will begin to turn to product A because of its more favourable relative price. If the price of B falls, then consumers will start to buy B instead of A. Products that are complements (e.g. computers and printers or software) will have negative values of XED. If the price of B goes up, the quantity demanded of B will drop and so will the complementary demand for A.

Assume the current average market price of a standard type of personal computer is $1000 and current sales are 100 units per day (see Figure 2.7). Consider what might happen if, following a 2% decrease in the price of laptop computers (a substitute product), demand for PCs falls from 100 units to 98 units per day at the original price (D_0 to D_1). Our calculation becomes:

$$XED = \frac{2\% \text{ fall in demand for PCs}}{2\% \text{ decrease in price of laptops}} = +1$$

The positive sign indicates that the products are substitutes.

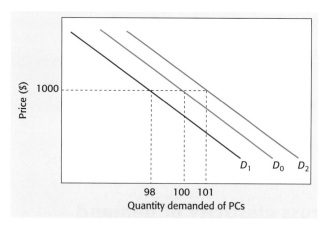

Figure 2.7 *A change in the demand for PCs*

What would have happened to the demand for PCs if, following the same change in the price of laptops, the XED had been +2? Redraw Figure 2.7 to illustrate this.

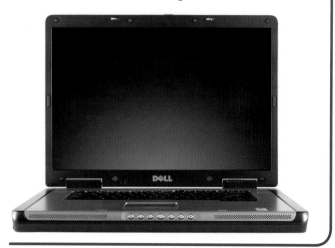

Now consider that the average price of software (a complement) falls by 5% – this encourages extra sales of PCs so that demand for PCs rises to 101 per day at the original price and the demand curve shifts from D_0 to D_2.

The cross elasticity calculation is:

$$XED = \frac{1\% \text{ increase in sales of PCs}}{5\% \text{ fall in price of software}} = -0.2$$

Note again that the sign indicates the nature of the relationship (a negative one between complements), and the numerical value indicates the strength of that relationship.

1 What would happen if demand for PCs had risen to 110 units per day? Calculate the XED and redraw Figure 2.7 to illustrate what has happened.
2 The owner of a local golf course loans out equipment to non-members who want to play occasional rounds. She estimates that in June and July, if she lowers the hire price of clubs by 10%, the number of non-members playing will increase by 25%. Calculate and comment on the XED. What other factors should the owner consider?

Business relevance of elasticity

Price elasticity of demand

Knowledge of PED is useful to help understand price variations in a market, the impact of changing prices on consumer expenditure, corporate revenues and government indirect tax receipts.

In Figure 2.8 you can see how variations in PED can lead to price volatility following a change in the conditions of supply (see below). D_e represents a demand curve with PED > 1 over the relevant price range. D_i represents a demand curve with PED less than 1 over the relevant price range. A decrease in supply resulting from an increase in, say, production costs, would result in a leftward shift in the supply

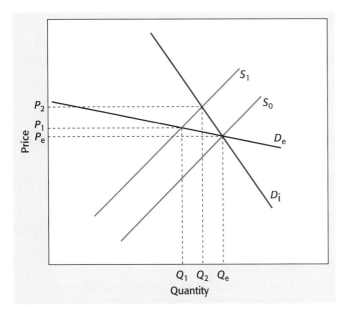

Figure 2.8 *Price volatility following a change in supply*

curve, from S_0 to S_1. Whilst we can see in both cases that the change in equilibrium leads to higher prices and a reduction in the quantity traded, the extent of the changes varies according to the PED. For D_e, as producers try to raise prices (to pass on the higher costs to their customers), consumer reaction is to stop buying this product. This reaction constrains the extent to which prices rise only from P_e to P_1 – quantity, therefore, takes the strain here and falls considerably from Q_e to Q_1. On the other hand, when demand is relatively price inelastic, producers have the scope to raise prices considerably (P_e to P_2) without suffering from a significant drop in sales (Q_e to Q_2).

SELF-ASSESSMENT TASK 2.14

This question has been adapted from one set by OCR. Read the feature and then answer the questions that follow.

Coffee break

Recent research has shown that 93% of UK households have bought instant coffee in the last year. Moreover, coffee as a drink continues to increase in popularity, as consumers try variations such as cappuccino, espresso, mocha and latte. This expansion in demand has also led to an increase in the types of manufactured coffee available, although instant coffee remains the largest seller.

Raw coffee, when it leaves the plantation, is pale green, hence the name 'green coffee' when it is traded. It is bought and sold on world commodity markets in London and New York. At any one time, the amount to be sold and the quantity that manufacturers and processors wish to purchase are key factors determining its price. Like any product, therefore, the price of raw coffee is determined where market supply and demand are equated.

The final price of raw coffee is very important for the economic well-being of millions of people living in countries such as Costa Rica, Kenya and Colombia which are heavily dependent on this crop. Typically, farmers in such countries practise small-scale production – their plots of land might be no more than 1 or 2 hectares. It is therefore unrealistic for them to sell their product direct to the world market. So what usually happens is that they sell their crop to a government-controlled agency which in turn releases stocks onto the world market, depending on market conditions.

A Kenyan coffee producer

An alternative approach, practised by major manufacturers such as Nestlé, is for coffee to be bought direct from local farmers. This happens only in countries where Nestlé manufactures locally and for export. In such circumstances, Nestlé offers a 'fair price' to farmers to ensure a regular supply of green coffee. This price is widely advertised as the minimum price that will be paid for supplies. It also follows that the higher the qualilty, the higher the price. This arrangement ensures that farmers continue to grow coffee, whilst providing Nestlé with regular supplies outside the uncertainties of the occasionally volatile world commodity market.

1 a How is the market price of raw coffee determined on world commodity markets?
b Excluding price, state and explain two other determinants of demand for raw coffee in world markets.
c Suppose a major coffee-producing country decides to reduce supplies to the world market. Assuming no change in demand, use a diagram to explain how this action would affect the world raw coffee price.
2 a Define elasticity of supply.
b Would you expect the price elasticity of supply for raw coffee to be relatively elastic or inelastic? Justify your answer.

c Would you expect the price elasticity of supply for instant coffee to be relatively elastic or inelastic? Justify your answer.
3 a The 'fair price' of raw coffee paid to small farmers by Nestlé in a particular developing country is usually fixed above the normal equilibrium price. With the aid of a diagram, explain how this affects the market for raw coffee in that country.
b Briefly describe the benefits of a 'fair price' for the producers of the raw coffee in this developing country.

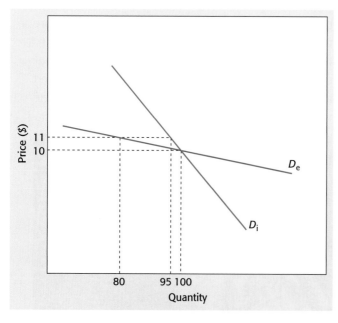

Figure 2.9 *Price elastic and price inelastic demand curves*

PED and total expenditure/ total revenue

PED can help us understand how total spending by consumers will change as price rises or falls.

$$\text{Total expenditure} = P \times Q$$
$$= \text{Total revenue of a firm}$$
$$\text{or industry}$$

In Figure 2.9, assume there are two products each with the same equilibrium price ($10) and quantity traded (100 units per day). Total expenditure by consumers per day = $10 × 100 = $1000 – this is, of course, equal to the revenue received by companies. Now, if the price rises to $11, the differences in PED indicate that consumers respond in different ways, and the total expenditure will change:

- D_e is relatively price elastic over the relevant price range, and quantity falls considerably to 80 units (PED = –2). Total expenditure is now down to $880 per day – the reason, of course, is that the relative fall in sales is greater than the relative increase in price.

- D_i is relatively price inelastic over the relevant price range and the quantity traded only

falls slightly to 95 units (PED = – 0.5). Total expenditure actually rises even though less is traded. The reason is that the increase in price exerts a more powerful influence in this case.

SELF-ASSESSMENT TASK 2.15

1 You used this demand schedule when we looked at PED on a linear demand curve at the beginning of this section. Figure 2.10 shows the resulting demand curve. Refer back to how PED varies along a linear demand curve – note, in the top half of the demand curve PED > 1 whereas in the lower half PED < 1.

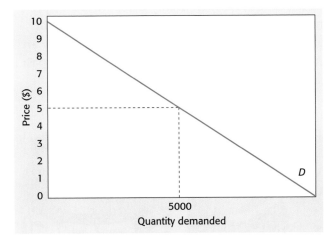

Figure 2.10 *The demand curve for product R*

a Use Table 2.8 to help you calculate the total expenditure (TE)/total revenue (TR) figures and graph the resulting values underneath the demand curve (put TE on the vertical axis and quantity on the horizontal axis – it will help if you use the same scale on the horizontal axis).

b What do you notice about TE/TR figures as the price is cut from $10 towards $5 per unit?

Price of product R ($/unit)	Quantity demanded of product R (units per week)	Total expenditure $ per week
10	0	
9	1 000	
8	2 000	
7	3 000	
6	4 000	
5	5 000	
4	6 000	
3	7 000	
2	8 000	
1	9 000	
0	10 000	

Table 2.8

c Why does this happen?
d What do you notice about the TE/TR figures as price is raised from $0 to $5?
e Why does this happen?
f Where is TE/TR maximised?

2 If a government is interested in raising more revenue from indirect taxes, such as VAT or excise duties, should it tax products that are price elastic or price inelastic? Explain and illustrate your answer with diagrams and examples.

Income elasticity of demand

Since YED provides information about how demand varies as income changes, the concept is potentially of great importance to business organisations and governments.

If the YED for a normal good exceeds unity, then demand for that product will grow more rapidly than consumer incomes during normal periods of economic growth – hence considerably greater productive capacity may be required. However, during a recession, when incomes fall, firms producing this sort of product will be extremely vulnerable, given the large reduction in demand that might be expected.

If YED is negative, then firms producing such inferior goods will see their sales decline steadily over time as the economy grows – however, they may be the sort of business to benefit from the hard times of recession.

SELF-ASSESSMENT TASK 2.16

1 What will happen to sales of a product whose YED = +0.6?
2 How could you use YED values to advise a company on how to produce a mix of goods and services that would reduce the risk often associated with only producing a very narrow range of products?
3 Why might government planners be interested in the YED values of different products?

Cross elasticity of demand

Many companies are concerned with the impact that rival pricing strategies will have on the demand for their own product. Remember that substitutes are characterised by a positive XED: the higher the price, the more likely it is that consumers will buy a cheaper substitute. In such cases there is a high degree of interdependence between suppliers, and the dangers of a rival cutting price are likely to be very significant indeed.

Companies are increasingly concerned with trying to get consumers to buy not just one of their products but a whole range of complementary ones, e.g. computer printers and cartridges. XED will identify those products that are most complementary and help a company introduce a pricing structure that generates more revenue. For instance, market research may indicate that families spend most money at restaurants when special deals are offered, even though the PED for meals is low. In this case, for example, the high negative cross elasticity between meal prices and the demand for soft drinks (such as Pepsi Cola and Coca Cola) means that although the revenue from food sales may fall the demand for soft drinks may increase. This indicates that the restaurant may need to introduce a more sophisticated pricing structure by looking at the relationships between the demand for all products and services offered.

Cautionary note

We have assumed that calculating elasticity values is straightforward. In fact there are enormous practical statistical problems, which mean that elasticity values are best seen as estimates. For instance, consider the difficulties of calculating PED values from historical data. Have the price changes only been caused by supply variations? Have there been any non-price demand influences at work? Remember, if we are to calculate the PED value accurately, we need to separate out all the other influences and just measure the impact of the price change alone on quantity demanded – the difficulty encountered here is known as the *identification problem*. Collecting data from other sources, such as market testing or surveys (using questionnaires and/or interviews), is costly in terms of time and money and may not be particularly valid or reliable. As such, many companies may prefer to make rough 'guesstimates' of elasticity values or to work with incomplete data, particularly if they are operating in markets where rapid change means past data ceases to be a good indicator of the future.

Close substitutes

Supply

To an economist:

> **supply** refers to the *quantities of a product that suppliers are willing and able to sell at various prices per period of time, other things being equal.*

Note the similarities below with the definition of demand on page 42:

- **Quantities** Once again we must emphasise that economists often deal with numerical values and very often try to represent information in a quantitative way.
- **Product** As with demand we are using the term to refer to any item that is being traded. It can be used for goods or services. We could also stretch this to include tradable items like money or other financial assets such as shares.
- **Suppliers** These are the sellers of the product and are often referred to as 'producers', although they may not necessarily be manufacturers of the product but again may simply be an intermediary in the production–consumption chain or they may be selling services. We could look at an individual company's supply of a product or, more usefully, we can aggregate to look at the supply for an overall market.
- **Willing and able to sell at various prices** Clearly, in a market economy, companies must gain from selling their products. The ability to earn profits is likely to be a major (but probably not the only) influence on company behaviour – the higher the price, other things being equal, the more profit companies are likely to make.
- **Per period of time** Supply must also be time related. It is of no use to say that Acer supplied 200 computers unless you specify the relevant time period. Clearly this needs to be consistent with the time period being used for demand.
- **Other things being equal** We will see shortly that there are numerous potential influences on the supply of a product. Analysing the connections between the various elements is very difficult if lots of these elements are changing simultaneously. So, we assume these other factors affecting supply remain unchanged.

The supply curve

We need to take the definition and represent it diagrammatically to construct what is known as a **supply curve**. We could do this for an individual firm selling PCs or, by aggregating each company's supply curves, we could get the industry or market supply curve for PCs. Assume again that we have collected statistical data about companies' selling intentions and that these plans can be represented by Table 2.6 (this is known as a market **supply schedule**). We can plot this supply schedule to see how the quantity of PCs depends upon variations in price. Figure 2.10 shows the supply curve (S_0) for the data in the table.

Price of a 'standard' PC ($)	Quantity supplied per week– supply curve S_0
800	1000
1000	2000
1200	3000
1400	4000
1600	5000
1800	6000
2000	7000

Table 2.9 *Market supply schedule*

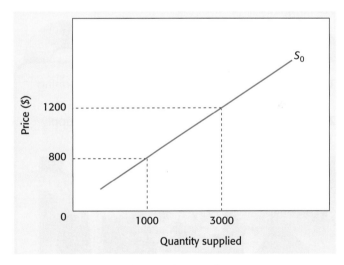

Figure 2.11 *The market supply curve for PCs*

What the supply curve in Figure 2.11 shows:

- A positive or direct relationship between price and quantity supplied. The **law of supply** is:
  - when price goes up there is an *increase* in *quantity supplied*
  - when price goes down there is a *decrease* in *quantity supplied*.

- Again notice the language that is being used – changes in price cause changes in quantity supplied. This is represented by movements up and down the supply curve (again some economists prefer to use the terms 'extension of supply' for a movement up the supply curve and a 'contraction of supply' for a movement down the curve).
- A causal relationship – we are saying that price changes cause the change in quantity supplied.
- A linear relationship – the supply curve has been drawn for simplicity as a straight line, but of course there is no reason why the supply curve should not be represented in a non-linear way, e.g. in the form of an upward sloping curve.
- A continuous relationship – we could look at the curve to find out how many PCs companies would plan to supply at a price of $1150.
- A time-based relationship – the time period again is weekly.

Note we are also assuming other things being equal – any other factor influencing supply is assumed to be unchanged.

SELF-ASSESSMENT TASK 2.17

1 How many PCs per week are companies planning to supply if the price is $1100?
2 What price would persuade companies to supply 1350 PCs?

3 What assumptions are you making when you answer these questions?
4 What might be the advantages and disadvantages of using a diagrammatic form such as in Figure 2.11 to represent supply?

Shifts in the market supply curve

Whilst the above is useful, one of the limitations is that companies' supply intentions are influenced by factors other than the price of the product (which, if you think about it, is the most tangible expression of consumers' buying intentions). Other things are most certainly not always equal. Changes in these **supply conditions** can be illustrated by shifts in the supply curve. A rightward shift indicates an increase in supply; a leftward shift indicates a decrease in supply. Notice again how the language changes when we are talking about a shift in the whole curve rather than simply a movement along it – a change in supply rather than a change in the quantity supplied (see Table 2.10 and Figure 2.12).

Price of a 'standard' PC ($)	Quantity supplied per week – supply curve S_2
800	2000
1000	3000
1200	4000
1400	5000
1600	6000
1800	7000
2000	8000

Table 2.10 *An increase in supply*

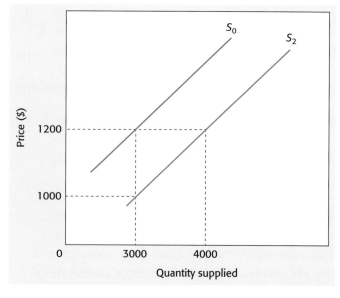

Figure 2.12 *A shift to the right in the market supply curve for PCs*

What the horizontal and vertical shifts in Figure 2.11 show:

- Horizontal shift – companies are now more willing and/or more able to supply PCs at each and every price. Previously they had only been prepared to supply 3000 units per week at $1 200; now they are prepared to supply 4000.
- Vertical shift – companies previously wanted $1200 per unit to persuade them to supply 3000 units per week; now they are prepared to accept $1000.

SELF-ASSESSMENT TASK 2.18

Use the information in Table 2.11 to draw a new supply curve (S_1). Explain what has happened to that supply curve – remember you are showing a decrease in supply. Draw in supply curve S_0 as well so that you can use it as the basis for your comparison.

Price of a 'standard' PC ($)	Quantity supplied per week – supply curve S_1
1000	1000
1200	2000
1400	3000
1600	4000
1800	5000
2000	6000

Table 2.11

Causes of shifts in the supply curve

Companies clearly differ in their willingness and ability to supply products and, as with demand, we could spend a long time building a list of possible factors other than price that will affect supply. If we were required to conduct a detailed analysis of supply conditions in a particular industry, that might be justified. For our purposes we need to simplify and generalise about the factors that can influence supply in most industries. As with demand, we can focus on three main influences:

- the **costs** associated with supplying the product
- the size, structure and nature of the industry
- government policy.

Let us discuss each in turn.

Costs

In a market-based economy, no firm (in the absence of government support) can exist indefinitely if it makes losses, so companies will make supply decisions on the basis of the price they can get for selling the product in relation to the cost of supplying it. What we are interested in is what factors can influence the position of the supply curve – in other words, what factors can cause an increase or a decrease in the costs of supplying each and every unit, since it is likely that this will impact on the price that companies charge per unit. Below are listed some potentially influential factors – if any factor pushes up costs, there is likely to be a leftward shift in the supply curve or a decrease in supply; if the factor lowers costs, there is likely to be an increase in supply:

- wage rates
- worker productivity (output per worker)
- raw material and component prices
- energy costs
- equipment maintenance costs
- transport costs
- the state of technology.

SELF-ASSESSMENT TASK 2.19

Go through each of the above factors in turn and work out what sort of change in that factor will cause:

a an increase in supply

b a decrease in supply.

The size and nature of the industry

If it is clear that if there is substantial profit to be made by selling a product, then firms inside and outside the industry are likely to react. Firms currently in the industry may invest in capital equipment in an attempt to grow bigger and take advantage of the situation. Firms outside the industry may try to enter this market and new firms may set up in business. If the size of the industry increases, because there are more firms or bigger firms, then it is likely that the supply of the industry will increase. Equally, if firms in the industry start to compete more intensively on price, it is likely that the supply curve will shift to the right as the effects of this price competition start to affect the price that all companies are willing to accept for their products. Of course if a fierce price war breaks out, then consumers, at least temporarily, may enjoy very much lower prices for any given level of supply.

SELF-ASSESSMENT TASK 2.20

1 Why might firms choose to leave an industry?
2 What is likely to happen to the industry supply if the size of the industry shrinks?
3 What might happen to supply if all firms decide to try and increase the amount of profit they make on each unit they sell?

Government policy

Governments influence company decisions in many ways. Legislation designed to protect consumers or workers may impose additional costs on companies and this may affect the supply curve. Governments may also impose a **specific tax** such as excise duties on the output of companies or an **ad valorem tax** such as value added tax on sales. The impact of tax is like a cost increase because companies may seek to pass the tax on to the consumer in the form of higher prices. As such, indirect taxes often result in a decrease in supply. On the other hand, a relaxation of certain types of legislation or government subsidies can increase supply by encouraging firms to reduce prices for any given level of output. Government policy in agriculture may involve the release of **stocks** to calm the otherwise volatility of markets associated with a poor harvest.

Other supply-influencing factors

These are varied and often specific to the particular industry or activity. For example, the supply of agricultural produce is often influenced by weather conditions. Adverse weather can lead to a dramatic reduction in supply; good weather conditions in contrast can result in bumper harvests for producers. Some manufacturers may be able to switch production from one product to another fairly easily, so the relative profitability of alternative product areas may be important. In financial markets, such as the stock market or the foreign exchange market, supply may be significantly influenced by expectations of future prices.

There is also the case of **joint supply**. A good example is in the case of soya bean production where part of the crop is used for human food products whilst what is left over is used to produce animal feed.

Once again the skill of the economist is to use theory, insight and observation to identify the key influences on supply in any situation to explain the past or to try to predict the future.

Price elasticity of supply

Price elasticity of supply (PES) is a numerical measure of the responsiveness of supply to a change in the price of the product alone. The supply could be that of an individual firm or group of firms; it could, of course, refer to the supply of the overall industry. It is expressed as:

$$PES = \frac{\% \text{ change in quantity supplied}}{\% \text{ change in price}}$$

Since the relationship between the price and quantity supplied is normally a direct one, the PES will tend to take on a positive value. If the numerical value of PES is greater than 1, then we say that supply is relatively price elastic, i.e. supply is responsive. If the numerical value of PES is less than 1, then supply is relatively price inelastic, i.e. supply is unresponsive.

SELF-ASSESSMENT TASK 2.21

Refer to the supply curve S_0 in Figure 2.12 (page 58). What would happen to this curve if the government introduced a tax of:

a $100 per computer?
b 10% on the pre-tax selling price?
c legislation that raised companies' costs by about 20% on average?

Figure 2.13 shows five supply curves each with different PES values.

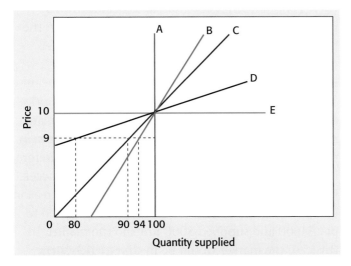

Supply curve	% change in quantity supplied/	/ % change in price		= PES and Description	
A	0	/ 10% decrease	=	0	Perfectly inelastic
B	6% decrease	/ 10% decrease	=	+0.6	Relatively inelastic
C	10% decrease	/ 10% decrease	=	+1.0	Unitary elasticity
D	20% increase	/ 10% increase	=	+2.0	Relatively elastic
E	Firms are not prepared to supply any at a price below $10 but will supply as much as they can at $10 (or above!)		=	+ ∞	Perfectly elastic

Figure 2.13 *Five different supply curves*

Factors influencing PES

The key words in understanding PES are supply flexibility – if firms and industries are more flexible in the way they behave, then supply tends to be more elastic. The main influences on PES include the following:

- The ease with which firms can accumulate or reduce stocks of goods. Stocks allow companies to meet variations in demand through output changes rather than price changes – so the more easily manufacturing firms can do this, the higher the PES. Companies that provide services are, of course, unable to build up stocks.

- The ease with which they can increase production. In the short run firms and industries with spare productive capacity will tend to have a higher PES. However, shortages of critical factor inputs (skilled workers, components, fuel) will often lead to an inelastic PES. This is particularly the case with agricultural products where it takes time to alter the type of crops produced.
- Over time, of course, companies can increase their productive capacity by investing in more capital equipment, often taking advantage of technological advances. Equally, over time, more firms can enter or leave an industry and this will increase the flexibility of supply.

Implications for business

You have already seen how variations in PED will influence the nature of a change in the equilibrium following a given shift in the supply curve. Figure 2.14 also confirms that the PES will influence the nature of a change in the equilibrium following a given shift in the demand curve. The diagram illustrates two alternative supply curves with different elasticities over the relevant price range. S_e is relatively price elastic, S_i is relatively price inelastic.

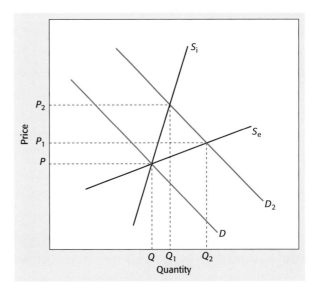

Figure 2.14 *Supply curves with different elasticities*

If the initial equilibrium is at PQ and then demand for a normal good increases, perhaps because of an increase in income, in both cases the new equilibrium price and quantity are higher. However, in the case of S_e, the greater flexibility in supply allows companies to respond to this increased demand without raising prices so much. In the case of S_i, the inflexible nature of supply means that companies raise prices more sharply in response to the surge in demand.

Putting supply and demand all together – markets in equilibrium and disequilibrium

Each side of the market has now been analysed separately and it is time to put it all together. At any point in time, there will be a given set of conditions influencing demand and a given set of conditions influencing supply (see Table 2.12). Let us say that these conditions are reflected in demand curve D_0 and supply curve S_0 from earlier on – these relationships have been combined in Figure 2.15.

Price of a standard PC ($)	Quantity supplied per week	Quantity demanded per week
800	1000	7000
1000	2000	6000
1200	3000	5000
1400	4000	4000
1600	5000	3000
1800	6000	2000
2000	7000	1000

Table 2.12 *Market supply and demand schedules for PCs*

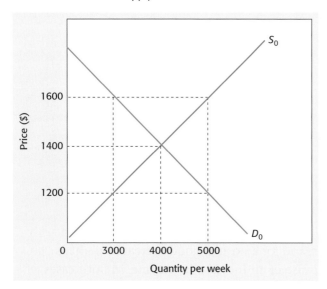

Figure 2.15 *Equilibrium price and output in the market for PCs*

The term **equilibrium** refers to a situation of balance where at least under present circumstances there is no tendency for change to occur. In this particular situation, equilibrium will exist when the plans of consumers (as represented by the market demand curve) match the plans of suppliers (as represented by the market supply curve).

The market equilibrium will, therefore, be at a price of $1400 with 4000 units bought and sold. These are referred to as **equilibrium price** and **equilibrium quantity**. Total consumer expenditure (and therefore industry **total revenue**) will be $5 600 000 per week. Just think about what would happen if for some reason companies thought that consumers were prepared to pay $1600 and supplied 5000 units to the market. In this case the market would be in **disequilibrium** (an imbalance where change will happen). At a price of $1600, under present circumstances, consumers are only planning to buy 3000 units. As such companies will build up excess stocks at the rate of 2000 PCs per week. There is disequilibrium due to excess supply. Companies would be irrational to carry on with this unplanned stock building. How might they react?

First of all, they could cut prices; they would also probably start to reduce the quantity they supply to the market. Of course, as they cut prices, some consumers who would not have been prepared to pay the higher price are now attracted back into the market – the disequilibrium starts to narrow. Provided there is no change to any of the conditions of supply or demand, and nothing prevented companies adjusting in this way, then eventually, perhaps through expert decision making or simply trial and error, the market price and quantity should move back to equilibrium.

Consumers can easily compare prices in superstores

Think now what would happen if the price was set at $1000. Again we have disequilibrium – this time of excess demand. Consumers are now keen to snap up what they consider to be a pretty good deal. However, given the low prices, supplies are fairly low and there are not enough PCs to meet demand – suppliers run out of stocks far quicker than they had expected, so there are unmet orders. Profit-oriented companies, if they are reasonably sharp, will recognise this and will start to raise price and increase the number of PCs available for sale. However, as prices rise, some consumers will decide that PCs have become too expensive and the quantity demanded will fall. Once again, as a result of trial and error and good management on the part of businesses, the market will adjust back to the equilibrium.

This process of market adjustment may not happen instantly; there will be time lags, perhaps quite lengthy ones if companies cannot react quickly. The point, however, is that there will always be a tendency for the market to move back to its equilibrium because that is where the underlying motives and plans of consumers and suppliers are driving it. When this position is reached, it is said that the market clears.

SELF-ASSESSMENT TASK 2.22

In Figure 2.16 symbols are used instead of numbers.

1 What is the market equilibrium price and quantity?
2 What area will show the total expenditure by consumers? This will be the same as the total revenue earned by companies.
3 What is the state of the market if the price is at P_1?
4 What is the state of the market if the price is at P_0?
5 Explain what will happen if the market is in a disequilibrium of:
 • excess demand
 • excess supply.
6 What advantages/disadvantages are there in using symbols, such as Ps and Qs, to analyse markets rather than actual numbers?

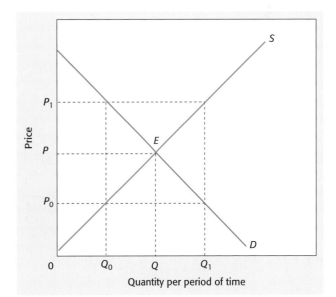

Figure 2.16

SELF-ASSESSMENT TASK 2.23

1 Review the factors that can cause the demand curve to shift.
2 Review the factors that can cause the supply curve to shift.
3 Review how disequilibrium positions are eliminated in a market.

Changes in the equilibrium

The equilibrium will change if there is a disturbance to the present market conditions – this could come about through a change in supply conditions (the supply curve shifts) or a change in demand conditions (the demand curve shifts).

A change in demand

Look at Figure 2.17 – notice we are using P and Q symbols again instead of actual numbers – if there is an increase in demand (D_0 to D_2), then, at the original price, there is now a disequilibrium of excess demand equal to $Q_1 - Q_0$. As suppliers begin to recognise this they will start to raise the price and increase the quantity supplied. The rise in price will lead some consumers to decide they do not want to buy the product at the higher price. Although the process may take some time, the market will move back towards the new equilibrium at $P^* Q^*$, where the market is once more in balance. Note that the new equilibrium is at a higher price with a larger quantity traded than in the original situation.

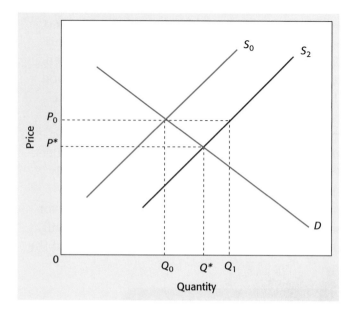

Figure 2.18 *The effect of a shift in the supply curve on equilibrium price and quantity*

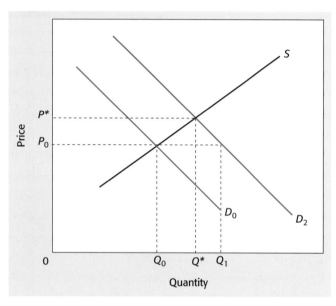

Figure 2.17 *The effect of a shift of the demand curve on equilibrium price and quantity*

A change in supply

Look at Figure 2.18 – if there is an increase in supply (from S_0 to S_2) then, at the original price (P_0), there is disequilibrium due to excess supply ($Q_1 - Q_0$). This would, of course, eventually be eliminated as price falls towards its new equilibrium level and the quantity traded in equilibrium rises from Q_0 to Q^* where the plans of consumers and companies once more coincide.

A change in supply and demand

The above analysis is useful to deal with simple situations. However, in many situations the conditions of both supply and demand may change

simultaneously. Look at Figure 2.19. The initial equilibrium is at P and Q with the demand curve D_0 and the supply curve S_0. The increase in demand for the product (caused by, say, the increase in the price of a substitute) puts upward pressure on price. However, the simultaneous increase in supply (caused by, say, a fall in raw material and energy costs) puts downward pressure on price. The resulting effect is that the equilibrium price remains unchanged, although of course there is a fairly significant increase in the quantity traded (from Q_0 to Q^*).

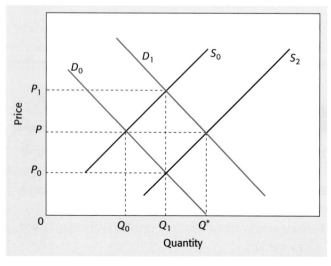

Figure 2.19 *An unchanged equilibrium price and a changed equilibrium quantity*

On 1 May 2009, the price of white sugar on the London commodity market reached a two and a half year high of $441 per tonne. Analysts put this down to an increase in demand from India, the world's largest consumer, and from Russia. A hefty 850 000 tonnes was heading for these two markets in May. With the imminent peak in the Brazilian cane harvest, it was expected that the increase in supply would bring prices down.

Using demand and supply diagrams:

1 Show how the increase in demand from India and Russia affected the market

2 Show how the increased supply of Brazilian sugar might affect the market.

3 What factors might mean that the world price of sugar will continue to increase in the future?

Consumer surplus

The underlying principles behind the demand curve are relatively simple to understand. They are also ones which many of us follow in our daily lives. For instance, when a product is on 'special offer' in a local shop, and its price has been reduced, more will be demanded and purchased.

For any good or service, though, there are always some people who are prepared to pay above the given price to obtain it. Some of the best examples where this happens are in the cases of tickets to popular rock concerts or, in England, to watch Premier League football clubs, such as Manchester United, or to see a major Test cricket series where all tickets are sold out. The stated price of tickets may well be

$40 per ticket, but there will always be some people who are willing to pay over $40 to obtain a ticket. Another example might be the case of a chocoholic who is prepared to pay over the odds to get a bar of his or her favourite chocolate. To the economist, such situations introduce the concept of **consumer surplus**.

Consumer surplus arises because some consumers are willing to pay more than the given price for all but the last unit they buy. This is illustrated in Figure 2.19 a where consumer surplus is the shaded area under the demand curve and above the price line. More specifically, it is the difference between the total value consumers place on all the units consumed and the payments they need to make in order to actually purchase that commodity.

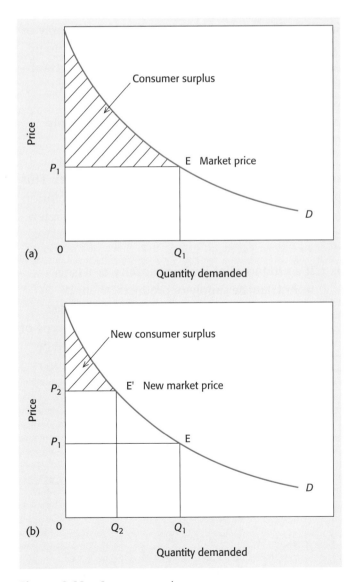

Figure 2.19 *Consumer surplus*

If the market price changes, then so does consumer surplus. For example, if the price increases, then consumer surplus is reduced as some consumers are unwilling to pay the higher price. This reduction is shown in Figure 2.20 b. The loss of consumer surplus is shown by the area $P_1P_2E^1E$. On the other hand, a fall in the market price will lead to an increase in consumer surplus. This is because consumers who were previously willing to pay above the new market price now end up paying less.

Prices as a rationing and allocative mechanism

It should be clear from the last part of this section that prices play a very important part in the allocation of resources in markets. The workings of the price mechanism as described are in the main automatic; in other words, price variations act as a signal in response to changes in demand or supply or both. This self-regulating mechanism (referred to by Adam Smith as 'the invisible hand') is an important feature of the market economy. It is a means by which equilibrium indicates where consumers' demand and the producers' willingness to supply meet.

In certain situations, this mechanism can also serve to **ration** resources in a particular market. This process can be achieved with or without intervention on the part of the government. Let us consider a few examples.

- If a producer has limited capacity or wishes to restrict the supply of products, then, if these products have a high price, the market mechanism will automatically result in a type of rationing occurring. A good example could be the ways in which exclusive car manufacturers

or designer fashion companies charge very high prices for their products. Price therefore limits demand and in turn seeks to ensure that it is in line with the quantity that is supplied.

- Governments may also wish to use the price mechanism as a means of rationing. A good example could be the way in which some governments try to restrict sales of alcohol or tobacco products through imposing very high rates of taxation on their consumptions. Another example could be the use of minimum price legislation, in this case to ration demand in relation to supply. This is shown in Figure 2.21. To be effective, the minimum price must be above the equilibrium price as determined in a free market.

- At the minimum price producers are willing to supply more than consumers are willing to demand. There is therefore excess supply. The price mechanism used in this way rations demand. In all of these cases, the government is interfering with the workings of the price mechanism in order to meet some other particular objective.

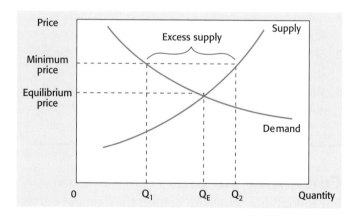

Figure 2.21   *The effects of a minimum price*

SELF-ASSESSMENT TASK 2.25

The feature below demonstrates how knowledge of demand, supply and the price mechanism can be applied in order to explain the global problem of rising food prices, particularly in the world's poorest economies in Africa and Asia. Read the feature and then answer the questions that follow.

Rising global food prices

In 2009, the World Bank reported that global food prices had almost doubled since 2005 and were forecast to continue to increase. The price of wheat especially had increased at an alarming rate of around 200% from 2008 to the end of 2009. The prices of maize (corn) and rice had also escalated.

In November 2009 the Indian government reported that annual food price inflation was over 21%, the price of pulses had risen by over 30% as had sugar prices. In Pakistan, food prices had also increased at a record rate amidst claims of hoarding by grain processors and retailers.

Normally, price changes for cereals can be attributed to short-term variations in supply caused by disruptive weather conditions. This was not so for the latest set of price increases which were caused largely due to demand side factors which included:

- the rising demand for meat in the booming economies of China and India; large quantities of grain are needed to feed chickens, pigs and cows, driving up prices
- a fall in domestic food production by increasingly affluent families in these countries.
- the increased demand for bio-fuels, especially in the USA and parts of Europe which has resulted in harvests being diverted from food processing to fuel processing factories, particularly for sugar cane and maize.

Supply side factors have exaggerated price increases and include:

- extreme weather conditions in 2008 and 2009, such as prolonged drought in parts of India, Australia and southern Africa and unexpected

frosts in parts of China, which had resulted in poor harvests; Europe's grain harvest was also affected by poor weather
- global stockpiles of grains were at a record low level, meaning that supplies could not be released onto the market to reduce price volatility.

In India, the problems of small farmers have been aggravated by the government's attempts to control prices. When domestic prices are rising, the government restricts export sales; when prices fall, farmers are paid subsidies. These actions seek to protect the interests of consumers and farmers alike. Because of uncertainty, many small sugar farmers abandoned sugar in 2008 when prices fell by 40%. In 2009 and early 2010, sugar prices surged. The obvious response would be for farmers to revert to sugar in the hope that high prices will persist.

Rising food prices have had a heavy impact on the poor in countries such as Bangladesh, India, Pakistan and those in sub-Saharan Africa. For people who have to live on less than $1 a day the rising price of food is devastating and can affect rural as well as urban communities. There have been riots in West Bengal in protest against subsidised food being sold on the informal market. In Senegal, Mauritania and in other parts of Africa, there have also been protests over rising food prices.

The World Bank has identified 36 countries where there are grave concerns over food security; 21 are in Africa, including Sierra Leone which lacks access to food from local markets due to its low level of income and the high prices of imported food.

1 Consider the factors that have contributed to rising food prices. Split these into demand factors and supply factors.

2 Using a demand and supply diagram, explain how the following factors have affected the market for food crops:
   a the increased demand for crops for biofuel
   b the increased consumption of meat in China and India.

3 The government of Sierra Leone has announced that it would start to produce its own rice, rather than rely on imports, from 2009. How might this affect the price of rice in Sierra Leone and on the global market?

4 Discuss whether rationing and an indirect tax on rice might produce a better allocation of resources in this market.

SPECIMEN EXAM QUESTIONS

The following questions have been set in recent CIE examination papers.

1 a Explain how an equilibrium price for a product is established in the market and how it may change. [8]

   b Discuss whether a firm's revenue would increase in response to price and income changes if the price elasticity of demand for its product became highly elastic. [12]

   [20 marks]

(October/November 2007)

The following question is taken from part of a recent OCR examination paper.

2 Air Passenger Duty (APD) is a flat rate indirect tax on passengers who fly from UK airports. It is collected by the airlines who add the tax onto ticket prices. At present, the tax is £5 for economy class passengers travelling on flights within the European Union.

   The table below summarises the likely effects of increases in APD on a typical flight.

New tax rate	£10	£15	£25	£35
% change in ticket prices	7%	14%	28%	42%
% change in quantity demanded	−5%	−15%	−40%	−66%

   a Calculate the price elasticity of demand for each of the new tax rates.
   b Explain the meaning of each of the figures you have calculated.

   c Suppose the UK government wishes to reduce the demand for air travel for environmental reasons. Comment on how it might use the price elasticity of demand estimates to achieve this objective.

(June 2009)

SUMMARY

In this core section it has been shown that:

- A market exists whenever people come together for the trade or exchange of goods and services.
- The buying side of the market is referred to by economists as the demand side. It is possible to derive a demand curve for any market – this shows how the quantity demanded varies with the price of a product.
- The demand curve shifts to the left or right when, 'other things being equal', the assumption is changed. Three important causes of this are a change in income, a change in consumer tastes or attitudes and a change in the price of related products.
- Price, income and cross elasticity of demand are relevant concepts that explain the extent of change in the quantity demanded and in demand respectively; they are all numerical measures that have substantial business relevance.
- It is possible to model the selling side of a market through a supply curve. This shows how the quantity supplied varies with the price of a product. The supply curve shifts when there are changes in the costs of supply, the characteristics of an industry and government policy.
- The price elasticity of supply is important in understanding how supply reacts to a change in the price of a product.
- Equilibrium occurs in the market where there is no tendency for change, when the plans of consumers match the plans of suppliers. A change to the equilibrium position will produce a new equilibrium price and quantity.
- Consumer surplus arises because some consumers are willing to pay more than the market price for a product.
- Prices are important in allocating and rationing resources in a market.

2 The price system
Supplement

- the law of diminishing marginal utility and its relationship to the derivation of an individual demand schedule and curve
- what a budget line is and how it can be used to show the income and substitution effects of a price change
- the short run production function: fixed and variable factors of production and the law of diminishing returns; the long run production function and returns to scale
- why the demand for labour is a derived demand, the factors that affect it and how a firm's demand for a factor of production such as labour can be explained using marginal revenue product theory
- what is meant by the supply of labour, the factors that affect it and the significance of net advantages
- how wages are determined in a free market, the role of trade unions and government in wage determination, wage differentials and economic rent
- the difference between the economist's and the accountant's definitions of costs, how various costs can be determined and how the shape of the short run average cost curve can be explained
- how to explain the shape of the long run average cost curve, the relationship between economies of scale and decreasing costs, internal and external economies of scale
- why firms grow and how small firms can survive
- how to explain the relationship between elasticity, marginal, average and total revenue for a downward-sloping demand curve
- the meaning of a firm and the industry
- the objectives of firms including the traditional one of profit maximisation
- what is meant by market structure and how this can be explained in terms of the number of buyers and sellers, the nature of the product, ease of entry and the nature of information
- the market structures of perfect competiton, monopoly, monopolistic competition and oligopoly
- what is meant by contestability and the features of contestable markets
- how firms behave in terms of pricing and non-price policies
- how the performance of firms is assessed in terms of output, profits and efficiency; how the above market structures compare in these terms.

Utility and marginal utility

Economists have long been interested in the way that consumers behave. Aspects of demand theory were introduced earlier in the Core section of this chapter. Here we shall look behind the demand curve and explore why it really is the case that consumers buy more of a good when its price falls.

The starting point is the notion of **utility**. This idea dates back to the nineteenth century and is a term used to record the level of happiness or satisfaction that someone receives from the consumption of a good. It is assumed that this satisfaction can be measured, in the same way that the actual units consumed can be calculated. Two important measures are:

- total utility – the overall satisfaction that is derived from the consumption of all units of a good over a given time period
- **marginal utility** – the additional utility derived from the consumption of one more unit of a particular good.

SELF-ASSESSMENT TASK 2.26

1 Table 2.13 shows the total utility gained from the consumption of lemonade in a week.

Quantity consumed (bottles)	Total utility
0	0
1	20
2	35
3	45
4	53
5	58
6	54
7	48

Table 2.13

a Calculate the marginal utility.
b Sketch the total utility and marginal utility curves (put utility on the vertical axis, quantity consumed on the horizontal axis).

2 If the price of lemonade increases from $1 to $2 per bottle, how might it affect consumption? Explain your answer using the data above.

The marginal utility gained from the consumption of a product tends to fall as consumption increases. For example, if you buy an ice cream you will get a lot of satisfaction from consuming it, especially in hot weather. If you consume a second one, you will still get some satisfaction, but this is likely to be less than from the first ice cream. A third ice cream will yield even less satisfaction. This aspect of consumer behaviour is referred to as the law of **diminishing marginal utility**. As consumption increases, there may actually come a point where marginal utility is negative, indicating dissatisfaction or disutility.

In considering the consumer's equilibrium, it is necessary to remember that Economics assumes that consumers have limited incomes, behave in a rational manner and seek to maximise their total utility. A consumer is said to be in equilibrium, assuming a given level of income, when it is not possible to switch any expenditure from, say, product A to product B to increase total utility. This is referred to as the **equimarginal principle** and can be represented:

$$\frac{MU_A}{P_A} = \frac{MU_B}{P_B} = \frac{MU_C}{P_C} \cdots = \frac{MU_N}{P_N}$$

where *MU* = marginal utility

P = the price

A, B, C and *N* = individual products

It is possible to use marginal utility to derive an individual demand curve. The fundamental principle of demand is that an increase in the price of a good will lead to a reduction in its demand. Using the above principle, this can now be proved. The value of the expression $\dfrac{MU_A}{P_A}$ will now fall as the price of A has increased. So, the marginal utility of A per $ spent will now be less than on any other goods. The consumer will therefore increase total utility by spending less on good A and more on all other goods. This will in turn reduce the value of their marginal utility. In other words, the consumer only maximises total utility by buying less of good A. The conclusion is that the demand curve for a good is downward sloping.

Budget lines

As shown in Chapter 2 Core, all consumers are constrained in what they are able to buy because of their income and the prices of goods they wish to buy. These two important underpinning principles of consumer behaviour are brought together in the idea of a **budget line**. This shows numerically all the possible combinations of two products that a consumer can purchase with a given income and fixed prices.

Suppose someone has $200 to spend on two products, A and B. Assume the price of A is $20 and the price of B is $10. Table 2.14 shows the possible combinations that can be purchased. Each of the combinations would cost $200 in total. Figure 2.22 a shows the budget line for this situation. Any point along this line will produce an outcome where consumption is maximised for this level of income.

If there is a change in the price of one good, with income remaining unchanged, then the budget line will pivot. For example, if the price of product B falls, then more of this product can be purchased at all levels of income. The budget line will shift outwards, from its pivot at point A. This is shown in figure 2.22b. So, if the price of B falls by a third, then 30 of good B can now be purchased with an income of $200.

Quantity of A ($20 each)	Quantity of B ($10 each)
10	0
9	2
8	4
7	6
6	8
5	10
4	12
3	14
2	16
1	18
0	20

Table 2.14   *Combinations of A and B with a budget of $200*

As the price of B has fallen relative to that of A, which is unchanged, consumers will substitute B for A. This is known as the **substitution effect** of a price change. It is always the case that the rational consumer will substitute towards the product which has become relatively cheaper. With the fall in the price of B, the consumer actually has more money to spend on other products, B included. Real income has therefore increased, which may mean that a consumer may now actually purchase more of product B. This is called the **income effect** of a price change.

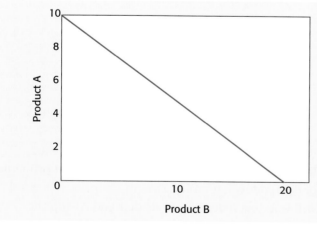

(a)   *Budget lines for an income of $200*

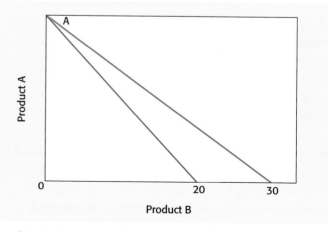

(b)   *Budget lines – a fall in the price of B*

Figure 2.22

SELF-ASSESSMENT TASK 2.27

1 Re-draw Figure 2.22a to show how it would change:
   a if the price of B increased, leaving the price of A unchanged
   b if the price of A decreased, leaving the price of B unchanged.
2 In your own words, describe the substitution and income effects of:
   a an increase in the price of a normal good
   b a decrease in the price of an inferior good.

Principles of production and the production function

Introduction

At the beginning of Chapter 1 we identified four factors of production. These were land, labour, capital and enterprise. In all cases, the demand for these factors of production comes from a producer who wishes to use them to make various goods or products. The producer is normally a firm or business whose demand for factors of production is derived from the needs of its operations. Let us take the case of a clothing manufacturer to elaborate this important point.

As a consequence of globalisation, many items of clothing are now produced in the developing economies of South East Asia, north Africa and central Europe. Designer labels, such as Nike, Reebok, Ellesse and Kappa, are no longer produced in the home country of their corporate producer. Producers in these countries need all of the factors of production in order to make their products for sale in markets which are mainly in developed economies. Their task is to combine the factors of production in an effective way to be efficient, competitive and profitable in the world market. The most important decision they have to make concerns the relative mixture of labour and capital. Therefore the task for the firm is to find the least cost or most efficient combination of labour and capital for the production of a given quantity of output.

Clothing is a typical example of a business where labour and capital are in direct competition with each other. If labour costs are relatively cheap, as is the case in developing and emerging economies, then the production process is likely to take place using much more labour than capital. In most developed economies, though, the reverse is true. High-tech machines can often be used to replace labour, largely because it is more cost effective to do so. So, in this case, the same amount of output is produced using more capital and far less labour than if it were taking place in a developing economy.

Firms therefore have to choose between alternative production methods. Returning to the case of the clothing manufacturer, Figure 2.23 shows three different methods of production, each of which combines different levels of labour and capital to make items of clothing. Line A shows a method whereby labour and capital are used in equal proportions; line B shows a production method which uses twice as much capital as labour and line C shows the output resulting from twice as much labour as capital being used. On these lines, points *X*, *Y* and *Z* show the respective amounts of labour and capital that are needed to produce 100 units of clothing. If we join these points, then it gives us what is known as an isoquant, a curve which joins points which give us a particular level of output. This isoquant can of course be extended for other combinations of labour and capital not shown on Figure 2.23.

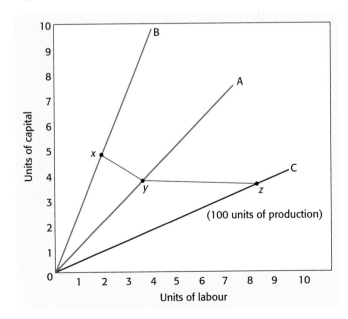

Figure 2.23 *Alternative production methods*

A clothing factory in India

The production function

To simplify our analysis, let us assume that the size of a clothing factory is fixed and that the only way in which the units of clothing produced can be varied is through varying the input of labour. This is referred to as the **short run**. Table 2.15 shows how the quantity of clothing produced depends on the number of workers employed. For example, if there are no workers in the factory, there is no output; with one worker, output is 100 units. When there are two workers, the total output is 180 units and so on.

Figure 2.24 is a graph of the first two columns of data in Table 2.15. It shows the relationship between the quantity of factor inputs (labour/workers) and the **total product** or quantity of output (clothing). It is called the **production function**. Column 3 of Table 2.12 shows the **marginal product**, the increase in output that occurs from an additional unit of input (labour in this case). The data in this column show that, when the number of workers goes from one to two, output increases by 80 units; when it goes from two to three workers, the marginal product is 60 units. As the number of workers increases, the marginal product declines. This property is referred to as **diminishing returns**.

The final column of Table 2.15 shows another important variable, **average product**. This is calculated by dividing the total product (output produced) by the number of workers employed. It is a simple measure of labour productivity, i.e. how much output is produced by each worker.

Number of workers	Output of clothing	Marginal product	Average product
0	0		0
		100	
1	100		100
		80	
2	180		90
		60	
3	240		80
		20	
4	280		70
		15	
5	295		59
		11	
6	306		51

Table 2.15 *Production data*

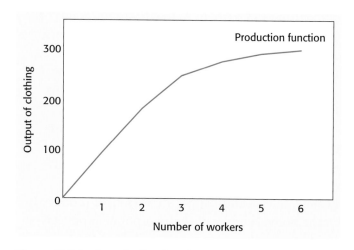

Figure 2.24 *A production function*

SELF-ASSESSMENT TASK 2.28

1 Using data from Table 2.15, draw a graph with lines to show:
- the marginal product of labour
- the average product of labour.

2 What do you notice about the shape of the two lines?

3 What implications do these lines have for a clothing firm planning how much to produce?

From short run to long run

As stated above, the short run is a period of time in Economics when at least one of the factors of production is fixed. The factor that takes the longest to change is capital. The factor that tends to be easiest to change is labour as we have already seen. Students often ask the question, 'How long is the short run?' This is not an easy question to answer, as it tends to differ for different industries. In the clothing **industry** it is likely to be no more than a few weeks: the time that is taken to install new capital equipment and to get this operational to produce clothing. In other industries, it will be much longer. A country building a new hydro-electric power station will, for example, take much longer to plan, install and make such a new facility operational. Ten years may well be a realistic estimate in this case. This time is still referred to as the short run since capital is fixed over this time.

In the **long run**, all factors of production are variable. This therefore gives the firm much greater scope to vary the respective mix of its factor inputs so that it is producing at the most efficient level. So, if capital becomes relatively cheaper than labour, or if a new production process is invented and this increases productivity, firms can reorganise the way in which they produce. Firms must therefore know the cost of the factors of production they use and see this in relation to the marginal physical output which accrues. The right combination of factors can be arrived at as their price varies. Firms should aim to be in a position where:

$$\frac{\text{marginal product factor A}}{\text{price of factor A}} = \frac{\text{marginal product factor B}}{\text{price of factor B}} = \frac{\text{marginal product factor C}}{\text{price of factor C}}$$

and so on for all factors of production they use. For them to be able to do this all factors of production must be variable.

If we go back to the principles introduced in Figure 2.23, it is possible to derive the long run production function for a firm by initially constructing an isoquant map. This shows the different combinations of labour and capital that can be used to produce various level of output. This is shown in Figure 2.25.

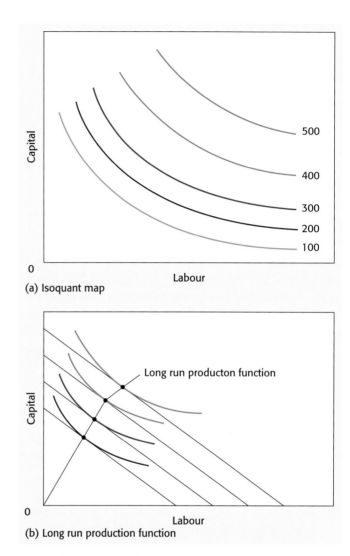

(a) Isoquant map

(b) Long run production function

Figure 2.25 *Isoquants and isocosts*

Let us again assume that this is for a clothing manufacturer. Figure 2.25 a consists of a collection of isoquants for output levels 100, 200, 300, 400 and 500 units of production. From this it is possible to read off the respective combinations of labour and capital that could produce these output levels. (Remember that this is only looking at output from a physical standpoint.)

If you look at the diagram carefully you will see that as production increases from 100 to 200, relatively less capital and labour is required per unit of output. This is referred to as **increasing returns**. As production expands further, increasing amounts of capital and labour are needed to produce 100 more units and so move up to the next isoquant. In contrast, this indicates **decreasing returns**.

In the long run, both labour and capital can be varied and, as stated above, the actual mix will depend upon their prices. Figure 2.25b shows what are known as isocosts: lines of constant relative costs for the factors of production. On this figure, therefore, each of the isocosts shown has an identical slope. In deciding how to produce, the firm will be looking for the most economically efficient or least cost process. This is obtained by bringing together the isoquants and isocosts, so linking the physical and economic sides of the production process. The point where the isocost is tangential to an isoquant represents the best combination of factors for the firm to employ. Hence, on Figure 2.25b, the expansion path or long run production function of the firm can be shown by joining together all of the various tangential points.

It is important to recognise that the above analysis is highly theoretical. In practice:

- It is often very difficult for firms to determine their isoquants – they often do not have the data or the experience to be able to do this.
- It is also assumed that in the long run it is quite possible to switch factors of production. This may not always be as easy as the theory might indicate.
- Some employers may be reluctant to switch labour and capital – they may feel that they have a social obligation to their workforce and will therefore not alter their production plans with a change in relative factor prices.

The labour market

Introduction

When you leave school or college (hopefully with a CIE Advanced Level in Economics), the wage or salary you get paid will be determined largely by what type of job you take. If you get a post as a clerk, you are likely to get more pay than if you are a street cleaner. Equally, if you go on to become a teacher, you will get paid more than a clerk. In turn, the manager of a multinational company will get paid more than a teacher. So, why is it that some workers get paid more than others? Why is it that some people with exceptional sporting talent, for example Cristiano Ronaldo, Tiger Woods or Amitabh Bachchan, are

so highly paid? The answer to these questions, like many such questions in Economics, is that it all depends on supply and demand. To understand why some people get paid more than others, economists have looked at the labour market and sought to put forward various principles based on the characteristics of this market.

Why are some sports personalities so highly paid?

Demand for labour

Many of the principles introduced in the Core section of this chapter can be applied to the labour market. However, there is one fundamentally different point: the demand for labour is a **derived demand**. By this, we mean that the firm's demand for labour is due to its decision to produce certain goods or services. Labour is therefore demanded not for its own sake but because it is essential for the production of goods or services. If we go back to our earlier examples, clerks are employed because they are necessary for a firm to carry out its business. The streets need cleaning, therefore street cleaners are employed. Children need education so teachers are required. This may seem obvious but it does underpin the whole basis of labour economics. A small number of film stars, rock idols and sports personalities have exceptional talents – the demand for their services is very high indeed and they can command a high fee for their services.

The analysis that follows is based upon two important assumptions:

- The firm wishing to hire labour is operating in a competitive market. There are many buyers and sellers of labour, and no single firm or worker can affect the wage that is paid.

- The firm is a profit-maximiser. Its demand and supply of labour are based on it maximising the difference between total revenue and total costs.

The marginal revenue product of labour

So far in our analysis of the demand for labour we have only been concerned with physical inputs and outputs. This is somewhat unrealistic because, in reality, the profit-maximising firm is concerned with how much this output is worth to the firm. We must therefore take into account the cost of employing labour – the wage rate. Let us assume that this is $600 per month and, using data from Table 2.15, let us assume that a unit of clothing sells for $10.

When the firm hires the first worker, this worker generates $1000 of revenue for the firm; this in turn represents $400 of profit. The amount of revenue generated by an additional worker is referred to as the **marginal revenue product** of labour. Adding a further worker generates another $800 and $200 profit. There comes a point when, after the third worker has been employed, a further worker adds more to costs than to revenue (it still costs $600 to employ the worker but only $400 worth of clothing is produced). So, above this level of employment, the value of the marginal product that is being produced is less than the wage. This clearly makes no sense to the firm. It can therefore be deduced that the firm should hire workers up to the point where the value of the marginal product of labour equals the wage that is being paid. The demand curve for labour can therefore be represented by the value of the marginal product curve. This is shown in Figure 2.26. So, in general terms:

- a firm should continue to hire labour as long as the additional worker adds more to revenue than he or she adds to the firm's costs
- the market wage is determined by the marginal revenue product of labour
- the marginal revenue product curve for labour is the firm's demand curve for labour
- if the wage rate rises or falls, then fewer or more workers will be employed.

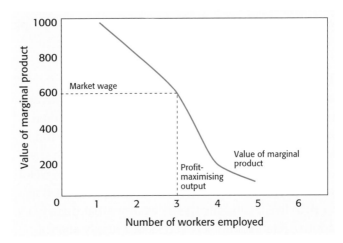

Figure 2.26 *The value of the marginal product of labour*

It follows from this analysis that the wages paid to workers are a direct reflection of their marginal revenue product. So, a street cleaner has a lower marginal revenue product than a clerk, who in turn has a lower marginal revenue product than a teacher and so on. It also follows that it is actually possible to measure marginal revenue productivity. This is a very big assumption to make. In a manufacturing firm it may be possible to do this, but in many occupations this is not possible. How, for example, can we measure the marginal revenue of a teacher? The answer is 'with great difficulty'. We therefore need to look at the other side of the labour market, that involving the supply of labour, to give a proper explanation of how wages are actually determined.

Supply of labour

The labour supply or supply of labour refers to the total number of hours that labour is able and willing to supply at a particular wage rate. The general principles of supply introduced in the Core section of this chapter apply here. However, it is important to remember that in this case we are talking about people and their willingness to participate (or otherwise) in the labour market depending upon the rate or price that they are offered for their services. It is useful to consider labour supply at three levels: that of the individual worker, that of a firm or industry and that of the economy as a whole. Different factors affect supply depending upon which of these levels we are dealing with. Let us look briefly at each in turn.

The individual's labour supply

As with any supply, price (or wage in this case) has an important bearing on the decision of any individual worker to enter the labour market. If the wage is too low, someone may determine that it is not worth the effort of going to work and decide to stay at home. Not many people are in this position – most of us need to work to live. Economic theory assumes that there is a positive relationship between labour supply and the wage rate. So, as the wage rate increases, more people are willing to offer their services to employers. This is shown diagramatically by the labour supply curve, which mainly slopes upwards (as shown in Figure 2.27). Beyond a certain point, though, individuals will take the view that they prefer leisure to work. This point is indicated by the backward-sloping curve from point X. Before this point, an individual worker is more willing to supply his or her labour as the wage rate increases. It must be stressed that this point depends on the individual's attitude to work and leisure – point X on any individual's supply curve will vary.

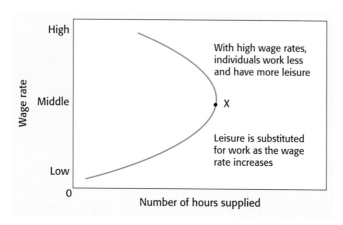

Figure 2.27 *An individual's labour supply curve*

A further factor that can affect an individual's supply of labour is the income tax rate. In all countries this tends to be progressive. Low-wage workers pay little or no tax. As wages rise, more of the increase is paid in tax to the government. In the UK, for example, the standard rate of income tax in 2009 was 20%, with a maximum rate of 50% for high-income earners. In many other countries this higher rate is above 50%.

The downside could be that a high tax rate stifles the incentive to work. Governments must therefore be very careful to not do this as it will adversely affect economic prospects if key workers are not encouraged to work because of the high tax rates.

Labour supply to a firm or industry

This supply curve consists of the sum of the individual supply curves of all workers employed in a firm or industry. It is usually upward sloping throughout (see Figure 2.28). As happens with an individual worker, the number of workers wanting to supply their labour increases with the wage rate that is offered. The slope of this supply curve is measured by the elasticity of supply of labour – the extent to which labour supply responds to a change in the wage rate. Figure 2.28 shows two different supply curves, one inelastic (L_1) and the other elastic with respect to the wages being paid.

There are various reasons for this difference. An obvious one is the skills required to carry out a particular occupation. In general, the more skills required, the more inelastic will be the supply of labour. This also applies to the amount of education and training that is required to carry out a particular job. Anyone who teaches has to spend at least four years acquiring the necessary qualifications. Supply to such an occupation will be more inelastic than to, say, road sweeping, where no skills and little or no education and training are needed.

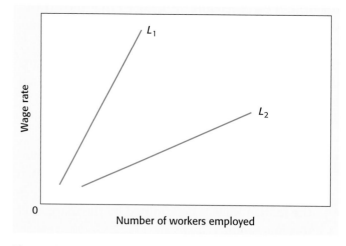

Figure 2.28 *The supply curve of labour to a firm or industry*

The supply curve L_2 in Figure 2.28 is therefore likely to be that for an industry where wages are low and where there is a plentiful supply of labour with no particular skills or training.

In a competitive labour market, the wage rates offered in all other industries or occupations will be important in determining the supply of labour to a particular industry. In developing economies, an obvious example could be the difference in wages in agriculture compared with wages in emerging manufacturing industries or food-processing industries which usually pay more to their workers.

The long run supply of labour

This is of particular significance to the economy as a whole. There are important contrasts here between developed and developing economies, involving wider economic factors including the following:

- **The size of the population** In some developed economies, the total population is relatively stable; in others it is increasing at a modest rate mainly due to increasing immigration. In contrast, the population of Italy is actually declining quite markedly. With life expectancy increasing, there are relatively fewer people of working age. In contrast, in most developing economies, there is an increase in the overall supply of labour from within as increasing numbers of young people join the labour market. This means the long run supply curve for labour shifts to the right, indicating that more workers are willing to supply their labour at a given wage rate.
- **The labour participation rate** This term is used to determine the proportion of the population of working age actually in employment. In many developed economies, workers often choose to leave the labour market, by taking 'early retirement', before the normal age for retirement, so reducing the labour participation rate. At the lower end of the age range, with more students electing for higher education, the labour participation rate is also falling slightly. The combined effect of these has been for a slight reduction in the labour participation rate, so shifting the long run labour supply curve to the left.

- **The tax and benefits levels** As we saw in Figure 2.27 for the individual, there comes a point where the work–leisure trade-off affects labour supply. This also affects the supply of labour for the economy as a whole, particularly in developed economies. Governments therefore have to be very careful in their taxation and social security policies to ensure that the long run supply of labour is not adversely affected through a reduction in the willingness of people to work. In the UK, as previously stated, the top rate of income tax is now 50% – 20 years ago it was much more progressive, with marginal tax rates as high as 80% of the increase in income for the highest paid. In such circumstances, there is clearly a huge disincentive for someone to stay in the labour market. The level of unemployment and social security payments can also affect the long run supply of labour in a similar way. Through their supply-side policies therefore governments seek to provide incentives for certain types of labour to remain active in the labour market (see Chapter 7).
- **Immigration and emigration** These affect the long run supply of labour in an economy. Where there are labour shortages, as was the case in the UK during the late 1950s and early 1960s, immigrants moved from Commonwealth countries, often to work in relatively low pay industries and the public services. This increased the supply of labour. Emigration from these countries in turn relieved pressures in their labour markets. In the past, the UK has faced labour shortages in nursing, teaching and 'high-tech' industries as well as in other skilled manual occupations. Since 2004, the geographical enlargement of the EU has seen a huge influx of migrant workers from the new member states in Central and Eastern Europe.

The above factors determine the long run supply of labour. Shifts to the left and to the right in the long-run supply of labour are shown in Figure 2.29.

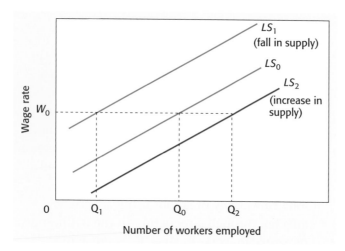

Figure 2.29 *Shifts in the long run supply of labour*

In the long run, the supply of labour to a particular firm, as distinct from the economy, is influenced by the **net advantages** of a job. These include **pecuniary advantages** and **non-pecuniary advantages**.

A pecuniary advantage includes things such as the weekly wage or monthly salary, any bonus payments, the opportunity to work paid overtime and pension prospects. Non-pecuniary advantages are numerous and cover an almost endless list of factors that have to be taken into account by a person considering whether to remain in a job, change jobs or even to change occupations. These include the hours of work, job security, holiday entitlement, promotion prospects, location of the workplace and whether the job is pleasant or satisfying. For many workers, these non-pecuniary advantages rather than pecuniary advantages often have a major bearing on their choice of occupation.

SELF-ASSESSMENT TASK 2.29

Read the feature below and then answer the questions that follow.

Polish migrant workers leave Britain in droves

When Poland and seven other Central and Eastern European countries joined the EU in May 2004, the UK experienced one of the largest single waves of immigration the country had ever seen. This was mainly because the UK, unlike other member states, gave free access to the citizens of these eight countries.

By 2008, there were well over 1m new migrant workers registered for work or who were self-employed in the UK. Around 700 000 were from Poland, the largest of the new member states. Their motives for coming to the UK were economic and included high unemployment in Poland, low wages at less than one quarter of the UK average, and an opportunity to send money back home to their struggling families.

Around 80% of the Polish migrants were less than 34 years old. Many went to London and to the Anglia region where there was a desperate shortage of agricultural labour. Unlike former

Commonwealth migrants, Polish workers went to almost every corner of the country in search of work. They continue to play an important part in the manufacturing, construction, hospitality and catering industries as well as in agriculture. Polish-owned businesses, restaurants and shops have also become a common sight.

As recession looms over Britain, Polish workers are leaving the country and going home in droves. Some of those leaving have become unemployed; others have become disillusioned by the high cost of living in the UK and the effects of the depreciation of the Polish zloty. They have also been attracted by the better state of the Polish economy and the consequent opportunity to work for a more realistic wage in their home country.

Source: Blume, C., VOA News, 31 March 2009 (adapted)

---

1 Use a diagram to explain the effects on the UK labour market of:
  a the influx of migrant workers
  b the return of Polish workers following the downturn in the UK economy.

2 Discuss the costs and benefits for
  a the UK economy
  b the Polish economy
  of labour migration on the scale reported above.

Wage determination under free market forces

So far, we have established two important features of the workings of the labour market. These are:

- the wage paid to labour equals the value of the marginal product of labour
- the willingness of labour to supply their services to the labour market is dependent upon the wage rate that is being offered.

In some respects, it might seem surprising that the wage can do both of these things at the same time. However, it is all tied up with how wages are actually determined in a competitive labour market.

The price of labour, the wage, is no different from any other price in so far as it depends on demand and supply. Figure 2.30 shows how the wage and quantity of labour adjust to balance demand and supply. As the demand curve reflects the value of the marginal product of labour, in equilibrium workers receive the value of their contribution to the production of goods and services. Each firm therefore purchases labour until the value of the marginal product equals the wage. Therefore, the wage paid in the market must equal the value of the marginal product of labour once it has brought demand and supply into equilibrium. The market therefore clears at the equilibrium wage.

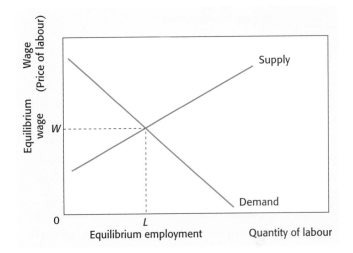

Figure 2.30 *Equilibrium in the labour market*

However, the labour market is dynamic, like any market – any change in the demand or the supply of labour will change the equilibrium wage. The value of the marginal product of labour will also change by the same amount, as, by definition, it must always equal the wage rate.

Let us now analyse how a change in the demand for labour and a change in the supply of labour affect the market equilibrium.

If we go back to the earlier example of clothing, we can see that an increase in the income of consumers in developed economies will shift the demand curve for clothing to the right, indicating that more will be demanded at any price. In turn, this affects the demand for labour producing the clothing – this is shown in Figure 2.31 by a shift to the right of the labour demand curve. The outcome is that the equilibrium wage rises from W_1 to W_2, and employment increases from L_1 to L_2. As before, the change in the wage rate reflects a change in the value of the marginal physical product of labour.

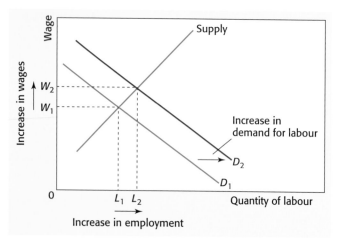

Figure 2.31   *Effects of an increase in demand for labour*

A change in the labour supply will also affect the market equilibrium. Suppose that there is an increase in the number of migrant workers and that this increases the number of workers who are able to produce clothing. When this happens, the labour supply curve shifts to the right. This surplus labour has a downward effect on wages, making it more profitable for firms producing clothing to hire more labour. As the number of workers increases, so their marginal physical product falls, as does the value of their marginal revenue product. The outcome in this case is that wages are reduced for all workers,

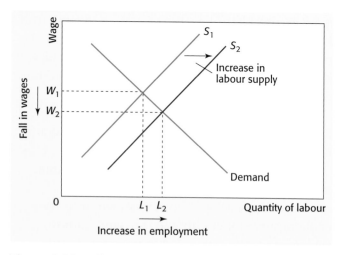

Figure 2.32   *Effects of an increase in the supply of labour*

although the level of employment rises. This is shown in Figure 2.32.

The role of trade unions and government in wage determination

So far in our analysis of how wages are determined we have assumed that the respective forces of demand and supply operate freely with no intervention. In many respects this is an unreal assumption as in many labour markets, the demand and supply of labour are affected by the actions of trade unions and the government. Such interventions produce what are sometimes referred to as imperfections in the labour market.

Trade union members protesting over job cuts

Trade unions are organisations that seek to represent labour in their place of work. They were set up and continue to exist because individuals (labour) have very little power to influence conditions of employment, including wages. Through **collective bargaining** with employers, they act on behalf of their members to:

* increase the wages of their members
* improve working conditions
* maintain pay differentials between skilled and unskilled workers
* fight job losses
* provide a safe working environment
* secure additional working benefits
* prevent unfair dismissals.

Traditionally, trade unions have been strong in manufacturing and less important in the service sector, transport excepted. As the structure of the UK economy has changed, so total membership has fallen to just 6 million workers in 2009, less than one in three of the working population. Many of these trade union members are employed in the public sector. Consequently, the power of the trade union movement is not as strong as it was when membership was over 10 million in 1985.

Economic analysis suggests that, in a competitive labour market, a powerful trade union is able to secure wages for its members above the equilibrium wage rate explained in Figure 2.30 (page 81). The basis for this claim is shown in Figure 2.33. At the equilibrium wage, the quantity of labour employed is L. If a strong trade union can force up wages to say W_u, which is above the equilibrium, the number of workers who are offered jobs by employers falls to L_u. At this wage though the number of people who would like to work is higher. This is shown by L_c. Consequently, there is a shortfall between those who want to work and those who can actually work, due to the influence of the trade union. This is shown in Figure 2.33 as the difference between L_c and L_u.

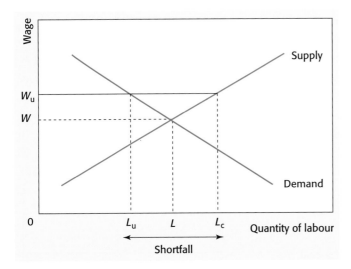

Figure 2.33 *The effect of a strong trade union in a competitive labour market*

In practice, it is really quite difficult to prove whether or not this theory actually applies in labour markets. A much quoted example is that of actors and actresses in the UK and USA where there are very strong unions which restrict the numbers able to work in films, television and theatres. The wages of their members are supposedly supported in this way. Other examples are likely to be in labour markets where a trade union has a monopoly over workers with a particular type of skill. Increasingly though the **closed-shop** policies of trade unions such as the above have been made illegal, so restricting their powers to act in this way. The case of the print unions in the UK was another example. However, new technology has removed their power to secure exceptionally high wages for their workers.

As globalisation increases, trade unions who try to behave in this way are playing a dangerous game with employers. The fear is that because of high labour costs and restrictive practices employers will go out of business or transfer production to countries where wage levels are lower. This threat has been particularly severe for UK car manufacturers – production has been switched to other EU countries, such as Spain and Poland, where labour costs can be as little as one-fifth of those in the UK. Consequently, trade unions have very little real influence over the wages paid to their members.

The labour market has seen explicit government intervention through the introduction of national minimum wages. In the UK, after considerable deliberation, the government's Low Pay Commission recommended a national minimum wage from early 1999 for all workers above the age of 21. The main aim of a minimum wage such as this is to reduce poverty and the exploitation of workers who have little or no bargaining power with their employers. In the UK, many women employed in shops, small businesses and low-skill jobs, such as home working and cleaning, were being paid very low wages and, in the eyes of the government, were being exploited. The introduction of the minimum wage was of particular significance for them.

Whether there should be a minimum wage is controversial. Some of the aims are given above. Additionally, it was argued that the amount of state benefits being paid to low-income families would be reduced with the introduction of a minimum wage. There might also be a small increase in tax revenue. Opponents were not convinced by these arguments, believing that jobs would be lost and that other low-paid workers would seek an increase to maintain their differential with the lowest paid. Cost-push inflation could well result, so affecting the economy as a whole.

The economics of a minimum wage are shown in Figure 2.34. The effect on an industry is particularly dependent upon the elasticities of demand and supply for labour in that industry. Figure 2.34a shows the effects where there is an inelastic demand for labour. The loss of jobs here is much less than shown in Figure 2.34b where the demand for labour is more wage elastic. In both cases there is an excess supply of labour at the higher minimum wage. This excess is more pronounced in (b) where both the demand for and supply of labour are relatively elastic. It can also be seen that the higher the minimum wage is set above the competitive equilibrium ($2.50 in the case of Figure 2.34), the greater will be the excess supply of labour willing to work at the national minimum wage.

Monopsony in the labour market

A **monopsony** occurs in the labour market when there is a single or dominant buyer of labour. In this situation the monopoly buyer is able to determine the price which is paid for the services of the workers that are employed. Unlike other examples we have looked at, in this situation we are now dealing with an imperfect rather than competitive market.

Figure 2.35 shows how the monopsonist can affect the market equilibrium. The monopsonist will hire workers by equating the marginal cost paid to employ a worker with the marginal revenue product gained from this employment. This is the profit-maximising position. The wage that the monopsonist pays to hire

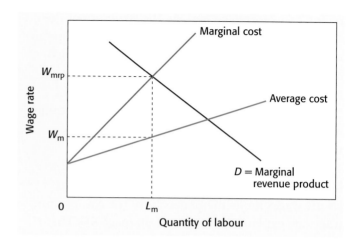

Figure 2.35   *A monopsony buyer of labour*

labour is W_m. This is actually below the wage that should be paid if they were paying the full value of their marginal revenue product, that is W_{mrp}. The level of employment is L_m.

In this situation the power of the employer in the labour market is of over-riding importance and the employer can set a low wage because of this buying power. Monopsonists often exist in local labour market situations, for example, where there is just one major employer in a town or where workers may be employed in an extractive industry located well away from where they may normally live. In this way the employer dominates the labour market, setting down wages and all other conditions of employment.

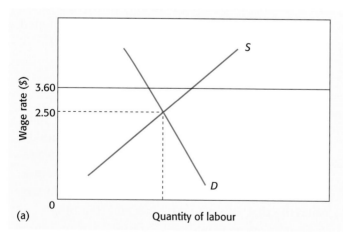

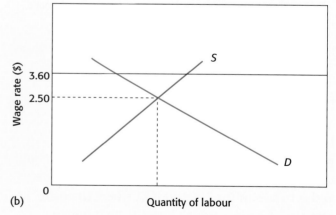

Figure 2.34   *The effects of the introduction of a minimum wage*

Transfer earnings and economic rent in the labour market

In our introduction to the labour market we posed the question:

Why is it that some people with exceptional sporting talent, for example Christiano Ronaldo, Tiger Woods or Amitabh Bachchan, are so highly paid?

The answer to this question can in part be given in the same way as to that as to why a teacher is paid more than a street cleaner – supply and demand. In order to answer why these differences in earnings occur, economists find it useful to split earnings into two elements:

1   **Transfer earnings**   This is the minimum payment necessary to keep labour in its present use.
2   **Economic rent**   Any payment to labour which is over and above transfer earnings.

Both are shown in Figure 2.36 a. Transfer earnings are indicated by the area under the labour supply curve. As we have seen, this is upward sloping. Although the equilibrium wage is W, at wage rates below this there are workers who are willing to offer their services to employers. In fact, at any wage rate from zero upwards, workers will join the labour market, until at wage W, L (labour supply) is available. In all cases up to W, the wage that a worker receives is their best alternative. For those workers willing to work for less than W, then any wages they get over and above what they will accept is their economic rent. This is shown by the triangular area in Figure 2.36a.

It follows, therefore, that different workers receive different amounts of transfer earnings and economic rent even in the same job. Take a bus driver as an example. Some people are very willing to drive buses for a low wage. These have low transfer earnings and large economic rent. Others though will be attracted just by the equilibrium wage paid to bus drivers. In such cases they have little or no economic rent, the wage almost entirely consisting of transfer payments.

The case of superstars can be explained using Figure 2.36b. Such people have a scarce and, in some respects, unique talent. Their labour supply curve

is completely inelastic and their earnings consist entirely of economic rent. In contrast, workers who have a completely elastic supply, such as many unskilled workers and others in menial jobs, have no economic rent at all as their earnings consist entirely of transfer earnings. Employers can hire an infinite supply of labour at the market wage, W. This situation is shown in of Figure 2.36c.

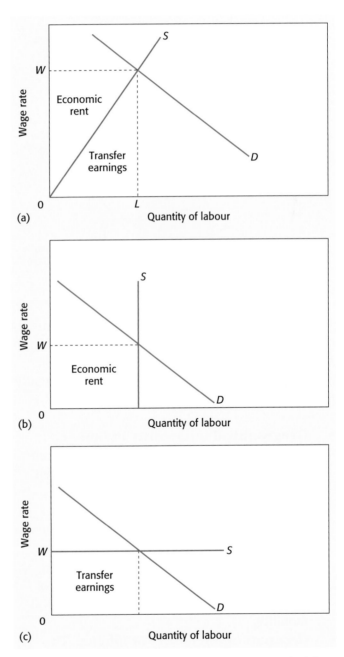

Figure 2.36   *Transfer earnings and economic rent in the labour market*

Other labour market imperfections

The basis of a competitive labour market is that workers are free to move in relation to demand. So, if there are vacancies in one geographical area or in one occupation, unemployed labour will be mobile and fill these vacancies. The **mobility of labour** is shown in Figure 2.37 where, in theory, labour will migrate to the South from the North in order to meet the former's demand for labour.

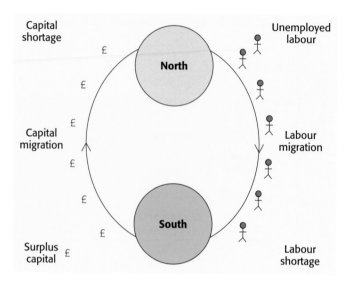

Figure 2.37 *Factor mobility in a competitive market*

The reality of the labour market is that this seemingly simple operation does not occur as economic theory might expect. In reality, much labour is immobile and not able to flow geographically or occupationally for the following reasons:

• **Geographical** immobility of labour
  Many people are reluctant to move away from friends and relatives and their local area even when unemployed. The cost of moving, in financial and personal terms, may also be prohibitive. In capital cities, for example, the cost of housing in areas with job vacancies usually prohibits workers from moving from the lower-cost areas where they live. A lack of information also tends to restrict geographical mobility.

• **Occupational mobility of labour**   This refers to a situation where labour is restricted in the type of job that can be taken up. For example, although a street cleaner cannot fill a vacancy for a teacher, a teacher is able to clean streets. This issue becomes much more difficult

in specialist occupations where extensive training is needed to complete a particular job. A good example is that of dentists, who have to study for a minimum of five years in order to be able to practise. An unemployed worker could clearly not take on such a position.

Another particular issue in labour markets is that of **wage differentials**, in other words the differences in wage rates for different groups of workers. The following differentials can be recognised:

• **Between different occupations**
  Non-manual jobs tend to pay more than manual posts, due to the high levels of skill that are required. The greater the skill, the higher the marginal revenue productivity of labour.

• **Between different industries**   Industries with a strong trade union, as shown earlier, are likely to pay more than those with a weak trade union. Capital-intensive industries usually pay more than labour-intensive industries as worker productivity is likely to be higher. Industries where there are risks, such as the chemical industry, are likely to pay higher wages than many other types of manufacturing.

• **Between males and females**   In all countries the average pay for women is below that for men. This is partly due to many women working part time and not full time, but it is also due to many more women being employed in occupations such as nursing and secretarial work, where pay levels are often very low.

SELF-ASSESSMENT TASK 2.30

Think about the labour market in your country.

1 What information might you obtain to determine whether labour is mobile, both geographically and occupationally?

2 What policies does your government use to improve labour mobility?

3 Explain the main wage differentials that apply. What information might you obtain in order to provide evidence for these differentials?

- **Between regions in the same country**
  This is certainly true in the UK where the average pay of workers in peripheral regions, such as Scotland and the north of England, is less than in one of the main cities, such as London or Bristol.

Theory of the firm

The firm's costs of production

The remainder of this chapter will concentrate on the firm. Although we have already referred to the firm we have not as yet defined it. The term 'a firm' is used by economists to describe a unit of decision making which has particular objectives such as profit maximisation, the avoidance of risk-taking and achieving its own long-term growth. At its lowest level the firm may be a sole trader with a small factory or a corner shop. The term is also used for national or multinational corporations with many plants and business establishments. In economic theory all firms are headed by an entrepreneur (see Chapter 1).

An entrepreneur must consider all the costs of the factors of production involved in the final output. These are the private costs directly incurred by the owners. Production may create costs for other people but these are not necessarily taken into account by the firm (see Chapter 3). The firm is simply the economic organisation that transforms factor inputs into goods and services for the market.

An accountant's view of a firm's costs is that they are incurred when the firm makes a recognised expenditure. They are production expenses paid out at a particular time and price. Profits are what is left when the expenses are deducted from the firm's income or sales revenue.

The economist's view of costs is wider than this. The accounting view does not fully recognise the private cost of economic activity. As well as money paid out to factors, there must be an allowance for anything owned by the entrepreneur and used in the production process. This factor cost must be estimated and included with the other costs. In addition, the concept of opportunity cost is relevant. As we saw in Chapter 1, opportunity cost involves the sacrifice of the next best alternative and is the value of what has been given up. The entrepreneur may have capital that could have been used elsewhere at no risk and would have earned an income. The entrepreneur will expect a minimum level of profit, reflecting what his or her capital and labour would have earned elsewhere. This is the concept of **normal profit**. Economists regard this element of the entrepreneur's reward as a cost of production, because without it there would be nothing produced by the firm. Profit, to an economist, is:

> Total revenue (unit price multiplied by number of units sold) minus total cost (including normal profit).

If this is positive, then it is **abnormal profit**. The prospect of making abnormal profit motivates the entrepreneur to take the business risks in supplying goods and services to the market. In order to understand cost structures in business, economists split costs into different categories and use specific cost concepts.

Short run costs

- **Fixed costs** These are the costs that are completely independent of output. Total fixed cost data when drawn on a graph would appear as a horizontal straight line. At zero output, any costs that a firm has must be fixed. Some firms operate in a situation where the fixed cost represents a large proportion of the total. In this case it would be wise to produce a large output in order to reduce unit costs.
- **Variable costs** These include all the costs that are directly related to the level of output, the usual ones being labour and raw material or component costs. In other words, costs that are incurred directly in the production process.

Important definitions are:

> Total cost (TC) equals total fixed cost (TFC) plus total variable cost (TVC)

From this information all the relevant cost concepts can be derived.

$$\text{average fixed cost (AFC)} = \frac{\text{total fixed cost}}{\text{output}}$$

$$\text{average variable cost (AVC)} = \frac{\text{total variable cost}}{\text{output}}$$

$$\text{average total cost (ATC)} = \frac{\text{total cost}}{\text{output}}$$

Marginal cost is the addition to the total cost when making one extra unit and is therefore a variable cost.

The most important cost curve for the firm will be the ATC, showing the cost per unit of any chosen output. For most firms the decision to increase output will raise the total cost, that is, the marginal cost will be positive as extra inputs are used. Firms will only be keen to do this when the expected sales revenue will outweigh the extra cost. Rising marginal cost is also a reflection of the principle of diminishing returns (see above). As more of the variable factors are added to the fixed ones, the contribution of each extra worker to the total output will begin to fall. These diminishing marginal returns cause the marginal and average variable cost to rise, as shown in Figure 2.38.

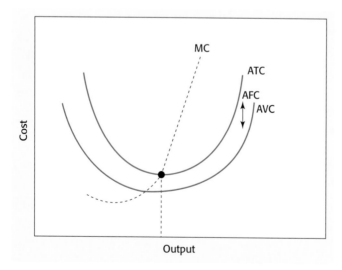

Figure 2.38 *Short run cost relationships*

The shape of the short run ATC is the result of the interaction between the average fixed cost and the average variable cost: AFC + AVC = ATC. As the

firm's output rises the average fixed cost will fall because the total fixed cost is being spread over an increasing number of units. However, at the same time, average variable cost will be rising because of diminishing returns to the variable factor. Eventually this will outweigh the effect of falling AFC, causing ATC to rise. This gives the classic 'U' shape to the ATC. On a graph of cost data, the MC will always cross AVC and ATC at their lowest point. In this situation, the most efficient output for the firm will be where the unit cost is lowest. This is known as the optimum output. It is where the firm is productively efficient in the short run, but the most efficient output is not necessarily the most profitable. For a firm wishing to maximise its profits, its chosen output will depend on the relationship between its revenue and its costs.

Costs in the long run

As we have already seen, the short run for the firm is a period of time when it cannot alter its fixed inputs. The level of production can only be changed by altering the variable inputs, such as labour. The time taken to alter fixed factors differs, depending on how easy it is to get new capital installed.

In the long run, the firm can alter *all* of its inputs, using greater quantities of land, capital and labour, operating on a bigger scale. All the factors are now variable.

In the very long run, technological change can alter the way the entire production process is organised, including the nature of the products themselves. In a society with rapid technological progress this will shrink the time period between the short run and the long run and suddenly shift the firm's product curves up and its cost curves down. There are now examples in consumer electronics where whole processes and products have become obsolete in a matter of months as a result of more powerful microchips increasing the volume and speed of the flow of information. In the case of airlines, the introduction of the jumbo jet suddenly raised the passenger miles per unit of input by 50%.

It is possible that a firm can find a way of lowering its cost structure over time. One way might be by increasing the amount of capital used relative to labour in the production process, with a consequent increase in factor productivity.

The long-run average cost (LRAC) curve shows the least cost combination of producing any particular quantity. Moving from its short run equilibrium shown in Figure 2.39a, part (b) of this figure shows a firm experiencing falling ATC over time. This would enable it to lower the price without sacrificing profit. Products such as laptops, digital cameras, DVD players and MP3 players are examples where prices have fallen through competition and changing technology.

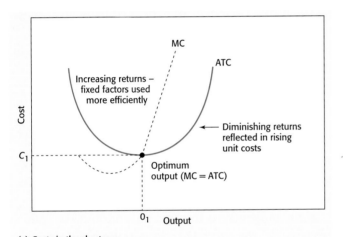

(a) Costs in the short run

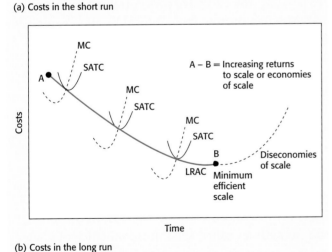

(b) Costs in the long run

Figure 2.39 *A firm's costs in the short run and in the long run.*

Economies of scale

Where an expansion of output leads to a reduction in the unit costs, the benefits are referred to as **economies of scale. Internal economies of** **scale** are the benefits that accrue to a firm as a result of its decision to produce on a larger scale. They occur because the firm's output is rising proportionally faster than the inputs, hence the firm is getting increasing returns to scale. If the increase in output is proportional to the increase in inputs, the firm will get constant returns to scale and the LRAC will be horizontal. If the output is less than proportional, the firm will see diminishing returns to scale or **diseconomies of scale**.

The key advantage for a firm obtaining economies of scale is a reduction in the cost per unit produced, i.e. a fall in the ATC. The nature of the possible economies depends on the nature of the economic activity. Some of the following may apply in a particular industry:

- **Technical economies**   This refers to the advantages gained directly in the production process. Some production techniques only become viable beyond a certain level of output. Economies of large dimensions occur in a number of business applications. For example, if a firm doubles the scale of the production of a box structure, its production costs will double. If it is being used as a container to transport goods, then the operating costs may not increase in proportion. The capacity of the container will have increased eightfold, generating a much larger potential revenue. The trick is to make sure that the extra capacity is fully used.

  Making full use of capacity is also important on a production line. Car production is the result of various assembly lines. The number of finished vehicles per hour is limited by the pace of the slowest sub-process. Firms producing on a large scale can increase the number of slow-moving lines to keep pace with the fastest, so that no resources are standing idle and the flow of finished products is higher. This is one of the reasons why in 2009 Tata Motors in Mumbai was able to produce the first of thousands of its Nano cars. At a price of around $2500, this no-frills vehicle puts car ownership within reach of lower-income poor families.

Car production in India – an example of technical economies of scale

- **Purchasing economies** As firms increase in scale, they increase their purchasing power with suppliers. Through bulk buying, they are able to purchase inputs more cheaply, so reducing average costs. One of the best examples of this is the US retail giant Walmart which uses its purchasing power to stock goods in its stores at rock bottom prices.

- **Marketing economies** Large-scale firms are able to promote their products on television and in newspapers at lower rates because they are able to purchase large amounts of air time and space. They are also likely to be able to make savings in their costs of distribution because of the large volumes of products being shipped.

- **Managerial economies** In large-scale firms these come about as a result of specialisation. Experts can be hired to manage operations, finance, human resources, sales, logistics and so on. For small firms, all of these functions often have to be carried out by a multi-task manager. Cost savings are expected to accrue where specialists are employed.

- **Financial economies** Large-scale firms usually have better and cheaper access to borrowed funds than smaller firms. This is because the perceived risk to the lender is lower.

- **Risk-bearing economies** These might explain why, as firms get larger, they become more diversified. It is a way of spreading business risks. A diversified conglomerate can cover any losses in one activity with the profits from another, an option not open to smaller firms.

Risks can be further reduced by co-operating with rivals on large capital projects.

The last example above may be an illustration of **external economies of scale** since firms can benefit from savings in research and development costs. This particular benefit is received by all the firms in the industry as a direct consequence of the growth of the industry and may be one reason for the trend towards the concentration of rival firms in the same geographical area. The advantages may include the availability of a pool of skilled labour or a convenient supply of components from specialist producers who have grown up to make the items for all the firms. They may all benefit from greater access to knowledge and research and the better transport infrastructure that will result from general expansion in the economic activities.

However, there are limits to economies of scale. A firm can expand its output too much with the result that unit costs start to rise. This may be the beginning of diseconomies of scale. The most likely source of these lies in the problems of co-ordinating large organisations and the effect size has on morale and motivation.

In the same way as internal diseconomies of scale are possible, the excessive concentration of economic activities in a narrow geographical location can also have disadvantages. External diseconomies may exhibit themselves in the form of:

- traffic congestion which increases distribution costs
- land shortages and therefore rising fixed costs
- shortages of skilled labour and therefore rising variable costs.

A firm that is producing at its optimum output in the short run and the lowest unit cost in the long run (sometimes called the minimum efficient scale), has maximised its efficiency. In industries where the minimum efficient scale is low there will be a large number of firms. Where it is high, competition will tend to be between a few large players.

The advantages of size in the form of economies of scale suggest that there will be a tendency for firms to get bigger over time. Why then do some markets feature a large number of small firms? The next section considers this question.

SELF-ASSESSMENT TASK 2.31

1 The following items are a selection of business costs:

- the rent of a factory
- taxes paid on business premises
- workers' pay
- electricity charges
- raw materials
- advertising expenditure
- interest on loans
- management salaries
- transport costs
- depreciation on fixed capital.

Indicate whether each one is likely to be fixed or variable in the short run.

2 Study Figure 2.40 and then answer the questions that follow.

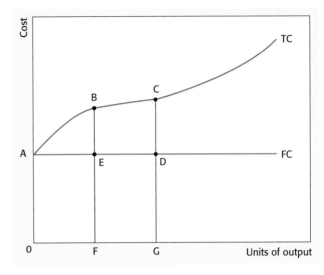

Figure 2.40

a What is the:
  i ATC at output G?
  ii AVC at output F?
  iii AFC at output G?
  iv TC at output F?

b What information would be required to determine profits at output G?

Reasons for the survival of small firms

At least 90% of business units in the UK are very small firms employing fewer than ten people. This is typical of most economies. Manufacturing firms tend to be bigger and here the definition of small firms is usually those employing fewer than 100 people. The reasons why so many small firms exist in a world where the economic power lies with big businesses are as follows:

- There are economic activities where the size of the market is too small to support large firms.
- The business may involve specialist skills possessed by very few people.
- Where the product is a service, e.g. solicitors, accountants, hairdressers, dentists and small shops, the firm will be small in order to offer the customers personal attention for which they will pay a higher price.
- Small firms can fill in the market niches left by the big ones.
- Small firms may simply be the big firms of tomorrow. Although the number of small firms

is high, it is misleading because of the fact that they have a very high 'death rate'.

- There are particular obstacles to the growth of small firms. Probably the largest of these is access to borrowed capital because of the perceived risk on the part of banks.
- The entrepreneur may not want the firm to get bigger because extra profit is not the only objective and growth might involve a loss of control over the running of the business.
- Recession and rising unemployment can trigger an increase in the number of business start-ups as former employees try to become self-employed.
- Small businesses may receive financial help under government enterprise schemes because of their employment and growth potential.
- The disintegration of large firms in an attempt to cut costs and focus on the more profitable core activities creates new business opportunities for small ones.
- It is sometimes cheaper for large firms to contract out some of the peripheral tasks such as design, data processing and marketing, to

specialist small firms. Manufacturing firms may buy in components from small suppliers producing for a range of companies, because it is cheaper than the large firm trying to supply small quantities itself.

- The increased access to technology through personal computers and mobile phones has reduced the optimum size of business unit and made small businesses more efficient and therefore competitive with the large ones.

- In the field of computing and technology, it is often the small firms which pioneer new products. This innovation is illustrated by the volume of computer software produced by people who previously worked for large organisations.

The growth of firms

Although the number of large firms is small, it is true that they dominate both national and international trade. Business growth is strongly linked with the pursuit of profit but the motives behind a firm's growth may include the following:

- **The desire to achieve a reduction in ATC over time through the benefits of economies of scale**   This allows firms to compete more effectively with rivals because they can afford to cut prices without sacrificing profits.

- **To achieve a bigger market share, which would boost sales revenue and therefore profits**   This is sometimes referred to as the monopoly motive, but it could be a defensive strategy to maintain market share in anticipation of action by rivals. In the global economy there is a strong argument that only big firms can compete in markets where multinationals are present.

- **To diversify the product range**   A multi-product firm has the advantage of being able to spread business risks. If one branch of its activity is stagnating or going into decline, there will still be the revenue from others to keep the firm afloat. Firms often see new business opportunities in related areas. This is at the heart of successful entrepreneurship. Sometimes

SELF-ASSESSMENT TASK 2.32

Read the feature below and then answer the questions that follow.

SMEs in Africa and Asia

An ever-increasing emphasis in developing economies is being placed on the role of small and medium-sized enterprises (SMEs). Although definitions vary between countries, small enterprises usually have 5–49 workers and medium-sized ones, 50–199 workers. Large enterprises have 200 workers and over. Enterprises that are run by self-employed people are particularly significant throughout large parts of Africa and Asia.

In Africa, SMEs are the main source of employment, comprising over 90% of business operations and contributing over 50% of employment and GDP. Many remain outside the formal economy yet harness their talent in the informal sector. Those that grow move into the formal sector, generating much needed taxes for governments. Over time, a small number of SMEs might even become listed public companies.

Small businesses in India

The bar charts in Figure 2.41 show how employment in eight Asian countries is distributed between different sizes of enterprise. The variation is striking.

SMEs across Africa and Asia are particularly prevalent in activities such as food provision and processing, certain types of local retailing, financial services, IT and a range of personal services. They invariably face strong competition from other SMEs and in some cases, increasingly, from multinationals. As such they are vulnerable; many do not survive due to competitive market forces.

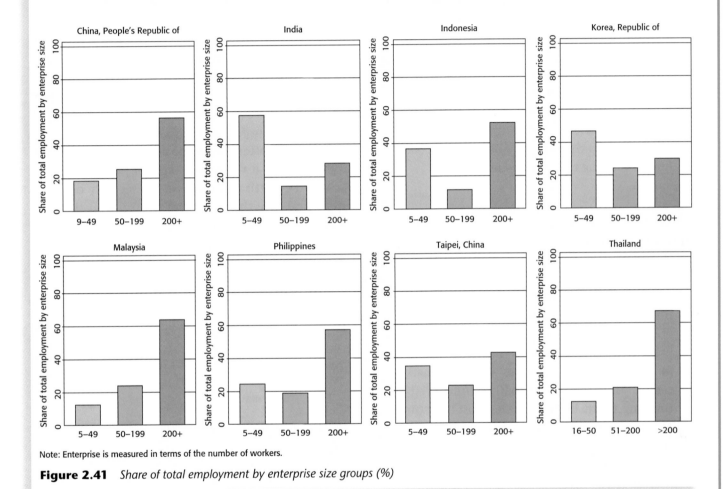

Note: Enterprise is measured in terms of the number of workers.

Figure 2.41   *Share of total employment by enterprise size groups (%)*

1 Describe the variations in employment by size of enterprise for the eight Asian countries shown in the bar charts.

2 Why is it that in some countries a large percentage of employment is in large enterprises, yet in others, SMEs employ the majority of the working population?

3 Discuss the extent to which SMEs are important economic agents in your country.

they can use the same production facilities as for their original activity, keeping the costs down. These benefits are called economies of scope.

- **To capture the resources of another business**   Sometimes, firms may realise that resources are being underutilised in another firm and that the real value of the firm is currently above its accounting valuation. The resulting takeovers and mergers can lead to the firm being brought back into profit or being broken up. This is because the sum of the parts sold separately is greater than the current valuation of the whole enterprise. It is sometimes called 'asset stripping' and the cash may be ploughed back into improving the core business.

How do firms grow?

Firms can grow internally or externally.

- **Internal growth**   A firm decides to retain some of the profit rather than pay it out to the owners. It is ploughed back in the form of new investment in order to increase the productive capacity. This is most likely to occur in capital-intensive activities where the market is expanding. The timing will be influenced by the stage of the business cycle, most investment occurring when the national economy is approaching a boom.
- **External growth**   The business expands by joining with others via takeovers or mergers. The objective in a takeover bid is to buy sufficient shares from the owners of the firm to get 51% of the total and therefore have control of the business. A merger often has the same result, a new larger legal entity, but the name implies less of a struggle and that both parties have agreed to the action. Mergers may be more numerous when there is a downturn in the economy or where there is a shrinking market and firms are left with excess productive capacity.

In practice, both types of growth can be going on at the same time. External growth may be a quicker and cheaper route for firms than internal growth, especially when there is high fixed cost. For example, it may be cheaper for one oil company to buy the assets of another than to expand existing operations, unless there are large recoverable reserves.

Firms can grow through integration and this may involve growth in several different directions as Figure 2.42 shows. Each of these offers specific advantages. The principal motives for horizontal integration are likely to be to achieve economies of scale and a larger market share. Vertical integration offers firms the chance to capture the profit margins at the other stages of production. Backward growth can increase the security of supply and give the firm more control over the quality of raw materials or components.

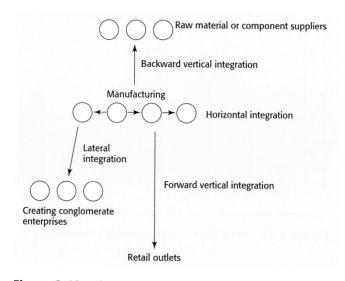

Figure 2.42   *The routes to integration*

Lateral integration is the beginning of diversification where the company goes into an activity quite closely related to its existing one. Some firms may also launch into new areas that have nothing to do with current production.

1 Read the feature below and then answer the questions that follow.

Competition up in the air

The large airline companies are having to cope with a situation of scarcity, not of aircraft but the lack of takeoff and landing slots at major international airports. This is one reason for their interest in a new generation of very large aircraft or superjumbos.

Aircraft production is clearly an effective duopoly. The European Airbus group has definite orders for at least 60 of its new A380s which can carry over 500 passengers at a time. They estimate that it cost at least $20 billion simply to get the first one in the air. At the same time, the American Boeing group is struggling to produce its prototype double decker superjumbo. These new planes will only make economic sense if they fly at full capacity all the time. The aircraft will offer operators the prospect of economies of scale and additional benefits of reduced emissions and fuel costs.

Competition between airline operators is fierce. Each firm is trying to strengthen its position through brand loyalty, offering frequent flyer discounts and improving the quality of the provision for business class travellers where demand might be less price elastic. Profits are higher on the long distance routes and new entrants on the European routes have increased competition by offering a lower price no-frills service. Some firms may have to use the long-haul profits to cover losses on the short routes.

a Why will aircraft production never have many firms competing for sales?

b Explain why the airline operators are so interested in the new products.

c What is the economic significance of low price elasticity in business travel?

d What do you predict will be the motives behind any horizontal integration of airline companies?

e With reference to both costs and revenue, how might the airline companies be able to increase their overall profits?

2 Read the feature below and answer the questions that follow.

Pharmaceutical industry mergers beat recession

Ten years ago the global pharmaceutical industry experienced a spate of mergers. That was when Glaxo and Astra Zeneca were created and Pfizer became the world's number one after taking over Warner-Lambert and in 2003, Schering-Plough.

In early 2009 three new multibillion dollar deals were announced. These were:

* Roche buying Genentech ($47bn)
* Merck's takeover of Schering-Plough ($41bn)
* Pfizer's purchase of Wyeth ($68bn).

Each of the newly merged giants has their specialisms. Roche is big in cancer-treating drugs, Merck in cholesterol-reducing drugs whist the largest of all, Pfizer, is big in vaccines, anti-depressants, oral contraceptives and impotence aiding products.

The global industry is not short of cash. The reasons for the latest mergers stem mainly from fierce ongoing competition from generic drug manufactures. These companies can make cheaper copies of drugs once patents have expired. Many such products are made in the emerging economies of southern Asia. The knock-on effects are that big conglomerates are cutting back on new product development. Instead they are concentrating resources on new products such as the Tamiflu vaccine which is difficult to copy. They are also buying new products from small businesses and then using their power to produce these for the global market.

Source: Townend, A., Daily Telegraph, *16 March 2009 (adapted)*

a What are typical reasons for business mergers?

b Why do these reasons not apply to the 2009 mergers in the global pharmaceutical industry?

c What benefits might consumers get from larger companies?

d How might increased horizontal integration affect SMEs in the global pharmaceutical industry?

International growth

Firms may take this route to expand either by exporting from a domestic base, setting up licence agreements or joint ventures with foreign firms or setting up directly in other countries. The reasons may include:

* saturation of their domestic market caused by too much competition
* domestic recession
* the prospect of economies of scale
* identification of growth markets
* access to materials, technology, patents or new management techniques
* risk spreading
* low labour costs.

Setting up direct production may also avoid import barriers and reduce some of the difficulties of exporting.

A multinational company is one that owns or controls production facilities in many countries and derives a substantial part of its total revenue from non-domestic sources. Its decisions are made in a global context, even though it has a domestic base. The objective is to maximise its profits by switching investment to areas that offer the highest return on capital employed. This strategy sometimes involves rationalising production and writing off investment in particular locations. Multinational conglomerates can become so large that they are difficult to manage. The decision then is sometimes to break them up, selling off the least profitable parts and concentrating on core activities.

The firm's revenue

In the theory of the firm, there are only two possible revenue relationships. In a competitive market, each firm has to accept the ruling market price. Its demand curve is horizontal at this level. Any firm in any other market will face a downward-sloping demand curve for its product. If the firm chooses to increase its output, the extra sales will depress the price. To look at it another way, the sales will only increase if the price is reduced from its present level. An increase in price would lead to a fall in the volume of sales. The following definitions are used by economists when looking at a firm's revenue:

Total revenue (TR) is price multiplied by quantity.
Average revenue (AR) is total revenue divided by output.

The firm's demand curve therefore is the average revenue curve or the price line.

Marginal revenue (MR) is the addition to the total revenue resulting from the sales of one extra unit. Because the firm can only sell more by reducing the price, it follows that the value for MR will always be lower than AR. Figure 2.43, derived from the accompanying data, shows that when the price moves from 9 to 8, the MR is 7. The addition to TR is gradually falling as the price falls until when five units are sold MR = 0. At this point total revenue is maximised.

Revenue data

Price (P)	Units sold (Q)	TR (P x Q)	MR
10	0	0	
			9
9	1	9	
			7
8	2	16	
			5
7	3	21	
			3
6	4	24	
			1
5	5	25	
			−1
4	6	24	
			−3
3	7	21	
			−5
2	8	16	
			−7
1	9	9	

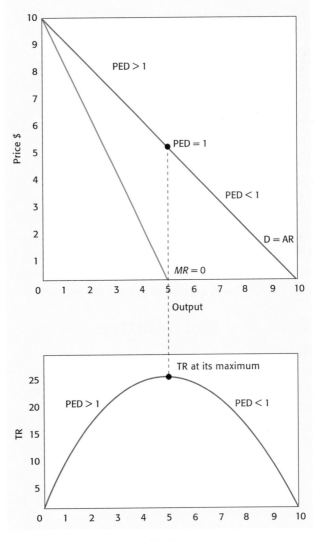

Figure 2.43 *The relationship between average revenue, marginal revenue and total revenue*

The relationship between price elasticity of demand and revenue

In the above example the firm would be facing a straight-line demand curve. Even so, the consumers' reaction to a price change varies at different prices due to the way in which the price elasticity of demand (PED) varies along the demand curve.

As the price falls in steps from $10, sales increase more than proportionally, giving PED a value greater than 1, until the output of 5 when total revenue is unchanged. This gives a PED value of 1. Beyond this output PED has a value less than 1 and the result is that further price cuts will reduce total revenue.

A relationship between elasticity and marginal revenue can also be seen. In the elastic part of the demand curve where PED > 1, the marginal revenue is positive and total revenue will be increasing. When the PED = 1, MR will be zero and total revenue will be maximised. When PED < 1, MR will be negative, reducing the total revenue

The most important thing about the concept of price elasticity from the firm's point of view is that it determines what happens to total revenue when the price is altered. It would make sense for any firm operating in the elastic part of the demand curve to reduce price and boost total revenue. Conversely, in the inelastic part, the firm should raise its price if it wants to see higher revenue. In this example revenue is maximised at five units of output with a price of 5.

With knowledge of the firm's cost structure and revenue situation, and the firm's objectives, we are now in a position to make some predictions about the output the firm will choose to put on the market.

A firm and the industry

A firm

As we saw earlier, a firm is a business organisation that buys or hires factors of production in order to produce goods and services that can be sold at a profit. The types might include:

- sole traders or one-person businesses
- partnerships
- co-operatives
- private or public limited companies
- state-owned firms
- multinational or transnational firms.

| **SELF-ASSESSMENT TASK 2.34** |

A small family-run engineering company has a production capacity of 9000 units per year. Market research suggests that the market will take up all of this output at a price of $8. The firm's cost structure is as follows:

- direct labour $1.50 per unit
- raw materials $0.50 per unit
- other variable costs $1.00 per unit
- the total fixed costs are $27 000 a year.

1 Calculate:
   a AFC
   b AVC
   c ATC
   d AR.
2 If the factory produced its capacity output, what would the firm's abnormal profit be?
3 Suppose that consumer tastes change away from the product and the firm has to reduce the price to $6 in order to get rid of unsold stock. What situation is the firm now in?

Firms can range from small simple organisations to ones that are almost too complex to control, and where there is some conflict of interests between the members. The characteristics and behaviour of the firm depend on the type of economic activity and the nature of competition. The factor mix in firms varies enormously, with some firms in the service sector being highly labour intensive. This contrasts with some manufacturing that is capital intensive. The decisions that firms take will vary according to the cost and availability of factors of production in different economic systems. There has been a trend in the rich western economies to make large parts of manufacturing more capital intensive to the point where some major activities, such as car manufacturing, can largely be done by robots and computer-controlled machinery. Another trend has been increased concentration of ownership in the hands of large multinational conglomerates.

The industry

In a competitive market structure, the industry is simply the sum of all the firms making the same product. This is the total market supply.

In other markets, the industry is taken to be the total number of firms producing within the same product group, i.e. things which are close substitutes for each other. It is sometimes difficult to draw the line between different industries, for example, are motor cars and motor cycles in the same product group? In reality many multi-product firms operate in more than one industry at the same time. A multinational conglomerate can be in several industries right across the global economy. A particularly good example is the Indian-owned Tata Group which has global interests in steel, vehicle production, upmarket hotels, telecommunications and electronics.

The industry is therefore a collection of business organisations which supply similar products to the market. When a firm's market share is discussed it tends to be in terms of the sales of the firm divided by the total sales of the entire industry. The terms 'industry' and 'market' are interchangeable in this context.

The firm's objectives

Profit maximisation

The standard assumption made by economists is that firms will seek to maximise their profits, i.e. maximise the gap between the firm's total revenue and total cost (including normal profit). A firm making the minimum level of normal profit is said to be producing at the break-even output. Firms will want to make abnormal profit as a reward for managing the resources and taking business risks.

If the firm produces up to the point where the cost of making the last unit is just covered by the revenue from selling it, then the profit margin will have fallen to zero and total profits will be at their greatest. In Figure 2.44, a firm producing an output to the left of Q is sacrificing potential profit. It can raise total profit by increasing its output, because each marginal unit sold adds more to revenue than it does to costs. A firm producing to the right of Q is making a loss on each successive unit, which will lower the total profit. It would be better off cutting

the output back to Q where MC = MR and the area of abnormal profit will be at its highest.

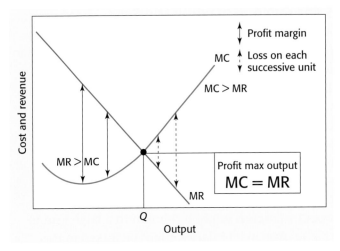

Figure 2.44 *The profit maximisation rule*

There may be several reasons why firms do not operate at the profit maximisation output:

- In practice, it may be difficult to identify this output. The firm may simply work out the average total cost and add on a profit margin in order to determine the selling price. This cost-plus pricing technique may not result in maximum profit.
- Short-term profit maximising may not be in the long-term interest of the company since:
  - firms with large market shares may wish to avoid the attention of government watchdog bodies, such as the Competition Commission in Britain
  - large abnormal profit may attract new entrants into the industry
  - high profits may damage the relationship between the firm and its stakeholders, such as the consumers and the company workforce
  - profit maximisation may not appeal to the management, who may have different objectives
  - high profits might trigger action by the firm's rivals and it could become a target for a take-over bid.

Alternative objectives to profit maximisation

Dissatisfaction with the simple assumption of profit maximisation has led to a number of alternative assumptions that have been labelled as managerial or behavioural theories.

Sales revenue maximisation

A firm may be prepared to accept a lower price and produce above the profit-maximising output in order to increase its market share in a growing market. This is a penetration pricing policy. A firm choosing to maximise its sales revenue would raise output beyond MC = MR until MR had fallen to zero. Extra sales after this would contribute nothing to total revenue, therefore it is at its maximum. There may still be abnormal profit if total revenue is higher than total cost. The reason why **sales revenue maximisation** might be chosen in a large firm is that management salaries might be linked to the value of sales. Shareholders might be more interested in profit. The solution to this conflict of interests is to offer management some shares as a bonus or link their salaries to profits.

Sales maximisation

This option maximises the volume of sales rather than the sales revenue. In **sales maximisation** the firm would increase output up to the break-even output where the total revenue just covered the total cost. A higher output implies loss-making behaviour. The only situation where this would be possible is where the firm could use the profit from some other activities to cover these losses using the principle of cross-subsidisation. It could be that in a state-owned firm, there are social objectives lying behind price and output decisions. The company might be instructed to keep prices down, to cover their ATC, or to make sufficient profit to be self-financing when it comes to new investment.

A firm in the private sector would not go beyond the break-even output in order to expand sales unless it is part of a diversified grouping where cross-subsidisation is being practised. Deliberately cutting the price to reduce profit might be a strategy to deter new entrants into the market. If they still appear, a price war may be a tactic to squeeze them out.

Satisficing profits

This behaviour would occur when a firm is determined to make a reasonable level of profits, sufficient to satisfy the shareholders but also to keep the other stake-holding groups happy, such as the workforce and, of course, consumers. The firm is seen as a coalition of interest groups, each with its own objectives which may change over time. Workers will expect pay rises and improvements in working conditions which may raise costs. Consumers may expect to see prices falling, particularly if there are rival producers. This is a long way from the simple profit-maximising theory as firms may choose to sacrifice some potential short-term profits to satisfy these expectations.

Where the firm's shareholders are divorced from control of the firm, there may be a conflict of interests. The management's motives may be concerned with growth rather than profit. They may place a lot of importance on comfortable working conditions, job security, status and fringe benefits, such as company cars, private health care and pension rights. Time and money spent on these issues can raise costs. If the firm has close rivals, it may make management more cautious because the risk of failure will threaten their job security and career advancement prospects. Firms may have charitable or environmental objectives which must be financed at the cost of profit.

Satisficing profits can also be a feature of firms that have enjoyed a high market share over a long period of time. Complacency can lead to firms losing their focus on the cost structure or failing to devote resources to either product or process innovation. Either situation can lead to a loss of profits.

One must be careful of sweeping statements concerning firms' short run behaviour and recognise the difference in objectives that can exist in different countries. Extra long run profits may follow from short-term sacrifices. As a working assumption, it is still valid to see profit maximisation as the major long-term objective of privately owned firms operating in a free market system. The search for abnormal profit will be a major factor in explaining firms' behaviour throughout the world.

Read the feature below which looks at some of the objectives of the firm, and then answer the questions that follow.

Chefaid plc

A row has broken out in the boardroom of Chefaid plc, a kitchenware company, over the firm's prospects and future direction. The marketing director announced a record level of sales for the last quarter and suggested that there should be a 10% target for the growth of sales revenue over the coming year. It was suggested to him that this was unwise. The firm's latest product, an exclusive set of kitchen tools, has yet to break even. The sales record owes a lot to the current popularity of cookery programmes on TV, but there is a danger that the sales boom is a flash in the pan.

The managing director was more interested in the firm's profitability. He was under pressure to declare higher future dividends and to get the funds to finance the planned new factory. He believed that a profit-maximisation strategy was the best way forward. The production director warned the meeting that cost pressures were building up and that industrial relations with the workforce were fragile because of the beginning of talks about wages and new working conditions. Management in general had been delighted with the new share option scheme and the bonus linked to sales performance.

It was suggested that the prospects for growth in general were good, because of the increase

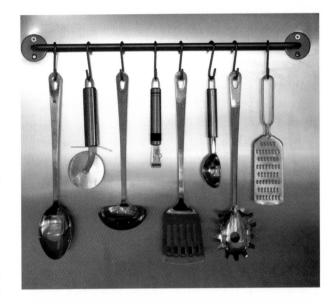

in consumer confidence, and the firm's market share had benefited from the closure of two large rivals during the recession. It was argued that the market was becoming less competitive and this might give an opportunity for price rises. The company must not lose sight of its long-term drive to raise profitability by reducing unit costs. This sparked further disagreement over the firm's sponsorship commitments, its promotions budget and its charitable contributions.

1 What do economists mean by the phrase 'the market is becoming less competitive'?
2 What will be the best output for the firm if the profit-maximising strategy wins the day?
3 What are the risks associated with this strategy?
4 What output would maximise turnover?
5 What does the phrase 'fail to break even' mean? What advice would you give to improve the performance of the new product?
6 Explain why the management may not favour profit maximisation.
7 To what extent does the case study show that businesses have a range of objectives?
8 Discuss the idea that each business decision to reach an objective has risks attached to it.

Market structures

The term 'market structure' describes the way in which goods and services are supplied by firms in a particular market. In economic theory, a range of models has been developed within what is called the spectrum of competition. These models are shown in Figure 2.45. The extreme or limiting models may only exist in theory but give a framework for understanding real-world competition. The following stages can help to identify a market structure within this spectrum of competition:

- By counting the number of firms. The bigger the total, the closer to perfect competition the market stucture will be.
- A better guide will be to use a **concentration ratio** to see the combined market share of the biggest 3, 4 or 5 firms in the industry as a percentage of total industry sales. The bigger the percentage, the closer the industry will be to the **oligopoly** and **monopoly** models.
- By considering how easy or difficult it is for new firms to set up and how easy it is for firms to exit the industry. These barriers are indicative of market structures on the right-hand side of the spectrum.
- By considering the importance of economies of scale to the firms. The more important they are, the closer the industry will be to an oligopoly.

Figure 2.46 provides an elaboration of the above. Understanding this figure is very important for the rest of this chapter.

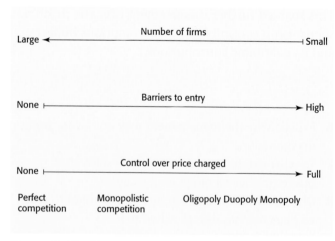

Figure 2.45   *The spectrum of competition*

Perfect competition

Perfect competition is a theoretical extreme. The main point of studying this model is that it acts as a benchmark for real-world competition. The performance of actual firms can be judged against this most efficient model. (Some of the characteristics are shared by the next most competitive model, which somewhat confusingly is known as monopolistic competition).

Perfect competition has the following characteristics:

1. There is a large number of buyers and sellers who have perfect knowledge of market conditions and the price.
2. No individual firm has any influence on the market price. Firms are described as being price takers. The ruling price is determined by the forces of market demand and the output of all the firms.
3. The products are homogeneous. This means that they are all of the same quality and are identical in the eyes of the consumer.
4. There is complete freedom of entry into and exit from the market.
5. Each firm will seek to maximise its profits.

The only industry which comes anywhere near this theoretical model is agriculture. The problem in searching for an example is in finding products that are homogeneous. Perfect competition has a lot of appeal as a yardstick because if it were to operate, there would be consumer sovereignty and efficient production with no possibility of exploitation.

In perfect competition, the firm cannot do anything that will influence the market price. Each individual firm makes such a small contribution to the industry output that no alteration in its own output can significantly affect the total supply. The firm can choose to produce any quantity it likes and will be able to sell all of it at the ruling price. The demand curve facing the firm is therefore perfectly elastic at this price. In this situation if the firm sells an extra unit of output, it will get the same price as the one before. The marginal revenue is therefore equal to the price or

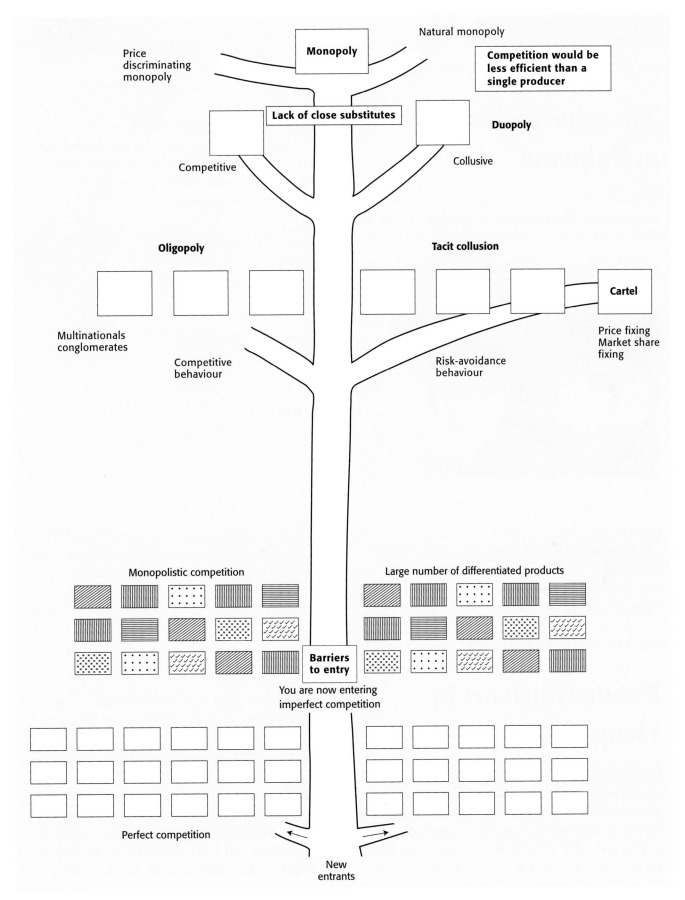

Figure 2.46 *A competition road map*

1 Read the feature below and then answer the questions that follow.

The telecom industry in Pakistan

Pakistan's telecommunications industry is one of the hottest in the emerging economies of Asia. In 2005, there were around 40 million mobile phone subscribers; by mid-2009, this figure had more than doubled to 95 million. As the market has grown, so too has competition. Table 2.16 million shows the estimated market shares of the main providers over this period.

	2005 (%)	2009 (%)
Mobilink	49	31
Ufone	21	21
Warid	14	19
Telenor	11	22
Instaphone	4	–
Paktel/Zong	1	7

Table 2.16
Source: http://telecomp.net3

a Calculate the four-firm concentration ratios for 2005 and 2009.

b Why are these not necessarily good indicators of change in the market structure?

c Discuss how telecommunication companies might compete in a growing market like Pakistan.

2 Read the feature below and then answer the questions that follow.

Public transport in Hong Kong

Hong Kong has a diverse public transport system consisting of a modern surface rail (KCR) and mass transit system (MTR), franchised bus services, tram services, various ferry services, minibuses and public taxis. All are privately owned. Unusually, no subsidies are paid for their operation by the Hong Kong government.

In 2007, the KCR and MTR companies were amalgamated to form a new integrated company. This move was designed to cut out wasteful competition and duplication whilst providing scope for the benefits of economies of scale.

Franchised bus companies are operated by five companies. Each has its own geographical group of services. Fares, frequency levels, types of vehicle, routes and even bus stops are all part of the franchise arrangement with the government.

charge very low fares. They are the only providers of their modes of transport although buses, taxis and road tunnels as well as private cars compete with them. They do though have a unique brand and a loyal customer base.

Hong Kong has 4400 minibuses, known locally as public light buses. The 2800 green topped ones can carry 16 seated passengers on fixed routes. The remaining red ones are more flexible and not as strictly regulated. The fares charged are competitive and can be determined by the driver. Many are owned by the driver or by small companies.

Finally, Hong Kong has 15 000 red urban Toyota taxis. Fares are strictly regulated by meter and vehicle numbers fixed by the government. Most are privately owned or leased from local companies by their drivers.

There are a few pinch points and stretches of route where they compete with each other.

The famous Star Ferry, with cross-harbour services, and the Hong Kong Tramways Company

a Use the evidence above to provide examples of monopoly, natural monopoly, oligopoly and monopolistic competition. Justify your answers.

b Explain what additional information you might need to be more certain of these market structures.

c Discuss the extent to which similar market structures can be found in the public transport system in your own country.

the average revenue. In Figure 2.47 (page 106), all the firm's revenue information is in the line:

$$D = AR = MR$$

Choosing the output is the only decision that the firm has to make. This will be done by considering the relevant costs of production. Given the assumption that the firm wants to maximise profits, the chosen output will be where MC = MR.

The firm's total revenue is the price multiplied by the output sold. If the total cost of producing this output is lower than the total revenue, then the firm will be making an abnormal profit. This is also known as **supernormal profit**. If TC = TR, then the firm would break even and be making a normal profit. It is possible that the costs could be higher than the revenue, in which case the firm may be about to exit the industry. This may not be immediate: a firm can continue in production

making short-term losses, as long as the price covers the AVC, that is the cost of paying the wage bill and buying the materials for production. This is the shut-down price. The firm would be making a loss equivalent to the amount of fixed costs. In this situation the firm's only hope is that the market price will rise to increase its revenue or that it can take action to reduce its costs of production. Firms where the revenue is lower than costs will be leaving the industry. If a lot of them do, the effect will be a reduction in the overall market supply which will raise the market price giving the rest an opportunity to continue producing and at least make normal profit. In the long run, firms will only supply the market if they can cover all their costs and make a normal profit. The minimum supply for the firm will be the optimum output. In perfect competition, firms will only make different amounts of profit from each other if they have different cost structures. Their behaviour is strictly limited and the only way

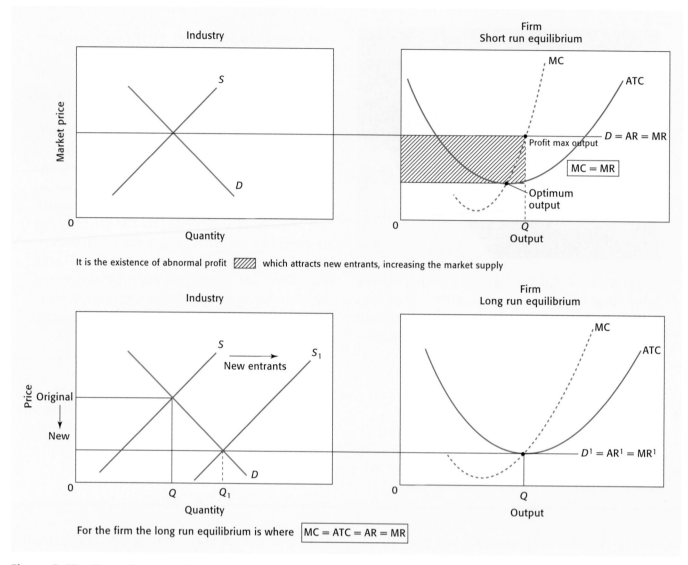

Figure 2.47 *The perfect competition model*

to boost profit would be to increase productivity and lower average total cost.

Abnormal profit will only be a feature of perfect competition in the short run. This is because its existence will act as an economic incentive for the entry of new firms. The absence of barriers means that the total supply in the market will rise. The effect of this on the existing firms is that the market price will fall and the abnormal profit will diminish. When the abnormal profit goes, the entry of new firms dries up, and the existing ones will simply be covering costs. It is the competitive force of large numbers of new entrants that destroys abnormal profit.

The long run equilibrium is therefore where the only firms left are the most efficient ones, making a normal profit.

In this situation, there is no action that the firm can take to prosper at the expense of rivals. It has no market power. Firms' behaviour is easy to understand. The appeal of this model is that abnormal profit is competed away and the only firms that participate in the market in the long run are productively and allocatively efficient. It is the efficient economic performance which occurs in perfect competition that can be used to criticise real-world competition.

SELF-ASSESSMENT TASK 2.37

1 Study the diagrams in Figure 2.48 and then answer the questions that follow.

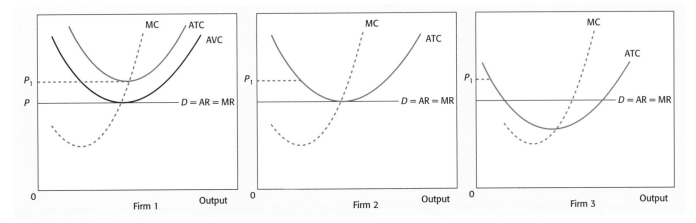

Figure 2.48 *Perfect competition – three different cost situations*

a Describe each firm's situation with respect to profit.

b If market demand increased and the price rose to P_1, how would it affect each of them?

c According to the theory what will happen next?

d What output does a firm in perfect competition choose?

e How can an individual firm increase its profits?

2 Read the feature below and then answer the questions that follow.

Shedding light on the competition

In Guangdong, people do not hide their light under a bushel. 'Guizhen: Lighting Capital of China', proclaims the sign beside the highway into the village (more of a town), which two decades ago was an unpaved track. Factory after factory, every one of them advertising light fittings, lines the road. In town, hundreds of shopfronts display their variations on a theme: street lights, chandeliers, bedside lights, halogen lights, lights of any sort, from the modern to the eternally tasteless. Guizhen has 60 000 registered inhabitants, says the party secretary, Mr Wu, frantically talking on his cellphone, and though there are officially

1000 lighting factories, 'there are also 600 or so underground ones…they all count.'

One resident in every 40 men, women and children, then, is a factory owner, and that does not take into account the wholesalers and shop owners. On top of that there are some 40 000 migrant workers. It is an intensely competitive industry. The Guizhen factories on average change their designs every fortnight. The specialist designers of light fittings have to come up with three new ideas a day. In return, they are paid 600 000 yuan ($72 000) a year, many times the salary of China's prime minister.

Since the first factory opened in 1986, little-known Guizhen has captured 46% of China's total domestic lighting market. One in every two light fittings you see in China has been trucked out past that bragging highway sign.

Source: Economist *survey of China, 8 April 2000 (adapted)*

a Is this an example of perfect competition or monopolistic competition? Justify your choice.

b Why is product innovation so highly rewarded?

c What is the economic significance of the migrant workers in this industry?

Monopolistic competition

This is the market structure closest to the model of perfect competition because of the large number of competing suppliers.

Monopolistic competition has the following characteristics:

1 There is a large number of buyers and sellers.

2 There are few barriers to entry into the market and it is easy for firms to recoup their capital expenditure on exit from the market.

3 Consumers face a wide choice of differentiated products. Each firm has a slight degree of monopoly power in that it controls its own brand.

4 Firms have some influence on the market price and are therefore price makers.

5 Each firm will seek to maximise profits.

Each firm is competing with a large number of similar producers. In this situation the demand curve facing the individual firm will be downward sloping but relatively price elastic because of the presence of substitutes. It might be an option for firms to reduce their price in order to increase total revenue. As in perfect competition, the firms can make abnormal profit in the short run but the key restraint on their power is the free entry of rivals. In the long run, the prediction is that the profit-maximising firms will only be able to achieve a normal profit covering all

the production costs and the opportunity cost of capital.

The clue to the behaviour of firms in this market structure lies in the concept of product differentiation. The development of a strong brand image must be seen as an act of investment on the part of the individual firm. This highlights the important role that advertising and promotions play in this market structure. Successful advertising will not only shift the firm's demand curve to the right at the expense of the rivals but will also reduce the price elasticity of demand if the consumers feel there are no close substitutes. This is what is meant by brand loyalty – people will not easily shift back to rival products. There are problems associated with advertising because it will be a competitive tool taken up by all the firms. In this case one could argue that the advantage will be temporary and that advertising will simply add to the firm's costs and bring little benefit to its demand curve. If advertising is not equally effective, the successful firms might take advantage of their greater market share and brand loyalty to charge a higher price. It would increase its sales revenue by doing this in the portion of the demand curve where price elasticity of demand has a value less than 1.

It is easy to see how each firm can try to strengthen its market power in the short run. The constraint on firms is that there is freedom of entry into the market, which will threaten the existence of abnormal profit in the long run. By a combination of marketing and product innovation, the individual firms may be able to postpone the long run equilibrium if the total market is growing.

At the heart of this model of competition is the fact that there are a large number of competitors using a combination of price and non-price competition to try and increase their market power. If there are few barriers to entry, then their success will only be temporary. There are many typical examples of this market structure in operation. Take-away food outlets and local privately owned restaurants are particularly good examples. They may appear to be selling similar products, but in reality, their products depend upon the skills and recipes of their owners. Local hairdressers' shops, driving schools and travel agents also exhibit the characteristics of this market structure.

Take-away food outlets in Singapore

Figure 2.49 shows the equilibrium price and output in monopolistic competition. In the short run, the profit-maximising firm will be seen to make abnormal profits. In time these will be competed away by the entry of new firms which will shift the original firm's demand curve to the left. The process will continue until all firms in the industry are making normal profit. A key point though is that in both the short and the long run the firm is inefficient. It operates above the minimum point of its average total cost curve giving a situation of excess capacity.

Barriers to entry

The existence of substantial **barriers to entry** of new firms into an industry differentiates oligopoly and monopoly from monopolistic competition and perfect competition.

Barriers to entry are a range of obstacles that deter or prevent new firms from entering a market to compete with existing firms. They give firms a degree of market power in that decisions can be made by existing firms without the risk of their market share or price being challenged from outside. The construction and maintenance of these barriers can become part of the firm's behaviour. Below are some of the main barriers:

- In some countries, it may be impossible for new firms to enter an industry because the economic activity is state owned or the good is produced

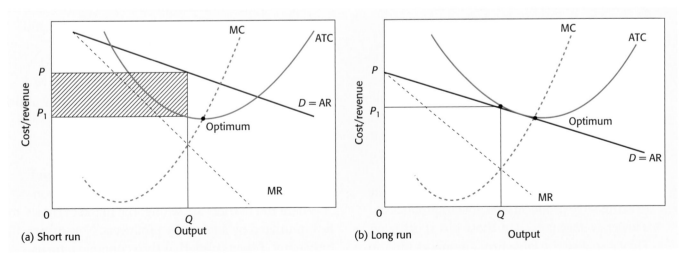

Figure 2.49   *Monopolistic competition in the short and the long run*

under licence from the government. This is a legal monopoly created to achieve social and political objectives. The economic justification might lie in the concept of a **natural monopoly**, where it is more efficient to have a single producer than to have competing firms. In countries where the state-owned resources have been privatised and the market has been deregulated, the economic justification has been that the injection of competition will bring economic and social benefits.

- The high fixed cost or setup cost in activities such as electricity generation, aircraft and car production and pharmaceuticals may deter potential entrants. The barrier here is access to capital. Only very large firms will be able to fund the necessary investment. Research and development costs will represent a high proportion of total costs and it will require high sales over a long period of time before the activity becomes profitable.
- If a firm is shutting down and these costs cannot be recovered because the resources are specialised and are not easily transferrable to other uses, they are regarded as sunk costs and act as a **barrier to exit** from the industry because the capital investment will be lost. It is therefore the risk of entering and the high cost of failure that deters potential entrants.
- Advertising and brand names with a high degree of consumer loyalty may prove a difficult obstacle to overcome. This explains why firms regard their expenditure on advertising and promotions as a type of investment. Existing firms can make entry more difficult through brand proliferation, giving consumers an apparent abundance of choice and closing market niches. Successful advertising cannot only shift a firm's demand curve to the right but it can also reduce its price elasticity of demand. This gives the firm greater market power because consumers do not see the rival firm's product as a close substitute.
- Economies of scale can be a barrier because the existing large producers are able to produce at a lower average cost than those just starting up. They also give the large firm an opportunity to cut its price in order to eliminate any high-cost

producers. This is the concept of predatory pricing which can be used to eliminate any new firms that do enter the industry.

- The production process or the products of a firm may be protected by a legal monopoly in the form of a patent, whereby competitors cannot copy without the permission of the owner. The idea is to guarantee a reward to entrepreneurs with original ideas for a reasonable period of time. The barrier here is access to either technology or information.
- Some existing firms may have a monopoly access to raw materials, components or retail outlets, which will make it difficult for new entrants. Vertically integrated manufacturing businesses will be protected by the fact that their rivals' costs will be higher.
- In activities such as consumer electronics, the pace of product innovation is so rapid that the existing firms will be working on the next generation of products whilst launching the current range. Unless the new entrants have original ideas or can exploit a new market segment, they are destined to fail.
- It may be possible for existing firms to hide the existence of abnormal profit by what is called entry limit pricing. This involves deliberately setting a low price and temporarily abandoning profit maximisation. It may be in the interest of all the players to do this and it therefore becomes a form of collusion through **price agreements**.
- Collaboration between existing producers to develop new products may act as a barrier in that the resources necessary to compete are beyond the means of single producers.
- Market conditions, such as a fall in demand resulting from economic recession, can leave producers with surplus production capacity and this will deter entry.

The concept of barriers to entry is central to understanding where the models of oligopoly and monopoly fit within the spectrum of competition.

Where the barriers are strong, the market is likely to be dominated by a few large producers. New firms will only enter if they think that the economic returns will be greater than the cost of breaking the barriers.

Oligopoly

Oligopoly is defined as a market situation where the total output is concentrated in the hands of a few firms. It is possibly the most realistic economic model but ironically the theory does not provide the definite predictions regarding the price and output of the firm that exist in every other model. An effective oligopoly can exist in an apparently competitive industry if a handful of firms dominates the market. Duopoly, where the market is shared between two big players, can be seen as an extreme form of oligopoly.

An oligopoly has the following characteristics:

1 The market is dominated by a small number of firms.
2 Their decisions are interdependent. Firms must decide their market strategy to compete with close rivals, but they must also try to anticipate their rivals' reactions and think what the next step should be in the light of this response.
3 There are high or substantial barriers to entry.
4 The products may be homogeneous or differentiated.
5 The uncertainty and risks associated with price competition may lead to price rigidity.
6 Firms may or may not choose to maximise profits.

The difficulty in studying oligopoly is that the behaviour can follow two very different routes. There are examples of aggressive competition in some industries whilst in others there is a suggestion of co-operation and even collusion.

Oligopolists are price makers but one of the dangers of using this weapon is that the firm can get drawn into a price war. An oligopolist would only start a price war if its costs of production were significantly lower than its rivals. A price war may be the natural outcome of economic events, such as overcapacity in the industry or the entry of new firms. Where the firms are highly diversified, a firm may be prepared to sacrifice profits by cutting the price, in an attempt to increase market share. Profits from some of its activities may be used to cover short-term losses on others.

Although they each have market power in the form of influence over the prices they charge, the uncertainty surrounding the outcome of competitive tactics means that firms may prefer non-price competition. The observation that prices tend to be similar between oligopolists and are stable with time might be explained by the kinked demand curve theory as shown in Figure 2.50.

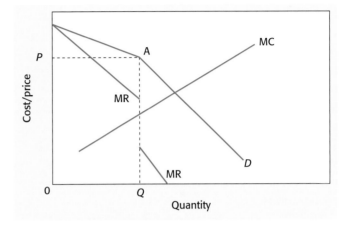

Figure 2.50 *The kinked demand curve*

The diagram illustrates a situation where one firm suspects that it faces a relatively elastic demand curve below the existing price. The temptation would be to cut the price in an attempt to increase total revenue. The outcome depends on the rivals' response. If they also cut their price, then the firm will sell relatively little extra output. It could even be worse off than it was before the price cut. It can also be seen that the firm could lose out if it chose to raise the price. Whatever the elasticity was, if rivals do not copy the price increase, then the firm will lose a disproportionate amount of sales because the product will look overpriced against that of rivals. The firm would be better off concentrating on non-price competition to increase revenue. This may include the following:

- advertising and promotions
- product innovation – the attempt to make the products more appealing to consumers.
- brand proliferation – where the firm produces lots of brands to saturate the market and to leave no gaps for rivals
- market segmentation – producers may decide that there are markets where the consumers have different characteristics and needs, and these market niches will be catered for through product innovation

- process innovation – usually seen as a way of reducing average costs, allowing the firm to cut the price without sacrificing profits.

One way for a firm to grow rapidly would be to take over one of its rivals. As seen earlier, this so-called horizontal integration may in fact be the cheapest way of getting growth in sales if the competing oligopolists are of a similar size. If a takeover or merger is likely to be resisted, a firm wanting to get rapid growth may prefer to look elsewhere. This leads to a prediction that diversification becomes a feature of businesses in an oligopolistic market. This could explain the growth of businesses which start to look for profits by producing in different countries and eventually become multinational corporations.

The difficulty of choosing competitive strategies and of predicting the response of rivals may change the objectives of the firm. Profit-maximising strategies may be replaced by satisficing (see page 100). The firm's management becomes more cautious, preferring to make just enough profit to keep the shareholders happy. The focus shifts towards maintaining market share.

Co-operation and collusion between oligopolists

There are situations where big firms find that it is in their interest to co-operate with rivals. One of the best examples is where the research and development costs are a high proportion of the total costs and where the pace of technical change is very rapid. It is in the interests of all the firms to pool their knowledge and agree on technical standards, perhaps taking part in joint ventures.

Collusion is altogether different. It is an anti-competitive action by producers. Informal or tacit collusion usually takes the form of **price leadership**, where firms automatically follow the lead of one of the group. The objective is to maximise the profits of the whole group by acting as a single monopolist. This illegal activity is difficult to prove since there is invariably no written evidence. A price agreement or output agreement is known as a **cartel** arrangement.

Collusion of any kind will work best when:

- there is a small number of participants
- a strong element of trust exists between them
- they have similar cost structures
- there is a clear leader
- the agreement can be policed
- there is no danger from new entrants
- the market conditions are stable
- the government will not intervene.

Collusion is more likely to be tacit where the behaviour of each firm is the result of an unwritten rather than formal agreement. One of the simplest forms is a follow-the-leader agreement, where each firm will only adjust its price following a move by the dominant firm. There are other price leadership models, such as using a typical firm as the yardstick for price. This will only change if a rise in costs affects the profit margin. The principle is the same: each firm will act in the same way in the interests of the group as a whole.

In practice, it is difficult to identify either tacit or formal agreements. This is because price similarities can be the result of either aggressive pricing in a competitive oligopoly or the outcome of a collusive agreement.

Monopoly

In theory, a monopoly is where a single firm controls the entire output of the industry. It is at the opposite end of the spectrum to perfect competition. In practice, a monopoly situation can arise when a firm has a dominant position in the market in terms of its market share. For example, in the UK, a legal monopoly is when a firm has more than 25% of the total market; if the share exceeds 40%, then the monopoly is seen as dominant.

A monopoly is protected from competition by the barriers to entry explained earlier. The word 'monopoly' conjures up an image of giant powerful firms. However, a local monopoly can exist where a relatively small firm dominates a local market either because it is too costly for others to enter or the prospect of profit is not high enough. Even when monopolists are large, the extent of power must not be exaggerated. Sometimes a domestic monopoly can be suddenly broken by new competition, say, from imported goods and services.

A single firm or pure monopolist in theory would face a downward-sloping market demand curve. In this situation it can decide on the price to charge or the quantity to supply, but not both. There may be situations where the monopolist is unable to make abnormal profits in spite of having market power. One such example would be where the fixed costs are so high that the necessary price would be outside the range that the consumers could afford. It may be that all the monopolist can hope for is that the revenue covers the production costs.

Figure 2.51 shows the equilibrium output of a monopolist. A profit-maximising monopolist would choose the output where MC = MR. This output will be somewhere over the price range where demand is price elastic and will be sold at the price consumers will pay. If the total revenue is higher than the production costs, it will make abnormal profit. This will be a permanent feature. In monopoly, there is no distinction between the short run and the long run because of the barriers that prevent the entry of competitors. There is no economic incentive for the monopolist to move away from the profit-maximising output Q.

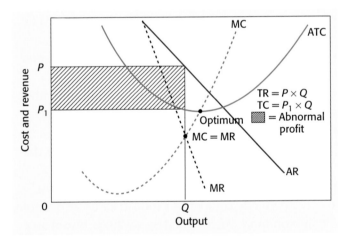

Figure 2.51 *The equilibrium of a monopoly*

The monopolist's profits could be increased in certain circumstances by a practice known as **price discrimination**. Price discrimination occurs where the monopolist chooses to split up the output and sell it at different prices to different customers. It is only true price discrimination if the quality of the product is identical in all market segments. The monopolist is making use of the fact that some consumers would have been prepared to pay more

than the single price (see Figure 2.52). At this price they would be enjoying some consumer surplus. The monopolist's aim is to charge what the consumers will pay and turn the consumer surplus into producer surplus in the form of abnormal profit.

It may be possible for a monopolist to use price discrimination to produce at a profit when competitive firms or a monopoly charging a single price could not cover costs. Figure 2.52 shows that at the single price profit maximisation output, the total revenue would be $3 \times 40 = 120$ and the total cost would be $3 \times 45 = 135$, giving a loss of 15. If the output was sold separately for what consumers would pay for each individual unit, the revenue would be $60 + 50 + 40 = 150$, giving an abnormal profit of 15. The monopolist has effectively tapped into the consumer surplus and turned it into producer surplus or profit. If triangle A in the diagram is the same size as triangle B, which is the shortfall in cost, the firm will break even, but if it is larger then it makes abnormal profit. As long as the consumers are prepared to pay the higher price, there is no consumer exploitation. The competitive market price would generate losses and therefore there would be zero output in the long run.

Price discrimination can only exist in particular circumstances and there are situations where it can

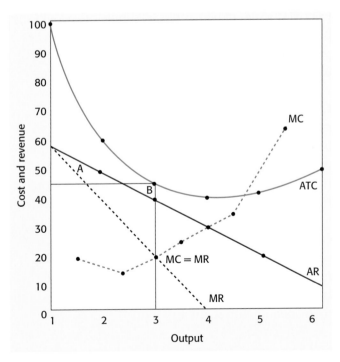

Figure 2.52 *A price discriminating monopolist*

113

be justified on economic grounds. If different groups of customers are charged different prices because the cost of providing the service differs, then it is quite acceptable. For example, at peak times of demand a firm might have to employ more staff. Price discrimination might in fact be used as a way of spreading out demand. This would account for out-of-season air fares and the lower price for off-peak telephone calls. Spreading out demand may improve efficiency, giving a further benefit to consumers. Price discrimination could be used to generate revenue on parts of a service, such as a rail network, so that the operator can cover losses on the least popular routes. Transport provides several examples of travellers being split into definite categories and charged different prices. There may be social motives for charging older people and children less than others. Consumer loyalty may be rewarded by discounts. The price of a journey may vary with the time of day or the day of the week.

If a firm wishes to split the market up into different segments and charge different prices, it must have a mechanism for keeping the markets separate. It must avoid the possibility of consumers buying in the cheaper part and the product being resold at a higher price. Price discrimination will only make economic sense if the market segments have different price elasticities of demand. The simple rule would be to charge higher prices where the demand is more price inelastic and lower prices where demand is price elastic.

Comparing monopoly with perfect competition

Figure 2.53 shows the equilibrium price and output of a monopoly charging a single price in a market free of government intervention and the situation that would occur in a perfectly competitive industry.

The classic case against monopoly is that its conduct and performance is undesirable when compared with that of firms in more competitive markets. The following observations can be made from the diagram comparing the equilibrium in both perfect competition and monopoly:

- The price in monopoly will be higher than it would be in perfect competition.
- The monopoly output is lower.

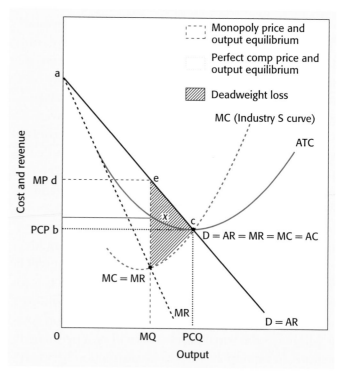

Figure 2.53 *A comparison of a perfectly competitive industry with a profit-maximising monopolist*

- The monopolist is making short and long run abnormal profits.
- The firm in perfect competition is productively efficient, producing the optimum output.
- It is also allocatively efficient, producing where price = MC.
- The monopolist captures consumer surplus and turns it into abnormal profit.
- The monopolist is productively inefficient, producing less than the optimum output in the search for extra profit.
- The price charged is well above marginal cost.
- If a perfectly competitive industry was turned into a monopoly, there would be a welfare loss of area *x* in addition to greater allocative inefficiency.

The criticisms of real-world monopolies based on a comparison with perfect competition may not be valid for two reasons:

1 Perfect competition is a theoretical ideal. Monopoly must be compared with the real-world models of monopolistic competition and oligopoly. These are also characterised by productive and allocative inefficiency. In addition they may involve a waste of resources in competitive advertising.

2 Figure 2.53 is drawn under the assumption that the costs in monopoly will be the same as in perfect competition. This ignores the possibility that the monopolist can achieve internal economies of scale which would reduce unit costs. It is possible that a monopolist could charge a lower price than would occur in perfect competition, making consumers better off, even though the monopolist is making abnormal profits.

A positive case can be made for monopoly in the following circumstances:

- A monopolist cannot always make abnormal profit – it depends how high its costs are. There may be situations where the fixed costs are so high relative to the total cost that the market price can just cover the average costs. In this case the monopolist would only make normal profit. This is a case of natural monopoly, where it would make no economic sense to have the product supplied by competing firms.
- The concept of abnormal profit must be considered carefully. One of the criticisms of a competitive market is the uncertainty of profits in the long run. A monopolist however can plan future investment and finance it through what are guaranteed profits. This may offer customers better products and the workforce greater security.
- The investment may take the form of process innovation, implementing new techniques of production with the objective of lowering unit costs.

- Alternatively, the profit could be used to finance product innovation which will add to consumer welfare in the future, either through an improvement in the product's performance or through widening consumer choice.
- If the benefits of economies of scale and greater investment are passed on to consumers, it could be argued that they have gained from the existence of abnormal profit.

One of the criticisms raised against state-owned monopolies is that the absence of competition makes them become less efficient. The essence of the argument is that firms with a guaranteed market can be complacent. Monopolists are said to suffer from x-inefficiency, which means that their cost levels are higher than they would be in competitive firms because they do not have the incentive for process innovation. They become less dynamic, doing things in a particular way simply through tradition. In addition, some of their investment may take the form of erecting barriers to maintain the level of abnormal profit by excluding potential rivals. This will add to costs in the short run. This may be true but there is the possibility that these inefficiencies are outweighed by economies of scale which lower the unit costs.

It is clear that monopolies can operate in ways that lead to inefficiency or consumer exploitation. However, one can make a positive case for monopoly. This explains why the investigation of monopoly practices is difficult and each case must be judged on its own merits. It is dangerous to assume that monopoly is always harmful; the performance of a monopolist may be little different from that of firms in oligopoly.

SELF-ASSESSMENT TASK 2.38

Read the feature below and then answer the questions that follow.

Does OPEC have a monopoly in the supply of oil?

The Organization of the Petroleum Exporting Countries (OPEC) is a cartel set up in 1960 by five countries. The membership has now risen to 11. OPEC is responsible for 40% of the world production of crude oil and 14% of the world's natural gas. However, its exports of oil represent 60% of the oil that is traded internationally, and it has 77% of the world's proven oil reserves. Its declared objective was to secure fair and stable prices for producers, an efficient, economic and regular supply of oil to consuming nations and a fair return on capital for those investing in the oil industry.

The cartel was in a very strong position. It had a geographic monopoly because the distribution of world oil deposits is uneven. The demand for oil has been rising on trend and has been an essential raw material with a low price elasticity of demand because of the lack of a close substitute. In this situation, any reduction in supply will increase the market price without much reduction in the volume traded. The revenue of the OPEC members will certainly increase. OPEC cut production in 1973–74 and 1979 in what have been described as oil crises. In the 1980s, oil prices fell because supply was greater than demand.

The only thing that will weaken OPEC's economic power is if new suppliers outside of the cartel appear or consumers take action that will reduce consumption. Technology may provide alternatives to oil in the future. The monopoly will weaken further if there is disagreement over the target price or the production quotas allocated to each member country.

OPEC denies that it is acting as a single monopoly, cutting output in order to charge high prices to consumers and points out that western

governments make more money from the tax on oil than the producing countries receive in revenues from selling the oil.

At the retailing end of the industry, the supply is in the hands of an oligopoly of oil companies who deny that they are charging too much, insisting that the profit margin is low because of fierce competition. Profits are only high because of the large turnover.

Some analysts predict that there will be further horizontal integration between oil companies that are already vertically integrated. The oil industry will continue to be dominated by a few big players mainly because of the high fixed cost and risks associated with exploration and drilling.

1 Is OPEC a monopoly or an example of collusive oligopoly? Justify your answer.
2 Explain the economic logic behind OPEC's decision to reduce output.
3 What factors may reduce the demand for OPEC oil over time?
4 How can the oil companies boost their profits if they have little control over the market price?

Contestable markets

So far, in dealing with market structures, the models shown in Figure 2.45 (page 102) have been analysed. A **contestable market** is not listed here although contestability increasingly features in many markets throughout the world. By definition, a *perfectly* contestable market is one in which there are no costs of entry and exit. So, only perfect competition matches this ideal; monopolistic competition, with few relatively costless barriers to entry and exit, can match it to some extent, as can oligopoly in certain situations.

A contestable market is not so much a market structure as a means by which governments have sought

to regulate industry and the provision of services. It has had particular significance in the UK since 1979, when the principle of contestability became central to the tremendous structural changes that have been made especially to the service sector of the economy.

The important features of a contestable market are as follows:

- Free entry, which implies that new and existing market providers will have the same cost structure as in a perfectly competitive market.
- The number and size of firms are irrelevant. If a contestable market has only a few large firms, any

cost differences should be a reflection of a decision by a particular firm to charge a given price.

- Normal profits only can be earned in the long run. If firms are making supernormal profits, then this is the signal for others to enter the market. This could be on a 'hit and run' basis – a firm sees an opportunity, enters the market, collects the gains and leaves at no cost.
- The threat of potential entrants into the market is over-riding. Oligopolists and even a monopolist are obliged to offer consumers the benefits that they would receive in a more competitive market structure. Otherwise, new firms will enter from the pool of potential entrants.
- All firms are subject to the same regulations and government control irrespective of size.
- Mechanisms must be in place to prevent the use of unfair pricing by established firms to stop new entrants from entering the market.
- Cross-subsidisation is eliminated since firms cannot make normal profits if they sell any of their services below cost.

The application of contestability to the airline market is particularly interesting since, prior to deregulation, routes were strictly regulated by governments and there was little competition. The 'open skies' policy of a deregulated market has led to lower fares and a greater choice of airline for passengers. This has particularly been the case in the US domestic market and in Europe, where new low-cost airlines such as easyJet and Ryanair have entered the market and challenged the established national carriers. A further outcome has been the response of these carriers to form alliances.

There are other examples of contestable markets in the UK including:

- local bus services and rail services
- the provision of public services such as electricity, gas and water supplies
- telecommunications, particularly through the choice of network suppliers.

In theory and in practice, any market, even a monopoly, can be contestable. This state of affairs will come about if there is a pool of potential entrants waiting to enter a market if they see existing firms making abnormal profits. The cost of entry and exit is the main factor that determines whether a market really is contestable. Deregulation, the removal of barriers to entry, is the main way in which markets can be opened up to competition.

This policy is one that has been implemented by many governments worldwide, often in markets where previously the government has been the only provider of a service. The global air transport market is a particularly good example.

SELF-ASSESSMENT TASK 2.39

Read the feature below and then answer the questions that follow.

Airline alliances

The international airline business is a particularly good example of an oligopoly. It has moved from an industry where 20 years ago individual carriers competed with each other on particular routes to one where networks compete with each other on a network basis. These networks are known as alliances. Three alliances cover most of the world's airlines. These are shown in Table 2.17.

Oneworld:	British Airways, American Airlines, Cathay Pacific, Qantas, JAL Japan Airlines plus 6 others
SkyTeam:	Air France, KLM, Aeroflot, China Southern Airlines, Delta Airlines, Kenya Airways plus 6 others
Star Alliance:	Lufthansa, Swiss, bmi, Singapore Airlines, Air China, Air Canada, United, Continental Airlines, Air New Zealand, Turkish Airlines plus 16 others

Table 2.17 *Airline alliances*

Continental Airlines is the latest addition to the Star Alliance. Having pulled out of merger talks with United Airlines, in August 2009 it announced its intention to withdraw from SkyTeam. Analysts see this switch as the next best thing, not least because United is also a member of the formidable Star Alliance.

The way the new battleground is shaping up since the US and the EU entered into an 'open skies' agreement earlier this year, Star competes with SkyTeam and both compete with Oneworld. Continental's switch to the Star Alliance was approved by the US Department of Transportation in July 2009 on the grounds that it will give the airline 'more flexibility, benefit consumers, enhance competition and preserve jobs'. In addition, it will create new service options and a wider range of fares for travellers.

Source: Airlinealliances.org

1 Explain the possible benefits to an airline of becoming a member of an alliance.
2 Explain the possible benefits to passengers of airline alliances.

3 The US Department of Justice remains concerned about the anti-competitive behaviour of airline alliances. Comment on this concern.

Conclusions – the conduct and performance of firms

The conduct or behaviour of firms has been discussed in each of the four main market structures. The ways firms carry out their businesses will be determined by their objectives and the actual market conditions. As we have already seen, a firm's market power, and hence its conduct, is directly linked to the ease or difficulty of entry into the market.

In setting their prices, only in perfect competition are firms truly price takers. Any firm that moves away from a policy of charging more or less than the prevailing market price will have to leave the industry in the long run. In all other market structures, firms are price makers to some extent, although there may be some **price competition**. Consequently, **non-price competition**, where firms compete in terms of product promotion through branding, packaging or advertising, is relevant in monopolistic competition and oligopoly. A monopolist though has complete control over the prices that are charged.

Other aspects of pricing were discussed in the cases of oligopoly and monopoly. Price leadership was stated as being prevalent in oligopoly. Here, a market leader may be the price leader. This firm sets prices and others follow. The rigidity of prices in this market was illustrated by the kinked demand curve, a clear recognition of the mutual interdependence of firms.

So, in imperfect competition, firms compete with others on a mixture of price and non-price competition. It is only when there are very close substitutes that their conduct becomes less predictable. In this way, firms are interdependent. The extent to which they feel they can take risks with regard to their rivals' responses can lead to a change in a firm's pattern of behaviour. The outcome is often one of collusion.

The perfect competition model is an ideal. All other market structures fail to match it in terms of efficiency and performance. Monopolistic competition, for example, is said to have excess capacity with firms operating at less than the optimum level of output. The prices charged will be higher than what they could charge if they were bigger.

The models of competition make an assumption that, whatever the market structure, each firm will seek to maximise its profits all of the time. In reality this is clearly not the case. There is a particularly strong argument for relaxing this assumption when investigating how oligopolists operate. Alternative motives therefore often make it difficult to predict the conduct of firms in respect of price and output.

SPECIMEN EXAM QUESTIONS

The following questions have been set in recent CIE examination papers.

1 a   Explain how a knowledge of long run average costs might be useful to a profit-maximising firm. [10]
  b   Discuss whether firms want, and are able, to maximize profits as suggested by economic theory. [15]

[25 marks]

(October/November 2008)

2 Airbus, a large aircraft manufacturing company, announced in 2007 that its goal was to increase its $475 million research budget by 25% in order to try to develop a more environmentally friendly aircraft that had lower fuel consumption.
  a   Explain why Airbus is likely to be in an imperfect rather than perfect market structure.   [10]
  b   Economics textbooks sometimes criticise firms in imperfect competition as being against the public interest. What does this mean and how far does the Airbus announcement prove the textbooks wrong?   [15]

[25 marks]

(May/June 2009)

SUMMARY

In this supplement section it has been shown that:

- The principle of diminishing marginal utility can be used to explain the shape and derivation of the demand curve.
- A consumer will choose a combination of goods where the value of the marginal utility divided by the price of the good is equal for all goods.
- A price change for a good can be divided into a substitution effect and an income effect.
- In the short run at least one factor of production is fixed; all factors are variable in the long run.
- The short run production function shows how the quantity produced varies with changes to the input of a variable factor of production, normally labour.
- The demand for all factors of production is a derived demand; in the case of labour, the firm's demand curve can be derived from the value of the marginal revenue product.
- The supply of labour to a firm depends upon the wage rate; the shape of the supply curve for labour depends upon the responsiveness of labour supply to a change in the wage rate.
- The wage rate in a market is like any other price and is determined by supply and demand; labour markets can be influenced by the actions of trade unions and the government.
- Transfer earnings and economic rent can be used to explain why some workers are paid more than others.
- Economists split a firm's costs of production into fixed and variable costs; marginal and average costs are particularly useful in explaining how costs vary with a firm's output.
- In the long run, as output expands, the benefits from falling average costs are known as economies of scale; these benefits can accrue both within and from outside of a particular firm.
- Although economic power rests with large firms, small firms are more typical and are able to survive for many reasons.
- The normal objective of a firm is profit maximisation; other objectives may also be relevant in some types of business activity.
- The structure of markets can be explained by various characteristics including the strength of barriers to entry, the number and size of firms, the nature of the product and the availability of information.
- Economists recognise various models of market structure, namely perfect competition, monopoly, monopolistic competition and oligopoly; these models are useful for making comparisons with real markets.
- Many real-world markets are increasingly contestable in their structure.
- Firms compete in various ways depending upon the market structure in which they operate.
- The main models of market structure themselves can be compared in terms of their relative output, profits and efficiency.

Government intervention in the price system
Core

Meaning of market failure

It is stating the obvious to say that **market failure** exists when a market fails. However, the question needs to be asked: 'Fail at what?' The answer is: 'Fail at delivering economic efficiency'. Market failure exists whenever a free market, left to its own devices and totally free from any form of government intervention, fails to make the optimum use of scarce resources. Using earlier terminology, it is when the interaction of supply and demand in a market does not lead to productive and/or allocative efficiency. There are though reasons why this may not be the case.

Look at the following different reasons why markets fail:

- where there are externalities in the market
- the cases of merit and demerit goods
- the cases of public and quasi-public goods
- information failure
- adverse selection or moral hazard
- where monopolistic elements operate in a market (supplement)
- where there are concerns about the distribution of income and wealth (supplement).

Externalities (negative and positive)

Defining externality

If the market system is to work well and lead to economic efficiency, it is important that those people who make economic decisions are those who are affected by those decisions. A transaction between a supplier and a consumer for a product needs only to affect the particular supplier and particular consumer involved. As long as this is the case, then both sides will act only so long as both feel that they will benefit from any action – all is well in the market. However, a problem could clearly arise if someone else not party to the economic decision is affected by that decision. This is the concept known as **externality**.

An externality is said to arise if a third party (someone not directly involved) is affected by the decisions and actions of others. For example, if you decide to play your radio in public, then others (third parties) not involved in making that decision are affected by the noise that is being made.

Private and social costs

Another way of understanding the same concept is to define an externality as any divergence between private and social costs or benefits. The **social costs** of any action are all of the related costs associated with that action. The **private costs** are those costs involved in an action that accrue to the decision-maker. The difference between the two is **external costs**.

Therefore, social costs equals private costs plus external costs.

Negative externalities

It is quite possible that these private and social costs are the same: all of the costs of an action accrue to the decision-maker and there are no further costs. If this is the case, then there are no externalities. However, it is possible that there will be a difference: private and social costs may not be equal to each other. For example, if you make a decision to take a journey in my car, you consider only the costs of the petrol and the time taken. However, you do not consider the further costs that you may be imposing on others in terms of your contribution to road congestion, to atmospheric pollution and to possible car accidents. In this situation, a **negative externality** exists, the cost of which is an external cost. The situation is illustrated in Figure 3.1. Here, private costs are part of the social costs involved in a decision. However, they do not represent all of the social costs. The difference shown between the

two is the external cost or the cost of the negative externality.

Private and social benefits

A similar situation can also exist with benefits rather than costs. The social benefits of a decision are all of the benefits that accrue from that decision. The **private benefits** are those that accrue solely to the decision-maker. Again, these may or may not be the same. Any difference between them is the **external benefits**.

Positive externalities

It is possible that the social benefits of a decision may exceed the private benefits. If this is the case, then a positive externality, or external benefit, is said to exist. For example, if you make a decision to go to the doctor to be inoculated against a particular disease, then clearly you receive the private benefit of not catching that particular disease. However, you may not be the only one to benefit. The fact that you do not get the disease has some possible benefit to all others with whom you come into contact, who will now not catch the disease from you.

The problem created by externalities

The main problem created by externalities is that where they are present they will lead to an inappropriate amount being produced: the free market will lead either to too much or too little production.

Consider a firm that produces a chemical. There are costs that the firm will have to meet in producing a certain quantity of this chemical. These would include such things as:

- raw material costs
- labour costs
- energy costs.

All such costs would be termed private costs: they have to be paid for by the decision maker (the firm). These costs form part of social costs. However, there are further costs likely to be involved as well. These might include the cost of dumping the chemical waste, perhaps in a local river, which in turn creates clean-up costs for a third party. In addition, any atmospheric pollution created might cause ill health and there is likely to be additional road congestion

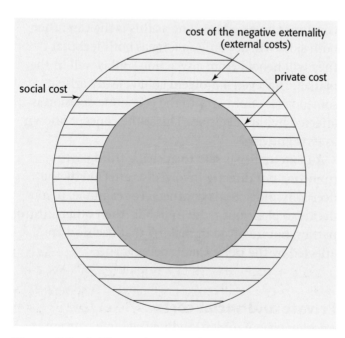

Figure 3.1 *A difference between private and social costs*

arising from the transportation of the chemicals. These are all negative externalities. The problem is that only the private costs of producing the chemical will be taken into account by the firm when making its pricing decision. The external costs, which are *real costs to society*, will not be taken into account. This will mean that the price will be lower than if all social costs were recognised and taken into account. Consequently demand and production will be higher than if full social costs had been considered. Thus, a negative externality will lead to too much of a product being produced. The situation can be seen in Figure 3.2.

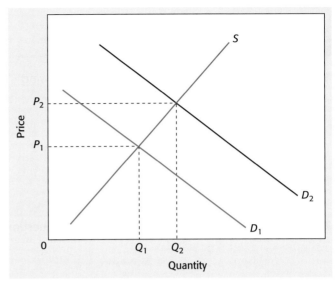

Figure 3.3 *Underproduction caused by a positive externality*

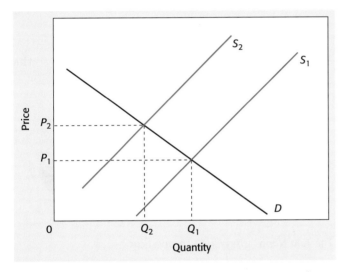

Figure 3.2 *Overproduction caused by a negative externality*

The price that will occur in the market will be P_1 where the supply schedule that takes account of the private costs, S_1, is equal to demand. This price is associated with production of Q_1. However, if the supply schedule took into account the social costs, S_2, which are greater than the private costs, then this would result in a price of P_2. This price is associated with a lower production of Q_2. Thus, the negative externality has led to $Q_1 - Q_2$, overproduction. Too many scarce resources are being devoted to the production of this product. The market has failed.

The opposite problem is true of a positive externality. Here, the problem is that too little of the product is being produced. If only the private benefits, and not the social benefits, are considered, then there will be underproduction. This is illustrated in Figure 3.3.

This time, the problem is with demand. If only the private benefits are registered, then demand is represented by the demand schedule D_1. This leads to a price of P_1 and an associated production of Q_1. However, if the further extra benefits to society were registered (which they will not be by the private decision-maker involved), then demand would be greater at D_2. This would lead to a price of P_2 and a production of Q_2. Thus there is an underproduction of $Q_2 - Q_1$ associated with the positive externality. Insufficient scarce resources are being devoted to the production of this good or service. The market has again failed.

Externalities are therefore a source of market failure as resources are not allocated in the ideal way: too few or too many resources are likely to be directed to the production of certain products.

Decision making using cost–benefit analysis

So far we have seen that there is market failure where there is a divergence between private and social benefits and costs. It is in such circumstances that **cost–benefit analysis** (CBA) has been used by economists as a means of decision making, not least to ensure that the right choice of action is being made. Here we are often concerned with situations where major economic projects produce substantial and often controversial side effects, in particular where there are costs and benefits which fall upon people and communities who have no direct

SELF-ASSESSMENT TASK 3.1

1 Identify and explain whether each of the following involves a positive or a negative externality:

    a a next-door neighbour playing his or her music loudly

    b a person being educated beyond the compulsory school leaving age

    c discarding a used battery in the road

    d smoking in a public place

    e a new, well-designed and pleasant public building

    f the use of pesticides in agricultural production.

2 Read the feature below and then answer the questions that follow.

India reveals world's cheapest car – but what are the bigger costs?

The world's cheapest car was unveiled by India's Tata Motors yesterday with a US$2500 price tag that brings car ownership into the reach of tens of millions of people, prompting fears about its environmental impact.

Critics say the Tata Nano will lead to millions more cars hitting the already clogged up roads in the country's teeming cities. They are concerned that this explosion will add to mounting air and noise pollution problems.

Company chairman, Ratan Tata, believes that the Nano will be the least polluting car in India and claims that it meets stringent EU emission standards. He also believes that this so-called 'People's Car' will provide India's growing middle classes with the personal mobility and

The Tata Nano – the world's cheapest car

status symbol they long for. For the masses though widespread poverty will limit car ownership. For a rickshaw driver in Delhi, earning just over US$2 a day, the so-called People's Car amounts to more than three years' earnings.

Source: Associated Press/Reuters, South China Morning Post, *11 January 2008 (adapted)*

a Identify and explain:

    i a private benefit and an external benefit

    ii a private cost and an external cost arising out of Tata's production of the Nano.

b Discuss whether the production of the Nano is a case of market failure.

3 Read the feature below and then answer the questions that follow.

e-wasted: waste dumped in poor countries

In this age of constant upgrades, where do all the old unwanted computers, mobile phones, TVs, cameras, batteries etc. go? Many end up in land-fill…and here is where the problems begin.

Most old electronic devices are laden with toxic heavy metals that can leach into water and soil or which are released into the air when burnt. An average 27 kg desktop computer can contain 2 kg of lead, a heavy metal that is known to cause blood and brain disorders in children.

If the estimated 500 million computers in the world were thrown out today we would be disposing of 2.8 billion kg of plastic, 7 million kg of lead and 286 000 kg of mercury! Annually, e-waste is between 20 and 50 million tonnes, with Asia accounting for 12 million tonnes. But because e-waste is highly toxic, proper disposal is expensive. Often, thousands of tonnes are exported to or dumped in developing and poor countries where

e-waste is highly toxic and expensive to dispose of

the waste is taken apart, melted or disposed of in unsafe conditions. This trade has been linked to environmental hazards and health problems from cancer to birth defects.

Source: New Sunday Times, Malaysia, 23 September 2007 (adapted)

a Explain why there is market failure in this case.
b Explain the various private costs and external costs identified in the feature.

c Discuss alternative ways in which the market could deal more efficiently with the problems of e-waste.

---

connection with the particular project, either as consumers or suppliers.

There are many situations where CBA can be used to aid decision making. In all types of economy there are numerous examples of environmental pollution which results in external costs being imposed on the local community. The so-called spillover effects upon third parties (those not involved in the particular project) can be far-reaching and substantial. CBA genuinely attempts to quantify the opportunity cost to society of the various possible outcomes or sources of action.

In developed economies, the UK especially, concerns continue to be raised over the increasing

number of new retail projects being built by major supermarkets and property developers. These developments can have a tremendous impact on local communities – not all of the perceived benefits are beneficial in the long run.

CBA is also widely used in the appraisal of major transport projects such as London's Crossrail extension and the Hong Kong–Zhuhai–Macau Bridge. Where huge investment is needed, CBA can provide justification based on taking a wide view of a project's impact on users of the facility and on the wider economy over a projected period of time.

The cost–benefit approach differs from private sector methods of appraisal in two main respects:

- It seeks to include all of the costs and benefits, not just private ones.
- It often has to impute a **shadow price** on costs and benefits where no market price is available, for example, how to value travel time savings, how to value the benefit of cleaner air or being able to live in a less noisy environment.

The framework of cost–benefit analysis

Whatever the problem under investigation, there are four main stages in the development of a cost–benefit analysis. These are shown in Figure 3.4.

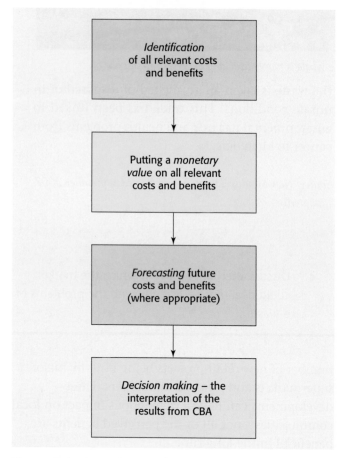

Figure 3.4 *Stages in a cost–benefit analysis*

The first stage is to identify all of the relevant costs and benefits arising out of any particular project. This involves establishing what are the private costs, the private benefits, the external costs and the external benefits. On the surface this may seem a relatively simple task. In reality, and with a little more thought, it is not so. There are particular problems when it comes to identifying external costs and benefits. These are often controversial, not easy to define in a discrete way and have the added difficulty that it is not always possible to draw the line in terms of a physical or geographical cut-off. The spillover effects of a new retail development, for example, are wide-reaching and often affect people and communities beyond the immediate vicinity of the proposed development.

The second stage involves putting a monetary value on the various costs and benefits. This is relatively straightforward where market prices are available. For example, in the case of a new retail development, a monetary value can be put on the jobs created or the increased profits arising from the development. For other variables, though, a monetary value must be attributed for costs and benefits where no market prices are available. This particular measurement difficulty has occupied economists for thousands of hours over the years. It has also been a very controversial matter in situations where cost–benefit analysis has come under close public scrutiny. A particularly good example of this is the issue of valuation of time, especially travel time and savings in travel time. Another relevant example is how to put a monetary value on the cost of accidents, particularly where serious injuries or a loss of life is involved.

The third stage applies in situations where projects have longer-term implications which stretch well into the future. Here, economists have to employ statistical forecasting techniques, sometimes of a very crude nature, to estimate costs and benefits over many years. This particularly applies to proposed projects where massive capital expenditure is involved. In other cases, this stage may not be needed, particularly if two alternatives are being considered (see Self-assessment task 3.2, question 2).

The final stage is where the results of the earlier stages are drawn together so that the outcome can be presented in a clear manner in order to aid decision-making. The important principle to recognise is that if the value of benefits exceeds the value of the costs, then the particular project is worthwhile since it provides an overall net benefit to the community (see Self-assessment task 3.2, question 2 for a simple example of such a situation).

The four stages in a cost–benefit analysis provide a coherent framework by which decisions can be made in situations of market failure. Any cost–benefit study or application should therefore be seen in these terms.

To conclude, it is relevant to recognise that in practice cost–benefit analysis is fraught with many difficulties. Some have already been stated such as:

- which costs and benefits should be included
- how to put monetary values on them.

Additionally, there are others, particularly when it comes to the acceptance of the outcome by the community as a whole. For example:

- CBA does not always satisfactorily reflect the distributional consequences of certain decisions, particularly where public sector investment is involved. In the case of a new retail development, external costs are likely to be highly localised whilst external benefits, in terms of employment creation for instance, are likely to be more widely spread.

- Many public sector projects can be very controversial and subject to much local aggravation from pressure groups. It may be the case that the outcome of the CBA is rejected for local political reasons, with the consequence that the most expedient decision may not be the one recommended by economists. Where this happens, it is easy to dismiss the technique of CBA as irrelevant. This is not a fair conclusion, not least as CBA has at least brought out the issues involved so that a decision can be taken on the basis of all of the information available. CBA is an aid and not a replacement for decision making.

SELF-ASSESSMENT TASK 3.2

1 Read the feature below and then answer the questions that follow.

Traffic problems in Bangkok

Bangkok, the capital of Thailand, is one of Asia's megacities. For its citizens, and those who visit as tourists or for business reasons, one thing that no one can get away from is its horrendous traffic congestion. The population is increasing at a massive 2% per annum and, as in all parts of Asia, vehicle ownership levels are increasing at a substantial rate as a consequence of economic advancement. This situation means increasing stress levels, deterioration in the quality of life and increasing health problems for its teeming population.

A recent government report has estimated that:

Morning rush hour in Bangkok

- the typical resident spends 44 working days a year stuck in traffic
- peak vehicle speeds have fallen to 6 km per hour
- lost production due to congestion is estimated to be 10% of Thailand's GDP

- much of the energy used to move vehicles is wasted because of the congestion
- one million people a year suffer from diagnosed respiratory diseases linked to the air pollution quality which has 18 times more CO_2 emissions than the WHO maximum guideline

- there is a high incidence of lung cancer amongst the adult population and children have unacceptable levels of lead in their blood
- thousands of people a year suffer strain and stress-related illness directly accountable to the severe congestion

- school children leave home for school at 5 a.m. to beat the congestion.

Unlike its 'neighbours' such as Kuala Lumpur, Singapore and Hong Kong, Bangkok does not have a rapid transit system, although one has been planned for at least 30 years. The time has surely come when this has to be authorised.

Suppose you have been asked by the authorities in Bangkok to produce a cost–benefit analysis for a new rapid transit system for the city.

a Using the above information as a guide, what costs and benefits would you include in your analysis?

b On what theoretical basis might you:
   - recommend that a new rapid transit system be constructed?
   - recommend that there is no case for a new rapid transit system?

c In each case, comment upon how confident you might be of your recommendations.

2 The following is an adaptation of an A level question set by UCLES. Read the feature and then answer the questions that follow.

Cavalier Pet Products

Cavalier Pet Products is a large privately owned manufacturer of canned pet foods based in Bolton, Lancashire, UK. The company, which employs 300 people, is long-established and has been on its present site since it was founded by its owners, the Fazackerley family, in 1906. It is a market leader, producing own-branded products, which are widely advertised and well known.

Because of the nature of its manufacturing processes, the company is a polluter of the local environment. The nauseating smells from the factory, particularly in hot weather, are the main source of complaint. The firm also creates noise disturbance and quite recently was successfully prosecuted for discharging effluent into a local stream running alongside the factory. There is increasing local pressure from residents for something to be done about the whole question of the firm and its operations.

The obvious answer is for the firm to move to another location. The Managing Director of Cavalier Pet Products, Basil Fazackerley, favours such a move but is quite adamant that, 'We will not pay the full cost. If the local council want us to move, then they will have to help us to do so.'

The decision to relocate the factory has long-term implications both for its owners and for the community. In particular, new jobs will be created as the firm increases output and the environment within the vicinity of the present site will experience environmental gain.

The local council has agreed to contribute to the relocation as it can see a benefit to the community. Cavalier Pet Products remains concerned that it should only pay a realistic contribution to the cost of relocation.

In order to sort out these difficulties, a local university was asked to carry out a cost–benefit analysis of the proposed relocation. A summary of its findings is given in Table 3.1.

Costs		Benefits	
Private costs of the relocation	1300	Private benefits	1500
Contribution from local authority	300	External benefits	1200
External costs	400		
Total costs	**2000**	**Total benefits**	**2700**

Table 3.1 *Estimated discounted[1] costs and benefits of the relocation of Cavalier Pet Products (£000)*

Note: [1]Discounting is a procedure whereby a present value is given to costs and benefits that will occur some time in the future.

a What is the specific purpose of the cost–benefit analysis in this case study?

b With reference to the proposed relocation, give an example of:
- a private benefit
- an external benefit

arising from the proposed relocation. Explain your choice.

c Use the information in Table 3.1 to state what conclusions you could draw from the cost–benefit analysis.

d You are asked to plan an investigation to estimate the various external costs and benefits of the proposed relocation. Explain how you might do this and comment upon some of the problems you might face.

Economic appraisal of Crossrail

Crossrail is a hugely ambitious rail project that will provide a much needed west–east rail link through from Heathrow Airport to East London. At an estimated cost of £16 billion, it will involve extensive tunnelling work in central London. The case for Crossrail, like any major new transport infrastructure project, has to be justified through an economic appraisal. This is based on cost–benefit analysis.

The projected user benefits of Crossrail are:

- Value of time savings for current public transport users and motorists. The rationale for this benefit is that once the new Crossrail link opens, many

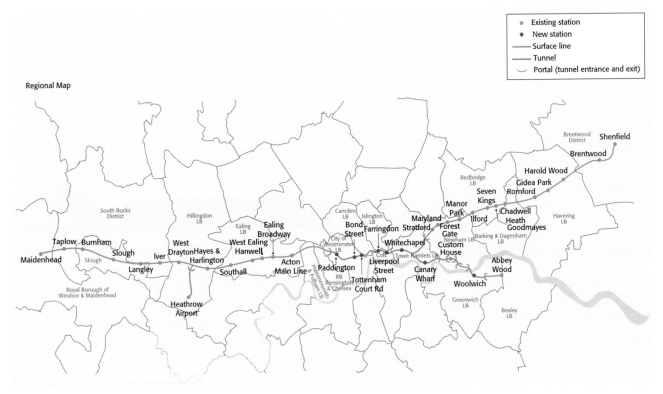

The Crossrail Heathrow East-London link

users will experience reduced travel times. The opportunity cost of these travel time savings is a benefit to such groups.

- A reduction in crowding and improved journey quality. This benefit will take the form of improved comfort for users transferring to Crossrail from other congested transport modes.
- Reduced operating costs for road users and a reduction in accidents. These benefits will accrue to road users who continue to make their journeys by road whilst a reduction in accidents will also generate some benefits to the local community and to health services.
- Benefits to mobility impaired passengers using Crossrail.

The costs of Crossrail are easier to identify and consist of:

- capital costs of construction
- maintenance costs
- operating costs.

Table 3.2 summarises the estimated monetary values of these benefits and costs. The benefits are split between trips made in the course of work and those made for leisure and commuting purposes.

User benefits		Costs	
	£m		**£m**
Leisure/ commuting trips		Capital costs	10 626
		Maintenance costs	1 606
– time savings	7 985	Operating costs	1 670
– improved quality	2 889		
– other	355		
Business trips			
– time savings	4 847		
– other	17		
Total benefits	**16 093**	**Total costs**	**13 902**

Table 3.2 *Projected user benefits and costs of Crossrail (present value)*

Source: *Cross London Rail Links, 2005*

As Table 3.2 shows, Crossrail is expected to generate over £16 billion of user benefits, with about one-third accruing for business trips that carry the highest

value of time savings per hour of travel time saved. Interestingly, the user benefit is the same as the projected construction costs in 2007.

So far this summary of the cost–benefit analysis has followed the normal methodology. In planning Crossrail, one of the objectives has been to facilitate the continuing development of London's Finance and Business Services sector. This is a spillover effect arising from Crossrail. Such effects are by no means easy to identify or quantify. Having said this, Cross London Rail Links (CLRL) has estimated likely job creation and moves to more productive jobs in central London. They believe that around 5000 new central area jobs will be created by 2016, rising to 33 000 by 2026. Some workers will be able to move to better jobs, representing a benefit to themselves and to the economy through higher tax revenues.

The overall value of the wider economic benefits is estimated at £7.2 billion. Table 3.3 summarises all of the respective benefits and costs.

	£m
Total costs	13 902
Less: Public transport revenue	– 6 149
Plus: Indirect tax reductions	1 207
Net cost to government	8 960
Transport user benefits	16 093
Wider economic benefits	7 161
Total benefits	23 254
Total benefits : net costs	2.60 : 1

Table 3.3 *Overall costs and benefits of Crossrail (present value)*

Source: *CLRL, 2005*

SELF-ASSESSMENT TASK 3.3

With reference to the cost–benefit analysis of Crossrail:

1 Explain why the valuation of travel time savings is an important item in this cost–benefit analysis.
2 Comment on why the cost–benefit analysis is an 'aid' rather than a clear mandate for Crossrail to be constructed.

Merit goods, demerit goods and information failure

Another way in which markets may fail is due to the existence of **merit goods** and **demerit goods**.

Sometimes, merit and demerit goods are simply seen as an extension of the idea of externalities as discussed above. A merit good may be described as a good that has positive externalities associated with it. Thus, an inoculation against a contagious disease might be seen as a merit good. This is because others who may not now catch the disease from the inoculated person also benefit. A demerit good is seen as any product that has negative externalities associated with it. Thus, cigarettes can be seen as a demerit good because secondary or passive smoking can be viewed as a possible cause of ill health (a clear negative externality). If this is all there is to merit and demerit goods, then they cannot be seen as a separate category of market failure from externalities.

However, merit and demerit goods can (and indeed should) be defined in a different way which makes them different from externalities. The essence of merit and demerit goods in this definition is to do with an **information failure** to the consumer. This arises because consumers do not perceive quite how good or bad a particular product is for them: either they do not have the right information or they simply lack some relevant information. This is why demerit goods are provided by the government for those who are deemed to need them.

Merit goods

With this idea of a failure of information, a merit good is defined as a good that is better for a person than the person who may consume the good realises. Given this definition, education is often defined as a merit good. The individuals who make decisions about how much education to receive (or how much to allow their children to receive) do not fully appreciate quite how much benefit will be received through being well educated. We do not appreciate how good education is for us. We do not perceive its full benefits at the time of making the decision about how much education to receive.

Demerit goods

Demerit goods, on the other hand, are those products that are worse for the individual consumer than the

A packet of cigarettes may be classed as demerit goods

individual realises. Cigarettes are taken to be a good example here. It is suggested that when a person makes a decision to smoke a cigarette, he or she is not fully in possession of all of the information concerning the harmful effects of smoking. If he or she were in possession of such information, then there would be a greater reluctance to smoke.

It is interesting to note that the example of a demerit good given here, namely smoking, is the same as the example of a product that can be seen as having negative externalities associated with it. However, the reason for identifying the product is different. Here, it is not due to the damage done to others that the issue arises, but rather due to the unperceived damage done to the person consuming the product. Hence, information failure.

Merit goods, demerit goods and value judgements

It may have been noticed in the above definitions that a significant question poses itself with regard to merit and demerit goods. Who is to say what is 'good' or 'bad' for a person? If an individual consumer makes a presumably rational decision to consume a product, what right has the rest of society to say that he or she is making a 'wrong' decision? It seems clear that if this is what is going on, we have entered the area of **value judgements**. If society is able to say to consumers that they do not fully realise what is good or bad for them, then we are accepting that 'society knows best' and has some right to make such a judgement. In effect, we are allowing **paternalism** to be a legitimate part of Economics. It is acceptable for us to say that society can judge what is, or is not, good for a person, regardless of what that person believes. In this area, then, we may have gone beyond our allegedly 'value-free' positive Economics that was introduced in the first part of the book.

The problems caused by merit and demerit goods

Why, then, might merit and demerit goods be identified as a failure of the market? The problem is that their existence will cause an inappropriate amount of the products concerned to be produced.

Merit goods will be underproduced in a free market situation. Insufficient scarce resources will be devoted to their production. The problem is that the lack of information about how good the product is for individuals will result in insufficient demand being registered for the product in the market. This is shown in Figure 3.5. Here, the 'correct' level of demand, if consumers appreciated the true value of the product to themselves, would be D_1. This would lead to a market price of P_1 where D_1 is equal to the supply of product, S. This price would be associated with a level of production and consumption of Q_1, the ideal quantity of the good. However, because consumers undervalue the product, demand is only registered as D_2. This leads to a market price of P_2 (where D_2 is equal to supply, S) which is associated with production and consumption of Q_2. This is below the optimum level: the market has failed.

Figure 3.6 shows the problem of a demerit good. Here, the 'correct' demand should be at D_1 which will lead to a price of P_1 and a production and consumption of Q_1. As consumers over-value the product, demand is registered at the higher level of D_2. This leads to a market price of P_2 and a production and consumption of Q_2. The market has failed: too many scarce resources are devoted to the production of this demerit good.

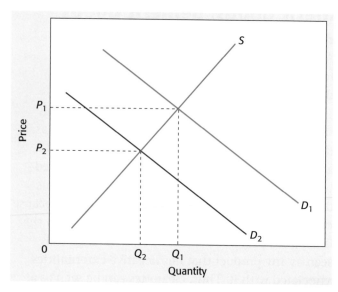

Figure 3.5   *The under-provision of a merit good by the market*

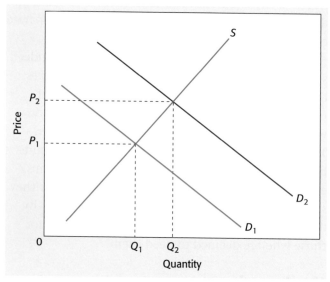

Figure 3.6   *The over-provision of a demerit good by the market*

Moral hazard and adverse selection

There are numerous other examples of market failure arising from information failure. In welfare Economics two types of situation can be recognised: **moral hazard** and **adverse selection**.

Moral hazard can best be explained in the context of the health care market. Why does anyone go to a doctor? The most usual reason is because we are not sure how to deal with a health problem, whether this be something trivial like a sore throat or something more serious. We visit the doctor to get information –

in doing this we recognise that the doctor is better informed than we are and that the whole point about making this visit is to accept the advice that is given. Moral hazard is when some person in the market (in this case the doctor) is better informed than those seeking advice. However, if the advice is wrong, we shall have made an undesirable choice of treatment. This will be a misallocation of resources and hence, market failure.

Adverse selection is rather different. In this case, the information failure is reversed because information may well be withheld or be inaccurate when it emanates from, say, someone requiring health insurance. This puts the insurer in a position where not all the necessary information is provided for risk to be established. If this happens, then the cost of the health premium will be too low. If this person then requires treatment for an undisclosed problem, the premiums for healthy people will have to rise. In the worst case, if premiums become too expensive, healthy people may no longer seek health insurance as it has become too expensive. This is not good news for the insurer who could be left only with 'bad risk' customers. It might even lead to the collapse of the market through the enforced withdrawal of insurers. Again, there is a misallocation of resources and hence, market failure.

SELF-ASSESSMENT TASK 3.4

Discuss whether each of the following is a merit or a demerit good:

a compulsory secondary education
b wearing a seat belt
c chewing gum
d visiting a museum
e playing loud music and shouting at a cricket match.

Public goods

A different type of good from a merit or demerit that may cause the market to fail is referred to as a **public good**. Here, it is not a matter of too much or too little provision of the good in question, but rather whether the product will be provided at all.

There are two specific characteristics that a good must possess if it is to be classified as a public good:

1 It must be **non-excludable**. This means that once the good has been provided for one consumer, it is impossible to stop all other consumers from benefiting from the good.
2 It must be **non-rival**. As more and more people consume the product, the benefit to those already consuming the product is not diminished.

Once one begins to think about these characteristics, there are a number of goods that can be seen as public goods. Take the example of a lighthouse. Once a lighthouse is built to warn one ship at sea away from a dangerous area of rocks, then by its very nature, this service will automatically be provided to all ships that sail within a certain distance of the lighthouse. It is non-excludable. Equally, the fact that other ships see the light given by the lighthouse and are warned away from the dangerous rocks does not reduce the benefit that any one particular ship receives from that warning. It is non-rival. Very few goods though are pure public goods in the sense that they match both of the above characteristics in full.

Quasi-public goods

While there may be some goods that can clearly be defined as 'public' in nature, there are others that have some of the attributes of such goods without fully possessing the two required characteristics stated above. Such goods are referred to as **quasi-public goods**. They are like public goods without truly being public goods.

In practice, it is not possible to classify all products as being either 'public' or 'private'. Many products lie somewhere in between these two extremes. A good that is closer to a public good than to a private good, but is not fully a public good, is called a quasi-public good.

A good example might be a sandy seaside beach. Such a beach is available to all those who wish to use it. It appears non-excludable. However, it is possible to think of ways of excluding consumers. Privately owned beaches do this. Equally, the beach is non-rival up to a point. If you are the first person on a pleasant beach on a warm sunny day, it does very little to diminish your enjoyment of that beach as a few more people arrive to enjoy the benefits themselves.

However, there may well come a point at which that is no longer the case. As the beach becomes crowded, space limited and other people's conversations and music become ever more audible, enjoyment may perceptibly reduce. Thus the beach has something of the characteristic of non-rivalry, but not the full characteristic. It is a quasi-public good.

The problem caused by public goods

The problem that may be caused in a free market by the existence of public goods is a serious one: the market may fail to produce them at all. There may be a consumer demand for such products (consumers are willing and able, in principle, to pay for the product's services), but the free market may not have a mechanism for guaranteeing their production.

This problem is referred to as the **free rider** issue. Some consumers attempt to gain a 'free ride' on the back of other consumers' purchases of the public good. It is entirely reasonable that they may attempt to do this. One of the key characteristics of public goods is that they are non-excludable. This implies that once one consumer has purchased the product, all other consumers cannot be prevented from benefiting from that product. Take the example of the lighthouse. Once one particular fisherman has provided a lighthouse close to some dangerous rocks for his own benefit, then all other fishermen in the area will benefit equally from the lighthouse. Their advantage, however, is that they do not have to pay for this lighthouse: they have received a free ride on the back of someone else's purchase. The logical thing to do, then, would seem to be for all fishermen to sit back and to wait for one fisherman to be foolish enough to provide a lighthouse so that those not purchasing can benefit without paying. Unfortunately, the implication of this is that the lighthouse will never be provided: everyone waits for everyone else to provide it, and nothing happens.

It could be argued that a more likely scenario to the one described above is that all fishermen in an area might agree to club together in order to make the purchase and thus the lighthouse would be provided. However, there is still a problem here as it is in the interest of any one fisherman to conceal his desire for the lighthouse, refuse to pay but still to gain the final benefit once it is provided. Again, if all fishermen behave like this, the lighthouse is not provided.

The existence of public goods may mean that scarce resources are not used in a way that would be desirable. People may wish for the provision of such goods (they yield utility), but the demand may never be registered in the market.

Private goods

Private goods are those bought and consumed by individuals for their own benefit. Most of the goods we consume are private goods. They have two important characteristics:

- **Excludability** It is possible to exclude some people from using a private good. This is normally done through charging a price. If the price is not acceptable, then that good will not be consumed. Once a private good has been purchased by one person it cannot be consumed by others.
- **Rivalry** The consumption by one person reduces the availablility for others. In some ways it seems obvious that when we purchase food, clothes or a textbook then this means that fewer of these goods are available for purchase by others.

SELF-ASSESSMENT TASK 3.5

Explain whether each of the following may be described as a private, a public or a quasi-public good:

a the local police service
b a chocolate bar
c a public park
d a firework display
e a stretch of road
f street lighting
g a berth for a cruise ship
h a public cricket pitch
i a museum.

Private goods can also be rejected if the price is too high or the quality is not what is expected.

These seemingly obvious qualities of private goods are useful since they help us understand what is meant by public goods.

Government intervention

You have only to glance at a newspaper or listen to the news or a political debate for a few minutes to realise that one of the more controversial areas of Economics is concerned with the extent and reasons for government intervention in markets. Governments throughout the world intervene to a greater or lesser extent and the reasons for intervention vary enormously between them. However, the justification for intervention is usually where there is market failure.

We shall now consider what forms intervention can take with respect to the instances of market failure analysed above.

Methods of government intervention

Regulation

The government uses different methods of **regulation** as a means of controlling a market. Legal and other methods are used to control the quality and quantity of goods and services that are produced and consumed.

Regulations have been important in combating negative externalities. For example, excessive levels of pollution are prohibited by regulations that apply to the manufacture of vehicles and the production of electricity. These are just two examples. Regulation may also refer to prices. Examples of price controls include minimum wage legislation and maximum price controls (see Supplement for a wider analysis).

Financial intervention: use of taxes and subsidies

Financial tools, such as **taxes** and **subsidies**, are frequently used by governments to influence production and the prices of commodities in an economy. For example, demerit goods which produce negative externalities are usually subject to high rates of indirect taxation. By contrast, subsidies, involving a direct payment by the government to a producer, make the price paid by consumers less than it should be. Typically, subsidies are paid for goods that give

positive externalities. They might be in the form of a partial subsidy, as in the case of staple food products and public transport, or total, as in the case of free school meals for children from low-income families.

Tax instruments may also vary. In the UK two different forms of taxation are currently applied to the use of vehicles. Vehicle Excise Duty is paid once every six or twelve months for any vehicle using roads. The same amount is paid whether the car is used daily or only once a month. In addition vehicle users pay **excise duties** and value added tax on petrol. In this case the total amount of tax paid rises with the number of miles driven. The first type of tax may deter ownership of a vehicle whilst the second deters use of the vehicle.

Governments also provide the finance that is needed to produce a good or service. It is very important to note that just because the government provides the finance for a product, it does not necessarily mean it has to produce the product. For example, the government could finance education but all schools, colleges and universities might be privately owned and run. Health care may be provided free (financial intervention) but the drugs used in prevention and cure of illness might be privately produced.

State production

In addition to providing the finance it is also possible for a government to take over the production of a good or service, either in whole or in part. In many countries state-owned industries such as electricity generation, coal mining, water provision and railways are entirely owned and managed by the state and are often referred to as *nationalised industries*. In many countries this is no longer the case following the major shift towards privatisation that took place during the 1980s and 1990s. It is also very common to find that some goods and services are produced by both the state and the private sectors. Education and health care are particularly good examples of these types of service industries. State-run hospitals function alongside private hospitals and independent schools operate alongside state schools.

The impact of government intervention on markets

The impact of the different methods of government intervention will vary according to the reasons for market failure and the conditions facing the markets.

135

Public goods

Public goods, such as defence, need to be financed by the government but they do not necessarily need to be produced by the government. The government will decide upon the optimal amount of defence expenditure and raise revenue through taxation to fund it. The problem facing the government is deciding on the best or fairest method of raising the tax revenue required. One approach is to tax individuals according their income. Thus those who have the highest incomes (or wealth) will pay most in taxation. Many governments use the 'ability to pay' principle as a basis for their tax systems and this is widely accepted amongst the electorate as being the fairest means of raising tax revenue. In most countries the government takes a larger percentage of income in tax from the rich than the poor. This is called a **progressive tax** system.

Externalities
Setting standards and regulation

Governments frequently use regulation to overcome market failures caused by externalities. Let us consider the case of an electricity company that pollutes the surrounding countryside. The government might intervene by setting standards which restrict the amount of pollution that can be legally dumped. The government would then need to regulate and inspect the company to make sure that these restrictions are enforced. It can do this in several ways, for example by imposing large fines on any company that contravenes the law. Exhaust fumes from cars pollute the atmosphere and to reduce this problem the government can set legal limits on the amount of carbon particles that are emitted from a car's exhaust pipe.

Financial intervention – taxes

An indirect tax would normally be imposed on the individual or firm that causes the negative externality. This is consistent with the so-called 'polluter pays' principle.

In Figure 3.7, in the case where there is no government intervention, the equilibrium occurs at point E, where supply, S_1, which is given by marginal private cost (MPC), equals demand, D, which is given by marginal private benefit (MPB). However, if

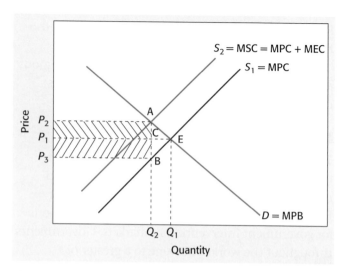

Figure 3.7 *External costs and use of taxation*

external costs are taken into account, then the supply curve becomes S_2 or marginal social cost (MSC). The vertical distance between these two supply curves is marginal external cost (MEC). The socially optimal level of output is now equal to Q_2, where S_2 cuts the demand curve. At this socially optimal level of output, the marginal external cost is equal to the vertical distance AB.

The government intervenes in this market and imposes a tax which is equal to the marginal external cost. This tax is added to the cost of producing the product and thus the supply curve S_2 is also equal to the MPC plus this tax. From the diagram, you can see that the price at which the product is sold has increased from P_1 to P_2. This is less than the tax applied by the government. At first sight this may appear a little strange, but the producer has accepted a cut in the price received from P_1 to P_3. The producer has borne the burden of part of the tax. The total tax paid is equal to the area P_2ABP_3, of which the consumer's share of the burden is P_2ACP_1 and the producer's share is P_1CBP_3. The effect of the negative externality is now internalised within the market.

Financial intervention – subsidies

Financial intervention to overcome market failure caused by positive externalities takes the form of a subsidy. This is shown in Figure 3.8. The equilibrium without government intervention is at point F where MPC = MPB or $D_1 = S_1$. In this case, marginal external benefit is added to the MPB curve to give the MSB

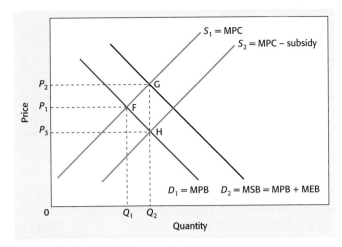

Figure 3.8 *External benefits and use of a subsidy*

or marginal social benefit curve. The MSB represents society's demand curve for the product.

If the government subsidises production of this product, then the supply curve moves to the right from S_1, which equals MPC, to S_2, which equals MPC minus the subsidy. The marginal cost of supplying the good is reduced by the amount of subsidy and the vertical distance GH is equal to the value of the subsidy. Thus the equilibrium after the subsidy is at point H, which is where D_1 crosses S_2 and the optimal amount of goods Q_2 is sold by the market.

As you might expect, there is considerable debate over which is the best method of government intervention when externalities are present in a market. If we accept the argument that education provides external benefits, then one solution would be to provide a subsidy for education. This can be seen where the government subsidises university education. Students still have to pay towards their education in the form of a fee, which can be represented by P_3 in Figure 3.8. The government provides the difference between P_2 and P_3 by providing a subsidy.

Maximum price controls and price stabilisation

We will conclude this core section by considering how governments impose maximum price controls in markets and how price stabilisation policies can be applied in agricultural markets.

Maximum price controls are only valid in markets where the maximum price imposed is below the normal equilibrium price as determined in a free

market. Governments use legislation to enforce maximum prices for:

- staple foodstuffs, such as bread, rice and cooking oil
- rents in certain types of housing
- services provided by utilities, such as water, gas and electricity companies
- transport fares where a subsidy is being paid.

Figure 3.9 indicates that at the price ceiling of P_1, production is not sufficient to satisfy everyone who wishes to buy the product. Consequently, as price cannot rise, the available supply has to be allocated on some other basis. The most likely way is by means of queuing, a much evidenced form of control in the former planned economies of Central and Eastern Europe (see Chapter 1). Rationing is another means of restricting demand – it inevitably leads to an informal market for the products involved, with consumers then having to pay inflated prices well above the ceiling price.

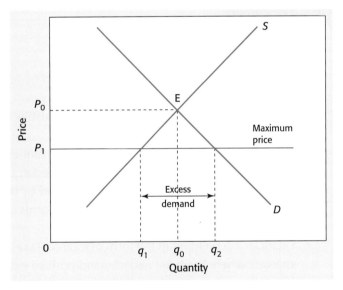

Figure 3.9 *The effects of maximum price control*

Price stabilisation policies, especially in agricultural markets, are designed to lessen the effects of unplanned fluctuations in supply. A producers' association or a government-backed marketing board regulates supply by releasing stocks on to the market in order to stabilise farm incomes. By releasing buffer stocks at times of shortage or by purchasing excess stocks at times of surplus production, price can be stabilised at a predetermined level. Although theoretically simple in terms of their economic logic, such policies are often criticised as they do not promote efficiency and tend to protect farmers from the full force of competition in world markets.

SPECIMEN EXAM QUESTIONS

The following questions have been set in recent CIE examination papers.

1 a Explain how resources are allocated in a market economy. [8]

b Discuss, with the aid of a demand and supply diagram, the effects on consumers and producers when the government introduces an indirect tax on a good. [12]

[20 marks]

(October/November 2007)

2 a Explain the market failure which arises from the characteristics of public goods. [8]

b Discuss whether the use of cost–benefit analysis helps to improve economic decision-making. [12]

[20 marks]

(October/November 2008)

SUMMARY

In this core section it has been shown that:

- Markets do not always operate as suggested by economic theory. There are various reasons why markets fail.
- Where negative and positive externalities exist in a market, the outcome is an inappropriate level of production.
- Using cost–benefit analysis can be an important aid to decision making.
- Merit and demerit goods will not be provided in the right quantities by the market.
- Public goods will not necessarily be provided by the market.
- Government intervention can take various forms including regulation, financial intervention and direct provision of goods and services.
- Financial intervention in the form of indirect taxes and subsidies has been widely advocated for use in markets where there are negative and positive externalities.
- Maximum price controls and price stabilisation programmes are other ways that governments choose to intervene in markets.

Government intervention in the price system
Supplement

Market failure

In the Core section it was suggested that there may be times when markets do not function well. Three particular reasons were identified:

1 The existence of externalities

- Both negative and positive externalities can cause a market to fail to work effectively.
- Negative externalities exist when the social cost of an activity exceeds the private cost. There is an external cost that is not paid by those directly involved in the transaction. This leads to overproduction of the product involved as the true cost does not directly have to be paid by the producers and consumers of this product.
- Positive externalities exist when the social benefit of an activity exceeds the private benefit. The full benefit to all of society is not gained by those directly involved in an activity. This means that the product is underproduced as demand will not be as great as it should be.

2 Public goods

- Public goods possess the twin characteristics of non-excludability and non-rivalry. Once the good (such as a lighthouse) is produced for one person, it is impossible to stop others from benefiting. Equally, as more and more people consume the product, the benefit is not diminished to existing consumers.
- Public goods may not be produced in free markets due to the problem of 'free-riding'. No-one is prepared to purchase the product as there is a strong incentive to wait for someone else to do so and then to enjoy the benefit without incurring any cost. If everyone behaves in this way, then the product is not produced.

3 Merit goods

- Merit goods can be defined either as products that generate positive externalities or as products that generate greater benefits to individuals than those individuals realise. Health care could be seen as a clear example.
- Merit goods are likely to be underproduced in a market as the full benefits are not recognised. The demand for the product is thus less than it ideally should be.

The purpose of this chapter is to build upon this earlier analysis and to consider some further ways in which markets fail.

When markets do not work well they are seen to fail. Market failure can now be defined in a more precise manner. It exists *when the operation of a market does not lead to economic efficiency*. A free market may fail to deliver either productive efficiency or allocative efficiency (or both). Resources are then not being used in the best way possible in that market. So for this reason, the market has failed.

Monopolies and market failure

One important way in which markets can be seen to fail is when a market is dominated by a single supplier, a monopoly.

A monopoly technically exists where there is just one firm in the industry. However, an industry can be deemed to be a monopoly when it is dominated by one firm. There are two reasons why monopolies might be expected to develop:

- **Economies of scale** Where there are significant economies of scale present in an industry, firms will have to be very large in order to effectively exploit those economies (see Self-assessment task 3.6 on Mauritius sugar industry).
- **The profit motive** It is assumed in Economics that firms aim to maximise profits. A very effective way of maximising profits is to destroy competitors. Given this, a free market may move towards a monopolistic market.

The problem with this tendency towards monopolistic markets is that there are economic reasons to expect such markets to be inefficient. They are unlikely to be either productively or allocatively efficient. In other words, there tends to be market failure in monopoly markets.

A useful way to understand the problems of monopolies is to try to compare the possible production point of an industry if it were a monopoly as opposed to being a competitive industry (see Figure 3.10).

In a fully competitive market (a state of perfect competition), price is determined by the interaction of supply and demand. The equilibrium price and quantity will be where the supply curve intersects the demand curve. This information can be seen on the diagram. The average revenue line (AR) is the same as the demand curve. In a perfectly competitive industry, the marginal cost curve (MC) is the same thing as the supply curve. Thus the equilibrium price in the perfectly competitive industry is P_1 and the quantity is Q_1.

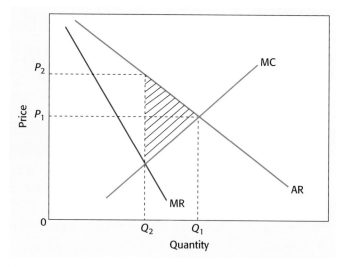

Figure 3.10 *A comparison of monopoly and a competitive market*

The situation is different in a monopoly market. Here, the firm has the power to set the price for the whole industry. Given this, the profit-maximising monopolist will choose to set the price at the point where marginal cost is equal to marginal revenue as this is the point of profit maximisation. On the diagram, this is indicated by the price of P_2 and the quantity Q_2. This suggests that price will be higher and quantity lower in a monopoly market than in a competitive market.

The problem is not simply that price is higher under monopoly. The essence of the problem is that price is above marginal cost (as is clear on the diagram). This means that there is not allocative efficiency. Price is higher than the cost of producing the last unit of production and thus demand and production are too low. There are insufficient scarce resources directed to the production of this product. There is inefficiency.

In addition to allocative inefficiency, there may also be productive inefficiency in monopolistic markets. It is possible that the cost curve indicated on the diagram may rise if the market is a monopoly compared to its position in a competitive market. This is due to *x*-inefficiency. This is a phrase used by economists to describe the tendency of costs to drift upwards in monopolies. The reason for this is easy to see. Monopolists do not have the same competitive pressures operating upon them as do firms in competitive markets. Whilst a monopolist may have the incentive of profits to keep costs as low as possible, there is not the same threat of bankruptcy.

A monopolist can 'get away with' higher costs as there are no rivals who will take away the trade if costs and thus prices are higher than is possible. Thus costs tend not to be at their lowest possible level. There is not productive efficiency.

The profit-maximising point is where marginal cost is equal to marginal revenue. It can be seen that this point is not the minimum point on the average cost schedule and thus that there is not technical efficiency.

The conclusion is clear: monopoly markets tend to fail. They do not lead to resources being used in an optimum way and thus there is economic inefficiency.

SELF-ASSESSMENT TASK 3.6

Read the feature below and then answer the questions that follow.

Mauritius sugar sector offers lessons for Kenya

The lush green fields of sugar cane farms in every village and every hamlet, every state and every city distinctively identify Mauritius as a top sugar producer.

Unlike the Kenyan bittersweet sugar story, the success of the Mauritius sugar industry boils down to favourable policies introduced by the government that amalgamated the factories.

The government has also created policies to push diversification and cogeneration among the millers that are now owned by private developers. Sugar cane is grown on about 90% of the cultivated land area and accounts for 25% of export earnings.

Sugar farms occupy 62 000 hectares of land out of the total country area of 204 000 hectares. And as Kenya mulls over switching to irrigation from rain-fed agriculture, in Mauritius large overhead sprinklers sustain the sugar cane fields all year round.

The sector also contributes up to 60% of the Indian Ocean island's electricity requirements, according to the director of the Mauritius Sugar Producers Association, Jean Li Yuen Fong.

One of the foremost reform policies that have spurred this development is the amalgamation of sugar factories. Initially, the country had over 250 factories. According to Mr Fong, essentially every large-scale farmer owned a mill.

Sugar cane processing factory in Mauritius

Over time though, the entrepreneurs were forced to centralise to achieve economies of scale.

The factories were reduced to 23, then seven. But the amalgamation is not over yet, stated Mr Fong.

'In the medium term, we shall have between four and five factories left. This is to optimise the efficiency while also bringing down the cost of production.'

Soon after he took over the reins at Kilimo House, Agriculture Minister William Ruto put forward an idea to consolidate the management of the existing factories to make the industry more competitive and achieve the economies of scale.

In his proposal, Chemelil, Miwani, Muhoroni and Agro Chemical Food Company could be merged into one large mill. Mr Ruto also stated that small factories stood no chance of withstanding competition from the region unless they diversified into ethanol and bargasse production.

In Mauritius, nothing goes to waste as the green sugar cane leaves are used as fodder while dry ones go into thatching houses and exclusive beach hotels. The residue from the factories is used as manure. The Mauritius Sugar Industry Research Institute is charged with crop development.

Every farm has a beacon that bears the cane varieties so far planted and the date of next planting. Each variety produces eight ratoon crops before a new one is planted.

Jean Ribet, the president of Mauritius Chamber of Agriculture states in an industry annual report that the subsector is still yet to relax as more reforms are lined up.

'With the coming into operation of the World Trade Organization and the Economic Partnerships Agreements, we face competition as the EU opens its market to other producers,' he said. 'This will see sugar prices go down by about 36% and we have now been forced to restructure our industry through further amalgamation and diversification.'

In contrast to Mauritius, Kenya remains at odds with itself on how to go about privatisation. And as Kenya struggles to find a compromise in the ownership of the millers lined up for privatisation, Mauritius law is very clear that 35% of the shareholding is left to farmers and employees.

Source: Menya, W., Business Daily, All Africa Global Media, 21 August 2009 (adapted)

1 Using the information above, explain the benefits to the economy of Mauritius of the on-going amalgamation of sugar processing factories.

2 The proposed merger of four companies will lead to a technical monopoly. Discuss the extent to which this may not necessarily be beneficial to the hundreds of sugar cane producers.

Deadweight loss

Market failure can also be understood through an economic concept known as **deadweight loss**. This term refers to the loss of economic welfare due to the fact that potentially desirable production and consumption does not take place. There is not as much producer and consumer surplus as there would be if all such desirable trade took place. This loss of surplus is called 'deadweight loss'.

Deadweight loss can be seen to occur in a monopoly market when comparing that market with a competitive market. This is also illustrated in Figure 3.10 (page 140). The competitive outcome is given in this diagram by price P_1 and output Q_1. This represents the optimum production and consumption position. Just the right amount of resources is being used to provide this product. This is in contrast to the monopoly outcome given by price P_2 and

quantity Q_2. Here, there is underproduction and underconsumption. Too few resources are used in the production of this good because the price is too high. A measure of the resulting loss of economic welfare is given by the shaded triangle in the diagram. This indicates the loss of net consumer and producer surplus due to the monopoly. It is the deadweight loss due to the monopoly.

Deadweight loss can also be seen to operate when a government imposes an indirect tax on a product. This is shown in Figure 3.11.

The price and quantity of the product are given by the intersection of supply and demand before the tax is imposed. This gives a price of P_1 and a quantity of Q_1. The imposition of the tax is the equivalent of an increase in the costs of production and thus it shifts the supply schedule to the left (S to S_1). This leads to a higher price, P_2, and a lower quantity, Q_2. This

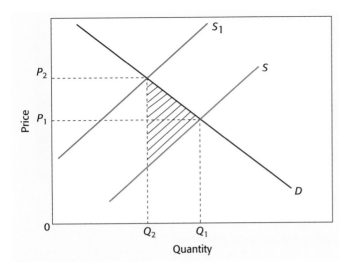

Figure 3.11   *Imposition of an indirect tax*

means a deadweight loss for the same reason as in a monopoly. Desirable production and consumption are discouraged because of the higher price. The resulting overall loss of economic welfare is shown by the shaded triangle. It gives a measure of the amount of deadweight loss due to the imposition of the tax. From a wider perspective, excessive taxes can undermine competitiveness in a market.

Government intervention to correct market failure

Introduction

In the Core section you read that when the market did not appear to work well (there was obviously market failure present) then the government intervened in order to try to improve the situation. Specifically, the following four forms of government intervention were identified.

1 Maximum prices

- If a price were seen to be too high, then the government might impose a maximum price.
- A maximum price could be imposed on a monopoly market in order to moderate the price. This is a policy used in some countries by regulatory bodies.
- A maximum price might also be used if there were concerns that consumers could not afford an important product, such as housing.
- The effect of a maximum price could be to create shortages as it could lead to demand exceeding supply.

SELF-ASSESSMENT TASK 3.7

Read the feature below and then answer the questions that follow.

Jam today, road pricing tomorrow?

Singapore invented it, Norway copied it, Stockholm spent 20 years and $1 billion before thinking again, whilst Hong Kong retreated at the last moment in the face of a popular revolt but is determined to try again. It is against this international context that in Summer 2005 the British government unveiled its plans for a national 'pay as you drive' system of charging for the use of roadspace. Since the announcement, there has been considerable opposition to this radical scheme. As a result, there has been an about-turn in policy, leaving road pricing decisions to particular towns and cities.

The bottom line is that politicians are terrified of road pricing; indeed they prefer not to be seen

to be interfering with the ability of the country's 28 million drivers to be able to use their vehicles when they want, where they want and at no additional cost above the massive levels of taxation that they are already pouring into the Exchequer from fuel duties, taxes on new vehicles and an annual road fund tax. The scale of the problems which the UK is facing is so serious that it cannot be ignored.

At the same time there is a remarkable consensus amongst economists that road pricing is the only way in which the country's congestion problems can be resolved. It is seen as a sensible way of dealing with the problem of a scarce resource, road space, which is inefficiently used and as a consequence, generates substantial costs to the community. Road pricing is not only the answer to congested city roads – it is a fair and logical outcome to a classic example of market failure.

Returning to Singapore, for many years now the government has imposed high customs duties on imported cars and set stiff registration fees and high annual road taxes. In addition it requires anybody buying a new car to get a permit, currently priced at between $27 000 and $49 000, well above the average annual income per head. If this were not enough, for the past 30 years, to enter a restricted city zone, drivers must pay a $2 flat rate charge in the morning peak period, falling to $1.30 at off-peak times. When the peak charge was extended to the rush hour in 1989, it further reduced traffic.

From Spring 1998, a new automatic 'pay-as-you-go' system replaced the above rather crude system. Using the latest micro-chip technology, charging is automatic (smart cards can be pre-loaded up to $150) and is based on the actual contribution to congestion made by individual car users. To the economist this is in many respects a 'dream ticket' – it matches in full the well-known 'polluter pays'

'Pay-as-you-go' system, Singapore

principle so strenuously advocated in text books yet so very rarely applied in practice.

But will it work in Britain? This is highly problematic, not least because, unlike Singapore, Britain does not have a world-class public transport system to provide a realistic alternative for urban travellers. If the country is serious about resolving its transport problem it must be as radical as the objections it faces. For a start, it could learn a lot from Singapore.

Source: The Economist, *6 December 1997 (adapted);* Bamford C G et al, *OCR A2 Economics, 2009.*

1 **a** Explain why traffic congestion is a classic example of market failure.
   b How in theory should a government deal with the problem of traffic congestion?
2 Suppose you have been invited to make a presentation to politicians and planners on how the experience of Singapore in dealing with its congestion problems might assist your country in reducing its urban transport problems. Briefly draft this presentation under the following headings:
   • the main benefits of road pricing in Singapore
   • the data you would need in being able to measure these benefits
   • why the experience of Singapore may not be entirely relevant for your own country.

2 Price stabilisation

• Some markets are susceptible to undesirable swings in the market price of the product. This is particularly true of the agricultural market.
• Prices may be stabilised by the government to protect the real incomes of both consumers and producers.
• In agriculture, the use of buffer stocks represents a way by which prices could be stabilised.

3 Taxes and subsidies

• Taxes can be used to discourage the production of a product. Subsidies encourage production.
• Taxes may be placed on products that generate negative externalities and would normally tend to be overproduced.
• Subsidies might be paid to producers of goods and services that have positive externalities and are merit goods. Such products, such as health

care and education, would be underproduced by the free market.

4 Direct provision

- The government may decide to provide some products itself.
- The main economic justification for the government providing goods and services is that they would not be produced otherwise. This can be seen to be the case with public goods.

The purpose of much of the remainder of this chapter is to consider further why governments intervene in markets and to analyse further policies that may be available for such intervention.

Objectives of government microeconomic policy

It is possible to identify two possible economic justifications for the government to intervene in the operation of free markets:

1 Governments may intervene in markets in order to try to restore economic efficiency. If markets are seen to be failing, for the sorts of reasons indicated earlier, then the government may try to move the market to a more efficient position through the use of various policies. Both productive and allocative efficiency could be improved through the introduction of appropriate government policies.

2 A further concern over the operation of free markets is to do with equity. Even if markets may be judged to be efficient, they may not be judged to be equitable.

Equity is to do with 'fairness'. The outcome of a free market may be judged to be 'unfair'. This can be seen in the comparison that is sometimes used between so-called 'political democracy' and 'economic democracy'. A free market is sometimes likened to an economic democracy. Consumers are the voters and money represents the votes. Those products that are 'elected' are those that receive most money votes. Thus, free markets produce allocative efficiency as they ensure that those products most in demand are those that are produced. There is, however, one important difference between these two democracies. The underlying principle of the political democracy

is that of 'one person – one vote'. This is clearly not true of the economic democracy. Here, the number of votes varies greatly between individuals. Some have very few, if any, whilst others have very large numbers of votes. Some would judge this to be inequitable and an undesirable aspect of market economies.

This area of Economics is not without difficulty. One person's judgement of what may be 'equitable' is not necessarily the same as another person's view. This is 'normative' economics: there are clear value judgements to be made between what is 'right' and 'wrong'. The role of the economist is usually seen as identifying the inequality and allowing others (such as politicians) to judge its desirability.

If the outcome of the market economy is deemed to be unacceptably inequitable, then governments can use policies to try to reduce the inequity. This could be within a country or it could be international in scale.

Government regulation

One further form of intervention available to governments mentioned briefly in the Core chapter is that of regulation. Regulation is the use of legal intervention to force consumers and producers to behave in certain ways. It is the use of government legislation in order to produce a more desirable economic outcome than that achieved by the free market.

Economists generally do not favour the use of government regulation. It is seen as a 'blunt' instrument. It forces consumers and producers to do (or not to do) certain things rather than to provide incentives. It can be seen as working against the market rather than with the market. However, governments may judge that regulation is sometimes required if a more desirable outcome is to be achieved.

Government regulation may be used in order to control the behaviour of monopolies. There are several forms of regulation that can be used for this:

- **Legislation that outlaws the formation of monopolies** This is usually referred to as merger policy. It takes the view that the formation of a monopoly in a market may be undesirable and thus, under some circumstances, mergers that would create a monopoly would not be allowed to occur.
- **Legislation that forbids certain types of monopoly behaviour** An example might

be 'predatory pricing'. This is when a powerful producer deliberately sets its price below that of its competition. It does this in order to try to destroy competition. Either a current firm is to be driven out of business or a potential new firm is dissuaded from entering the market. It thus maintains or strengthens the monopolist's position and can lead to inefficiency.

- **Laws that insist on certain standards of provision** These try to ensure that there is a guaranteed quality of product provided in monopoly markets.
- **Regulations that insist on certain levels of competition in an industry** A range of possibilities exists here. This policy has often been used in the telecommunications industry.

Government regulations can be used in other areas to try to overcome market failures, for example, to tackle environmental problems. A common approach suggested by economists is to use indirect taxes to tackle negative externalities that lead to excessive environmental costs and to give subsidies to encourage environmentally friendly production techniques. However, a more direct approach is simply to legislate and outlaw certain behaviour that creates environmental damage.

Laws may be passed by governments that disallow certain types of pollution. Any producers found to contravene such laws are prosecuted and thus pollution is reduced. Laws are seen as necessary in some situations to stop the excessive depletion of natural resources. There is no marginal cost for the using up of scarce resources such as public pasture by cattle herders. However, there is a cost imposed on others if the pasture becomes over-grazed. Thus regulations are needed. A similar situation can be seen with the over-fishing of fish stocks. Without regulation fishing stocks become dangerously depleted (see Self-assessment task 3.8).

SELF-ASSESSMENT TASK 3.8

Read the feature below and then answer the questions that follow.

China's fishing fleet sets challenge to US

China is the world's major fishing power. With an estimated 300 000 motorised fishing vessels and 8 m fishermen, in 2007 around 17 m tonnes of fish were caught. This is four times that of Japan, its nearest competitor, and way above what is netted by the US and other Pacific countries. These mind-blowing statistics leave little doubt about the severe strain of over-fishing that is being felt across the world's fishing areas. There are also wider concerns of sovereignty as Chinese fleets trawl further and further away from home as China's own resources have been fully exploited, with many areas facing almost complete exhaustion.

At any one time, there are close to 300 Chinese vessels operating in West African waters. Here, they tend to fish for mackerel and other low-value species. This fishing is often legal; at times

it is not, for example off the coast of Sierra Leone where fisheries protection vessels are essential in maintaining the country's territorial limits. The worry is that Chinese practices could take away the livelihoods of local fishermen and exaggerate the food crisis in Africa and elsewhere.

China has signed various bi-lateral fishing agreements with neighbouring states. It has also taken steps to protect some of its own coastal waters and to pay subsidies for fishermen to scrap their vessels. China has though refused to ratify the UN Fish Stocks Agreement, in force since 2001. On a more encouraging note, for over a decade the US Coast Guard has been co-operating with China's

Fisheries Law Enforcement Command to enforce a UN prohibition on drift net fishing in the North Pacific. If fish stocks are ever to return to environmentally sustainable levels in many parts of the world's oceans it is essential that the Chinese government makes positive moves to co-operate in the development of meaningful regulations to restrict the volume of catches made by its own fleet and by the fleets of other major producers. If not, then an environmental catastrophe seems inevitable.

Source: Asia Times Online, *August 2009 (adapted)*

---

1 Why is the depletion of fish stocks a case of market failure?

2 Use a demand and supply diagram to explain how the enforcement of regulations limiting the volume of catches affects the market equilibrium.

3 Apart from regulations, discuss the ways in which governments can intervene in the market to prevent over-fishing.

Government policies to redistribute income and wealth

There are three main types of policies that are available to reduce inequality in the **distribution of income** and wealth. These are:

- monetary benefits
- the tax system
- direct provision of goods and services.

Monetary benefits

A simple way to redistribute income is to pay benefits out of **government expenditure** to those on low incomes. Money is raised through the tax system and then paid to low income individuals and families in order to increase their disposable income. There are two types of such benefits:

- **Means-tested**   These benefits are only paid to those on low incomes. They are targeted directly at those who are seen to be most in need. An example would be unemployment benefit. However, such benefits are not always claimed

by those for whom they are designed. They can also create a disincentive to work (see Chapter 2 Supplement). If such benefits are reduced through an individual earning more, then there is an incentive not to earn more. This is the so-called **poverty trap**.

- **Universal benefits**   These are paid out to everyone in certain categories regardless of their wealth and income. Examples include universal state pensions and child benefit. Such benefits overcome the two problems associated with means-tested benefits. However, they imply paying out money to many who do not need it and therefore tend to be expensive to operate.

The tax system

The tax system can be used in order to reduce inequalities in income and wealth. This is specifically through the use of **progressive taxation**. Progressive taxes lead to those earning higher incomes being taxed a higher percentage of their income than those on lower incomes. Thus income differentials are reduced. Most **income tax** systems are progressive in nature. The average rate of tax rises as people earn higher incomes. Indirect taxes on products which are bought usually tend to be **regressive**.

Taxes can also be imposed upon wealth in order to reduce wealth inequalities. One example might be inheritance tax. Individuals who inherit more than a certain amount of wealth may have to pay some of the value of that wealth in tax to the government.

Direct provision of goods and services

A further way of reducing inequalities in society is for the government to provide certain important services free of charge to the user. Such services are financed through the tax system. If such services are used equally by all citizens, then those on lowest incomes gain most as a percentage of their income. Inequality is thus lowered.

The two most significant examples of such free provision in many economies are health care and

SELF-ASSESSMENT TASK 3.9

Read the feature below and then answer the questions that follow.

Income inequality in Pakistan

The distribution of income in Pakistan remains a serious economic and political issue. Although estimates vary, and some of the data is unreliable, the general picture is that the rich are getting richer and the poor becoming poorer. Moreover, income inequality is now more than in any other time in Pakistan's history. Table 3.4 provides a perspective on this problem.

The distribution of income in Pakistan is a serious problem

	1978	1988	1999	2002	2005[+]
Income share of lowest 20% population (%)	7.2	8.8	7.8	7.0	6.6
Income share of highest 20% population (%)	45.6	43.5	46.5	47.6	50.0

Table 3.4 *Inequality measures*

Note: [+] *estimate*

There are many varied reasons for this state of affairs. Two very relevant ones are the distribution of assets and the tax system. The poor have few or virtually no assets; the incidence of tax on the poor has also had an effect in so far as in recent years, the poor have experienced an increase in their tax burden whilst there have been no particular changes for the highest earners. This is surely against the whole concept of a progressive tax system.

Source: www.pakistan.gov *Employment and Income Distribution, Paper No. 14*

1 Use the data above to describe the changes in the income distribution of Pakistan from 1978 to 2005.

2 Discuss the policy measures that could be used by the government of Pakistan to reduce income inequality.

junior and secondary education. These markets are characterised by various market failures. However, these failures do not, according to standard economic theory, justify free provision to the consumer. The justification must thus be on the grounds of equity. The view is that everyone should have access to a certain level of health care and education regardless of wealth and income. Thus, these services are provided universally free: they are the material equivalent of monetary universal benefits.

The effectiveness of government policy

In principle, government policies to reduce market failures make economic sense. They increase the level of economic efficiency in markets and thus must be judged to be economically desirable. However, in practice, all may not work out as planned. Governments may themselves fail. There are reasons why government intervention may in fact create further inefficiencies and thus not improve the use of scarce resources in a society.

There are three main reasons why there may be **government failure**, through problems of:

- information
- incentives
- distribution.

Problems of information

Once the government starts to intervene in the running of markets, it needs information. The correct policies can only be introduced if governments have the correct information. The problem is that governments may have inaccurate information. In this case, they may introduce policies that lead to greater economic inefficiency. Some examples of this problem could be the following:

- There is a lack of information about the true value of a negative externality. It is often very difficult to give an accurate figure for the value of a negative externality such as pollution. It is difficult both to put an accurate figure to all of the costs imposed and to trace the source of the pollution itself. The problem with this is that it then becomes very difficult to impose the correct value of a tax that attempts to reduce production

to an efficient level. The wrong level of tax will lead to the wrong level of production.

- There is a lack of information about the level of consumer demand for a product. If the government is providing a product free of charge to the consumer, then some estimation of the level of consumer demand is required. This could be the case with a public good. However, the government must try to provide the right amount of such goods. If it does not estimate the level of demand accurately, then the wrong amount will be produced and thus there is inefficiency.

Problems of incentives

A further problem arises with government intervention in the economy due to the creation of undesirable incentives. These can create inefficiencies. Some examples of the ways in which this can happen are as follows:

- The imposition of taxes can distort incentives. The most obvious example of this is the possible impact of an income tax upon the incentive to work. High marginal rates of taxation can create disincentives for people to work harder and gain more income. If this happens, then scarce resources are not being used to their best effect and there is inefficiency. A similar point can be recalled from the earlier discussion of the deadweight loss of a tax. The disincentive to consume and produce created by the tax led to the wrong amount of a product being produced.
- Politicians may be motivated by political power rather than economic imperatives. Politicians are often seen as being motivated principally by the desire to remain in government. If this is so, then economic policies may be designed by governments to try to retain power rather than to try to ensure maximum efficiency in the economy. Thus, an unpopular tax on a product that produces negative externalities, such as car use that creates pollution and environmental damage, may be avoided due to the government's fears that it could lead to a loss of votes.
- Those running public services may have inappropriate incentives. Once products are provided by the government, then the profit

motive of the private sector is largely removed. The question then remains as to what may motivate those in charge of providing public services. There is no entirely clear answer to this question. At its worst, it could become a total lack of incentive to produce the product well or attempts to defraud the system.

Problems of distribution

Government intervention in the running of the economy is often justified by the need to reduce inequality. However, it is possible that government intervention might sometimes increase existing inequality. This is simply understood by recognising that the imposition of any tax will have a distributional effect. Thus, a tax on energy use that aims to reduce harmful emissions of greenhouse gases will have different effects on different groups of people. If the tax is on the use of domestic fuel, then older members of society may feel the greatest effect as they use proportionately more domestic fuel for heating than others in society. This could be seen as unfair and increasing inequality in society.

SELF-ASSESSMENT TASK 3.10

Explain why each of the following is an example of government failure.

a An underestimation of the full benefit to society of public transport that means only a small subsidy is being provided by the government.

b The building of a new road that has unclear benefits in an area where the government fears that it could lose votes at the next election.

c A high tax on health care that forms a significant part of many poorer people's budgets.

d A high level of unemployment benefit that means that people can sometimes earn more by not entering paid employment.

Privatisation

In a simple sense, **privatisation** refers to a change in ownership of an activity from the public sector to the private sector. In many instances, as in the UK, privatisation has returned activities that had previously been nationalised to new private owners. In a modern sense, privatisation means more than this and is now recognised to include the following:

- **The direct sale of government-owned and operated activities to the private sector**
  The nature of the sale can be diverse and includes offering shares to the public, management and worker buyouts, the direct sale to new owners and, in some cases, a partial sale with the government retaining some share in the new business.
- **Deregulation** through the removal of barriers to entry which had protected the public sector from outside competition. Through this action, a contestable market can be created (see Chapter 2 Supplement).
- **Franchising** This can give a new private sector owner the right to operate a particular service or activity for a given length of time. In some cases, the franchise might be an exclusive one; in other cases, some competition may be experienced.
- **Contracting out of services** previously provided in-house by public sector organisations. Normally, this involves activities that are deemed not to be core to those organisations. In some cases, contracting out allows public sector-based organisations to openly compete with private sector businesses for a particular contract.

By any yardstick, privatisation in the UK economy since 1979 (when a right-wing Conservative government led by Mrs Thatcher was elected) has been substantial. In 1979, the nationalised industries accounted for about 9% of GDP and 7% of employment. By 2000, these statistics were just 2% in each case. Table 3.5 shows the extent of privatisation in this period.

As this table shows, the principal privatisations were in the fuel and power and transport sectors. Both were nationalised in the late 1940s, and under government ownership both relied heavily on various forms of subsidy to cover their losses. Under public ownership, it was also recognised that the government was unable to fund the extensive investment programmes needed to enable them to compete in a rapidly changing UK economy. The table also shows how the government withdrew its support from a wide range of manufacturing activities. In many cases, this support had been

Fuel and power

National electricity generation and regional supply

National gas production and regional supply

Coal production

Nuclear power production

Transport

Railways, passengers and freight

Local and national bus services

Some major airports

British Airways, the national airline

Some road freight services

Some ferry services and ports

Other

Water supply

Telephones and telecommunications

Various manufacturing companies including British Steel, British Aerospace, British Petroleum, British Sugar Corporation, Rover Group, British Shipbuilders

Table 3.5 *Privatisation in the UK economy between 1979 and 2000*

essential in order to keep 'lame duck' companies solvent and safeguard employment. In many respects, the UK has led the way when it comes to privatisation. Other economies, developing as well as developed, have drawn upon the UK's experience to pursue their own privatisation policies.

Why privatise?

Taking the UK economy as a particular example it is possible to recognise various reasons for the extensive privatisation shown in Table 3.5. Some are economic, others much more concerned with political motivation. For example:

- In the early phase of privatisation, there is little argument that there was a deliberate commitment *to reduce government involvement in the economy*. A return to market forces was seen as necessary for many nationalised industries to achieve an efficient allocation of resources. Public ownership was believed to be a serious obstacle to these industries meeting their particular objectives.

SELF-ASSESSMENT TASK 3.11

Read the feature below and then answer the questions that follow.

Rail privatisation rolls across the continent of Africa

For the national governments, the value of these concessions has been threefold. First, subsidies and government expenditures have been significantly reduced, and in some cases, eliminated. Also, given that roads in most parts of Africa are provided by the government, traffic carried by rail has reduced congestion and public investment in roads. This has eased the financial burden of the railway on governments, suggesting that it could allocate funds to other priority areas in dire need of funding such as education and health care. Second, governments have earned, and continue to earn revenues from annual concession fees averaging about 4–6% of turnover and tax from the operator. This is in addition to the modest lump sum typically paid at the start of the concession.

Finally, the revitalisation of the railway has provided regeneration benefits along its routes, particularly in agriculture and mining.

Despite this positive track record, the World Bank reports that only one concession has operated in an uninterrupted manner for five years, and one national concession, in Gabon, has been cancelled outright. Inconsistent or inadequate investment in infrastructure, the continued decline in passenger service, staff issues and selective service provision – not to mention civil war and natural disasters – are all challenges that many countries must resolve.

Understandably, concessionaires are reluctant to invest in infrastructure with a life beyond the duration of their concession, or where the long-term economic and political risk is high, as it is in most African countries. They also do not usually generate enough revenue to cover the cost of infrastructure improvements by themselves.

It means that governments are left with the burden of funding infrastructure improvements, but these are often subject to long delays. In Malawi, the concessionaire and the government are at odds over who should pay to rebuild a bridge which was washed away. This deadlock means poor service and reduced income for the concession.

Passenger service is another contentious issue. Passenger traffic is often unprofitable, and concessionaires are usually uninterested or unwilling to maintain passenger services unless government subsidy is provided. This is the case in the joint concession of the Senegal–Mali railway, where only a limited passenger service is being provided until the government provides new rolling stock, which it has agreed to do. In other countries, such as Tanzania, the concessionaires are expected to cross-subsidise passenger services with freight, which many are not keen to do, because in many countries, buses are far cheaper than trains for passengers. Where the railway provides the only means of transport, it generally retains a service.

Rail freight in Africa

Another key social issue is human resources. Staff levels on most state-run railways in Africa are high, often the result of trying to achieve political ends rather than an attempt to improve the railway. Until recently, the soon-to-be-concessioned Nigeria Railways Corporation, which carried approximately 60 000 tonnes in 2004, employed 13 000 staff. It is no surprise that in almost every case, rail concessioning has led to massive staff cuts. These are often resisted by staff, unions, or political groups, causing delays in the process.

Source: Roy, M-A. and Kieran, P., International Railway Journal, *March 2006*

---

1 Explain the benefits of rail privatisation in Africa.

2 Comment on why some countries have continued to rely on the state to operate their national rail networks.

- There was also a deliberate policy *to widen share ownership* amongst the population and amongst the employees of the privatised companies. In this way, people who previously had no opportunity to own shares could purchase small quantities of shares in businesses where they were consumers. From an employee's standpoint, share ownership was seen as a way of enhancing motivation and improving labour relations in a company.

- Privatisation can generate *benefits for consumers* in the form of lower prices, wider choice and a better quality product or service. *x*-inefficiency would be likely to be reduced as firms become more aware of the need to control costs to stay in business. Consumers and shareholders therefore become pivotal in the affairs of privatised companies. Under state ownership consumers often took second place to the needs of the producers.

- The sale of nationalised industries has *generated substantial income* for the UK government over a long period of time. This has been estimated to be £70–£80 billion and has been very important in helping the economy to cope with deficits on the trading account of the balance of payments (see Chapter 4).

- It is further believed that privatised companies can be successful in raising capital, lowering prices and cutting out waste. In other words they are more efficient, with managers able to operate in a market-led way, without the restriction of trying to satisfy government objectives for their companies. Managerial freedom and a highly motivated workforce become the means by which economic efficiency is realised.

One of the most successful privatisations in the UK has been the sale of the nationalised rail freight business to the English, Welsh and Scottish Railway (EWS), now DB Shenker. Seemingly in terminal decline under government ownership, and unable to compete effectively with road freight, EWS has enjoyed considerable success since 1995.
For example:

- goods moved by rail had increased 70% by the end of 2007
- EWS had invested heavily in over 200 new freight locomotives and had begun a massive investment in freight wagons
- new customers, who had previously used only road freight, were switching some business to rail.

The case against privatisation

The experience of the UK economy has been that privatisation does not necessarily always produce the full range of benefits stated above. Let us briefly consider some of these arguments:

- In some situations, a private sector monopoly has replaced a public sector monopoly. The outcome therefore remains the same, namely a lack of competition. This has occurred in the UK in many of the privatisations shown in Table 3.5 (page 151), often on a regional rather than national market basis. Good examples are in water supply, rail passenger services and local bus operations. In such circumstances, firms can practise many of the practices of monopoly listed in Chapter 2 Supplement.
- Some economists argue that where there are natural monopolies, then these are best left to the public sector. Water, gas and railways are good examples where the unnecessary

duplication of services is wasteful, inefficient and not in the best interests of consumers.
- The sale of nationalised industries clearly generates substantial revenue for the government. This income though is a 'one-off stream', not to be repeated. Where governments may need further flows of funds, then privatisation sales may not be a future option for them.
- A regular complaint about privatisation is that there are often negative externalities associated with the change in ownership. One of the best examples is that of unemployment – many jobs are lost in all sorts of activities once a private sector owner has taken over a former public sector activity.
- Privatisation has to be accompanied by the setting up of regulators to ensure that competition is fair and that consumers are not being exploited through high prices and excessive profits for the new owners.

So, all in all, the decision on whether to privatise may not be as straightforward as it may seem. In general though it has been the prevailing view in many economies that the benefits usually outweigh the likely costs. It is for this reason that privatisation is firmly on the agenda of former centrally planned economies as they move towards market liberalisation and the generation of more competition.

SELF-ASSESSMENT TASK 3.12

1 For your own country, take each of these activities:
   - water supply
   - rail transport
   - telephone services.
   a Establish whether these activities are operated by the government or private sector businesses.
   b If government owned, how might the private sector help to improve the economic efficiency of these activities?
   c Why in your country might the government not wish to pursue a policy of privatisation?

SELF-ASSESSMENT TASK 3.13

Read the feature below and then answer the questions that follow.

Water privatisation in sub-Saharan Africa

Water privatisation, either by direct sale or through public–private partnerships, is now the favoured way forward for tackling Africa's serious problems of water provision. This may seem a little odd, given that the supply of water is best provided by a monopoly to avoid any problems of wasteful duplication.

Most countries in sub-Saharan Africa have a lack of clean water and adequate sanitation. As a consequence, water-borne diseases such as cholera and dysentery are rife and result in high infant and child mortality rates. The problems are acute in rural areas and in the teeming shanty towns in most of the large cities.

The push for privatisation is now required by the International Monetary Fund as a condition for countries receiving loans. It is a further requirement that a market price for water supplies must be established. The UK's Department for International Development took a similar line before giving funding for water privatisation in Ghana.

Queuing for water at a communal tap

The effects on local populations have been particularly controversial. The problem is that water tariffs have to be set by private companies at a market price which is often way beyond the means of most poor families. As a consequence, many cases of water-borne disease occur, not because of a lack of infrastructure, but because those in most need lack the meagre finances to be able to pay for this life-saving facility.

1 Discuss the case for and against the privatisation of water supplies in sub-Saharan Africa.

2 Comment on whether water should be provided free of charge to poor communities in sub-Saharan Africa.

Privatisation and the transition to a market economy

The task of transforming a centrally planned economy into a market economy is enormous. Not only must the foundations of a fully functioning market economy be put in place but the government needs to react to the inevitable problems during transition. If these issues are not complex enough, governments must conduct this transformation lacking any explicit prior experience on which they can draw. Although the major reforms can be identified, there is little guidance on the speed or the sequence in which the

reforms should be implemented. Some countries have chosen to follow the 'shock therapy' approach recommended by some economists. This approach involves extensive privatisation, strict monetary and fiscal policies to reduce inflation and the forces of supply and demand to determine internal market prices and the external exchange rate.

Others have chosen to adopt the 'gradual' approach to transition, arguing that consumers and producers needed time to adapt to the new economic system and that, to maintain public support for the reforms, the pain of transition needed to be softened. The transition to the market economy was arguably the largest structural experiment conducted in the twentieth century. It has had a profound and lasting impact on many economies.

The reforms which are needed on the road to the market economy are considered in the final part of this chapter.

Price liberalisation

The key to microeconomic reform is to allow prices to be determined by supply and demand. By freeing prices from state control, former centrally planned economies should enjoy benefits in the long term. Figure 3.12 shows the efficiency gains which are likely from such price liberalisation. In a command economy, prices bore no relationship to demand and supply. This is represented by a price (P_c) below the market equilibrium (P_m). At this price consumers demand a quantity of Q_2 but the supply is fixed by planners at S_p, with the result that excess demand of $Q_2 - Q_1$ manifests itself through lengthy queues for the product. Price liberalisation causes the price to 'jump' to P_m, encouraging an increase in supply to Q_e in the long run. Producers are better off by the area $P_cP_m$eb (the increase in producer surplus) and consumers are better off by the area $P_mP_c + Qae$ (the increase in consumer surplus). This change in consumer surplus arises because the effective price of the good under the command system was $P_c + Q$ as the price to consumers is raised by the time spent

queuing. Similar gains are possible by allowing domestic prices to reflect world prices more closely.

Removal of subsidies

In order to fully realise the gains from price liberalisation the government must also remove the various subsidies to state-owned enterprises (SOEs) which kept prices low. As these subsidies are removed prices will 'jump' even further. Some governments, most notably the Russian government, delayed the introduction of such price reforms for fear of the effect of price rises on the real wages of workers. Sensitive prices, such as food, housing and energy, were not fully liberalised. Another fear was that, if prices were liberalised before competition was introduced, the former SOEs might take advantage of their monopoly power and raise prices even further. Some countries, therefore, delay price liberalisation.

Privatisation

To create a fully functional market economy, SOEs need to be turned into profit-motivated, private sector firms. The privatisation of small-scale SOEs has created few problems – shops, restaurants and bars have largely been handed over to their former managers or, where they could be identified, their former owners. Where those who manage the firm are also its owners and free to make profit, changes can be rapid. Such small-scale privatisation has been the visible sign of transition for many consumers, with a rapid change in the appearance of the 'high street' in terms of window displays and the range of goods and services on offer. Outside the major cities, the typical Central and Eastern European 'restaurant', for example, may still exist, but the growth in fast-food outlets and trendy bars is apparent. Small-scale privatisation has been an important means of generating employment, much needed as large-scale SOEs shed labour in the quest for greater efficiency.

Large-scale privatisation has been much more of a problem. The key to such privatisation is to ensure that firms respond to the new market signals by seeking opportunities to reduce losses and improve profitability. Incentives need to be put in place so that firms become profit maximisers. In market economies these incentives exist in what is called the market for 'corporate control'. Briefly, firms are owned

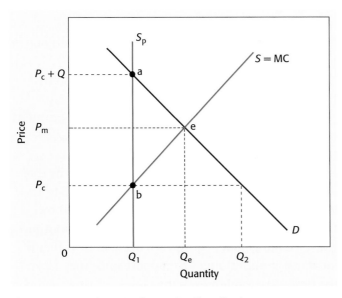

Figure 3.12 *The gains from price liberalisation*

155

by shareholders who appoint managers to look after their interests. If shareholders feel that managers are not maximising profits, they can either replace the managers or sell their shares on the stock market. The role of the stock market is crucial. As shareholders sell their shares, prices fall and firms become subject to takeover. Managers are kept on their toes by the threat of takeover and businesses are restructured by the new owners after a takeover. However, during the transition phase active share markets are absent or are only partially developed, causing some governments to delay the privatisation process.

Those governments that have privatised large-scale SOEs have had to think carefully about how to privatise. A number of different ways have been attempted:

- auctioning them to the highest bidder for cash
- issuing privatisation vouchers to the general public and then auctioning the SOEs in return for the vouchers
- allowing existing managers, workers and/or foreign companies to buy the SOE
- handing over the SOE to managers and/or workers for free.

Private ownership, of whatever kind, is not enough on its own to guarantee success. There is also a need to improve management techniques, especially in the areas of stock and quality control, financial management and marketing. Existing managers, of course, lack such skills and it may take some time for them to be acquired. This has convinced some governments of the need to delay the privatisation process whilst the necessary 'restructuring' takes place. Others have 'imported' the required management techniques by selling (wholly or partially) SOEs to foreign multinational companies, such as the sale by the Czech government of Skoda to the German car giant Volkswagen and the sale of Hungary's largest supermarket chain to Tesco, the UK's biggest grocery retailer. In other words, the type of privatisation during transition is as, if not more, important than the scale of privatisation.

Trade liberalisation

Liberalising prices does not make much sense without trade liberalisation. Since a lot of industry is monopolised by SOEs, liberalising trade can create the competition which might otherwise not exist. However, for trade to be liberalised it is necessary for the currency to be convertible into other currencies, at least for transactions involving goods and services (so-called current account convertibility). As will be seen in Chapter 4, international trade brings important benefits. By allowing resources to be allocated on the basis of comparative advantage, economic efficiency is improved and there is a spur to greater dynamism in the long run.

In theory, trade liberalisation can be achieved fairly quickly by removing the state monopoly on trade and all tariffs, quotas and non-tariff barriers to trade, and by allowing the currency to be convertible. Some temporary protection of domestic industries might, however, be justified, given the inefficient state of many SOEs, the need for the government to raise revenue in the early phase of the transition process and the need to stop the 'monetary overhang' being translated into a big surge in the demand for imports and a consequent deficit on the current account of the balance of payments. But tariffs on imports will cause problems for those industries trying to export because they will increase the cost of their imported inputs.

The transition economies of Central Europe have been in a fortunate position with regard to trade. Geographically close to the European Union, they have been able to find alternative markets for their exports after the collapse of COMECON, unlike some Eastern European states. In addition, they have gained tariff-free access to the EU which for many has paved the way for full membership. Consequently, their pattern of trade has undergone a major change as they are becoming more closely integrated with the economies of Western Europe.

Currency convertibility means that the government has to take some view on what sort of exchange rate regime it is going to adopt (see Chapter 6). Freely floating exchange rates cause problems as the exchange rate will have a tendency to depreciate and this will add to the uncertainty already caused by the transition from one economic system to another. Fixed exchange rate regimes are likely to be difficult for transition economies to support since they lack the necessary foreign exchange reserves. However, if the exchange rate is fixed at a low enough rate and against the 'right' currency, there is every chance that not much speculation will take place and this will minimise the amount of intervention needed to support the currency.

Reform of the financial sector

As we have seen, many of the reforms required as part of the transition process require a fully functioning financial sector. The elements of a typical reform package should include:

- establishing a central bank to control the money supply and interest rates independently of government and to act as a lender of last resort to the commercial banks
- creating banking institutions for collecting savings and channelling these savings to former SOEs so that they can invest and re-structure themselves
- setting up a framework to supervise and regulate the activities of the financial sector
- creating a market in which governments can sell bonds to finance any excess of expenditure over taxation receipts.

Given the nature of the financial system inherited from the years of planning, these reforms are a major task for governments and one that is likely to take many years to complete. The experience of financial sector reform has been very mixed. In Hungary, for example, the government refused to bail out banks which had made poor lending decisions, and started to sell them to foreign investors. In addition, there were tough bankruptcy laws ensuring that banks could recover their bad loans. The result was that, by 1996, almost 50% of Hungarian banks were foreign-owned and their bad debts small. In the Czech Republic, in comparison, almost 50% of loans made by banks are unrecoverable. Here banks remained in state ownership and they were encouraged by the government to finance many of the privatisations of SOEs, creating a conflict of interest. Instead of calling in the bad loans, Czech banks (essentially the owners of the former SOEs) gave out more and more loans. The legal framework tends to favour those who are in debt rather than giving power to the banks to recover their money. Consequently, the Czech government has been forced to bail out the banks for fear of a collapse in the financial system and has belatedly begun the process of privatising the banking system.

In pursuing a programme of economic reform, former centrally planned economies have experienced mixed success. The extent and pace of introducing reforms are obviously relevant, as is the degree to which monetary and external stability is achieved. Three further factors should also be recognised. These are:

- the ability to attract aid to underpin the economic reform process
- the ability to attract foreign direct investment from the USA, EU member states and Japan
- the extent to which there is political stability and a political commitment to persist with the process of economic reform shown in Figure 1.11 (see page 32).

SPECIMEN EXAM QUESTIONS

Question 1 has been set in a recent CIE examination paper.

1 Large firms necessarily become monopolistic. Monopolies adopt practices that are undesirable. Therefore, large firms should be regulated by governments. Discuss whether there is any truth in this argument. **[25 marks]**
(May/June 2008)

2 In India the post is delivered partly by private courier and partly by the government-owned India Post. The government is keen to increase its share of the market.
   a Explain why a government might wish to increase its control over private firms. [10]
   b Discuss whether an increase in government control necessarily improves efficiency in an organisation. [15]
[25 marks]

SUMMARY

In this supplement section it has been shown that:

- The operation of markets sometimes does not lead to economic efficiency.
- Monopoly power can create market failure. Monopolies can lead to both allocative and productive inefficiency.
- Deadweight loss is a measure of the welfare loss due to monopolies and the imposition of an indirect tax.
- Governments often intervene in markets in an effort to overcome market failures.
- Government microeconomic policy has two main purposes: to overcome market failures and to reduce inequality in the distribution of income and wealth.
- Government regulations can be used to try to overcome some market failures.
- Governments may use taxes and benefits to try to reduce inequalities of wealth and income in society.
- When governments intervene in markets they may themselves introduce further inefficiencies. These are called government failures.
- Governments may privatise an industry for various reasons including efficiency.

4 International trade
Core

On completion of this core section you should know:

- the principles of absolute and comparative advantage and their real-world limitations
- other explanations/determinants of trade flows
- the arguments put forward for free trade and why protectionist measures are applied to limit international trade
- what types of protection are used in international trade and what are their likely effects
- what is meant by *economic integration* and the main characteristics of free trade areas, customs unions and economic unions
- what is meant by the *terms of trade* and how it can be estimated
- the main components of the balance of payments of an economy.

The global economy of the twenty-first century

International trade is the lifeblood of virtually all modern developed and developing economies. As such, it involves the buying and selling of goods and services across national frontiers. At a personal level this is clearly seen through the many imported items that can be found in supermarkets and other retail stores. Products such as Coca-Cola, Fujifilm, Apple iPods, Nike trainers and Nescafé coffee are brands that are available throughout the world.

Increasingly, through international trade, economies have become more and more economically dependent upon each other. For example, the well-being of the US economy affects the well-being of many other economies in Central and South America, Europe, Asia and Africa. This was obvious with the onset of recession in 2008. This dependency can be seen by looking at the respective contributions of **exports** and **imports** to a country's Gross Domestic Product (GDP) (see Chapter 5). For Pakistan, in 2005, these were approximately 15% and 23% respectively. In other economies, this percentage was much greater.

Trade provides an important link between developed and developing economies. From a very general standpoint, the developed economies provide a range of consumer goods, capital equipment and financial services in exchange for raw materials, certain types of agricultural products and, increasingly, for a range of manufactured goods from the developing economies. Also included in international trade are the ever-increasing global receipts from international tourism. These are of very substantial importance, both domestically and as a source of foreign exchange, for many developing economies in the Caribbean, East Africa and Asia.

On the surface, it may seem best if we 'buy local'. After all, this promotes sales of home-produced goods and restricts the drain on foreign currency reserves caused by the need to pay for imports. But if all countries followed this strategy, there would be very little international trade except for certain essentials that could not be produced in the home market. As we shall see in this chapter, this state of affairs is very wasteful and the world economy as a whole would be poorer as a consequence.

Trade permits countries to specialise in products and commodities which they can produce relatively efficiently. There are many reasons for this specialisation and include the availability of particular factors of production. Economies which have naturally occurring resources, such as oil or copper, can exploit these and trade them on the world market. Alternatively, the climate or soils of a country may make it a good source of certain types of food product or a good destination for international tourists. Other economies may have a highly skilled workforce or have unit labour costs below that of others so enabling them to produce clothing, electronics or vehicles at competitive prices. These examples are a very clear link to the factors of production identified in Chapter 1.

From an accounting standpoint, the **balance of payments** in an economy is a financial record of all such international transactions. In principle, receipts from exports of goods and services can be used to pay for imports which cannot be produced as efficiently or which cannot be produced at all. The nature of the global economy though is that this is not as simple an exchange process as it might seem. Some economies, such as Germany, Japan and China, have traditionally had export surpluses. In contrast, others, such as the UK, the US and many developing economies, have spent more on imports than exports. Although by definition the world economy's trade flows balance, for individual countries this may not happen. If the imbalance is other than marginal, corrective action has to take place (see Chapter 7).

SELF-ASSESSMENT TASK 4.1

Think about the main types of goods:

- imported into your country
- exported by your country.

Make a list of these and see if you can come up with a simple explanation as to why this is so. Mention the factors of production in your explanation.

The principles of international trade

The economic logic which has underpinned the development of international trade has its origins over 200 years ago in the writings of classical economists who firmly advocated what we now refer to as **multilateral trade**. Their principles of absolute and, particularly, of comparative advantage have modern relevance in the objectives of the World Trade Organization (WTO), which exists to promote freer trade amongst all of its member countries.

The simple economic principles involved are summarised below. These show that trade will take

place when countries have a clear-cut or **absolute advantage** over other countries in what they produce. If we look at the UK's position, for example:

- India has a clear-cut advantage over the UK in the production of tea.
- The Windward Islands can produce bananas, which the UK cannot produce.
- France has an obvious advantage in producing wine for export to the UK.

A list like this can be quite extensive; we could also compile a similar list of items for the trade of any economy.

What is obvious is that, under certain circumstances, trade can also be beneficial where a country may not have such clear-cut advantage. Provided it has a relative or **comparative advantage** in the production of a particular good over another country, trade can produce gains for both partners.

Summary of the principles of absolute and comparative advantage

The following assumptions are made:

- There are just two countries involved in trade (say, France and India).
- Each can produce just two products (say, cloth and cheese).
- Productivity differs between them, so varying quantities of each are produced.
- Production costs and opportunity costs are constant for each product.

The production possibilities are shown in Figure 4.1.

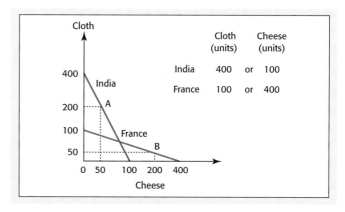

Figure 4.1 *Production possibilities – absolute advantage*

If each country was self-sufficient and devoted half of its resources to each product, then the situation would be as shown at points A and B on these production possibility frontiers.

India is clearly better at cloth production; France is better at producing cheese. India is said to have an absolute advantage in cloth, France in cheese. If, however, they subsequently specialised, concentrating on those products where they had absolute advantage, each country would actually be better off as a result of trade taking place (see Table 4.1).

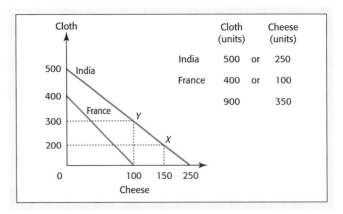

	Cloth (units)		Cheese (units)
India	500	or	250
France	400	or	100
	900		350

Figure 4.2 *Production possibilities with one country having absolute advantage in both products*

	Before trade (half of all resources to each industry)		After trade (all resources to chosen industry)	
	Cloth (units)	Cheese (units)	Cloth (units)	Cheese (units)
India	200	50	400	0
France	50	200	0	400
Total world production	250	250	400	400

Table 4.1 *The gains from trade under absolute advantage*

India could now import 200 units of cheese from France, an overall gain of 150 units, without losing any cloth production. France can similarly benefit from buying cloth from India.

The above situation, sometimes called reciprocal absolute advantage, means that one country is better at producing one product, the other is superior in the production of the other. This rather obvious situation can be developed a stage further through the principle of comparative advantage – this states that trade between two countries should still take place and be mutually beneficial provided the domestic opportunity costs of production differ.

Going back to our earlier example, let us assume that India has a clear-cut advantage over France in the production of both cloth and cheese (somewhat unlikely, but remember this is no more than a simple model!). Factor endowments, including more advanced machinery, good pasture land and a more productive workforce, could provide this advantage. On the surface, there may seem little point in the two countries trading because India has the edge in producing both cloth and cheese. This is shown in Figure 4.2.

If India decided not to trade at all, opting for self-sufficiency, each time it wanted more cloth, say, it would have to divert resources from cheese production. This trade-off, applying the concept of opportunity cost, can be shown by a movement on the production possibility frontier from X to Y. As India gained 100 units of cloth, it had to sacrifice 50 units of cheese production – the opportunity cost being that each unit of cloth gained resulted in a loss of half a unit of cheese. A reverse movement would produce a gain of one unit of cheese for every two units of cloth sacrificed. In the case of France, to gain an extra unit of cheese, there would be an opportunity cost of four units of cloth whereas each additional unit of cloth produced would result in a loss of a quarter of a unit of cheese.

The outcome of this principle is that countries should specialise in those goods in which they have the greatest relative efficiency over their trading partners. In other words, they should produce those products where there is least comparative cost. So, using the data above, India should concentrate on producing cheese, France on cloth. If this were to happen, and all resources were re-allocated in this way, total production would increase. This is shown in Table 4.2.

	Cloth (units)	Cheese (units)	
India	0	500	Total production has increased by **50 units**
France	800	0	
	800	500	

Table 4.2 *The gains from trade under comparative advantage*

The simple principles explained above are based on the following assumptions:

- The production possibility frontiers are linear.
- The exchange rate operating for international transactions must be between the respective domestic opportunity cost ratios. Otherwise trade will not be mutually beneficial. Indeed, where the differences between these opportunity costs are widest, then the potential for trade is greatest.
- No transport costs are charged. In today's global economy, this is very unrealistic, but it does reinforce the point made immediately above. There will be a gain from trade if the production benefit is greater than the transport costs.
- The two-country, two-product assumption is again a long way from reality in the twenty-first century. Countries might specialise in narrowly defined product areas, for example, high-quality woollen cloth, not cloth in general, and there are many potential trading partners in the global economy.
- Production costs are most unlikely to be constant. As countries specialise, for example, then they are likely to benefit from economies of scale as specialisation proceeds. They may also experience diseconomies of scale if specialisation goes too far.
- There are no restrictions on free trade between those countries which possess absolute and comparative advantage. This is clearly a very unrealistic assumption that has to be made.

Notwithstanding these assumptions, there are clear gains from international trade as the principles of absolute and comparative advantage indicate. These principles are, of course, extendable to any number of countries and any number of products – the more of each, the greater the total gains from trade, as long as the principle of comparative advantage is followed.

Multilateral trade free from restrictions is therefore beneficial for the overall well-being of the world economy. It ensures that goods are produced in those countries that are the most efficient producers, minimising the waste of scarce resources. Conversely, it is clear that restrictions on trade will reduce the gains that free trade can produce. In the interests of economic efficiency tariff barriers and any other measures which protect the free movement of goods are to be frowned upon.

Other explanations and determinants of trade flows

The principles of absolute and comparative advantage clearly have their weaknesses when it comes to explaining the reasons underpinning international trade. Alternative theories have been put forward including the following:

- **Competitive advantage** This theory focuses on the actual cost of production and how in reality, firms are continuously striving to reduce their unit costs. This is evidenced in the way that multinational companies are continuously seeking to move production to low-cost economies in order to gain competitive advantage. A typical example is the way in which VW has progressively moved its car production from Germany to lower-cost countries such as Czech Republic, Brazil and Mexico where labour costs are much cheaper.
- **Factor endowment** To some extent this is taken into account in the principles of absolute and comparative advantage. This model of trade stresses the importance of the quantity and quality of the factors of production. Some countries possess natural resources such as oil, natural gas, gold and diamonds. These resources obviously affect what they can produce. Over time, an increase in the quantity and quality of labour and capital could provide the overriding reasoning for an economy's pattern of trade.
- **Government policy** A government may decide that it does not wish to over-specialise and that its best strategy is to diversify production so that it has a range of products available in the event of any dislocation or interruption of supplies. This is clearly a strategic decision which over-rides the underlying assumptions of the principles of absolute and comparative advantage.

Types of protection and their effects

Since free trade leads to a rise in world economic welfare, why should any country adopt policies

The letters below were published in the *Daily Telegraph* on 3 March 2006 in response to an article on the relative merits of cane and beet sugar. Read them and then answer the questions that follow.

Cost of cane and benefits of beet

Sir – As Europe's main cane sugar refiner (Rose Prince: 'Buying sugar is as much a moral choice as a hazard to our waistlines', *Weekend*, 25 February), Tate & Lyle acts as the most important bridge to Europe for African, Caribbean, and Pacific least developed countries.

This access is independent of EU market demand, but commands an EU price, giving suppliers between £250 million and £300 million more for their sugar than would otherwise be the case. Last year this meant that 300000 direct employees in some of the world's poorer economies benefited from additional income for their raw sugar, compared with what they would have received by selling in the world market, competing with producers such as Brazil, Australia and Thailand. These funds are vital to sustaining their economies and employment.

Robert Gibber
Tate & Lyle
London EC3

Sir – Rose Prince indulged in the nation's favourite pastime – farmer bashing. Yes, beet pulp from refining is used for animal feed, but what is wrong with that? It ensures there is no waste and it is not a 'foul smelling mass', just innocuous, sweet smelling shreds.

Beet farming does not have a 'corrosive effect' on the soil; it has its place in the crop rotation and uses no more pesticides than other crops. Subsidies help with the higher cost of European production. Most cane sugar is grown on farms in the Caribbean and South America, subsidised by very low wages, long working hours and a disregard for health and safety conditions, not just by small farmers seeking fair trade.

Beet sugar is produced, refined and consumed in this country, so demands no unnecessary food miles – something Rose Prince has applauded in previous articles.

Helen Bletcher
Appleby, Lincs

UK's first bioethanol facility, Wissington, Norfolk

a Using information from the Tate & Lyle letter, explain the effects of the increased export earnings that are paid to sugar cane farmers.

b Comment upon the arguments put forward for producing sugar beet in the UK.

which prevent free trade? Sometimes policies are adopted which distort market forces in order to give a competitive advantage to the domestic industry of an economy. Such policies are called **protectionist** policies because they provide some degree of protection from foreign competition. We discuss below various methods of protecting domestic industry in this way.

Tariffs

A **tariff** is a tax on imports. It can be either specific, that is so much per unit, or ad valorem, which is a percentage of the price. Like all indirect taxes, tariffs have the impact of reducing the supply and raising the equilibrium price of the import. This gives a competitive advantage to home-produced goods and services, which become more attractive to consumers, resulting in a fall in imports.

Consider the situation in Figure 4.3. If this country did not engage in world trade, consumers would pay price P and consume quantity Q. This would be determined by the domestic supply and demand for the product. If the economy engaged in international trade, then consumers would benefit from international specialisation. World supply is shown as Supply (world). Under these circumstances prices would fall to P_1. Consumption of the product would rise from Q to Q_4. At this price, however, only Q_1 would be supplied by the domestic producers. This means that domestic production has fallen from Q to Q_1. Lower-cost overseas producers have free

access to the market, which has benefited consumers, but domestic producers have suffered, leading to a fall in employment in the industry. The imposition of a tariff, like all indirect taxes, would shift the supply curve upwards. This would increase the price to domestic consumers from P_1 to P_2. Production by domestic producers would increase from Q_1 to Q_2. Some jobs in the domestic economy would be saved.

Clearly, tariffs distort market forces and prevent consumers from benefiting from all the advantages of international specialisation and trade.

Quotas

A **quota** is a restriction on the maximum quantity of imports. Its effect is to reduce the supply of imports on the domestic market. This will lead to a higher equilibrium price than would occur in a free market. As with tariffs the impact is to prevent the domestic consumer from benefiting from all the advantages of international trade. One difference is that whereas the government gains revenue as a result of tariffs, with quotas the increased price paid by consumers results in the foreign firm which supplied the imports earning higher profits. The other effect of a quota is to restrict the import bill of the country which imposes the quota. An alternative might be for the government to sell licences to foreign firms to allow them to sell some allocation of the quota on the domestic market. The prospect of raised profits would ensure a market for the import licences.

Exchange control

One way of preventing excessive spending on imports is to set legal limits on the dealings in foreign currency that a country's citizens and businesses can make. If importers are limited in their access to foreign currency, they cannot pay for sufficient imports to meet the existing domestic demand. Imports will fall to a level below that which will occur in a free market. Again the consumer would suffer. All member states of the European Union abandoned exchange controls in 1993. This is not the case with all developing economies. In 1998, for example, the Malaysian government introduced temporary exchange controls to protect its exchange rate during the Asian financial crisis. Other developing economies use exchange controls to reduce their external debt.

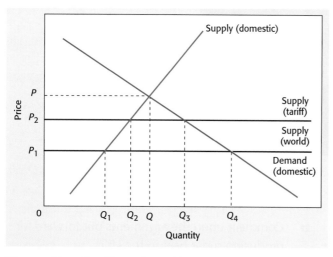

Figure 4.3 *The effects of a tariff*

Export subsidies

We have defined 'protectionism' in terms of any policy that distorts market forces to give competitive advantage to domestic industry. Sometimes, this is achieved through direct subsidies on exports. The impact of an export subsidy is to increase the supply of an industry's exports on the world market, which will have the effect of reducing prices below those determined in a free market. Foreign consumers will enjoy an increase in their economic welfare as the price of the good falls. Those employed in the domestic market might also benefit as production increases to match demand for the lower-priced goods. They might enjoy higher wages and their jobs might be more secure but only as long as the subsidy lasts. Those who lose out are the taxpayers who have to pay for the subsidy. In addition, as firms divert output to the overseas market, the supply of goods may fall in the domestic market, leading to rising prices and reduced welfare for domestic consumers.

The methods of protectionism described so far are all quite clear and obvious ways in which domestic industries can be given a competitive advantage over foreign industry in order to reduce imports and/or boost exports. Because these methods so obviously distort international market forces in pursuit of the more narrow national interest, they are all generally forbidden, except under very limiting circumstances, under the terms of international trading agreements such as the former General Agreement on Tariffs and Trade (GATT).

Protectionist policies are sometimes called expenditure switching policies because their aim is clearly to switch expenditure, both domestic and foreign, to the output of goods and services of the domestic economy (see Chapter 7).

An assessment of the arguments in favour of protectionism

International specialisation and free trade are justified because they lead to an optimal allocation of resources on a world scale and to a rise in the economic welfare of consumers. Any arguments advanced in justification of protectionist policies can only be assessed if the impact on world resource allocation and consumer welfare is also considered.

It is often argued that protectionism is justified for the reasons discussed below.

To safeguard employment in the home economy

An examination of the UK's trade accounts over the last few years will reveal the extent to which imports of manufactured goods have increased. The import penetration ratio is the proportion of the domestic sales of a product which is taken up by imports. For example, in 1968 the import penetration ratio in textiles was 16%. This means that out of every £100 spent on textiles in Britain, £16 was spent on imported textiles. By 2007 the figure had risen to 73%. In the category radio, television and communications equipment, the import penetration ratio was as high as 98% in 2007. As import penetration rises, domestic firms come under increasing pressure to maintain sales. The less successful will have to lay off workers and some may close down completely. This can result in considerable structural unemployment and can lead to calls for some degree of protection from imports.

Very often interest groups, such as trade unions, will call for tariffs when faced with a flood of cheap imports from abroad. There is no real economic justification in favour of import controls to protect jobs. These measures can only be justified on social grounds. To maximise economic welfare, labour should be considered as a resource that must be swiftly allocated and reallocated to its best use. This process can be aided by any measures to improve the occupational and geographical mobility of labour. Looked at in this way 'a flood of cheap imports' should be welcomed as a benefit to the consumer rather than seen as a threat to jobs.

To correct balance of payments disequilibria

Typical policies include raising income taxes and interest rates to prevent consumers purchasing imports. These policies are sometimes known as expenditure dampening policies. In addition to preventing imports, such policies also reduce consumer spending on the output of domestic industry, so the side effect is a rise in unemployment. This results in a call for these policies as an alternative way of protecting the balance of payments and the exchange rate. These policies will be analysed in detail in Chapter 7.

To prevent the exploitation of labour in developing economies

Very often when cheap goods are imported into a market there are claims that the goods are cheap because labour in the exporting countries is paid a very low wage. It is further claimed that labour, sometimes child labour, is exploited by unscrupulous business owners. This results in a call for import controls on moral grounds. There are often also calls for import controls on the grounds that firms in the importing country cannot compete with the cheap imports because they have to pay higher wages. This argument in favour of import controls is often combined with the argument that they are required in order to protect jobs.

Such arguments in favour of import controls have no economic justification whatsoever. If labour is cheap in an economy this is a reflection of that economy's factor endowment. A large supply of unskilled labour will lead to low wages and usually low priced products. The principle of comparative advantage states that this will lead to increased economic welfare as those economies with cheap labour specialise in those products in which they have the lowest comparative costs. This will be those products which are highly labour intensive. It should be noted that there may well be moral arguments to justify protectionism in this case, but it should also be considered that any measures which reduce imports from such countries are likely to make the problem of low wages worse. This is because any fall in demand for imports from such economies will reduce the demand for labour further and make wage rates fall even lower.

To prevent dumping

Dumping describes the process of selling goods in an overseas market at a price below the cost of production. This is a form of price discrimination because consumers in the home market will pay a higher price than those in the overseas market. The purpose of dumping might be to destroy existing competition in the overseas market or to prevent new firms in the overseas market from becoming established. Dumping can be achieved through export subsidies provided by the home government or through ensuring that consumers in the home market pay a sufficiently high price to more than cover total costs. Alternatively, firms might be prepared to suffer losses in the short term if this allows them to destroy competition and create a monopoly, increasing excess profits in the long term.

Clearly, if dumping leads to anti-competitive behaviour in the long run and prevents the realisation of comparative advantage, then import controls on products dumped in a market can be justified. It should be noted, however, that firms which face competition through cheap imports will often claim that goods are being dumped, when in reality the low prices of such goods are merely a reflection of the greater efficiency of the exporting firm. Whether a good is truly being dumped on a market needs careful investigation before import controls can be justified. This argument is particularly controversial in the case of clothing products from China being dumped in EU markets.

To safeguard infant industries

As shifts in comparative advantage occur, conditions for setting up industries in particular economies can become favourable. Establishing a fledgling or **sunrise industry** can be quite difficult in the early years especially if a new firm faces competition from a long-established overseas company. The **infant industry argument** is that a firm with only a small part of the market will not be able to benefit from all potential economies of scale and will be unable to compete in the market. It will be in the interests of established firms to try to drive the new firm out of business and they might cut prices fiercely to retain their market. If the infant industry does have the potential to develop into an efficient producer in line with comparative advantage, then import controls may well be justified in this case. It should be noted, however, that many industries call for protection in their fledgling state but they then develop a vested interest in maintaining this protection once they have become established. Interest groups develop to lobby politicians to prevent import controls from being removed.

Read the feature below and then answer the questions that follow.

After seven years of talking, the future of free trade faces a sticky end over bananas

World trade talks that began with bold promises seven years ago to open up markets and help poor countries are in danger of collapse this week – and nothing illustrates why more effectively than the banana.

On the eve of the summit in Geneva, negotiations have failed to reach agreement over imports of fruit into Europe. Latin American countries want a better deal for their exports, while African and Caribbean producers are vowing to oppose them.

The banana dispute is one part of a giant jigsaw of about 30 outstanding issues that make up the Doha Round of talks so fiendishly complex. As negotiators from 152 countries gather for a make or break week, they know that failure risks plunging the world into a bout of protectionism. This would leave future deals to be struck piecemeal, and could also lock developing countries into poverty for decades.

Impoverished Latin American nations such as Costa Rica and Honduras are desperate for lower EU tariffs so that they can sell their bananas. However, poor Caribbean states such as Jamaica and St Lucia could see their economies suffer to the point of ruin from the resulting loss of exports. As members of the ACP group of countries, they have had preferential access into EU markets.

Banana production in Jamaica

The World Bank is keen for the talks to succeed. It has estimated that a deal could generate US$287 billion extra trade by 2015, helping to lift some developing countries out of poverty.

France, Portugal and Spain are resisting any move to make concessions as they believe it would hurt their former colonies. The Latin American bloc is unsatisfied and is pushing for bigger changes.

Source: Charter, D. The Times, 21 July 2008 (adapted)

1   Explain what might happen if world trade in commodities such as bananas was completely free of restrictions.

2   Discuss whether there are any economic reasons why the EU is seemingly reluctant to reduce restrictions on trade with developing economies.

From theory to reality: trade and globalisation

Over the last 30 years or so, international trade in the world economy has grown more quickly than GDP growth. This trend is expected to persist, as the various economies of the world become more dependent upon each other through **globalisation**. Markets across the world are becoming more integrated, with developed and developing economies becoming much more economically dependent upon each other. For developing economies, trade is the main way in which they can realise the benefits of globalisation.

Consistent with the simple economic principles referred to earlier:

- Consumers in developing countries have an increasing variety of products to choose from as multinational corporations, such as Nestlé, Kelloggs, Sony, Microsoft, Coca-Cola, Toyota and so on, import goods into these countries and companies such as DHL, Schenker, Maersk and China Shipping provide the logistical support for this to take place cheaply and efficiently.
- Imports provide additional competition especially for domestic producers of food and drink products. It also exposes them to the best practices of such corporations.
- In turn, exports enlarge the markets for the products of developing countries, benefiting producers and their employees.
- Trade gives firms in developing countries access to improved capital inputs, such as machine tools, so improving their own productivity.
- There has been a substantial re-allocation of resources in the world economy. This can be seen through the ongoing shift in manufacturing activity from industrial countries to developing economies. International tourism growth has also benefited many developing economies.

The World Trade Organization (WTO), set up in 1995, has sought to create an environment in the world economy conducive to unrestricted multilateral trade. The most sensitive task it has faced to date has been to reduce trade barriers on international trade in agricultural products. These products provide genuine opportunities for many developing economies to trade in world markets. Unfortunately, some of the wealthy countries (the USA especially) have blocked moves to reduce tariffs and quotas on such trade, fearing competition from lower-priced imports. Notwithstanding, more developing countries have joined the WTO, recognising its importance in promoting their interests in the continued liberalisation of world trade.

Economic integration

Despite the work of the WTO, the structure of international trade in the twenty-first century is such that the benefits are being realised, not so much on a global scale, but through the increasing role of 'regional' trading blocs. Much of world trade takes place within these blocs, although the WTO continues to press for greater exchange between the blocs and developing countries.

There are four main organisations. These are:

- European Union (EU) – 27 member states in Western, Central and Eastern Europe (see Figure 4.4)
- North American Free Trade Agreement (NAFTA) – this includes the USA, Canada and Mexico
- The Association of Southeast Asian Nations (ASEAN) – 10 members including Singapore, Malaysia, Indonesia and Thailand
- Union of South American Nations (UNASUR) – formed in 2009, with the amalgamation of MERCOSUR and the Andean Community it has 12 members.

Table 4.3 shows their relative strength in 2007. As this shows, the EU is by far the most important overall.

	Total exports	**Total imports**
EU	5320	5574
NAFTA	1853	2684
ASEAN	864	774
MERCOSUR	224	184
Andean Community	76	70

Table 4.3 *Merchandise trade of selected regional trade agreements in 2007 (US$ bn)*

Source: World Trade Organization, 2009

The process by which these trading blocs have been established is referred to as **economic integration**. It refers to deliberate ways in which national economies agree to merge their economic affairs into a single economic organisation. Consequently, there is a 'blurring' of their boundaries as their economies become more closely linked to each other.

Table 4.4 (page 170) shows the three main forms of organisation, which are described below:

- **Free trade area** The loosest form of organisation involving the systematic removal

From six to 27

1958
Belgium
France
Germany
Italy
Luxembourg
Netherlands

1973
Denmark
Ireland
UK

1981
Greece

1986
Portugal
Spain

1995
Austria
Finland
Sweden

2004
Cyprus
Czech Republic
Estonia
Hungary
Latvia
Lithuania
Malta
Poland
Slovakia
Slovenia

2008
Bulgaria
Romania

European Economic Community 1958–1985

European Community 1986–1994

European Union 1995–date

Figure 4.4 *The New Europe*

of trade restrictions between members. In practice, this may be for just a selected range of commodity types, such as manufactured goods. The sensitive nature of trade in agricultural goods has meant that these have often been either excluded or partially excluded. A free trade area is the typical form of organisation, the EU excepted.

- **Customs union** The crucial feature is that members agree to erect a common external tariff on trade with non-members. This tariff may be on all trade or, as is the case with the EU, mainly on imported goods which member

states are able to adequately produce themselves. Agriculture has always been a very sensitive issue in the EU, with policy being to protect the interest of EU member states very clearly. Consequently, developing countries are highly critical of this policy, despite preferential access for the agricultural products of some developing countries.

- **Economic union** This involves the removal of restrictions on the movement of factors of production (labour, capital and enterprise) between members. In the case of the EU, it has also meant the development of various common

Type of organisation	Characteristics	Comments
Free trade area	Removal of tariffs and quotas on internal trade	Members are free to determine their own external trade policy towards non-members. NAFTA, ASEAN and UNASUR are still at this stage
Customs union	As above but with the agreement of a common external tariff on trade with non-members	Results in some trade being deflected from outside the union to within. Applied to the EC before moves to EMU
Economic union	As above but with more harmonisation and centralisation of economic policies	EU has moved beyond this with single currency and European Central Bank single interest rate

Table 4.4 *Main forms of economic integration*

policies in areas such as agriculture, transport, regional and social affairs. There has also been the deliberate harmonisation of other aspects of economic affairs in order to ensure a highly competitive environment. Controversially for most member states, the EU is now progressing towards an objective of Economic and Monetary Union (EMU), with a single currency (the euro), a single exchange rate and centralised economic policies.

Within the context of this section, the most important issue is whether these regional trading blocs actually enhance, or detract from, global economic welfare. This is a very difficult question to answer. Economists do though point to two main effects:

- **Trade creation** – consistent with absolute and comparative advantage, trade is generated between members over and above what might otherwise have happened. Greater specialisation occurs and less-efficient producers lose markets as imports from within the group replace their production. Resources are therefore more efficiently allocated. All of the organisations referred to in Table 4.4 aim to gain these benefits.
- **Trade diversion** – more difficult to explain and only occurs when external trade restrictions are imposed. Trade from outside the group is replaced by trade from within; this is not consistent with an efficient allocation of

resources as the prices paid for such goods will be higher than if purchased on the open world market.

Figure 4.5 shows an analysis of intra-EU imports and exports of goods for selected member states. In particular, it indicates how, through increasing economic integration, trade creation has taken place, bringing the economies much closer to each other. In some respects, the UK remains the 'odd European out', with a lower percentage of exports than imports compared to its main trading partners.

In the case of the UK's membership of the EU, former Commonwealth countries especially have had a decreasing share of imports to the UK. This is crude evidence of trade diversion. For many poor countries in Africa and Asia, this diversion has had a particularly negative impact on their economies through reduced employment and a destabilising of their balance of payments. This aspect of international trade globalisation has most certainly not enhanced their economic well-being.

A more recent feature of globalisation has been the extent of economic integration into the world economy of the BRIC (Brazil, Russia, India and China) group of emerging economies. Figure 4.6 (page 172) shows an index of the economic relationships that these countries have with 170 others. The emerging powers integration index measures a country's trade with the BRIC economies as a percentage of total trade and GDP. It also incorporates foreign direct investment and labour

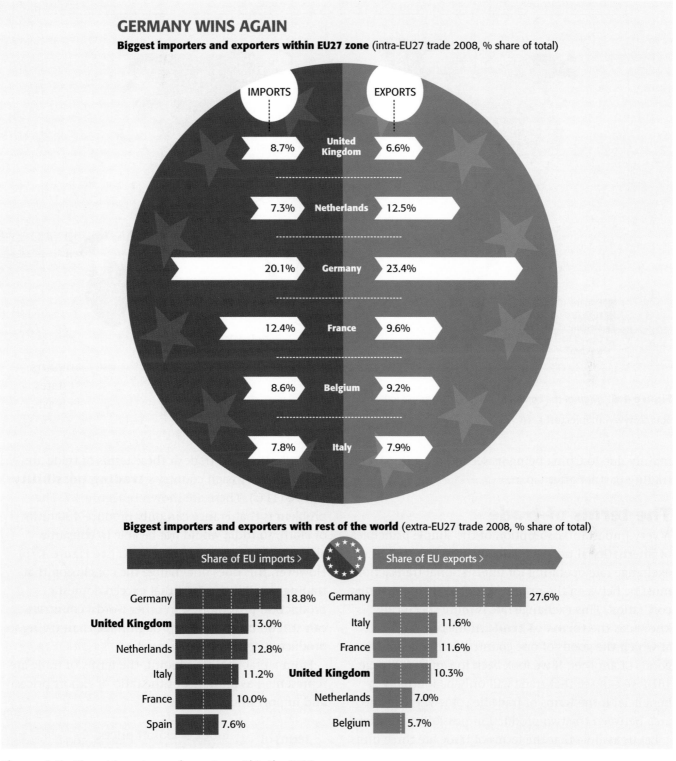

GERMANY WINS AGAIN

Biggest importers and exporters within EU27 zone (intra-EU27 trade 2008, % share of total)

IMPORTS

EXPORTS

8.7%	United Kingdom	6.6%
7.3%	Netherlands	12.5%
20.1%	Germany	23.4%
12.4%	France	9.6%
8.6%	Belgium	9.2%
7.8%	Italy	7.9%

Biggest importers and exporters with rest of the world (extra-EU27 trade 2008, % share of total)

Share of EU imports >

Share of EU exports >

Imports		Exports	
Germany	18.8%	Germany	27.6%
United Kingdom	13.0%	Italy	11.6%
Netherlands	12.8%	France	11.6%
Italy	11.2%	United Kingdom	10.3%
France	10.0%	Netherlands	7.0%
Spain	7.6%	Belgium	5.7%

Figure 4.5   *Biggest importers and exporters within the EU27 zone*

Source: Daily Telegraph, *18 September 2009*

migration flows. Four levels of integration have been identified. The figure identifies the ten countries that are most integrated with the BRIC'S economies. In general, the BRIC'S group are most established with regional neighbours, in countries with mineral deposits and in politically unstable or repressive states. Of the developed economies, Australia is most integrated with BRIC'S,

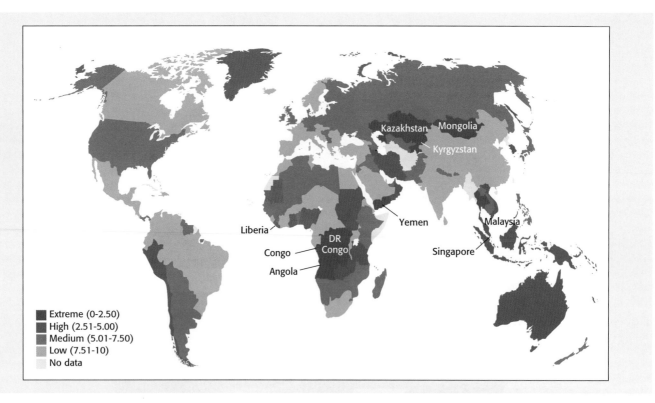

Figure 4.6 *Map of the emerging powers integration index*
Source: www.maplecroft.com

mainly due to China being its second most important trading partner after Japan.

The terms of trade

A very important assumption of the simple principles of international trade explained above was that 'the exchange rate operating for international transactions must be between the respective domestic opportunity cost ratios'. This exchange rate is more specifically known as the **terms of trade**. It measures the rate at which the goods of one country exchange for the goods of another. If we look back to Figure 4.2 (page 161), we can see that trade will only be mutually beneficial if the terms of trade lie somewhere in the area between the two production possibility frontiers.

Let us assume that the terms of trade are three units of cloth for one unit of cheese. With these terms, India could buy 750 units of cloth if it specialised in cheese production and sold it all to France. In turn France could buy 266.7 (800/3) units of cheese if it specialised in cloth and sold it all to India. If this were to happen, then each country would be consuming outside of its production possibility curve (PPC). The consumption combinations possible through

specialisation and trade at these terms of trade are represented by each country's **trading possibility curve** (TPC). These are shown in Figure 4.7. The problem is that France can only produce 400 units of cloth, so India would not be able to consume along the dotted section of its TPC (see Figure 4.7b). However, this does not change the conclusion that trading possibilities exist that exceed domestic production possibilities. In other words, countries can still do much better through trade than trying to produce everything for themselves.

From a practical standpoint, the terms of trade are represented as an index of the ratio of export prices and import prices:

$$\text{terms of trade index} = \frac{\text{index of export prices}}{\text{index of import prices}} \times 100$$

The ratio is calculated from the average prices of the many thousands of goods traded in world markets. In turn, these prices are weighted by the relative importance of each good traded. It is therefore a very complex calculation to work out for any type of economy.

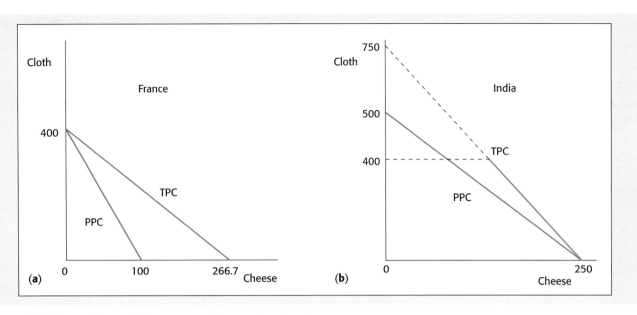

Figure 4.7 *The trading possibility curve and the benefits of trade*

Official statistics show the terms of trade as a single index in relation to a given base year. For example, if year 0 has a base year index of 100, then if in year 1 the terms of trade index is 102.4, this means that on average a country is receiving relatively better prices for its exports than it is having to pay other countries for its imports. So, in this case, the terms of trade have improved.

In contrast, if in year 1 the terms of trade index is 98.4, this means that on average a country is having to pay a relatively higher price for its imports than it is receiving for its exports. In this case, the terms of trade have deteriorated.

Relatively minor changes on a year-by-year basis have only limited economic significance. On a longer-term basis though, the time trend in the terms of trade can have a very marked impact on an economy. In general, the reality of the global trade market is as follows:

- The terms of trade for most developing economies were deteriorating up to around 2000. This means that year by year they had to export more and more goods (especially primary agricultural products) to support a given volume of imports. Since then, commodity prices have been volatile, reaching a peak in 2008. This is clearly shown in Figure 4.8.

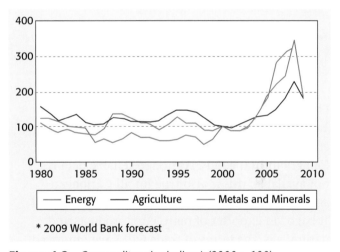

Figure 4.8 *Commodity price indices* (2000 = 100)*
Source: Global Commodity Markets, World Bank, 2009

- Fuel-exporting developing economies have been in a much stronger position, although in recent years, there has been considerable volatility in their terms of trade as the world price of crude oil has fluctuated widely. This hardly makes for sensible long-term economic planning.
- The terms of trade for most developed economies have shown longer-term improvement. This means that they have continued to receive increased real prices, especially for their exports of manufactured consumer goods.

Table 4.5 shows the terms of trade indexes for selected countries in Latin America from 1995 to 2004. For Chile, there was a large favourable increase in its terms of trade from 2003 to 2004 due to an increase in the world prices of copper and copper ores, the country's principal exports. In the case of Argentina, fuel exports account for the recent improvement in its terms of trade.

Country	1995	2000	2001	2002	2003	2004
Argentina	96.0	100	99.3	98.7	107.2	109.2
Brazil	107.6	100	99.6	98.4	97.0	97.9
Chile	102.1	100	93.3	97.2	102.8	124.9
Costa Rica	103.1	100	98.4	96.9	95.5	91.9
Ecuador	72.7	100	84.6	86.8	89.8	91.5
Mexico	83.1	100	97.4	97.9	98.8	101.6
Latin America area	89.7	100	96.3	96.6	98.7	104.0

Table 4.5 *Terms of trade index, 1995–2004 (2000 = 100)*

Source: Annual statistics of Latin America and the Caribbean, CEPAL, *2005*

Elsewhere, and for other countries not shown in Table 4.5, the terms of trade have deteriorated due entirely to the fall in typical commodity prices for agricultural goods. Although reliable data is not available, this is also true for all Caribbean agricultural exporting countries. For Trinidad and Tobago, an exporter of petroleum products and natural gas, the terms of trade will have improved due to large price increases since 2003. The same is true for Barbados with respect to its exports of aluminium. Some benefit from rising commodity prices will have been lost through the increased prices for manufactured imports. A crude indication of these price trends is shown in Table 4.6 for selected typical Caribbean export products.

The balance of payments

It is important that governments have an accurate record of all the transactions that take place between residents of their country and all other countries in

Product	1995	2000	2001	2002	2003	2004
Bananas	104.7	100	138.8	125.5	89.4	125.1
Sugar	162.4	100	105.6	84.2	86.7	87.6
Coffee	154.3	100	70.4	63.6	65.6	82.0
Aluminium	116.6	100	93.2	87.1	92.4	110.7
Crude oil	61.1	100	77.3	85.9	102.5	127.9
Natural gas	40.0	100	91.8	77.9	127.2	136.8

Table 4.6 *Price indexes for export commodities, 1995–2004 (2000 = 100)*

Source: Annual Statistics of Latin America and the Caribbean, CEPAL, *2005*

the rest of the world. These transactions are recorded in the balance of payments. In practice, this record is a very complex financial statement – though there is an internationally agreed method for its presentation. This is recommended by the International Monetary Fund (IMF) and permits economists to make international comparisons. The basics of this method are outlined below.

The balance of payments consists of the **current account**, the **capital account** and the **financial account**. We can use the UK as a typical example to explain the various components of the accounts.

It should be noted that the balance of payments accounts are simply a record of flows of money between residents of the UK and non-residents. Following basic accounting principles this means that every credit (+) entry is matched by a debit (–) entry. For example, if a UK resident exports goods abroad, this is recorded as a credit entry (+) in the accounts. We also have to record how foreign residents paid for these exports. Perhaps the foreign resident had a bank account in the UK and used this to pay the exporter. This would be shown in the accounts as a debit entry as a decrease in UK liabilities abroad (–). This means that the foreign resident has less of a claim on a UK bank account. The important point is that we have accounted for the spending and recorded both sides of the transaction. Since every credit item is matched by a debit item in the accounts, it follows that in an accounting sense, the balance of payments must always balance. In practice, however, we cannot have fully accurate information. As a result, a section of the accounts is entitled 'Net errors and omissions' to allow for discrepancies in the calculations.

The current account

The current account consists of:

- trade in goods
- trade in services
- income
- current transfers.

Trade in goods

The goods account covers items that can be touched, weighed or counted as they are traded. For this reason, they are sometimes known as visibles. For example, the import of cars from Germany is a debit item in the current account of the UK, whereas the export of cashmere sweaters to Japan is a credit item. The difference between visible exports and imports is referred to as the **balance of trade**.

Trade in services

The services account covers exports and imports of services. For example, if a UK resident purchases an airline ticket from a foreign airline, this has the same impact as the import of a good and is recorded as a debit item. However, if a merchant bank in the City of London raises a loan for a foreign firm, the fee charged by the bank is equivalent to an export and will be recorded as a credit item. The difference in trade in such items is known as the *invisible balance*.

Income

The income account is made up of income from investments abroad. This covers any earnings from foreign investment and financial assets and liabilities. For example, any dividends paid on foreign shares held by UK residents are recorded as credits, whereas interest paid to foreign holders of deposits in UK financial institutions is recorded as a debit item.

Current transfers

Current transfers are made up of central government transfers, e.g. payments and receipts from the EU, and other transfers by private individuals such as gifts of cash. The latter includes payments that are sent home by migrant workers.

Capital account

The capital account records transactions which involve the transfer of ownership of fixed assets and the acquisition or disposal of non-financial assets. An example of the former might be a government investment grant to undertake a large construction project, such as a water purification plant abroad. An example of the latter might be land purchased or sold by a foreign embassy.

Financial account

The financial account was formerly known as the capital account. This section of the accounts records the forms of investment overseas by UK residents and the inward flow of investment funds from foreign residents. It is this flow which gives rise to flows of investment income in the current account.

Net errors and omissions is a balancing item.

Balance of payments examples

Table 4.7 (page 176) shows a summary of the balance of payments current accounts for selected countries in 2007. (For ease of comparison all of the data are shown in US$.) It shows some interesting contrasts such as:

- The UK has traditionally experienced a deficit in its annual trade in goods and services. This is particularly the case for trade in goods; the positive invisible balance has helped to reduce this deficit.
- The USA has a massive deficit on trade in goods and services; in contrast, both Germany and Japan have substantial surpluses.
- Most developing economies invariably have a deficit in their trade in goods and services; China and Malaysia though have substantial export earnings from manufactured goods.

	Exports	Imports	Current account balance
Developed economies			
Germany	1326.5	1059.4	+150.7
Japan	712.8	621.0	+210.5
Spain	242.0	373.6	−145.3
UK	435.6	617.2	−115.2
USA	1163.2	2017.0	−738.6
Developing economies			
China	1218.0	955.8	+249.9
India	145.2	216.7	−9.4
Malaysia	176.2	146.9	+28.9
Pakistan	17.4	32.6	−8.3
South Africa	69.8	91.0	−20.6

Table 4.7 *Balance of payments current accounts for selected countries in 2007 (US$000 m)*

Source: World Development Report, *2009*

Looking at the balance of payments over time is in many respects more relevant to the economist than the information for just one year, as given in Tables 4.7 and 4.8 (see Self-assessment task 4.5). In this way, medium- and longer-term trends can be identified and analysed and appropriate policies put in place to deal with any problems that are identified. These policies will be analysed in Chapter 7.

SELF-ASSESSMENT TASK 4.4

Obtain an outline of the balance of payments account for your own economy. Summarise this in terms of the main headings used above and write a few sentences on what the data show.

SELF-ASSESSMENT TASK 4.5

Read the feature below and then answer the questions that follow.

Trade surplus narrows as export growth slows

China's politically sensitive trade surplus grew less than expected last month as Beijing's efforts to slow exports took hold and surging oil prices bloated import costs. Still, the trade gap for 2007 surged to a record US$262 billion, a sign that pressure to accelerate Yuan appreciation is unlikely to ease any time soon.

China's thirst for commodity imports of foodstuffs and oil products saw imports rise by 26%; export growth was 22%. Beijing is trying to engineer a slowdown in exports to reduce trade tensions with the United States, which continues to accuse China of deliberately depressing the value of the Yuan to help its own manufacturers. The EU has taken the same stand as the US.

Chinese exports en route to the EU

China already has the world's biggest foreign exchange reserves at a reported US$1.52 trillion.

Table 4.8 shows the balance of trade for 2007 between China and its ten largest trading partners.

	Exports to	Imports from	Balance
European Union	245.2	111.0	+134.2
United States	232.7	69.4	+163.3
Hong Kong	184.4	12.8	+171.6
Japan	102.1	134.0	−31.9
ASEAN group	94.2	108.4	−14.2
South Korea	56.1	103.8	−47.7
Russia	28.5	19.7	+8.8
India	24.0	14.6	+9.4
Taiwan	23.5	101.0	−77.5
Australia	18.0	25.9	−7.9

Table 4.8 *Top 10 trading partners (US$ bn)*

Source: South China Morning Post, *12 January 2008*

1 Table 4.8 shows that China has a balance of trade surplus with five countries and a balance of trade deficit with five countries. Discuss the extent to which this state of affairs can be explained by the principles of absolute and comparative advantage.

2 Explain how an appreciation of the yuan against the euro and the US$ is likely to affect the balance of trade between China and these trading partners.

SPECIMEN EXAM QUESTIONS

The following questions have been set in a recent CIE examination paper.

1 a How might opportunity cost help to explain the pattern of international trade. [8]

b Discuss whether the formation of regional trading groups such as ASEAN and NAFTA is desirable. [12]

[20 marks]

(October/November 2008)

SUMMARY

In this core section it has been shown that:

- International trade is an essential and beneficial feature of the global economy of the twenty-first century.
- The principles of absolute and comparative advantage can be used to show the benefits of free trade.
- Tariffs, quotas, exchange control and export subsidies distort the benefits of multilateral trade for the world economy; in certain circumstances, protection may be relevant especially for developing economies.
- Increasingly, economic integration can bring benefits to the members of such organisations.
- The terms of trade index measures the rate at which the goods of one country exchange for those of another.
- The balance of payments is an important financial record of the international trading transactions of a country.

Theory and measurement in the macroeconomy
Core

On completion of this core section you should know:

- what constitutes the labour force in an economy
- what is meant by labour productivity and how it can be measured
- how to measure unemployment and determine trends in employment and unemployment
- how to measure the general level of prices in an economy; money and real data
- the determinants of aggregate demand and aggregate supply and the shapes of these functions
- the interaction between aggregate demand and aggregate supply.

The labour force

The **labour force** in an economy is defined as the total number of workers who are available for work. It therefore refers to all males and females, normally 15–16 years and over, who can contribute to the production of goods and services. As well as those actually in employment, it also includes those who are unemployed as these people are available for work. The size of the labour force depends upon a wide range of demographic, economic, social and cultural factors, such as:

- the total size of the population of working age
- the number of people who remain in full-time education after leaving secondary school
- the normal retirement age for males and females
- the number of women who join the labour force on a full- or part-time basis.

Table 5.1 shows the size of the population for selected economies in 2008 projected to 2050. In themselves these aggregate statistics have little meaning – they really need to be seen in relation to the productive potential of these economies. However, they do give a very crude indication of the relative strength of these countries from an economic standpoint. In virtually all developed economies, the labour force has increased at a steady rate over the past generation. However, some have been slowing down in more recent years, largely as a result of workers retiring before the statutory retirement age and an increase in the number of school leavers remaining in higher

education. By 2050, according to Table 5.1, Japan and Russia will have experienced large falls in population. In contrast the growth in southern Asia is substantial and has major implications for the future balance of power in the global economy.

	2008	2050	% change
EU 27	498	494	−0.8
USA	304	438	+44.1
Russia	142	110	−22.5
Japan	128	95	−25.8
China	1325	1437	+8.5
India	1150	1755	+52.6
Pakistan	173	295	+70.5

Table 5.1 *Population projections for selected countries in 2050 (m)*

Source: Population Reference Bureau, United Nations, *2009*

An essential complementary measure is the **labour force participation rate**. This refers to the percentage of the total population of working age who are actually classified as being part of the labour force. Table 5.2 shows these rates for selected economies. In developed economies the rate is typically 50–70%. A lower participation rate usually indicates that an economy has a high participation rate in higher education and a relatively large number of people opting for early retirement. In the case of some developed economies, government policy in recent years has been to increase the higher education participation rates as a supply side policy to enhance competitiveness.

Comparable statistics for most developing economies are unreliable for various reasons including:

- the existence of a large subsistence sector
- differences in the official secondary school leaving age
- differences in attitudes towards married women seeking paid employment
- practical problems of data collection.

Table 5.2 indicates that there are substantial variations between developing economies. These differences are most likely due to the contribution of women to the labour force being constrained by social and cultural factors.

From a general perspective the following demographic trends are having an important influence on the size of the labour force in most developing economies:

- Contrary to developed economies **birth rates** exceed **death rates** in developing economies. Consequently, the total population and hence the labour force in these countries is increasing.
- Dependency ratios in most developing economies are high as a result of high birth rates

and an increasing life expectancy. Consequently, there are relatively more economically inactive people than those who constitute the labour force.

- Many developing economies have experienced a rapid growth in their urban populations, as there has been significant **migration** from rural areas. This ever-increasing **urbanisation** has made it very difficult for these economies to provide enough jobs to meet the needs and aspirations of its labour force. Rural dwellers unfortunately are often unaware of the realities of life in grossly over-populated cities.

Labour productivity

Productivity refers to the quantity of goods and services that a worker is able to produce in a particular period of time. (It should not be confused with production which is an aggregate measure not directly related to a particular input.)

In looking at measurement in the macroeconomy, it is invariably true that variations in living standards between economies can often be explained in terms of variations in the productivity of the main factors of production (see Chapter 6 Supplement). Labour is not a uniform resource. Variations in the productivity of labour depend on the education, training, experience and skills of the workforce. Clearly, when

	Male		Female		Total	
	15–24	25+	15–24	25+	15–24	25+
France	40.3	66.5	33.0	53.9	36.7	59.9
Italy	37.8	64.4	26.9	39.6	32.5	51.4
Poland	37.5	68.2	30.7	50.0	34.2	58.5
USA	63.3	75.5	57.9	59.6	60.6	67.3
Pakistan	72.2	90.5	18.6	22.4	45.9	56.8
Malaysia	n/a	n/a	n/a	n/a	n/a	64.1
Maldives	58.6	85.3	47.1	56.3	52.8	70.8
Sierra Leone	35.9	81.6	48.3	73.5	42.2	77.1

Table 5.2 *Labour force participation rates in 2006*
Source: Key Indicators of the Labour Market, ILO, *2009*

a skilled workforce is equipped with large stocks of capital and technological know-how, productivity is invariably higher than when this is not the case. The formal relationship between all inputs and outputs is represented in the production function (see Chapter 2 Supplement). The importance of productivity is in recognising that although the labour force in an economy is a key resource, the output it is able to produce is to a large extent directly related to the technical knowledge, skills and motivation of that workforce.

Employment and unemployment

Countries measure the numbers in employment and the numbers of those unemployed. The sum total of these is the labour force or **working population** as described above.

SELF-ASSESSMENT TASK 5.1

Read the feature below and then answer the questions that follow.

Labour productivity growth in Pakistan

Vulnerable employment is a relatively new term. It is defined as the number of family workers and own account workers as a percentage of the total employed. There are strong linkages between this, working poverty and labour productivity.

Productivity increases can be obtained through investment, trade, technological progress or changes in working practices. The significance is that such increases can lead to increases in spending on social protection and poverty reduction. Vulnerable employment may also be reduced. Although there is no guarantee, without productivity growth and hence induced economic growth, improvements in the quality of life are highly unlikely. Pakistan has millions of people living below the poverty line although the trend is falling. Productivity growth is vital if the percentage is to continue to fall especially as the total population is projected to increase

There is no clear pattern in labour productivity growth rates since 1990. Negative rates were recorded in the late 1990s, although more recently, the positive growth rates have seen a corresponding reduction in poverty. Economic and social reforms

Family-owned business in Pakistan

have paved the way for higher economic growth rates. A particular challenge though is to improve the position of women in the labour market. Participation rates are low and there is a need to give women better access not only to jobs but to quality jobs. If achieved, this would help to reduce vulnerable employment and poverty.

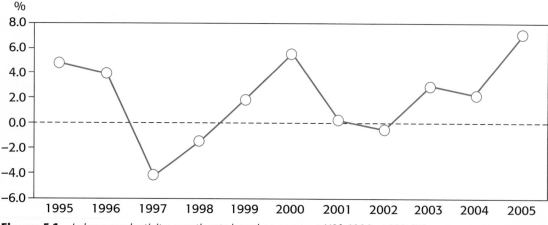

Figure 5.1 *Labour productivity growth rate based on constant US$ 1990 at PPP (%)*

1 Give some likely reasons for the volatile annual changes in labour productivity shown in Figure 5.1.

2 As well as more women entering the labour force, analyse other policies that might be used by the Pakistan government to increase labour productivity.

This is calculated:

working population = total number of workers in employment + total number of workers who are unemployed

Data on Pakistan's working population is shown in Figure 5.2.

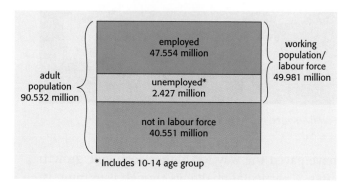

Figure 5.2 *Composition of adult population of Pakistan, 2007*

Data such as that in Figure 5.2 is usually collected annually through a **labour force survey**. For Pakistan in 2007, this survey recorded that 2.8 million people aged 10–14 years were also in employment. Compared to developed economies, the adult population not in the labour force is high at around 45%. As explained above, this is largely due to a low female activity rate of around 21% in 2007. The **dependency ratio** was also high at 68%.

The measurement of employment and **unemployment** is very important from the standpoint of the macroeconomy. For example, if there is unemployment in an economy:

- Output will be below its potential level. The economy will be operating inside its production possibility curve (see Chapter 1). Resources are not being used to the full, but, as the number of employed increases towards full employment, the economy will reach its production possibility frontier.

- The tax revenue received by the government will be lower than with a higher level of employment. If applicable, the amount of money paid out in the form of state benefits for the unemployed will in turn be lower (see Chapter 7).

- A high level of unemployment may result in civil unrest, increased crime rates and substantial social problems for those unemployed and their families. The gap in economic well-being between those in work and those who are unemployed can be substantial, particularly in developing economies where the degree of state support is limited.

Unemployment can cause significant social problems

The level of unemployment should be distinguished from the rate of unemployment. The level of unemployment refers to the total number of people who are unemployed whereas the rate of unemployment is the number of unemployed people divided by the labour force. So, in an economy with a labour force of 50 million people, 4.3 million of whom are unemployed, the rate of unemployment is 8.6%.

There is no universal measure of employment, but the term does cover some or all of the following:

- those in full-time paid employment
- those on recognised training schemes
- those working for a minimum number of hours per week.

Normally, those working in subsistence non-monetarised situations would be excluded, as would unpaid volunteers.

There is though a standard international definition of unemployment. This covers

- those who are not classified as employed
- those available for work
- those actively seeking work.

Most developing countries including Pakistan do not include the latter in their unemployment data.

Material on the difficulties of measuring unemployment can be found on page 261.

Material on the difficulties of measuring unemployment can be found on page 261.

SELF-ASSESSMENT TASK 5.2

1 For your own country, see what information you can obtain on:
   - the number of people in employment
   - the number of people who are unemployed.
2 Can you identify any trends in these important variables over the past ten years?
3 Comment on the macroeconomic significance of the size of the working population and the dependency ratio.

The general price level and price indices

A further important macroeconomic variable is the general price level. This is measured by governments in all types of economy and is a recognised measure of the **cost of living** in an economy at any one point in time. Changes in the general price level on a year-by-year basis in turn are a measure of the rate of inflation in an economy (see Chapter 6 for more details).

In its simplest form, the general price level in an economy is calculated periodically using some form of **consumer price index**. In the UK, the **Retail Prices Index (RPI)** is a measure of changes in the prices of consumer goods bought by people in the UK. Much attention is paid to this index by the media, politicians, business people and consumers.

The RPI is a weighted price index. Its calculation is a major statistical task, involving three main stages:

1 A survey to find out what families buy and how much they spend on particular items – this provides the **weights.**
2 Recording how much the prices of some 600 selected items have changed – this information is

collected from all main types of retail outlet, as well as from gas, water, electricity and transport suppliers at a **base date.**

3 The percentage change in price for each item is then multiplied by its weight – from this the average change in the RPI is determined.

Although not all countries have such a comprehensive price index as in the UK, the basic principles of construction remain the same irrespective of the level of sophistication.

SELF-ASSESSMENT TASK 5.3

Read the feature below and then answer the questions that follow.

So you think London's expensive? It isn't any more

It might be surprising for Londoners to hear that the capital city has fallen down a league table of the world's most expensive cities, sliding from second to 22nd.

The precipitous slide in the pound from the heady heights of $2.11 in November 2007 to $1.41 in January 2009 has triggered a sudden drop in the cost of living in London, according to research by UBS, the investment bank. Oslo is now the world's most expensive city, followed by Zurich, Copenhagen, Geneva, Tokyo and New York.

Oslo is now the world's most expensive city

Other big fallers include Moscow, Mexico City and Seoul, where the cost of living was also hit by currency devaluations and, in the case of the Russian capital, falling oil prices.

The cheapest cities are Kuala Lumpur, Manila, Delhi and Mumbai, according to the UBS calculations, which are based on a basket of 144 goods and services.

Within these categories, London residents suffer because their rail travel is the most expensive. A second-class, one-way ticket for a 125-mile rail journey costs £58.69 – double the fare for a comparable distance in some other Western European cities.

Oslo tops the league because of its strong currency and its relative strength during the global economic crisis. Residents also pay some of the highest taxes and social security contributions in the world. The gap in the cost of living between Eastern and Western Europe has not narrowed quickly, despite the huge changes in the former communist bloc.

The basket was roughly 35% cheaper in the cities of Eastern European EU member states than in their Western counterparts – down from 38% in 2006. UBS expects a catch-up in prices to take more than a decade.

And, as the pound falls, Eastern European workers in the UK will have to work harder to send the same amount home. Polish people with a job in London have to put in an extra hour and a half each month, compared with 2006, to send home £200.

Someone earning the average wage in Zurich and New York can afford an iPod Nano after nine hours of work, while employees in Mumbai need to put in 20 nine-hour days, or about a month, to purchase the same music player.

Tokyo workers have to spend only 12 minutes at their desks before they can buy a Big Mac for lunch, while their counterparts in Nairobi, the Kenyan capital, have to work for more than two and a half hours.

However, going out for a meal is an expensive business for the average resident of Tokyo, where a three-course dinner without wine comes to an average of £53, compared with £33 in London.

Prices for postage stamps and cleaning services showed the greatest variation, with stamps almost 90% more expensive in some cities than others.

Employees in Asian and Middle Eastern cities are spending much longer at work, averaging 2119 and 2063 hours per year respectively. The treadmill is at its most demanding in Cairo, where the average employee clocks up 2373 hours per year, followed by Seoul with 2312 hours.

In contrast, French workers are at their jobs for much shorter times. Staff in Lyon and Paris put in, respectively, 1582 and 1594 hours per year.

Source: The Times, *20 August 2009 (adapted)*

---

1 Account for the variation in the cost of living between cities.

2 Discuss the use and limitations of the information contained in the article.

$$\text{cost of living index, year 1} = \sum_{i=1}^{n} \frac{W_{i1}P_{i1}}{W_{i0}P_{i0}} \times 100$$

where W = weight of item in family expenditure
P = price of item
n = total number of items in index.

If the index is calculated to be over 100 in year 1, then the cost of living has increased compared with the base date, year 0. For example, if the index is 105, then the cost of living has increased by 5% since the base year. An index of below 100 in year 1 would indicate a fall in the cost of living.

Table 5.3 is a summary of the annual change in the monthly Consumer Price Index for Mauritius for the period December 2007 to December 2008. It stood at 108.2 at the start of this period; by December 2008 it was 115.5, a net increase of 7.3 points or 6.7%. The most substantial increase was for food and non-alcoholic drinks. Rice, meat, bread and vegetables also increased in price. The impact of this increase would be felt most by the poorest families.

Category	Weight	% change Dec'07–Dec'08
Food and beverages	286	+11.7
Alcohol and tobacco	92	+5.6
Clothing and footwear	51	+5.3
Housing	131	+2.2
Furnishings	64	+5.1
Health	30	+5.3
Transport	147	+6.6
Communications	36	−3.5
Recreation	48	−0.6
Education	32	+4.9
Restaurants and hotels	43	+13.6
Miscellaneous	40	+4.3
	1000	+6.7

Table 5.3 *Consumer Price Index, Mauritius*
Source: Central Statistics Office

1 With reference to your own country, briefly describe how you might construct an appropriate price level index.
2 If such an index exists, how does it compare with your own ideas on how it might be constructed?

Money and real data

Finally, a word of caution when handling data such as that on prices in the last section. The data quoted in the self-assessment task above and in Table 5.3 is given in monetary terms. This is also known as a **nominal value** since no allowance is made for inflation. Any remaining increase will be a real increase in prices due to market forces.

The **real value** shows how prices change over time once the effects of inflation have been removed. With a price index, this occurs when the data is expressed at constant prices using a base year.

The shape and determinants of aggregate demand

Aggregate demand is the total spending on an economy's goods and services in a given time period. It consists of four components: consumption, investment, government spending and net exports. So $AD = C + I + G + (X - M)$. Figure 5.3 shows a typical aggregate demand curve.

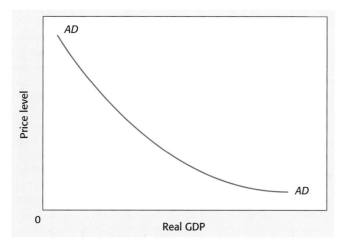

Figure 5.3   *The aggregate demand curve*

It slopes down from left to right because a lower price level will:

- raise demand for net exports because the country's goods and services will have become more price competitive
- increase the purchasing power of households with savings in the form of bank and building society deposits and other financial assets because their wealth will enable them to buy more
- reduce the rate of interest and so stimulate consumption and investment.

A change in the price level causes a movement along the *AD* curve. If, however, any of the components of *AD* change for reasons other than a change in the price level, the *AD* curve will shift. Figure 5.4 illustrates an increase in aggregate demand. This could occur because of, for example, a rise in expectations about the future, a cut in direct tax, an increase in the money supply, a fall in the exchange rate and a rise in the quality of domestically produced products.

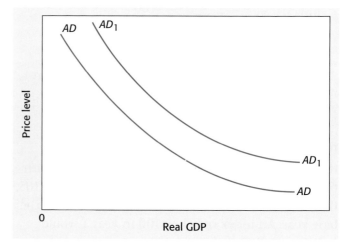

Figure 5.4   *An increase in aggregate demand*

Aggregate supply

Aggregate supply (AS) is the total output that firms in an economy are willing and able to supply at different price levels in a given period of time.

It is possible to distinguish between short run aggregate supply (SRAS) and long run aggregate supply (LRAS). Short run aggregate supply is the output which will be supplied at different price levels in a period of time when the prices of the factors of production remain unchanged. Figure 5.5 shows a typical *SRAS* curve. It slopes up from left to right.

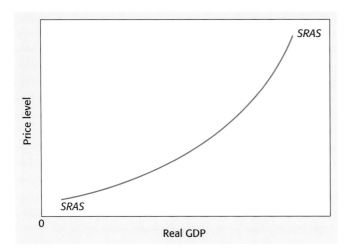

Figure 5.5 *The short run aggregate supply curve*

This is because a higher price level will enable firms to meet any extra unit costs in the form of, for example, overtime payments, and to enjoy higher profit margins.

The *SRAS* curve will shift if productivity or the payments to factors of production change. For example, an increase in wage rates, not matched by an increase in productivity, will shift the *SRAS* curve to the left, as illustrated in Figure 5.6.

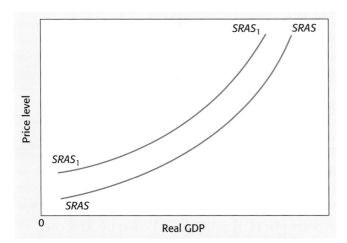

Figure 5.6 *A reduction in short run aggregate supply*

Long run aggregate supply is the output which firms would produce after the price level and factor prices have fully adjusted after any shift in aggregate demand. Keynesians often represent the *LRAS* curve as perfectly elastic at low levels of output, then upward sloping over a range of output and finally perfectly inelastic. This is to emphasise their view that in the long run the economy can operate at any

level of output and not necessarily at its full capacity. Figure 5.7 shows that from 0 to Q, output can be raised without increasing the price level. When output and hence employment are low, firms can attract more resources without raising their prices. As output rises from Q to Q_1, firms begin to experience shortages of resources and bid up wages and the cost of land and capital equipment. When output hits Q_1, the economy reaches the maximum output it can make with existing resources.

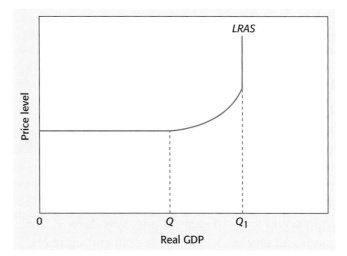

Figure 5.7 *The long run aggregate supply curve*

New classical economists illustrate the *LRAS* curve as a vertical line because they believe that, in the long run, the economy will operate at full capacity. This version of the *LRAS* curve is shown in Figure 5.8.

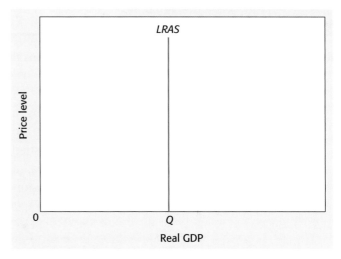

Figure 5.8 *A vertical long run aggregate supply curve*

Both Keynesian and new classical economists agree that the factors which will shift the vertical part of the *LRAS* curve are changes in the quantity and quality of resources as these will affect the productive capacity of the economy.

The *LRAS* curve will shift to the right if there is an increase in the quantity and/or quality of resources. For example, improvements in training will raise the quality of the labour force and an increase in investment will raise the quantity and, possibly, the quality of capital goods. Both of these changes will increase the maximum amount of output the country can produce. Other causes of changes in the *LRAS* include changes in technology, the quality of education and net immigration (see also Chapter 7).

Interaction of aggregate demand and supply

The equilibrium level of output and the price level are determined when aggregate demand and aggregate supply intersect, as shown in Figure 5.9.

If the price level was initially below *P*, the excess demand would push the price level back to the equilibrium level, whereas, if price was above *P*, some goods and services would not be sold and suppliers would have to cut their prices.

An increase in aggregate demand resulting from, for example, an increase in government spending is likely to increase output and raise the price level, at least in the short run. This outcome is illustrated in Figure 5.10.

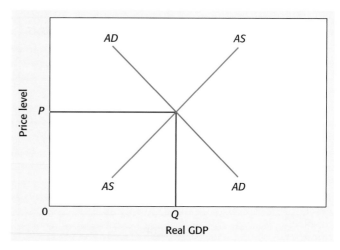

Figure 5.9 *The interaction of aggregate demand and aggregate supply*

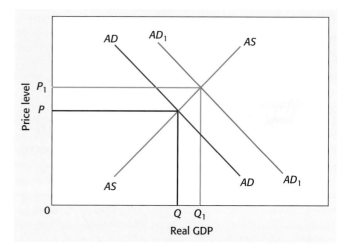

Figure 5.10 *The effect on output and the price level of an increase in aggregate demand*

SELF-ASSESSMENT TASK 5.5

Read the feature below and then answer the questions that follow.

In December 2000 Mexico was experiencing a shortage of skilled labour. This had begun to create bottlenecks to increased growth and pushed up wage rates. For example, in Chihuahua, a northern border state, a centre for assembly-for-exports plants, real wages had risen by 32% over the year. The government was seeking to raise productivity, in the short run, by introducing more flexible labour laws and, in the long run, by improving education and training.

1 Using a Keynesian LRAS curve, explain at what position on the curve the Mexican economy was seemingly operating in December 2000?

2 Illustrate, and explain, the effect of:
  a a rise in wage rates on the SRAS curve
  b improved education and training on the LRAS curve.

An increase in aggregate supply will also be likely to raise output and so lower the price level, as shown in Figure 5.11.

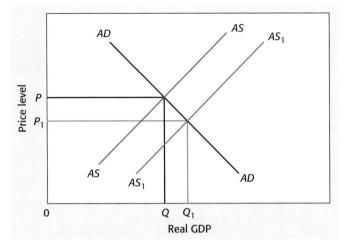

Figure 5.11   *The effect on output and the price level on an increase in aggregate supply*

SELF-ASSESSMENT TASK 5.6

Identify the effects of the following on aggregate demand, aggregate supply, output and the price level:

a   a reduction in the rate of interest
b   an increase in government spending on health care
c   advances in information technology
d   an increase in the quality of training
e   a cut in income tax
f   an increase in wealth.

SPECIMEN EXAM QUESTIONS

1 **a**   Explain the possible reasons for a change in size of a country's labour force. [8]
   b   Discuss the likely effects on the macroeconomy of a large increase in inward migration into a country. [12]

[20 marks]

SUMMARY

In this core section it has been shown that:

- The measurement of certain macroeconomic variables is important for economists to understand differences between various types of economy.
- The labour force is an important economic resource; variations in both its size and participation rate can be measured across different types of economies.
- The productivity of labour has an important bearing on the living standards in an economy.
- Unemployed labour is a resource which can be used to help an economy achieve its productive potential.
- The general price level in an economy can be measured by means of a weighted price index.
- Aggregate demand is total spending on goods and services produced in an economy at different price levels.
- The aggregate demand curve is downward sloping.
- Aggregate supply is total output in an economy at different price levels.
- The long run aggregate supply curve will shift to the right if the quality and/or quantity of resources increases.
- Equilibrium output and the price level are determined where the AD and AS curves intersect.

5 Theory and measurement in the macroeconomy
Supplement

On completion of this supplement section you should know:

- how national income statistics can be used as measures of growth and living standards
- the difference between money and real data and how the GDP deflator is used
- how economic growth rates can be used to compare living standards over time and between countries
- that there are other indicators of living standards and economic development
- the difference between broad and narrow measures of the money supply
- about the nature of a government's budget and deficit financing
- what is meant by the circular flow of income
- the key principles of Keynesians' and Monetarists' views on how the macroeconomy works
- what is meant by aggregate expenditure, its components and determinants
- how national income is determined
- how inflationary and deflationary gaps can be analysed
- the difference between the equilibrium level of income and the full employment level of income
- what is meant by the multiplier process
- the difference between autonomous and induced investment
- what is meant by the accelerator
- why and how the money supply can increase
- how commercial banks can create credit
- how to explain the relationship between the money supply, the price level and output
- what constitutes the demand for money
- the different theories of interest rate determination.

Introduction

In drawing up their policies, governments and their advisors rely on data about the current and forecasted performance of the economy. They also draw on a wide range of tried and tested concepts. Over time more aspects of the economy have come to be measured and professional economists have promoted changes in the schools of economic thought. In this section we will explore some of the key measures used by governments and consider differences between the Keynesian and Monetarist approaches.

National income statistics

Use of national income statistics

A government measures the total output of a country in order to assess the performance of the economy.

An economy is usually considered to be doing well if its output is growing at a high and sustainable rate. A government uses a variety of measures of the country's output. These are collectively known as **national income** statistics. This is because the total output of the country is equal to total income (and total expenditure).

The most widely used measure of national income is known as **Gross Domestic Product (GDP)**. Gross means total, domestic refers to the home economy and product means output. So, for example, Pakistan's GDP is a measure of the total output by the factors of production based in Pakistan. GDP is calculated by adding up consumers' spending, government spending on goods and services, total investment, changes in stocks and the difference between exports and imports.

From GDP, a number of other measures of national income can be found. GDP plus **net property income from abroad** gives **Gross National Product (GNP)**. Net property income from abroad is the income which the country's residents earn on their physical assets (such as factories and leisure parks) owned abroad and foreign financial assets (such as shares and bank loans) minus the returns on assets held in the country but owned by foreigners. So GNP gives a measure of the income of a country's residents.

GNP minus capital consumption gives **Net National Product (NNP)**. This is also referred to as national income. Capital consumption, depreciation or replacement investment covers investment undertaken to replace worn out and out-of-date capital. GDP minus capital consumption gives **Net Domestic Product (NDP)**. So gross measures include all investment whilst net measures only include investment which *adds* to the capital stock.

GDP is first measured at market prices, that is, the prices charged for goods and services in shops and other types of retail businesses. However, all the measures are recorded in terms of both market prices and factor cost. The latter is the value of output excluding indirect taxes and subsidies. So, to convert a measure from market prices to factor costs, indirect taxes are deducted and subsidies are added.

The ways of measuring GDP

There are three ways of calculating GDP. These are the output, income and expenditure methods. They should give the same total because they all measure the flow of income produced in an economy. So the value of output is equal to the incomes which it generates, that is wages, rent, profit and interest. If it is assumed that all incomes are spent, expenditure will, by definition, equal income.

The output measure

The output method measures the value of output produced by industries such as the manufacturing, construction, distributive, hotel and catering and agricultural industries or sectors.

In using this measure it is important to avoid counting the same output twice. For example, if the value of cars sold by manufacturers is added to the value of output of tyre firms, double counting will occur. Value added is the difference between the sales revenue received and the cost of raw materials used. It is equal to the payments made to the factors of production in return for producing the good or service, so that if a TV manufacturing firm buys components costing £60000 and uses them to make TVs which it sells for £130000, it has added £70000 to output. It is this £70000 which will be included in the measure of output.

The income measure

The value of output produced is based on the costs involved in producing that output. These costs include wages, rent, interest and profits. All these payments represent income paid to factors of production. For instance, workers receive wages and entrepreneurs receive profits. In using this measure it is important to include only payments received in return for providing a good or service. So transfer payments, which are transfers of income from taxpayers to groups of individuals for welfare payments, are not included.

The expenditure measure

What is produced in a year will either be sold or added to stocks. So, if additions to stocks are added to expenditure on goods and services, a measure is obtained which will equal output and income. In using this method it is necessary to add expenditure on exports and deduct expenditure on imports. This is because the sale of exports represents the country's output and creates income in the country,

SELF-ASSESSMENT TASK 5.7

Which of the following should be included in measuring GDP by the income method:

- government subsidies to farmers
- the pay of civil servants
- the pay of nurses
- supernormal profits
- state pensions?

whereas expenditure on imports is spending on goods and services made in foreign countries and creates income for people in those countries. It is also necessary to deduct indirect taxes and add subsidies in order to get a value which corresponds to the income generated in the production of the output.

Money and real GDP

Money (or nominal) GDP is GDP measured in terms of the prices operating in the year in which the output is produced. It is sometimes referred to as GDP at current prices and is a measure which has not been adjusted for inflation.

Money GDP may give a misleading impression of how well a country is performing. This is because the value of money GDP may rise not because more goods and services are being produced but merely because prices have risen. For example, if 100 million products are produced at an average price of $5, GDP will be $500 million. If in the next year the same output of 100 million products is produced but the average price rises to $6, money GDP will rise to $600 million. So to get a truer picture of what is happening to output, economists convert money into real GDP. They do this by measuring GDP at constant prices, that is at the prices operating in a selected base year. By doing this they remove the distorting effect of inflation. For example, in 2009 a country's GDP is $800 billion and the price index is 100. Then in 2010, money GDP rises to $864 billion and the price index is 105.

$$\text{real GDP} = \text{money GDP} \times \frac{\text{price index in base year}}{\text{price index in current year}}$$

So: $\$864\text{bn} \times \dfrac{100}{105} = \$822.86\text{bn}$

The price index used to convert money into real GDP is called the **GDP deflator**, which measures the prices of products produced rather than consumed in a country. So it includes the prices of capital as well as consumer products and includes the prices of exports but excludes the prices of imports.

SELF-ASSESSMENT TASK 5.8

In 2008 a country's GDP is $1000 billion. In 2009 nominal GDP rises to $1092 billion and the price index increases by 4%. Calculate:

a real GDP
b the percentage increase in real GDP.

Comparison of economic growth over time and between countries

Changes in real GDP are used to calculate economic growth rates. So, for example, if the real GDP of a country grows from $50 billion in 2008 to $52 billion, the annual economic growth rate for 2009 is 4%. Table 5.4 shows the average annual economic growth rates for a range of countries during the period 2000 to 2006.

	%		%
Argentina	4.7	Singapore	5.8
China	10.2	South Africa	4.3
France	1.7	Tanzania	2.5
Hong Kong	5.2	UAE	8.2
Indonesia	5.1	UK	2.6
Malawi	3.2	USA	2.7
Pakistan	5.8	Zambia	−5.7
Saudi Arabia	4.1	Zimbabwe	−4.4

Table 5.4 *Real GDP: average annual change 2000–2006*
Source: World Development Report, *2009*

In comparing economic growth rates over time and between countries, care has to be taken over a number of issues. One of these is that the official real GDP figures may understate the true change in output. This is because of the existence of, and changes in, what is called the hidden, informal or underground economy. These terms refer to undeclared economic activity. There are two main reasons why people may not declare their earned income to the authorities. One is that they are seeking to evade paying tax. For example, a plumber may receive payment for undertaking jobs in his spare time and not declare the income he receives to the tax authorities. So some of the services he produces will not be included in GDP. Another reason for not declaring economic activity is that the activity is itself illegal, for example smuggling goods.

Illegal market traders in West Africa

Some idea of the size of the hidden economy can be found by measuring any gap between GDP as measured by the expenditure and income methods. This is because people will be spending income they have not declared!

If the size of the hidden economy is relatively constant, the rate of economic growth may be calculated reasonably accurately. However, even a stable hidden economy can make international comparisons of economic growth rates difficult. This is because the size of the hidden economy varies between economies. It is influenced by the marginal rates of taxation, the penalties imposed for illegal activity and tax evasion, the risk of being caught and social attitudes towards, for example, different illegal activities. Table 5.5 shows some research findings into the scale of the underground economy in a number of diverse economies. Of the most developed economies, Greece had the highest percentage of unmeasured economic activity, 28%, and the USA the lowest, 8%. Higher levels were recorded in Central and Eastern European countries and in most developing economies.

Official GDP figures may also not provide an accurate measure of output and changes in output because of low levels of literacy, non-marketed goods and services and the difficulties of measuring government spending.

In countries with low levels of literacy, it will be difficult for government officials to gather information about all economic activity. Some people will be unable to fill out tax forms and others will fill them out inaccurately, so estimates will have to made for some output. This is a particular problem in Pakistan, which had an adult literacy rate of just 50%

Developed economies	%	CEE economies	%	Emerging economies	%	Developing economies	%
Austria	10.9	Azerbaijan	61.3	China	15.6	CAR	46.1
Belgium	21.0	Estonia	40.1	Vietnam	17.9	Dem Rep Congo	49.7
Greece	28.2	Georgia	68.0			Nigeria	59.4
Ireland	15.3	Hungary	26.2			Sierra Leone	43.9
Italy	25.7	Poland	28.9			Zimbabwe	63.2
Japan	10.8	Russia	48.7				
Switzerland	9.4	Ukraine	54.7				
UK	12.2						
USA	8.4						

Table 5.5 *Estimated underground economy (% official GDP), 2002–2003*

Source: Schneider, F. and Bajada, C. An International Comparison of Underground Activity, 2005

in 2005. The female literacy rate was much higher than that for males.

Estimates also have to be made for non-marketed goods and services. The GDP figures only include marketed goods and services, that is goods and services which are bought and sold and so have a price attached to them. Goods and services which are produced and which are either not traded or which are exchanged without money changing hands go unrecorded. For example, domestic services provided by home owners, painting and repairs undertaken by home owners and voluntary work are not included in the official figures. The proportion of goods and services which people produce for themselves and the amount of voluntary work undertaken vary over time and between countries.

It is also difficult to value the output of government goods and services which are not sold, such as defence. In the past in the UK the output was valued at cost, normally in terms of the value of inputs. This gave a somewhat distorted view of what was happening to output. For instance, if productivity increased in the fire service, fewer firefighters might have been needed. This would have reduced the cost of providing the fire service. Output as officially recorded would have fallen, although the level of service provided might have been unchanged or may even have increased. To overcome

this problem, the Office for National Statistics (ONS) in the UK developed a system for measuring government outputs of services other than through the value of inputs. This method covers education, health and social security – around 50% of the public sector – and uses a variety of key performance indicators (such as student numbers for education and claimant numbers for social security) in order to estimate output.

The nature of economic growth

In comparing economic growth rates it is also important to consider the nature of economic growth. A very high rate of economic growth may initially appear to be very impressive. However, this may not be sustainable in either the short run or long run.

For a few months a country's output may increase by a rate greater than the rise in the productive potential of the economy (trend growth) because, in response to high demand, machinery may be worked flat out and workers may be persuaded to work long hours of overtime. However, this cannot be sustained since a time will come when machines have to be repaired and when workers will want to reduce the number of hours' overtime they work.

High growth, achieved by depleting natural resources and creating pollution, will also not be sustainable in the long run. Increasing fish catches,

SELF-ASSESSMENT TASK 5.9

Read the feature below and then answer the questions that follow.

Nature is taking a hammering from the law breakers

Nature is taking a hammering from the law breakers. To damage the environment in the process of industrialising a country and making its people wealthy – as occurred in Europe, America and parts of Asia – is bad enough; to do so before achieving prosperity is even worse.

That is the risk faced by Ghana. With the economy still struggling to maintain consistent growth, Ghana's environment – and several industries

that could contribute to future economic success, including logging and tourism – are threatened by deforestation, desertification and pollution. 'We have serious environmental problems,' says Lee Ocran, deputy minister for environment, science and technology.

Ghana's forests, which once covered much of the south and centre of the country with mahogany and other valuable trees, will need a ruthlessly efficient protection programme if they are to survive for more than a decade.

Forest depletion in Ghana

At the turn of the twentieth century, Ghana had 8.2 million hectares of forest, falling to half that amount by 1950 – according to the ministry – 1.4 million hectares today, although environmentalists say the true figure is well under 1 million hectares.

It is estimated that the sustainable yield of the remaining forest is about 1 million cubic metres of timber a year, but farmers, illegal timber merchants and the big logging companies whose trucks can be seen on the roads to Takoradi port are thought to be extracting 2.3 million–3 million cubic metres annually. The installed capacity of the saw-milling industry is even higher.

Source: Victor Mallet, Financial Times, *29 November 2000*

1 Explain what is meant by sustainable economic growth.

2 What evidence is provided in the feature to suggest that Ghana's economic growth is not sustainable?

chopping down more areas of tropical rainforests and rapidly increasing manufacturing output may appear attractive ways of raising economic growth. However, such methods may reduce future generations' ability to achieve economic growth if fish stocks are exhausted, new trees are not planted or the environment is destroyed by pollution, which in turn reduces the fertility of the land and the health of the labour force.

Comparison of living standards over time

Real GDP per head figures have traditionally been used as one of the main indicators of living standards. If a country's real GDP per head is higher this year than last year, it is generally expected that the country's inhabitants will be enjoying higher living standards. This is indeed often the case but it is not always so.

Real GDP per head is found by dividing total real GDP by the country's population to give an average figure. However, real GDP is not evenly distributed. It is possible that, whilst real GDP per head rises, some people may not experience rises in income and some may even suffer reductions in their income. For instance, in the mid-1990s the Indian economy grew

at 7.5% a year but the proportion of Indians living in poverty dropped just 1% to 34%.

The change in real GDP figures may not reflect the true change in the quantity of goods and services that consumers can enjoy if the level of undeclared economic activity changes over time. A rise in the hidden economy may mean that people are experiencing a higher standard of living than first appears to be the case as described earlier.

To assess changes in living standards, changes in the type of products produced and the ways in which they are made must be considered. A rise in real GDP does not guarantee a rise in living standards. During a war, output may rise because more weapons are being produced but not many people will say that the quality of their lives is improving. The recruitment of more police to cope with more crime will again increase real GDP but will be unlikely to cause people to feel better off.

The type of products which raise people's living standards are better consumer goods and services, such as housing, food, clothing and transport. A shift of resources from consumer products to capital goods will enable more consumer products to be produced and enjoyed but only in the future. However, in the short run if the economy is operating at the frontier of its production possibility curve, such a move will cause people to enjoy fewer consumer products (see Chapter 1).

Even if people are able to enjoy more consumer goods and services it does not necessarily mean that they will be happier. As access to more and higher-quality products rises, the desire for even more and better products may increase at an even faster rate. For example, people who do not have a car are happy when they buy their first car but often within a short space of time they want a better model. This has particular implications for people in China and India where incomes and car ownership are increasing rapidly.

Real GDP measures the quantity of output produced but not the quality. Output could rise but if the quality of what is produced declines, the quality of people's lives is likely to fall. In practice, though, the quality of output tends to rise over time.

Working conditions also tend to improve over time and working hours usually fall. If real GDP per head stays constant from one year to the next but working conditions rise and/or working hours fall, people's living standards will rise.

However, whilst workers tend to enjoy improved conditions over time, the quality of the environment in some countries declines as a result of pollution and, for example, deforestation. A decline in environmental conditions will lower living standards but not real GDP. Indeed, if more resources have to be devoted to cleaning up the environment, real GDP will increase whilst living standards decline.

Figures 5.12 and 5.13 show a comparison of the quality of life in a number of the world's cities. It is based on an annual survey by William M. Mercer which ranks cities on the basis of 39 criteria that constitute the quality of life, ranging from recreational and transport facilities to crime and education. New York, which ranked 49th, is used as the base for this survey and is given an index of 100.

European cities dominate the top positions. Within Asia, Singapore has the top ranking and is 32nd in terms of the survey's criteria. Elsewhere, Kuala Lumpur is 75th. Pakistani cities score badly in terms of personal safety factors which are seen by the report's compilers as being very important when businesses are seeking to attract top managers. Within Africa, Cape Town and Port Louis (Mauritius) are the cities with the best quality of living; Lagos, Port Harcourt and Bangui are regarded as having the

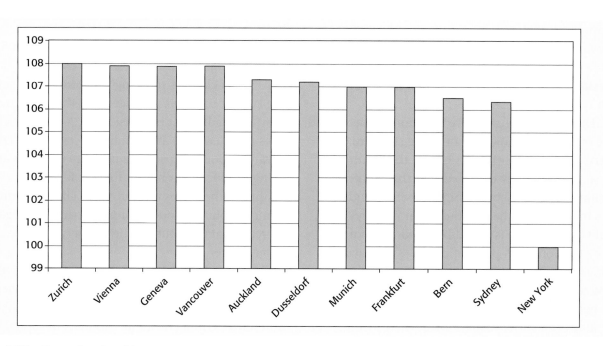

Figure 5.12 *Top performing cities*

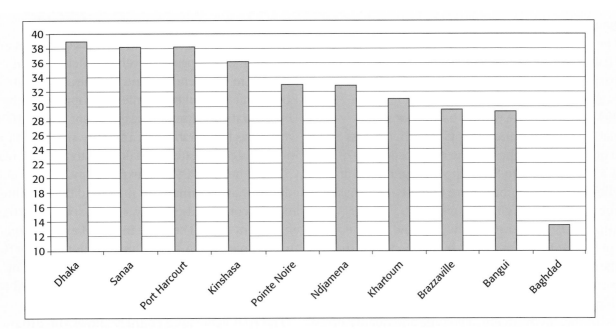

Figure 5.13 *Worst performing cities*

poorest quality of life. Results from surveys such as this do though need to be interpreted with caution. For example, a European living in Kuala Lumpur (KL) may well have a better quality of life than a person living in London which has a ranking of 38th. For the same rent, an apartment in a good part of KL is likely to be much bigger, with access to a pool and other facilities. In addition, the cost of living in KL is much lower than in London.

Comparison of living standards between countries

The citizens of a country with a higher real GDP per head are likely to enjoy higher living standards than people living in a country with a lower real GDP per head, but this is not necessarily the case.

Real GDP figures may give a misleading impression of a country's output because of the same problems of measurement as stated earlier in comparing living standards over time.

To compare living standards between countries we need to convert the real GDP per capita into a common currency. To avoid the comparison being distorted by exchange rate changes, economists usually adjust exchange rates to take into account their purchasing power parities. For example,

suppose the exchange rate is 6 Malaysian ringgits equals US $1 and the USA has a real GDP per head of $25 000 whilst Malaysia has a real GDP per head of 6000 ringgits. From this information it might appear that, when Malaysia's real GDP per head is converted into dollars ($1000), people in the USA are, on average, 25 times better off than people in Malaysia. However, if $1 can buy more goods and services in the USA than in Malaysia, then using the exchange rate to convert ringgits into dollars will exaggerate Malaysia's output. In terms of ability to buy products (purchasing parities), 12 ringgits may be worth $1. Using this as the basis for converting Malaysia's output into dollars would show that people in the USA are 50 times better off than people in Malaysia.

Even if a country is found to have a higher real GDP per head than another country using purchasing power parities, it does not necessarily mean that its inhabitants will enjoy higher living standards. For example, Kuwait has a very high real GDP per head but some immigrant workers in the country receive relatively low wages. Where income is very unevenly distributed, only a small number of households may benefit from a high average income.

When assessing living standards consideration must be given to factors that are not measured in real GDP per head, just as we do when making comparisons over time. One difference is in working hours. A study by UBS, a Swiss bank, published in 2009 found that the world's hardest working population lived in Cairo, Egypt. Measured across a range of professions, the average worker spent 2373 hours a year at work; in Seoul, it was slightly less at 2312 hours. Working hours were highest across Asia and the Middle East, typically over 2000 per year. Working hours were lower in the USA and Europe with people in Paris, for instance, only working an average of 1594 hours. Other factors which are not measured in real GDP per head include working conditions, political freedoms, fear of crime and the quality of the environment. The type and quality of products produced also has to be taken into account.

Other indicators of living standards and economic development

In assessing living standards, economists can use a wide range of indicators, e.g. the number of TVs per household, infant mortality rates and energy use per capita. What they normally do is to use composite indicators which include a number of indicators of living standards. For example, in 1972 two American economists William Nordhaus and James Tobin developed a new measure of economic welfare. They called this Net Economic Welfare (NEW), although it is now sometimes also referred to as Measurable Economic Welfare (MEW). This measure seeks to give a fuller picture of living standards by adjusting GDP figures to take into account other factors which have an impact on the quality of people's lives. Factors which improve living standards such as increased leisure hours are added to the GDP figure, whilst factors which reduce living standards, including rising crime and pollution levels, are deducted. Of course, in practice, it is difficult and expensive to measure the value of non-marketed economic 'goods' and 'bads'.

Economic development involves a wider meaning of living standards as it encompasses an improvement in people's welfare, including an increase in their choices and abilities. The best-known measure of economic development is the United Nations Human Development Index (HDI) which has been published annually since 1990. The index is a composite one, taking into account real GDP per head (PPP$), life expectancy at birth and educational attainment as measured by adult literacy and the combined primary, secondary and tertiary enrolment ratio. These are included as it is thought that people's welfare is influenced not only by the goods and services available to them but also by their ability to lead a long and healthy life and to acquire knowledge.

The HDI value for a country shows the distance a country has to make up to reach the maximum value of 1. Table 5.7 (see Self-assessment task 5.11 on page 201) shows the HDI indexes and the data from which these have been computed for a range of countries in 2007. A country's ranking by HDI does not always match its ranking in terms of real GDP per capita as is the case with Ireland and the USA. Indeed, in some cases there are marked differences.

A more recent composite measure from the UN has been the Human Poverty Index, HPI-1. This measures longevity (probability at birth of not surviving to 40), adult literacy and deprivation in terms of the percentage of people not using improved water sources and the percentage of children under 5 who are underweight. As expected the lowest ranked HPI-1 countries are in Africa. Some of the highest ranking countries are the former socialist republics of Central and Eastern Europe. A third measure is HPI-2. Figure 5.16 summarises the data from which each is compiled.

The money supply

The **money supply** is the total amount of money in an economy. This consists of currency in circulation plus relevant deposits. Governments measure the money supply to gain information about trends in aggregate demand, the state of financial markets

Read the feature below and then answer the questions that follow.

'Big Mac' economics

The Economist's Big Mac Index offers a light-hearted, but relevant guide to whether currencies are at their correct levels, based on 'purchasing power parity'.

This states that exchange rates should adjust to equalise the price of a basket of goods and services across all countries; the Big Mac PPP is the exchange rate at which a Big Mac, a standardised product, would cost the same in America as in other countries. In 2008, a Big Mac cost $3.54 in the US. So if the price of a Big Mac in dollars is above $3.54, a currency is dear or over-valued; if the price is below $3.54, then the currency is cheap, or undervalued, relative to the dollar. So as shown in Figure 5.14, the Swiss franc and the Norwegian krone are seriously over-valued against the US dollar. In contrast, the South African rand and Chinese yuan are under-valued.

The Big Mac concept can also be used to show variations in the purchasing power of international wage rates (Figure 5.15). Here, compared to the UK, the data shows a worker in Nairobi has to work around 12 times longer than one in London to earn the local price of a Big Mac lunch.

Figure 5.14   *Big Mac index*

Figure 5.15   *Time taken to earn a Big Mac*

Source: The Economist, *22 January 2009 (adapted)*

1   Explain what is meant by purchasing power parity.
2   Explain what effect using an under-valued exchange rate for the Polish zloty would have when comparing the GDP of Poland with that of the USA.
3   Explain how information on the purchasing power parity of wage rates can be used to draw conclusions about the cost of living in different countries.

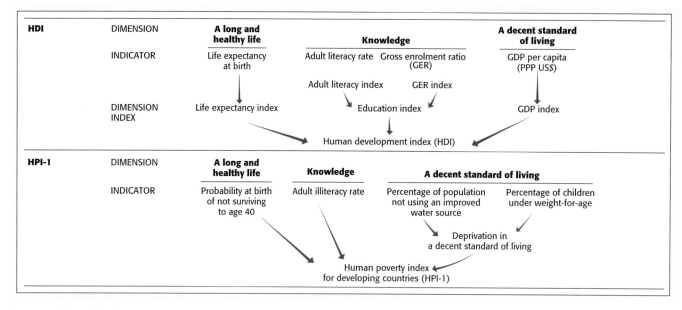

Figure 5.16 *Calculating the HDI and HPI-1*

and to help them in determining the direction of monetary policy.

Measuring the money supply is not as easy as it might appear from the above definition. This is because it is difficult to decide what to include in any measure of money – it is further complicated because governments in different economies use different measures of their money supply.

Economists define items as money if they fulfil the functions of money described earlier in Chapter 1. However, the extent to which items carry out these functions varies and can change over time. As a result governments use a variety of measures of the money supply which are occasionally altered to reflect developments in the roles carried out by particular items.

There are two main measures of money supply:

- **Narrow money** is money which is used as a medium of exchange and consists of notes and coins in circulation and cash held in banks and in balances held by banks at the central bank. This is sometimes referred to as the monetary base.
- **Broad money** consists of the above plus a range of items that are commensurate with money's function as a store of value.

Within the Caribbean, for example, the control of the money supply lies with the various central banks such as the Central Bank of Barbados and the Bank of Jamaica. The standard measures of money supply used are shown in Table 5.6.

Measure	Definition
M0	Currency in the hands of the public plus reserves held on behalf of commercial banks.
M1	Notes and coins outside the banking system plus current account balances.
M2	M1 plus short-term time and savings deposits, foreign currency transferable deposits, certificates of deposit and repurchase agreements.
M3	M2 plus travellers cheques, short-term bank notes, long-term foreign currency time deposits and money market mutual funds.
M4	M3 plus treasury bills, negotiable bonds and pension funds

Table 5.6 *Standard measures of the money supply*

SELF-ASSESSMENT TASK 5.11

1 Use Figure 5.16 to compare the difference between HDI and HPI-1.

2 Table 5.7 shows that Russia has a higher GDP per head than Malaysia, but a lower HDI value. How might this be explained?

3 Make a few notes on how the information produced by the HDI and HPI-1 might be used by UN policy makers.

Rank	Country	Life expectancy at birth	Adult literacy rate	Combined primary, secondary, tertiary enrolment	GDP per head, PPPUS$	HDI value
	Very high					
1	Norway	80.5	99.0	98.6	53 433	0.971
5	Ireland	79.7	99.0	97.6	44 613	0.965
13	USA	79.1	99.0	92.4	45 592	0.956
23	Singapore	80.2	94.4	n.a.	49 704	0.944
	High					
43	Hungary	73.3	98.9	90.2	18 755	0.879
66	Malaysia	74.1	91.9	71.5	13 518	0.829
71	Russia	66.2	99.5	81.9	14 690	0.817
81	Mauritius	72.1	87.4	76.9	11 296	0.804
	Medium					
92	China	72.9	93.3	68.7	5 383	0.772
95	Maldives	71.1	97.0	71.3	5 196	0.771
102	Sri Lanka	74.0	90.8	68.7	4 243	0.759
141	Pakistan	66.2	54.2	39.3	2 496	0.522
	Low					
176	DR Congo	47.6	67.2	48.2	298	0.389
179	CAR	46.7	48.6	28.6	713	0.369
180	S. Leone	47.3	38.1	44.6	679	0.365
182	Niger	50.8	28.7	27.2	627	0.340

Table 5.7   *Human Development Index, 2007*

Source: Human Development Report, UNDP, *2009*

Table 5.8 shows the money supply for Barbados at the end of December 2005. The control of M1 and M2 is particularly important.

Notes in circulation		532 824
Coins in circulation		43 038
Less: Treasury and Bank Cash	127 296	
Total currency with public (M1)		448 566
Demand deposits		2 738 895
Total money supply (M2)		3 187 461

Table 5.8 *Money supply in Barbados (BDS$000)*

Source: Central Bank of Barbados

Because of an increasing quarterly inflation rate, M1 has consistently increased on a month-by-month basis. More specifically, in July and December especially, increased seasonal demand forced the Bank to increase the total value of notes in circulation. The change in M2 has been less consistent, with falls recorded in five months of 2005 as the Bank sought to control the amount of lending by commercial banks in order to reduce the rate of inflation.

The budget and deficit financing

Managing the economy is a complex task. The annual **budget** is eagerly awaited and attracts much media attention as the overall outcome is a very clear indicator of the state of the economy. In the budget statement, the Finance Minister, or Chancellor of the Exchequer as the person is known in the UK, outlines the government's spending and taxation plans for the year ahead. The direction taken in the budget should give a clear indication of the government's macroeconomic priorities.

In principle, there are three types of budget:

- **Budget deficit** In this situation, projected government spending exceeds projected revenue from the many forms of taxation. This is where the government sees the need to reflate the economy by increasing aggregate demand. Normally this is in response to a situation where there is a need to expand the economy in order to create more jobs and income to get the economy moving out of recession.

- **Budget surplus** In contrast, this describes a budget where government revenue from taxation exceeds the government's projected expenditure on social protection, health care, education, transport and so on. Here the government has identified a need to deflate the economy by cutting back aggregate demand. This is normally in response to a situation where the rate of inflation in the economy is higher than the government feels to be appropriate. It could also be in response to a deteriorating deficit on the balance of trade.

- **Balanced budget** As its name suggests, this is a neutral situation where projected revenue and government spending are equal. Within the budget though there is likely to be some re-allocation of taxation and expenditure.

Within the budget, governments may use **discretionary fiscal policies** to make changes to government spending and taxation. These policies are discretionary in the sense that it is the government's decision as to whether the changes should be made. As will be explained later, the government can boost demand by cutting taxes or increasing its own expenditure.

In contrast, **automatic stabilisers** are incorporated into the budget. These stabilisers are the revenue received from certain types of taxes and the expenditure on certain forms of government spending. Both change automatically with fluctuations in real GDP. For example, if real GDP increases, the government will automatically receive increased tax revenue from income tax and indirect taxes due to the rise in incomes. It is also likely to experience a fall in spending due to an increase in the number of people in employment. Alternatively, a fall in real GDP will result in less tax revenue for the government and the need for additional expenditure to support those who have been thrown out of work.

If the government is using a deficit budget to promote an expansion in real GDP, this is likely to mean that more borrowing has to take place. In turn, the **national debt** will increase unless the deficit can be funded from accumulated surpluses from previous years. For many economies this is highly unlikely. With the increase in real GDP, an expansionary budget should lead to a rise in real incomes and hence, tax revenue. This will in part offset some of the projected borrowing requirement.

Where economies have experienced strong economic growth, tax revenue has invariably grown and resulted in governments being able to repay debt. In the UK, for example, the so-called 'Golden Rule' has been applied since 1999. In simple terms, this works on the principle that over the medium term the government should only borrow to invest, not to fund current spending. So, debt accumulation in the long run will be accompanied by higher output and tax revenue without needing a change in tax rates. The challenge that is facing the UK government is to stick to this principle. This seems virtually impossible

SELF-ASSESSMENT TASK 5.12

Read the feature below and then answer the questions that follow.

China's budget deficit to jump nine-fold in 2009

China's budget deficit is expected to reach 950 billion yuan this year, nine times higher than that of last year. The additional deficit included the anticipated issuance of 200-billion-yuan worth of bonds for supporting local government projects. The draft budget deficit would be deliberated during the country's top legislative conference scheduled for early March.

Meanwhile, the National People's Congress Financial and Economic Affairs Committee had already held in-depth discussions on expanding fiscal spending and upping state debt. Opinions were divided, the Economic Observer (EO) learned.

A source close to the matter told the EO that, during the discussions, some committee members claimed that a massive deficit was necessary in order to maintain 8% economic growth and safeguard employment.

Others pointed out that the deficit's proportion of China's gross domestic product (GDP) was expected to be under 3% – the internationally accepted level, according to the source. However, another camp argued that the massive deficit would likely incur more risks, especially if the

local governments failed to pay off the bond's principal interests and issuance costs on time, said the source.

Over the past two years, China has kept its fiscal deficit under 1% of its GDP – 0.8% and 0.4% for 2007 and 2008 respectively. The EO learned that such massive deficits were far beyond market expectations.

Last December, Chinese officials had projected a budget deficit of 500 billion yuan for 2009, but the figure was upped to 650 billion yuan a month later. Then again in late January, the Chinese central government announced a plan to issue 200-billion-yuan in bonds on behalf of the local governments to support local-level public investment. The move would skirt existing laws that prohibited local governments from running a budget deficit, thus also barring local authorities from raising funds through issuing bonds.

As of the latest information the EO obtained, the Ministry of Finance has put forward a deficit budget of 950 billion yuan.

The multiple reviews of budget deficits in such a short span of time puzzled Lin Shangxi, Vice

Director of the Research Institute of Fiscal Science which is part of the Ministry of Finance. Liu said given the widening gap between this year's fiscal revenues and expenditures, such frequent reviews could add more pressure for imbalance.

In January, State fiscal revenues had seen a decline of 126.5 billion yuan, or 17.1% down from a year earlier. Meanwhile, China's state spending had increased – it invested some 700 million yuan in battling the recent drought that struck 15 northern provinces, and it also spent some 300 billion yuan on its ongoing medical care reform this year.

Source: Xi Si, Economic Observer (EO) News, *23 February 2009*

The 'Birds Nest' Stadium is an example of a public investment project in China

1 Explain why China has found it necessary to increase its budget deficit in 2009.

2 What are the consequences of successive budget deficits for an economy?

due to the vast sums it has borrowed to avoid the collapse of some of the country's banks. Increased taxes are inevitable.

The circular flow of income

When governments spend more than they raise in taxation, they add to the **circular flow of income**. This process is shown in Figure 5.17 for a **closed economy**. The inner circle shows the real flow of products and factor services and the outer circle the money flow of spending and incomes. This figure is a simplified diagram; it assumes that all income is spent and that households and firms are the only sectors involved in economic activity. In practice, there are **leakages** – some income is saved, some is taxed and some is spent on imports. Some expenditure is also additional to the spending which comes from the incomes generated by domestic output. These extra items of spending are investment, government spending and spending by foreigners on a country's exports. A diagram can be drawn showing how some income and some expenditure 'leaks' out of

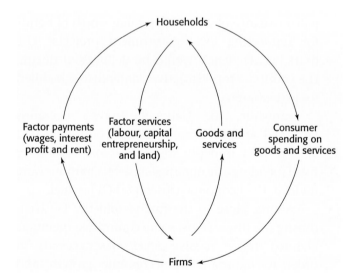

Figure 5.17 *The circular flow of income in a closed economy*

the circular flow in the form of saving, taxation and imports whilst other spending is 'injected' into the circular flow in the form of investment, government spending and exports. The circular flow of income for an **open economy** is shown in Figure 5.18.

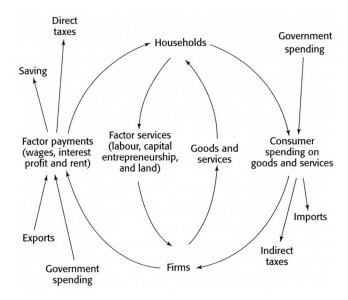

Figure 5.18 *The circular flow of income in an open economy*

Keynesians and monetarists

Keynesians are economists whose ideas and approach are based on the work of the British economist John Maynard Keynes (1883–1946). They believe that if left to market forces there is no guarantee that the economy will achieve a full employment level of GDP. Indeed, they think that the level of GDP can deviate from the full employment level by a large amount and for long periods. In such cases they favour government intervention to influence the level of economic activity. If there is high unemployment they argue that the government should use a deficit budget to raise the level of spending in the economy. They believe that a government can assess the appropriate amount of extra spending to inject into the economy in such a situation. For most Keynesians, the avoidance of unemployment is a key priority.

In contrast, for **monetarists**, the control of inflation is seen as the top priority for a government. This group of economists, the best-known of whom is the American economist Milton Friedman (1912–2006), argue that inflation is the result of an excessive growth of the money supply, so they believe that the main role of a government is to control the money supply. They also maintain that attempts to reduce unemployment by increasing government spending will only succeed in raising inflation in the long run. They think that the economy is inherently stable unless disturbed by erratic changes in the growth of the money supply.

One of the interesting consequences of the global recession from 2008 has been an upsurge of application by governments of Keynsian principles. In the US and UK, for example, massive government borrowing has been necessary in order to avoid the collapse of some financial institutions. This has meant that government debt has had to increase, leaving a legacy that will take many years to pay off.

John M. Keynes

Milton Friedman

Aggregate expenditure

Aggregate expenditure is the total amount which will be spent at different levels of income in a given time period. It is made up of consumption (C), investment (I), government spending (G) and net exports, that is exports minus imports $(X - M)$.

Consumption

Consumption or consumer spending is spending by households on goods and services to satisfy current wants, for example, spending on food, clothes, travel and entertainment. The main influence on consumption is the level of disposable income (income minus direct taxes plus state benefits). When income rises, total spending also usually rises. Rich people spend more than the poor.

However, whilst total spending rises with income, the proportion of disposable income which is spent tends to fall. Economists refer to this proportion as the **average propensity to consume** (apc).

$$\text{apc} = \frac{\text{consumption}}{\text{income}} = \frac{C}{Y}$$

When a person, or country, is poor most if not all disposable income has to be spent to meet current needs. Indeed, consumption may exceed income with people or countries drawing on past savings or borrowing. This situation can be referred to as **dissaving**. However, when income rises some of it can be saved. **Saving** is defined as disposable income minus consumption. The **average propensity to save** (aps) is the proportion of disposable income which is saved and is equivalent to 1 minus apc. As saving rises, the actual amount saved and aps tend to increase. The rich tend to have a lower apc and a higher aps than the poor.

The rich also have a lower **marginal propensity to consume** (mpc) and a higher **marginal propensity to save** (mps) than the poor. The mpc is the proportion of extra income which is spent:

$$\text{mpc} = \frac{\text{change in consumption}}{\text{change in income}} = \frac{\Delta C}{\Delta Y}$$

1 – mpc gives mps which can also be calculated by:

$$\frac{\text{change in saving}}{\text{change in income}} = \frac{\Delta S}{\Delta Y}$$

The relationships between consumption and income and saving and income can also be investigated by using the consumption and saving functions. The consumption function indicates how much will be spent at different levels of income. It is given by the equation: $C = a + bY$, where C is consumption, a is autonomous consumption (that is, the amount spent even when income is 0 and which does not vary with income), b is the marginal propensity to consume and Y is disposable income. bY can also be defined as income-induced consumption, because it is spending which is dependent on income. For example, if $C = \$100 + 0.8Y$ and income is \$1000, the amount spent will be $\$100 + 0.8 \times \$1000 = \$900$.

The saving function is, in effect, the reverse of the consumption function and is given by the equation: $S = -a + sY$, where S is saving, s is the marginal propensity to save, Y is income and a is autonomous dissaving (i.e. how much of their savings people will draw on when their income is 0; this amount does not change as income changes). The figure sY is induced saving, that is saving which is determined by the level of income. The saving function can be used to work out how much and what proportion households will save at different income levels. For example, if $S = -\$200 + 0.2Y$ and income is \$4000, then:

$$S = -\$200 + 0.2 \times \$4000 = \$600.$$

The average propensity to save will be \$600/\$4000 = 0.15. This will also mean that apc is $1 - 0.15 = 0.85$.

A number of factors, other than income, influence consumption. These include the distribution of income, the rate of interest, the availability of credit, expectations and wealth. If income becomes more evenly distributed because of, for example, an increase in direct tax rates and state benefits, consumption is likely to rise. This is because the rich have a lower mpc than the poor. When rich people lose income they are unlikely to cut back on their spending significantly, whilst the poor who gain more income will spend most of the extra.

Households will also usually spend more when interest rates are low. This is because the return from saving will be reduced, buying goods on credit will be cheaper and households who have borrowed before to buy a house, for example, will have more money to spend. If it becomes easier to obtain loans it is likely that total spending will increase. However, people are unlikely to borrow and to increase their spending if they are pessimistic about the future. Indeed, expectations about future economic prospects are thought to be a significant influence on consumption. When people become more optimistic that their future jobs are secure and that their incomes will rise, they are likely to increase their spending. An increase in wealth, which may result, for example, from a rise in the value of houses or the price of shares, will also probably increase consumption.

Investment

Investment is spending by firms on capital goods, such as factories, offices, machinery and delivery vehicles. The amount of investment undertaken is influenced by changes in consumer demand, the rate of interest, changes in technology, the cost of capital goods, expectations and government policy.

If consumer demand rises, firms are likely to want to buy more capital equipment to expand their capacity. Similarly, a fall in the rate of interest is likely to stimulate a rise in investment. This is for two key reasons. One is that the cost of investment will fall. Firms which borrow to buy capital goods will find it cheaper and firms which use retained profits will find that the opportunity cost of investment will fall. The second reason is that a lower interest rate is likely to raise consumer demand.

Advances in technology will raise the productivity of capital goods and so will probably stimulate more investment. Similarly, a fall in the price of capital equipment and/or cost of installation of capital goods is likely to raise investment.

As with consumption, expectations can play a key role in determining investment. When firms are optimistic that economic conditions are improving and demand for their products will rise, they will be encouraged to raise their investment. Governments can also seek to increase private sector investment by cutting corporation tax (the tax on company profits) and by providing investment subsidies.

Government spending

This covers spending on items such as the wages of teachers in state schools, medicines used in state hospitals and government investment in new roads and new hospitals. The amount of government spending which is undertaken in any period is influenced by government policy, tax revenue and other factors, including demographic changes. If a government wants to raise economic activity it may decide to raise its spending. Higher government tax revenues will enable a government to spend more, without resorting to borrowing. Pressure for a rise in government spending may come from an increase in the number of children (education) and/or an increase in the number of elderly people (health care and state pensions).

Net exports

The level of net exports is influenced by the country's GDP, other countries' GDP, the relative price and quality competitiveness of the country's products and its exchange rate. When a country's GDP rises, demand for imports usually increases. Whereas when incomes rise abroad, demand for the country's exports is likely to increase. A rise in exports may also result from an improvement in the competitiveness of the country's products, due for example to a rise in productivity or improved marketing.

The level of the exchange rate can be a key influence on net exports. If the exchange rate falls in value, the country's exports will become cheaper and imports will become more expensive. If demand for exports and imports is elastic, export revenue will rise whilst import expenditure will fall, causing net exports to fall (see Chapter 7 Core).

SELF-ASSESSMENT TASK 5.13

Read the feature below and then answer the questions that follow.

The Merlion fights back – Singapore's recent economic growth

Singapore is a particularly good example of a successful open economy. The basis of its progress since the split with Malaysia over 50 years ago is sometimes referred to as the Singapore Model. Lacking natural resources and heavily dependent on immigrant workers, Singapore's growth has been due largely to the performance of its electronics, chemicals, port and financial business services industries.

Up to 1999, real growth typically averaged 8% per year. In 2000 it was 9.9%. However, economic downturn in the US, EU and Japan saw a slump in the global demand for electronics products. In 2001, for the first time ever, real growth was negative at minus 2%. Recovery was slow, not helped by the SARS outbreak in 2003. By 2005, there was a return to normality when real growth was 6.4% and in 2006 it increased to 7.9%. Once again growth was export-led, from manufactured goods and financial business services. With global recession, it is though inevitable that this high growth performance will once again be affected by events that are outside of the control of the Singapore government.

Singapore's financial district

1 How and why is Singapore an open economy?
2 Explain how Singapore's real growth rate is susceptible to external events in the global economy.

3 Discuss two factors which could increase another component of Singapore's aggregate expenditure.

Income determination

The level of income in an economy is determined where aggregate expenditure is equal to output. If aggregate expenditure exceeds current output, firms will seek to produce more. They will employ more factors of production and so will cause GDP to rise. Whereas if aggregate expenditure is below current output, firms will reduce production. So output will

change until it matches aggregate expenditure, as shown in Figure 5.19.

This diagram is often referred to as a Keynesian 45° diagram. It measures money GDP on the horizontal axis and aggregate expenditure on the vertical axis. The 45° line shows the points at which aggregate expenditure equals national income (GDP). Output is determined where the $C + I + G + (X - M)$ line cuts this 45° line.

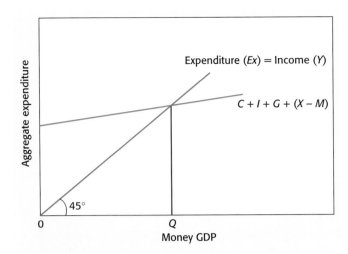

Figure 5.19 *The Keynsian 45° diagram*

If, for example, consumption and investment increase because consumers and entrepreneurs become more optimistic about the future, aggregate expenditure will rise and output will increase from Q to Q_1. Figure 5.20 shows this increase in GDP.

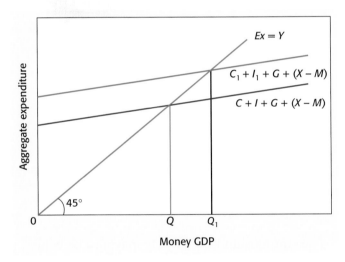

Figure 5.20 *Impact of a rise in aggregate expenditure*

Withdrawals and injections

For income to be in equilibrium it is also necessary for **injections** of extra spending into the circular flow of income to equal **withdrawals** (also called leakages) from the circular flow. As noted earlier, possible injections into the circular flow are investment, government spending and exports, whilst the possible withdrawals are saving, taxation and imports. Figure 5.21 shows equilibrium income in a two-sector economy (households and firms).

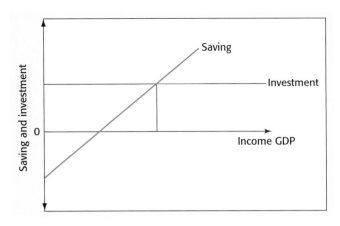

Figure 5.21 *Equilibrium income in a simple economy*

A rise in investment would in turn cause a rise in GDP. This is shown in Figure 5.22.

A fall in saving would have a similar effect. Figure 5.23 shows equilibrium income where $I + G + X = S + T + M$ in a four-sector economy (households, firms, the government and the foreign trade sector).

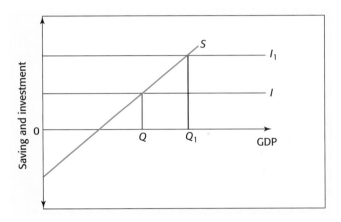

Figure 5.22 *A rise in investment in a simple economy*

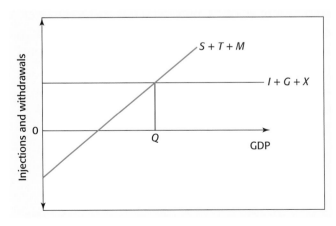

Figure 5.23 *Equilibrium income in an open economy*

209

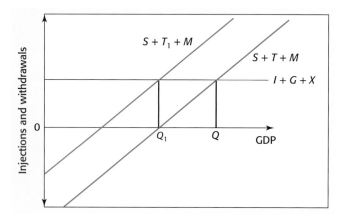

Figure 5.24 *Impact of a rise in taxation on equilibrium income*

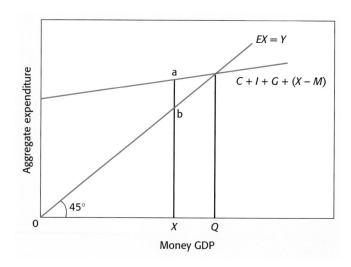

Figure 5.25 *An inflationary gap*

If, for example, tax rates should rise without any change in government spending, GDP will fall, as shown in Figure 5.24.

A rise in saving will also cause GDP to fall. Indeed, a decision by households to save more can result in them saving less. This is because higher saving can reduce income and hence the ability of households to save. This is referred to as the **paradox of thrift**.

Inflationary and deflationary gaps

In the short run, and Keynesians argue also possibly in the long run, an economy may not achieve full employment. An inflationary gap will occur if aggregate expenditure exceeds the potential output of the economy. In such a situation not all demand can be met, as there are not enough resources to do so. As a result the excess demand drives up the price level. Figure 5.25 shows that the economy is in equilibrium at a GDP of Q, which is above the level of output, X, that could be achieved with the full employment of resources. The distance ab represents the inflationary gap.

A government may seek to reduce an inflationary gap by cutting its own spending and/or by raising taxation in order to cut consumption.

Figure 5.26 shows a reduction in government spending moving the economy back to the full employment level.

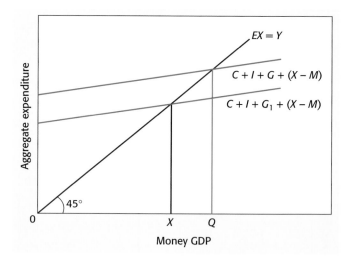

Figure 5.26 *Impact of a cut in government spending*

The equilibrium level of GDP may also be below the full employment level. In this case there is said to be a **deflationary gap**. Figure 5.27 shows that the lack of aggregate expenditure results in an equilibrium level at a GDP of Q, below the full employment level of X. There is a deflationary gap of vw.

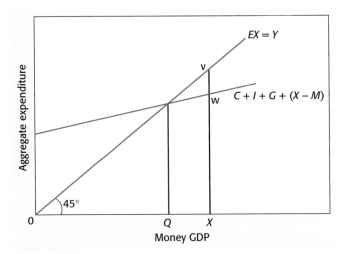

Figure 5.27   *A deflationary gap*

The Keynesian solution to a deflationary gap is increased government spending financed by borrowing. Figure 5.28 shows an increase in government spending eliminating the deflationary gap. As explained earlier, this in theory is the approach that many governments have implemented to get out of recession.

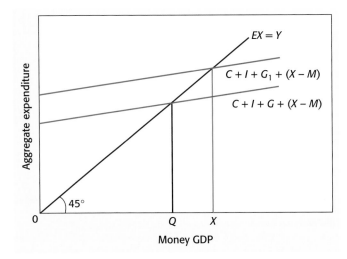

Figure 5.28   *Impact of an increase in government spending*

The multiplier

Figures 5.27 and 5.28 show that a change in government spending results in a change in GDP of greater magnitude. This tendency for a change in aggregate expenditure to result in a greater rise in GDP is known as the **multiplier** effect. This effect occurs because a rise in expenditure will create

incomes, some of which will, in turn, be spent and thereby create more incomes. For example, if people spend 80% of any extra income, an increase of government spending of $200 million will cause a final rise in GDP of $1000 million. This is because the initial $200 million spent will create higher incomes. People will spend $160 million of these incomes thereby generating a further rise in incomes. Of the $160 million, $128 million will be spent. This process will continue until incomes increase to $1000 million and the change in injections is matched by a change in withdrawals.

In the example above, GDP rises until the $200 million of extra government spending is matched by an extra $200 million of saving. The value of the multiplier is calculated by using the formula:

$$\frac{\text{change in income}}{\text{change in injection}} = \frac{\Delta Y}{\Delta J}$$

In the example above, the multiplier is:

$$\frac{\$1000\,\text{million}}{\$200\,\text{million}} = 5$$

The multiplier can also be estimated in advance of the change by using the formula:

$$\frac{1}{\text{marginal propensity to withdraw}}$$

The multiplier and equilibrium income in two-, three- and four-sector economic models

As we saw with the circular flow, economists often seek to explain their analysis first in a simplified form and then go on to include more variables. This is also the case with the multiplier where economists start with a simple model of the economy which only includes two sectors and then move on to a model which includes three sectors and then finally one which includes all four sectors.

Two-sector economy

In a two-sector economy (households and firms) there is only one withdrawal, one saving and one injection investment. In such an economy the multiplier can be found by using the formula:

$$\frac{1}{\text{mps}}$$

where mps is the marginal propensity to save. Because in this model income is either spent or saved, it can also be calculated by using the formula:

$$\frac{1}{1 - \text{mpc}}$$

Equilibrium income will occur where aggregate expenditure equals output, which in this case is where $C + I = Y$ and injections equal withdrawals, $I = S$.

A two-sector economy is sometimes referred to as a closed economy (that is one which does not engage in international trade) without a government sector.

Three-sector economy

The additional sector is the government sector. The model is still based on a closed economy but there is now an additional sector, the government, and so an extra injection, G, and an extra withdrawal, T (taxation). The multiplier is now:

$$\frac{1}{\text{mps} + \text{mrt}}$$

where mrt is the marginal rate of taxation (the proportion of extra income which is taxed). Equilibrium income is achieved where aggregate expenditure equals output, $C + I + G = Y$, and injections equal withdrawals, $I + G = S + T$.

Four-sector economy

This is the most realistic model as it includes all four possible sectors and is an open economy: households, firms, the government and the foreign trade sector. Again, equilibrium income is where aggregate expenditure equals output, but this is now where $C + I + G + (X - M) = Y$, and injections equal withdrawals, which is now where $I + G + X = S + T + M$. The multiplier is:

$$\frac{1}{\text{mps} + \text{mrt} + \text{mpm}}$$

where mpm is the marginal propensity to import (the proportion of extra income which is spent on imports).

SELF-ASSESSMENT TASK 5.14

In an economy, mps is 0.1, mrt is 0.1 and mpm is 0.2. GDP is $300 billion. The government raises its spending by $6 billion in a bid to close a deflationary gap of $20 billion. Calculate:

a the value of the multiplier

b the increase in GDP

c whether the injection of extra government spending is sufficient, too high or too low to close the deflationary gap.

SELF-ASSESSMENT TASK 5.15

Read the feature below and then answer the questions that follow.

International tourism – a mixed blessing

International tourism is arguably the biggest single item in world trade. The development of international tourism has been central to the economic development strategies of many developing economies, particularly those in the Caribbean area, southern and South East Asia and East and South Africa. The attraction of hoards of wealthy tourists descending on countries that are struggling to advance is obvious … or is it?

International tourism creates jobs in the tertiary sector. It also leads to jobs being created in agriculture and certain areas of manufacturing in order to meet the needs of tourists for food, drink, souvenirs and other products. This is the so-called 'tourism multiplier effect'. Figure 5.29 is a representation of this process within the context of a new hotel development.

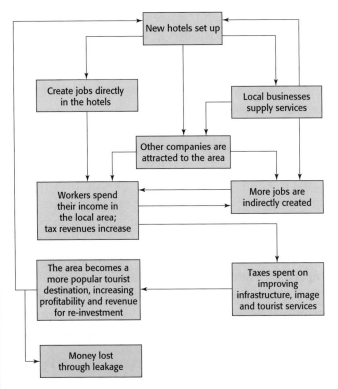

Figure 5.29 *Tourism multiplier effect*

Luxury resort in West Malaysia

The extent to which international tourism really benefits a local economy is heavily dependent on the leakages that take place. These take the form of payments for imported goods demanded by tourists, payments to foreign airlines and tour operators and in many cases, repatriated profits generated by multinational corporations who own hotels and resorts in tourist areas. A recent study has claimed that the multiplier effects of international tourism are often exaggerated. In parts of the Caribbean, for example, as much as 80% of all money spent by international tourists is lost through leakages; in Thailand, the figure is 70% yet in India it is only 40%. By way of contrast, in New York, it has been estimated that every dollar spent by tourists generates a massive $7 for the state's economy.

1 Calculate the value of the tourism multiplier for the Caribbean, Thailand and India.
2 Explain the likely reasons for the differences in the values you have calculated.

3 Discuss how governments in developing economies might introduce policies to make international tourism more beneficial than seems to be the case.

Autonomous and induced investment

Investment can rise or fall by significant amounts and it interacts with changes in income to cause significant changes in economic activity.

Investment which is undertaken independently of changes in income is known as **autonomous investment**. For example, a firm may buy more capital goods because it is more optimistic about the future or because the rate of interest has fallen. In this case, the aggregate expenditure line will shift upwards, as shown in Figure 5.30 (page 214). As a result of an increase in investment from I to I₁, GDP rises by a multiple amount, from Q to Q₁.

In contrast to autonomous investment, **induced investment** is illustrated by a movement along the expenditure line. This is because induced investment is investment which is influenced by changes in income. If income and hence demand increases, firms will be likely to buy more capital equipment. However, they will only continue to add to their capital stock if GDP continues to rise.

The accelerator

The **accelerator** theory focuses on induced investment and emphasises the volatility of investment. It states that investment depends on the rate of change in income (and hence consumer demand), and that a

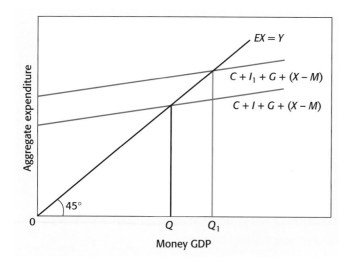

Figure 5.30 *An increase in autonomous investment*

change in income will cause a greater proportionate change in investment. If a £1 million increase in GDP causes induced investment to rise by £3 million, the accelerator co-efficient is said to be 3.

If GDP is rising but at a constant rate, induced investment will not change. This is because firms can continue to buy the same number of machines each year to expand capacity. However, a change in the rate of growth of income can have a very significant influence on investment. An example may help to show this.

In Table 5.9 it is assumed that the firm starts the period with eight machines, that one machine wears out each year and that each machine can produce 100 units of output per year.

The table shows that when demand for consumer goods rises by 25% (from 800 to 1000) in the second year, demand for capital goods rises by 200%

(from 1 to 3). When the rate of growth of demand for consumer goods slows in year 4, demand for capital goods falls. In the last year when demand for consumer goods falls, investment falls to zero with the worn out machine not being replaced, and hence productive capacity is reduced.

However, an increase in demand for consumer goods does not always result in a greater percentage change in demand for capital goods. For instance, firms will not buy more capital goods if they have spare capacity or if they do not expect the rise in consumer demand to last. It may also not be possible for firms to buy as many capital goods as they wish if the capital goods industries are working close to full capacity. In addition, with advances in technology, the **capital-output ratio** may change with fewer machines being needed to produce a given output.

Increase in the money supply and the creation of credit

As noted above, one of the causes of an increase in aggregate demand is an increase in the money supply. There are three main causes of an increase in the money supply:

* an increase in commercial bank lending
* an increase in government spending financed by borrowing from the banking sector
* more money entering than leaving the country.

Credit creation

Commercial banks, also called high street and retail banks, make most of their profits by lending to

Year	Consumer demand	Machines at start of period	Number of machines required	Replacement investment	Induced investment	Total investment
1	800	8	8	1	0	1
2	1000	8	10	1	2	3
3	1600	10	16	1	6	7
4	1800	16	18	1	2	3
5	1800	18	18	1	0	1
6	1700	18	17	0	0	0

Table 5.9 *Changes in investment*

customers, and when they lend they create money. This is because when a bank gives a loan (also called an advance by bankers), the borrower's account is credited with the amount borrowed. So every loan creates a deposit. Banks are in a powerful position to create money because they can create more deposits than they have cash and other liquid assets (that is items which can be quickly converted into cash).

From experience, banks have found that only a small proportion of deposits are cashed. When people make payments, especially large payments, they tend to make use of cheques, credit cards, electronic transfers and direct debits. These means of payments involve a transfer of money using entries in the records that banks keep of their customers' deposits rather than by paying out cash. So, banks can create more deposits than they have liquid assets.

Nevertheless, they have to be careful when calculating what liquidity ratio (the proportion of liquid assets to total liabilities) to keep. The lower they keep the ratio, the more they can lend. However, they have to be able to meet their customers' demands for cash. If they miscalculate and keep too low a ratio or if people suddenly start to cash more of their deposits, there is a risk of a run on the banking system. This was evidenced in 2008 when there were fears over the liquidity of some US and UK banks, the result being enforced government involvement. Indeed, banking is based on confidence. Customers have to believe there is enough cash and liquid assets to pay out all their deposits even though, in practice, this is not going to be the case.

The credit multiplier

By estimating what liquidity ratio to keep, a bank will be able to calculate its credit multiplier. This is also referred to as a bank or credit creation multiplier, and shows by how much additional liquid assets will enable banks to increase their liabilities. It is given by the formula:

$$\frac{\text{total value of new deposits created}}{\text{value of change in liquid assets}}$$

For example, if total deposits rise by £600 million as a result of a new cash deposit of £100 million, the credit multiplier is £600 million/£100 million = 6. It is also possible to calculate the credit multiplier by using the formula:

$$\frac{100}{\text{liquidity ratio}}$$

If a bank keeps a liquidity ratio of 10%, the credit multiplier will be 100/10 = 10. Knowing this enables a bank to calculate how much it can lend. It first works out the possible increase in its total liabilities. This is found by multiplying the change in liquid assets by the credit multiplier. So, if the credit multiplier is 10 and liquid assets rise by £40 million, total deposits will rise by £40 million × 10 = £400 million.

To work out the change in loans (advances), the change in liquid assets is deducted from the change in liabilities. This is because the change in liabilities will include deposits given to those putting in the liquid assets. In the example the change in loans will be £400 million – £40 million = £360 million.

In practice, however, a bank may not lend as much as the credit multiplier implies it can. This is because there may be a lack of households and firms wanting to borrow or a lack of credit-worthy borrowers. If banks persist in lending to borrowers with poor credit ratings, as was the case in the US sub-prime market, the risk of default is high and can have serious consequences on a bank's liquidity.

A bank may also change its liquidity ratio if people alter the proportion of their deposits they require as cash, if other banks alter their lending policies or if the country's central bank requires banks to keep a set liquidity ratio.

A central bank may seek to influence commercial banks' ability to lend. For example it may engage in open market operations. These involve the central bank buying or selling government securities to change bank lending. If the central bank wants to reduce bank loans it will sell government securities. The purchasers will pay by drawing on their deposits in commercial banks and so cause the commercial banks' liquid assets to fall.

SELF-ASSESSMENT TASK 5.16

A bank keeps a liquidity ratio of 5%. It receives additional cash deposits of $20 000. Calculate:

a the credit multiplier
b the potential increase in total liabilities (deposits)
c the potential increase in bank lending.

Deficit financing

As seen earlier in this section, if the government spends more than it raises in taxation it will have to borrow. If it borrows by selling government securities, including National Savings certificates, to the non-bank private sector (non-bank firms and the general public) it will be using existing money. The purchasers will be likely to draw money out of their bank deposits. So the rise in liquid assets resulting from increased government spending will be matched by an equal fall in liquid assets as money is withdrawn.

However, if a budget deficit is financed by borrowing from commercial banks or the central bank, the money supply will increase. When a government borrows from its central bank it spends cheques drawn on the bank. This spending increases commercial banks' liquid assets, which will increase their ability to lend. Commercial banks will also be able to lend more if the government borrows from them by selling them short-term government securities. This is because these securities count as liquid assets and so can be used as the basis for loans.

Total currency flow

The **total currency flow** of the balance of payments refers to the total outflow or inflow of money resulting from international transactions as recorded in the current account, financial account, capital account and balancing item (see Chapter 4). If there is net inflow of money into, for example, Malaysia the excess surplus currency will be converted into ringgits, thereby adding to Malaysia's money supply.

Relationship between the money supply, price level and output

As we saw earlier in this chapter, monetarists believe that changes in the money supply can have a significant effect on the price level and output in an economy. This relationship will be analysed in Chapter 6 Core when the Quantity Theory of Money is explained. Monetarists are very clear that a change in the money supply will cause an equal proportionate change in the price level. This is disputed by Keynsians who believe that the relationship is by no means as clear and simple as monetarists would have us believe. In other words, although the change in the money supply has some relevance, there are other factors that must be taken into account when explaining a change in the price level.

Interest rate determination and the demand for money

Monetarists and Keynesians also disagree over how the rate of interest is determined. Most monetarists support the **loanable funds theory**. This states that the rate of interest is determined by the demand and supply of loanable funds, as shown in Figure 5.31.

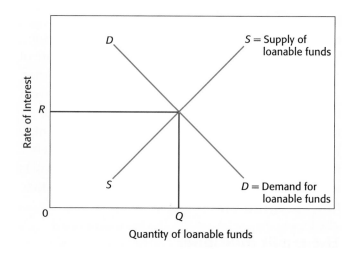

Figure 5.31 *Interest rate determination*

The demand for loanable funds comes from firms wanting to invest, households wanting to (say) buy a car on credit and from the government seeking to fund a budget deficit. Government demand for loanable funds is not very sensitive to a change in the rate of interest but a rise in the rate of interest will lower firms' and households' demand so the demand for loanable funds curve slopes down from left to right. The supply of loanable funds comes from savings. A higher rate of interest will increase the return from savings and so the supply curve is upward sloping.

An increase in the supply of savings will lower the rate of interest and cause an extension in demand for loanable funds, as shown in Figure 5.32.

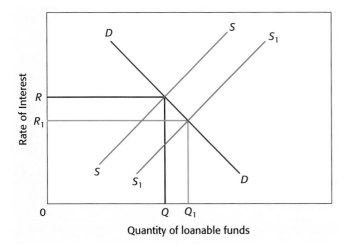

Figure 5.32 *The effect of an increase in savings on the rate of interest*

In contrast, Keynesians argue that the rate of interest is determined not by the demand and supply of loanable funds but by the demand and supply of money. It is assumed that the supply of money is determined by the monetary authorities and is fixed in the short run.

Keynes developed the **liquidity preference** theory to explain the demand for money. He identified three main motives why households and firms may decide to hold part of their wealth in a money form. The motive most people will be familiar with is the **transactions motive**. This is the desire to hold money to make everyday purchases and meet everyday payments. How much is held by a household or firm is influenced by the income received and the frequency of the income payments. Generally, the more income received and the more infrequently the payments are received, the higher the amount which will be held.

Firms and households also usually hold rather more of their wealth in a money form than they anticipate they will spend. This is so that they can meet unexpected expenses, and take advantage of unforeseen bargains. This is known as the **precautionary motive**. Money resources held for the transactions and precautionary motives are sometimes referred to as **active balances** as they are likely to be spent in the near future.

They are relatively interest inelastic so that, for example, a rise in the rate of interest will not result in households and firms significantly cutting back on their holdings of money for transactions and precautionary reasons.

In contrast, the third motive for holding money balances, the **speculative motive**, is interest elastic. Households and firms will hold what are sometimes called **idle balances** when they believe that the returns from holding financial assets are low. One financial asset which firms and households may decide to hold is government bonds. These are government securities which represent loans to the government. The price of government bonds and the rate of interest (in percentage terms) move in opposite directions. For example, a government bond with a face value of £500 may carry a fixed interest rate of 5% of its issue price. If the price of the bond rises to £1000, the interest paid will now represent 2.5% of the price of the bond. Households and firms are likely to hold money when the price of bonds is high and expected to fall. This is because they will not be forgoing much interest and because they will be afraid of making a capital loss, whereas, the speculative demand for money will be low when the price of bonds is low and the rate of interest high. Figure 5.33 shows the combined transactions, precautionary and speculative motives for holding money in the form of liquidity preference (or demand) for money. The rate of interest is at R since this is where the liquidity preference curve intersects the supply of money curve.

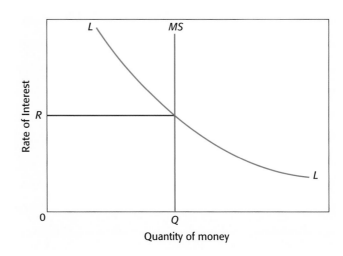

Figure 5.33 *The liquidity preference theory of interest rate determination*

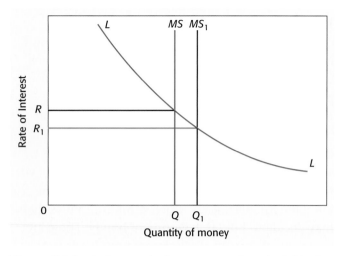

Figure 5.34 *An increase in the money supply and a fall in the rate of interest*

increasing the money supply. He described this situation as the **liquidity trap** and thought it could occur when the rate of interest is very low and the price of bonds very high. In this case, he thought that speculators would expect the price of bonds to fall in the future, so if the money supply was to be increased they would hold all the extra money; they would not buy bonds for fear of making a capital loss and because the return from holding such securities would be low. Figure 5.35 shows that at a rate of interest of R, demand for money becomes perfectly elastic and the increase in the money supply has no effect on the rate of interest.

An increase in the money supply will cause a fall in the rate of interest, as illustrated in Figure 5.34. The rate of interest falls because the rise in the money supply will result in some households and firms having higher money balances than they want to hold. As a result they will use some to buy financial assets. A rise in demand for government bonds will cause the price of bonds to rise and so the rate of interest to fall.

The liquidity trap

Although it is expected that an increase in the money supply will cause the rate of interest to fall, Keynes described a situation where it would not be possible to drive down the rate of interest by

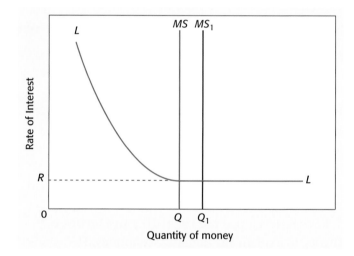

Figure 5.35 *The liquidity trap*

Read the article below and then answer the questions that follow.

Japan's gesture

When Masaru Hayami was appointed governor of the newly independent Bank of Japan two years ago, he had a reputation for stubbornness. Now he has demonstrated that trait with a vengeance.

In recent weeks he has faced a barrage of calls for him to stick with the Bank's ultra-loose monetary policy which has kept overnight rates at about zero by flooding the markets with liquidity. But on Friday Mr Hayami persuaded the Bank's policy board to raise the overnight money rate to 0.25%. For the first time in 10 years, Japanese interest rates moved up rather than down.

The immediate economic effects of ending the zero interest rate policy instituted in February 1999 may be modest.

As Bank of Japan officials point out, Friday's decision in itself is hardly likely to tip Japan's economy into recession. A rise of 0.25% is small, and still leaves interest rates at remarkably low levels.

Nor will it necessarily translate into an immediate rise in borrowing costs for all companies. Corporate loans are pegged not only to overnight market rates but also to the official discount rate, which remains at 0.5%. Economists estimate that typical corporate lending rates might rise by just 0.1%.

Bank of Japan, Tokyo

Japan has for many years looked like John Maynard Keynes' description of an economic slump in which businesses become so fearful that there is nothing monetary policy can do to persuade them to spend. Cutting interest rates in those conditions is as useless as 'pushing on a string'. But if cutting rates in Japan had little impact, then raising them may turn out to be considerably more significant.

Source: Gillian Tett and Ed Crooks, Financial Times, *14 August 2000 (adapted)*

1 Define liquidity.
2 Explain why 'flooding the markets with liquidity' would be expected to keep interest rates low.
3 Discuss the possible effect that the rise in Japanese corporate lending rates may have on investment.

4 Explain why cutting interest rates can be 'as useless as "pushing on a string"'.

SPECIMEN EXAM QUESTIONS

The following questions have been set in recent CIE examination papers.

1 The World Bank has given a loan to support the Ugandan government's road development programme. Improved roads into economically productive rural areas will have a major impact on the country's economy.

   a Explain why projects such as road building are often undertaken by the government rather than by the private sector. [10]

   b Use economic analysis to discuss why there will be a major impact on the economy from the road development programme. [15]

[25 marks]

(October/November 2007)

2 a It is feared that if the government increases taxes the level of national income will fall. Explain whether this is necessarily true. [10]

   b Discuss whether a fall in the level of national income is a good indicator that there has been a decline in the standard of living in the country [15]

[25 marks]

(May/June 2008)

SUMMARY

In this supplement section it has been shown that:

- Economic growth is an increase in real national output.
- GDP is measured by the output, income and expenditure methods.
- Real GDP is money (nominal) GDP adjusted for inflation.
- In measuring economic growth rates care has to be taken to ensure the quality of the information is good and that the size of the hidden economy and value of non-marketed goods and services are taken into account.
- Sustainable economic growth is economic growth which can be sustained over generations.
- An increase in real GDP per head is likely to mean higher living standards but may not do so if, for example, the size of the hidden economy falls, people have less enjoyment from the products produced, working conditions deteriorate, working hours rise and pollution increases.
- In using economic growth rates to compare living standards between countries, it is advisable to convert exchange rates using purchasing power parities.
- Other indicators of living standards and economic development include healthy life expectancy, the Human Development Index, the Human Poverty Index and Measurable Economic Welfare.
- Measures of the money supply include items which carry out the functions of money. Narrow money measures focus on items used as a medium of exchange, whereas broad money measures cover items used both as a medium of exchange and store of value.
- Budgets are statements of government spending and taxation plans for the next financial year.
- Deficit financing occurs when a government spends more than it raises in taxation.
- The circular flow of income shows the flow of money and resources around the economy.

- Keynesians believe that output and employment can deviate from the full employment level by substantial amounts and for long periods. In contrast, monetarists believe that the economy is inherently stable and that a government's key role is to ensure that the economy is not moved from the long run equilibrium by excessive increases in the money supply.
- Aggregate expenditure is total planned spending at different levels of income and is composed of consumption, investment, government spending and net exports.
- Equilibrium national income is achieved where aggregate expenditure equals output.
- An inflationary gap occurs if aggregate expenditure exceeds the full employment level of output, whereas a deflationary gap exists if aggregate expenditure is below the full employment level of output.
- Any change in injections and leakages will have a multiplier effect on GDP.
- Induced investment is undertaken due to increases in GDP, whereas autonomous investment occurs due to changes in other influences such as advances in technology, changes in the cost of capital equipment and changes in expectations.
- The accelerator theory states that investment depends on the rate of change of GDP and that changes in GDP create greater percentage changes in investment.
- The money supply can increase as a result of increases in bank lending, government borrowing and a net inflow of money into the country.
- Commercial banks create money because they lend more money than they have liquid assets.
- Monetarists believe that increases in the money supply cause proportionate increases in the price level. In contrast, Keynesians argue that there is no direct, proportionate relationship between changes in the money supply and the price level.
- The loanable funds theory states that the rate of interest is determined by the demand and supply of loanable funds. In the liquidity preference theory, it is the demand and supply of money which determines the rate of interest.

6 Macroeconomic problems
Core

Introduction

Every day stories appear in the newspapers and on the news about how the economy is performing. Some recent ones have been:

- 'Pakistan: food price inflation hits quake survivors' (*Irin News*, 24 August 2009)
- 'Food prices double in Sierra Leone' (*Daily Telegraph*, 27 March 2009)
- 'US trade deficit is collapsing at its fastest rate ever' (*New York Times*, 2–3 May 2009)
- 'Renminbi on the way to being the world's most important currency' (*The Independent*, 12 June 2009)
- 'Land of the rising yen' (*International Herald Tribune*, 8–9 August 2009).

These stories appear in the media because, in all cases, the events affect the lives of people and in turn and over time, economic well-being. Each of the problems analysed in this section has significance for all economies, whether developing or developed.

How the economy is performing can have a major impact on people's lives. In this chapter we shall look at problems which arise from:

- a persistent increase in the general price level in the economy
- disequilibrium in the balance of payments
- fluctuations in the **foreign exchange rate**.

SELF-ASSESSMENT TASK 6.1

A good newspaper or newspaper website contains a lot of information on the macroeconomy. In some cases this information is for the home economy. In other cases features make comparisons with other economies. For your own country, see what recent articles you can find on:

- inflation
- the balance of payments
- the foreign exchange rate.

From these articles, produce a short summary of:

- the perceived causes of the problems
- the consequences for your country's economy in the short- and long-term.

Inflation

Inflation refers to a situation in the economy where there is a general and sustained increase in prices, measured in terms of the indices described in Chapter 5 Core. In virtually all economies over the last 20 years or so, the control of inflation has been the main priority of government economic policy. Price stability is crucial for governments to achieve all of their macroeconomic objectives.

A few important points should be made:

- An increase in a small number of prices does not constitute inflation. The key thing is for the increase to be measured across a wide range of items that affect the spending of consumers. One of the few exceptions to this is the price of oil. When increasing, it can have a substantial adverse effect on inflation and across the economy as a whole.
- The rate of increase recorded on an annual basis, as in Table 6.1, is likely to be variable. Although there are are a few exceptions like Zimbabwe and to a much lesser degree the former Russian republics and some South American economies, inflation in the 21st century has been more controlled than at any stage since the mid-1970s.
- A low and steady rate of inflation may not be a bad thing for an economy. This puts pressure on businesses to be competitive and at the same time, produces a situation where there is broad confidence in the macroeconomy.

Virtually all developed economies have managed to contain inflation to less than 5% per annum over the last decade. Emerging and developing economies have not found this to be the case, although global inflation rates are now much more under control than in the the mid to late 1990s. Table 6.1 shows the estimated consumer inflation rates for selected developing economies in 2008.

It is clear from Table 6.1 that all economies have been experiencing mild inflation and, in some cases, much greater inflationary pressures. Including the unique case of Zimbabwe, for most sub-Saharan African countries, inflation remains a serious underlying problem. Table 6.2 is useful

Africa	% change on 2007
Botswana	12.6
Ghana	16.5
Sierra Leone	11.7
South Africa	11.3
Zimbabwe	11 200 000
Asia	
Bangladesh	8.9
Indonesia	9.9
Pakistan	20.3
Thailand	5.5
Middle East	
Bahrain	7.0
Egypt	18.3
Saudi Arabia	9.9
Caribbean	
Barbados	5.5
Grenada	3.7
Trinidad and Tobago	12.0
Central Europe	
Hungary	6.1
Poland	4.2
Ukraine	25.2

Table 6.1 *Estimated inflation rates for selected developing economies in 2008*

Source: World Fact Book, *CIA, 2009*

when determining the broad extent of the severity of inflation as a macroeconomic problem.

The recent inflationary history of Japan is particularly interesting as well as being unusual. This is shown in Figure 6.1. Even before 2003 retail prices were falling. This prompted and indeed was hastened by price cuts at many food stalls and the growth of discount stores selling cheap imported clothing and household items. Even McDonalds saw the need to slash prices. Despite increased corporate profits and a massive injection of government spending, job losses persisted and prices continued to fall until 2007 when it appeared that economic normality had

% change per annum over a period of time	Outcome
<5	Very mild inflation which can actually aid competitiveness.
5–9	Mild inflation, which must be kept under control to avoid future difficulties.
10–19	Inflationary pressures build up with increased wage demands and high interest rates; savings begin to be affected. Strict policies essential if problem is to be resolved.
20–50	Serious inflation. Economic relationships in real danger of breaking down. Confidence in money is seriously eroded.
50 and above	Signs of hyperinflation. Depending on severity, domestic economic structures collapse and currency becomes worthless on foreign exchange markets and also internally.

Table 6.2 *Degrees of inflation*

returned. Throughout the entire period, Japan has had a big balance of trade surplus.

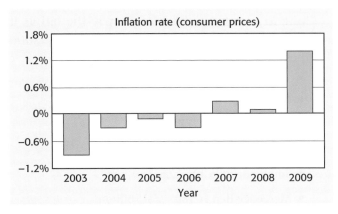

Figure 6.1 *Japanese inflation rate, 2003–2009*

Main causes of inflation

The persistent high rates of inflation that have been recorded by some countries have led to considerable interest amongst economists as to the causes of this inflation. A good starting point, as noted in Chapter 5, is **monetary inflation** and what the well-known US economist Milton Friedman had to say about inflation. He said that 'inflation is always and everywhere a monetary phenomenon'. In other

SELF-ASSESSMENT TASK 6.2

Read the feature below and then answer the questions that follow.

The millionaires who cannot afford to buy anything

The 100 billion Zimbabwean dollar note that went into circulation this week was officially worth just over 50p. On Harare's burgeoning undercover markets it was worth just 16p. Hours after printing, the price of a loaf of bread shot up by about 40% to Z$130000. These new notes are strictly speaking not currency – they are 'bearer cheques' signed by the governor of the central bank and have an expiry date of 31 December 2006.

Zimbabwean 100 billion dollar bill

At present, the highest denomination banknote is Z$50 000. A typical restaurant meal for four is about Z$15 million – it is likely to take almost as long to count out the notes to pay the bill as it does to eat the meal! Other prices in May 2006 include:

- 1 litre fresh milk – Z$80 000
- 1 litre Coca-cola – Z$120 000
- 1 chicken – Z$1.2 million
- Small portable TV – Z$23 million
- Mercedes-Benz C180 – Z$15 billion

For Zimbabwe's people, everyday life is a misery. They stand in shops with two bags: one full of money, the other for the food they are purchasing. Many cannot afford public transport and many of those in employment get up in the middle of the night to walk to work. The currency is worth less each day. A barter system is rapidly emerging and farm workers invariably prefer to be paid in produce rather than a stack of banknotes that lose value as soon as they are received. Only condoms, which cost Z$300 because they are heavily subsidised by the international community, seem to be inflation-proof.

Source: The Times, 8 May 2006 (adapted)

1 Zimbabwe is clearly experiencing severe hyperinflation. What effects is this having on the internal and external operation of the macroeconomy?

2 See what you can find out about how countries such as Argentina, Brazil and Nicaragua have dealt with similar hyperinflation problems.

words, periods of inflation coincide with increases in the money supply. So:

$$\uparrow \text{money supply} \longrightarrow \uparrow \text{rate of inflation}$$

There is though an important qualification; namely, that this will only occur if the rate of growth of the money supply is greater than the increase in the level of output in the economy, so forcing up prices. This has been an obvious cause of inflation for some of the economies shown in Table 6.1 above, particularly Zimbabwe where the printing of money has been reckless. The Quantity Theory is an example in the macroeconomy of supply being greater than demand. This is illustrated in Figure 6.2 which shows that:

- the demand curve for money is like any other demand curve – people want to hold a larger quantity of money when the value falls as they need more money to buy their particular purchases
- the supply curve for money is vertical since it is fixed by the central bank

- at the initial equilibrium (X), the demand for money and supply of money are balanced – the value of money is at v and the price level at p
- an increase in the supply of money (for example by printing more notes) shifts the supply of money from S_1 to S_2
- the outcome is that there is a new equilibrium position at Y where the value of money has halved and the price level has doubled.

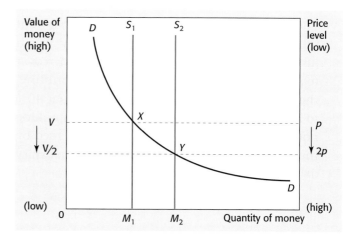

Figure 6.2 *The effects of an increase in the money supply*

Monetarists such as Friedman make use of the so-called **Quantity Theory of Money**. This theory is based on an interpretation of the equation

$$MV = PT$$

where M is the money supply, V is the number of times money changes hands, P is the price level and T is the output or transactions in the economy.

This equation (or Fisher equation as it sometimes known) has to be true since both sides represent total expenditure in the economy. By holding V and T constant, as they are unaffected by changes in the money supply, it follows that a change in the money supply causes an equal percentage change in the price level.

This is a highly simplified representation of what is a most complex situation, but it can be used to show quite clearly how the reckless printing of money can result in an increase in the general level of prices. This has clearly happened where governments have sought to get out of debt and finance their own spending by simply printing more money. It is by no means the only reason – where there is war, political upheaval and civil unrest, high inflation can result as people panic and lose confidence in the money supply, preferring to hold their assets in physical rather than monetary forms (see below).

There are two other recognised causes of inflation. Most developing economies rely heavily on imported oil. There have been times when actions by the Organization of the Petroleum-Exporting Countries (OPEC) have resulted in oil supplies being restricted. As demand is largely unaffected, basic economics tells us that prices will rise. So, in this case of what is known as **cost-push inflation**, prices are forced upwards. Higher oil prices quickly lead to a rise in domestic inflation across all oil-importing countries. Relatively, developing economies are more seriously affected than their developed counterparts and have to suffer:

- higher raw material costs (metals as well as oil)
- higher prices for imported consumer goods
- escalating food prices due to inceasing demand and supplies being used for bio-fuels
- increased demands for higher wages to cover the increased cost of living

so triggering a cost-induced inflation. Cost-push causes were clearly an important cause of the rates of inflation shown in Table 6.1. Another cause of cost-push inflation, again of particular relevance for developing economies, is where there is a substantial fall in the foreign exchange rate of their currency. The Brazilian cruzeiro and the Thai baht are two recent examples of currencies which have been affected in this way. The fall means that the price of imports into their domestic economies increases rapidly, although export prices, in terms of other foreign currencies, are lower. A worrying consequence of a substantial fall over a short period is that people lose confidence in that currency, both at home and in the international market. In turn, this further fuels inflation.

The third main cause of inflation is **demand-pull inflation** which occurs when there is an increase in the total demand for goods and services in an economy. It is so called because this increase in demand 'pulls' prices upwards if the economy does not have spare capacity to meet these increased needs. This cause of inflation has been used to explain inflation in many more developed economies at various periods over the past 40 years, mainly when an increase in consumer spending (often government induced) at a time of low unemployment has pulled up the price level.

Finally, though, an important word of warning. Inflation in practice is a complex phenonomen. Its causes are often complex, not necessarily just one of the simple reasons stated above – so much so in fact that economists invariably disagree about the actual line of causation.

Consequences of inflation

The effects of inflation depend on:

- the rate at which it is rising
- whether the rate is accelerating or stable
- whether the rate is the one which had been expected
- how the rate compares with that in other countries.

The inflation rate

An inflation rate of 20% is likely to cause more problems than an inflation rate of, say, 2% because money will be losing its purchasing power at a rapid rate. A very high rate of inflation is known as **hyperinflation** and when this occurs, people will lose confidence in money and may even go back to barter for their day-to-day needs.

In Germany, between 1913 and 1923, the price level rose 755 700 million times and people switched from using cash to using cigarettes to buy goods. More recently in Georgia in 1994 when inflation reached 15 000%, a wheelbarrow was needed to carry enough money to purchase a loaf of bread. The more recent case of Zimbabwe where inflation was around 11 million% from 2007 to 2008 was an all too clear illustration as to how an economy can just disintegrate when monetary controls are completely and utterly discarded.

Hyperinflation can also cause political instability. People become dissatisfied with the government's failure to control the high rise in prices and may look to parties offering radical solutions to the problem. Again, in Zimbabwe, this has been the case. Even less dramatic inflation rates of, say, 10% can cause problems. People who are on a fixed income or on an income which does not rise as fast as inflation will experience a fall in their purchasing power.

High rates of inflation also mean that people and companies may lose considerable purchasing power if they keep money lying idle and not earning interest. Economists refer to this as **shoe leather costs**. These are the costs involved in moving money from one financial asset to another in search of the highest rate of interest. The term can also be applied to firms and consumers spending more time searching out the lowest prices.

Inflation makes it more difficult to assess what is happening to the price of goods and services. A rise in the price of a good may now not mean that it has become more expensive relative to other goods – indeed it may have risen by less than inflation and so have become relatively cheaper. This tendency for inflation to confuse price signals is referred to as inflationary noise. It can result in consumers and producers making the wrong decisions. For example, producers seeing the price of their good rising may increase output when this higher price is the result of inflation rather than increased demand. This will result in a misallocation of resources.

Firms will also suffer from **menu costs**. These are the costs involved in changing prices. For example, catalogues, price tags, bar codes and advertisements have to be changed. This involves staff time and is unpopular with customers.

Whilst there are clear disadvantages of a high rate of inflation there can be advantages of a low, stable rate of inflation of, say, 2%. If the rise in the general price level is caused by increasing aggregate demand, firms can feel optimistic about the future. They will also benefit if prices rise by more than costs since this will mean that profits will increase.

Inflation may also stimulate consumption. This is because real interest rates may be low or even negative as the nominal rate of interest does not tend to rise in line with inflation. So debt burdens may fall and people may be able and encouraged to spend more. For example, those who have borrowed money to buy a house may experience a fall in their mortgage interest payments in real terms. At the same time the price of their house is likely to rise by more than inflation, which may make them feel better off, and so they may spend more.

The existence of inflation may also help firms which need to reduce costs to survive. For most firms the major cost is wages. With zero inflation, firms may have to cut their labour force. However, inflation would enable them to reduce the real costs of labour by either keeping nominal (money) wages constant or not raising them in line with inflation. During inflation workers with strong bargaining power are more likely to be able to resist cuts in their real wages than workers who lack bargaining power. At a time of recession and low inflation, job losses are inevitable.

Accelerating versus stable inflation

An accelerating inflation rate is likely to have more serious consequences than a stable rate. If, for example, inflation three years ago was 5%, two years ago it was 8% and last year it was 15%, people and firms will be likely to expect a further rise in inflation. The way they react is likely to bring about what they fear. For example, workers may press for higher wages, firms may raise prices to cover expected higher costs and consumers may seek to purchase goods now before their prices rise further. Accelerating, or indeed fluctuating, inflation will also cause uncertainty and may discourage firms from undertaking investment. The need to devote more staff and effort to estimating future inflation will also increase administration costs. If, on the other hand, inflation is stable it will be easier to predict future inflation and hence easier to plan and protect people from the harmful effects.

SELF-ASSESSMENT TASK 6.3

The rate of inflation in Pakistan was reported to have been 20.3% in 2008. Explain what this figure means and how it might have been calculated.

Anticipated versus unanticipated inflation

Anticipated inflation is when the rise in the general price level is the one, or close to the one, expected. If firms, workers, consumers and the government have correctly predicted the inflation rate then, as mentioned above, they can take measures to avoid the harmful effects. For example, firms can adjust their prices, nominal interest rates can be changed to maintain real interest rates, consumers may be able to distinguish between changes in the general price level and relative prices, and the government can adjust tax thresholds and index-linked pensions, benefits and civil servants' pay in line with anticipated inflation.

In contrast, **unanticipated inflation** occurs when inflation either was not expected or is higher than had been expected.

Unanticipated inflation can bring with it a number of problems. As people and firms have been caught unawares they are likely to be uncertain about future inflation. This can result in a fall in consumption and investment.

There can also be an arbitrary redistribution of income. Borrowers tend to gain and lenders to lose. This is because nominal interest rates usually rise more slowly than the inflation rate. So real interest rates often fall with inflation. This is very much the case in many countries where interest rates have fallen to zero per cent or thereabouts.

Income may also be transferred from the old to the young as the former tend to be net savers whilst the latter tend to be net borrowers. This transfer also happens because as state pensions are raised in line with inflation, they fall behind wages which usually rise at a faster rate than inflation.

International price competitiveness

Inflation may make a country's goods less price competitive. This may result in balance of payments problems. Consumers at home and abroad may turn away from buying the country's goods and services, which may cause a deficit in the trade in goods and the trade in services sections to increase. The uncertainty that arises from inflation may also discourage financial and capital investment in the country.

In a **floating exchange rate** system (see below), a fall in demand for a country's goods and services and a reduction in the inflow of investment from abroad will reduce the exchange rate. This in turn will lower export prices and, at least initially, restore price competitiveness. However, there is a danger that a vicious cycle will develop with inflation causing a lower exchange rate which in turn results in higher import prices, cost-push inflation and then a fall in the exchange rate. Also, if the root cause of the inflation is not tackled, it will continue.

However, inflation will not necessarily have adverse effects on the country's international trade position. If the country's inflation rate is below that of its main competitors, its goods and services will become more price competitive. In addition, if a country's goods and services were originally cheaper than their rivals, even with a higher inflation rate they may still be at a lower price.

Balance of payments problems
Introduction

The structure of the balance of payments was outlined in Chapter 4. In principle, the overall deficits and surpluses for any economy should balance – this is a function of the way in which the accounts are drawn up and how the inclusion of a balancing item (net errors and omissions) produces an outcome which is seemingly in equilibrium. The same is true on a global scale. A surplus on the balance of payments for one country for example, is offset by a deficit or deficits elsewhere. So, if this is the case, why are economists concerned about balance of payments problems?

In order to answer this question it is necessary to distinguish between equilibrium and disequilibrium in the balance of payments. In this context, equilibrium has a rather different meaning to the way the term was introduced in Chapter 2. In a balance of payments context, equilibrium refers to a situation where manageable deficits are cancelled out by modest surpluses over a period of time. Under such circumstances there is no particular tendency for the exchange rate to change (see below). So, on a short-term basis it does not necessarily mean that a deficit is bad and a surplus is good.

Two situations of equilibrium are described below:

- **Where the imports of goods and services exceeds exports but where this is offset by an inflow of foreign direct investment**. In other words, a current account deficit is counterbalanced by a financial account surplus. The UK economy is a good example of this.

- **Where the exports of goods and services exceed imports but where there is substantial investment abroad by companies and residents**. Here, a current account surplus is recorded, but matched by a deficit on the financial account.

It is difficult to put a time period on these short-term positions – the crucial thing is not to look at the balance of payments of an economy on a one-year only basis.

Disequilibrium occurs when, over a particular period, a country is recording persistent deficits or surpluses in its balance of payments. It has to be recognised that the exchange rate is either overvalued or undervalued on the foreign exchange market. In such situations, particularly in the case of a deficit, corrective action is required in order to prevent the economy draining its foreign currency reserves or ending hopelessly in debt.

Figure 6.3 shows the rather extreme case of the US economy which historically has moved from a position of persistent annual trade surpluses to one

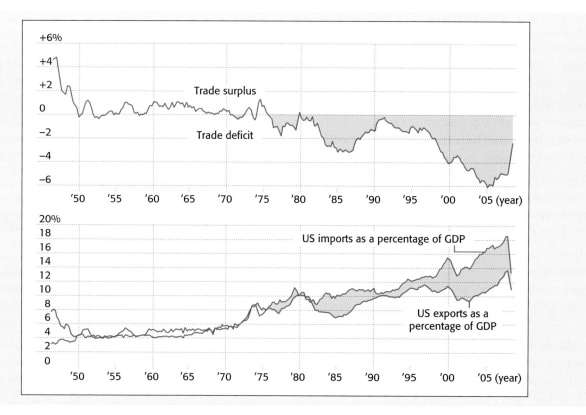

Figure 6.3 *US trade surplus or deficit as a percentage of gross domestic product*

Source: Bureau of Economic Analysis, *via Haver Analytics, reproduced in* New York Times, *2–3 May 2009*

of persistent annual trade deficits since the mid-1970s. The main reason for the US deficits is the way in which American consumers have increased their demand for imported manufactured goods, anything from clothing and electronics goods to motor vehicles. Since the onset of recession in early 2008, the deficit has virtually halved. The pain from the decline in American consumption has been felt in those countries that supply exports to the US market, notably China but also other South East Asian economies and Germany. Declining trade deficits in the US have been matched by declining trade surpluses in these and other countries that have been net exporters of manufactured goods. This is one reason why China has embarked on a massive government-funded stimulus programme and why the previously strong German economy has faltered with recession. There is therefore clear evidence that 'when the US sneezes, the rest of the world feels the effects'. This evidence is further supported by a fall in US exports, albeit at a lower rate than the fall in imports. This too is shown in Figure 6.3.

The problem of debt will be analysed in the Supplement section. The significance for the balance of payments of many developing economies is that large sums of capital were borrowed from commercial banks in the 1970s and early 1980s to fund development projects from which it was expected future income streams would be generated. Many such projects have turned out to be very poor investments. In other cases the money has been spent on other things or has been used corruptly by recipients. The legacy is one of chronic balance of payments deficits. The problem for many developing countries is that a very substantial part of their export earnings has to be paid annually in order to service this debt.

With this in mind, disequilibrium in the balance of payments can arise where:

- the imports of goods and services exceed exports and the financial account is in deficit
- exports of goods and services may just exceed imports but there is a persistent deficit on the financial account
- exceptionally, there is a large surplus on the current account, generating an overall balance of payments surplus. A pertinent example of an economy in this situation for many years has been the case of Japan.

Current account contrasts in emerging and developing economies

Some of the largest South East Asian economies are still running large trade surpluses despite recession in the global economy. This is clearly shown in Table 6.3, notably in the case of China, but also for Indonesia, Malaysia, Singapore and Thailand. All are exporters of a wide range of consumer goods to markets in the US, the EU and Australia. Singapore is also a major provider of financial and other business services.

	Trade balance (US$ bn)	Current account balance (US$ bn)
China	+250.6	+364.4
Hong Kong	−22.2	+31.4
India	−82.6	−26.6
Indonesia	+14.8	+4.4
Malaysia	+34.9	+36.7
Pakistan	−14.4	−8.9
Singapore	+18.6	+21.4
Thailand	+13.9	+13.2
Argentina	+16.4	+10.4
Brazil	+26.4	−17.6
Mexico	−14.6	−14.0
Egypt	−25.2	−4.4
Saudi Arabia	+212.0	+134.0
South Africa	−3.7	−15.8

Table 6.3 *Estimated current account contrasts for emerging economies, October 2008–October 2009*

Source: The Economist, *17 October 2009*

SELF-ASSESSMENT TASK 6.4

1 What is the difference between the trade balance and the current account balance of a country?

2 Use the information in Table 6.3 to compare the current account positions of Hong Kong and Brazil. What reasons might explain the differences?

In contrast, virtually all developing economies in Africa have deficits on merchandise trade and on current account balances. This is due to their need to import expensive oil, raw materials, manufactured goods and in some cases, food. Table 6.4 shows the position in 2007 prior to the onset of global recession. For some countries, in 2007, the price received for most primary agricultural products was relatively high and this boosted export revenue. The benefits though are likely to be short-lived as in 2009 many commodity prices had fallen back to the 2005 level. Many African countries are facing the added problem of substantial external debt as shown in the final column of Table 6.4.

	Trade balance (US$m)	Current account balance (US$m)	External debt (% GNI)
Central African Republic	−35	n/a	53
Congo, Dem. Rep.	−350	n/a	119
Ghana	−3660	−1040	21
Kenya	−5070	−526	26
Liberia	−333	−138	1128
Nigeria	+39000	+24202	9
Sierra Leone	−160	−101	10
Zambia	+862	−505	9
Zimbabwe	−370	n/a	110

Table 6.4 *Current account positions and external debt for selected African economies in 2007*

Source: World Development Report, *2009*

SELF-ASSESSMENT TASK 6.5

Give some possible reasons for the wide variation in the current account positions and external debt of the countries shown in Table 6.4.

Causes of balance of payments disequilibrium

Let us assume that disequilibrium is due to the first two of the situations identified earlier. This type of problem can be experienced by all economies. Three main causes of the disequilibrium can be identified:

1 The economy has a high propensity to import goods. Consequently, substantial deficits are recorded annually on the trading account. The UK is typical – the balance of trade in goods for all recent years except for 1997 has been in deficit, particularly with respect to trade with the rest of the EU. UK citizens like to purchase imported cars, clothing, footwear, food, drink, electronic goods and so on, even though all of these items can be produced in the UK. The perception of many people is that 'British is not best'. There are similar problems in developing economies. The cause though is different – such countries have very limited domestic production and have to rely on imported goods for much of their consumer demand. As far as exports are concerned, developing economies often rely heavily for their export revenue on sales of primary products on world markets. As shown in Chapter 4, the terms of trade are often unfavourable, meaning that they have to continually export a greater volume of goods for the same export revenue. It is therefore easy to see why many have trading deficits on their trading accounts.

2 There may be lack of confidence in a particular economy, resulting in few capital inflows. There may even be an exodus of capital from the economy. The determinants of the level of confidence is a complex phenomenon related to the macroeconomic variables referred to in Chapter 5, often set within a political context. Confidence may also be severely affected by one particular event, often of a political rather than of an economic origin, and this may well deter foreign investors.

3 From a shorter-term standpoint, a period of expansion in the macroeconomy, leading to increased consumer spending power, could produce a situation where much of this is spent on imported rather than locally produced goods. Imports are therefore 'sucked in' to the economy, with potentially serious problems for the overall balance of payments.

SELF-ASSESSMENT TASK 6.6

Using data you have collected, decide whether the balance of payments of your country is in equilibrium or disequilibrium. Can you explain why this is so?

Consequences of balance of payments disequilibrium

There are consequences of disequilibrium in the balance of payments for

- the domestic economy
- the external economy.

For the domestic economy, the consequence is that there will be a pressing need for corrective action (see Chapter 7). This need will be evidenced through a domestic economy which is characterised as having a very narrow type of economic structure and still heavily dependent on agriculture in the case of developing countries. For most developed economies, vast sectors of industry have suffered de-industrialisation, so increasing the demand for imported goods. Long-term unemployment therefore is an obvious consequence.

A second domestic consequence is that because of low business confidence, foreign investors are increasingly reluctant to invest in an economy with a balance of payments disequilibrium because of the risks that are involved. Economic prospects will be uncertain and there is a likely possibility that the currency may be devalued (see below). A situation like this hardly encourages new foreign investors to invest in an economy.

A third consequence is that for consumers there are likely to be fewer stocks of certain exotic imported consumer goods (e.g. perfume, designer clothes and specialist food items) and the general range will be restricted, often to products not produced domestically. Imports are also likely to have a much higher rate of tax imposed on them in order to restrict consumption.

For the external economy, it is often the case that disequilibrium in the balance of payments will put pressure on the government to introduce or upgrade some of the methods of protection described earlier in Chapter 4.

A second consequence is shown in Figure 6.4. Suppose the economy starts from the disequilibrium position shown in Figure 6.4a where at r_1 the total demand for foreign currency exceeds the supply of foreign currency by $Q_1 - Q_2$. This is a consequence of imports of goods and services exceeding exports, but

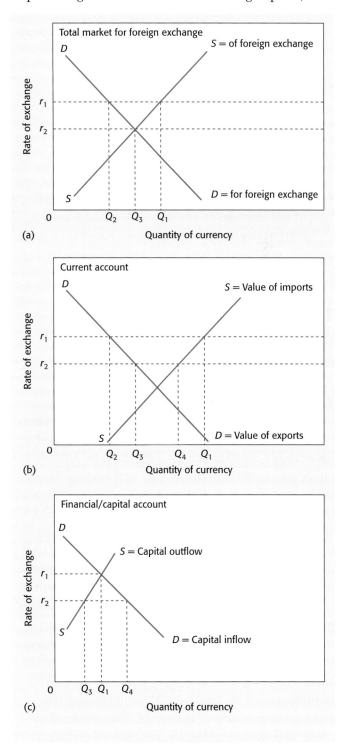

Figure 6.4 *Disequilibrium and equilibrium in the balance of payments*

233

with a balanced capital inflow and outflow –
see Figures 6.4b and 6.4c respectively. As will be
elaborated in Chapter 7, the corrective action that is
needed is for the exchange rate to be devalued. This
results in overall equilibrium (at r_2, Q_3) in diagram
(a), with a reduced current account deficit and a
financial account surplus.

In turn, though, the consequences for the domestic
economy should be recognised. For example:

- import prices will rise, in turn increasing
  the cost of living and fuelling cost-push
  inflation
- export prices will fall – depending on the
  products involved, revenue may increase, as
  indeed will employment
- confidence in the economy might be affected
  in the short term, possibly due to the fear of a
  further devaluation.

Material on the **Marshall-Lerner** condition and the
J-curve is on page 263.

The causes and consequences of fluctuations in foreign exchange rates

The measurement of exchange rates

When international rather than domestic trade takes
place, there is a crucial difference. If a UK resident,
for example, purchases a product made by UK
factors of production in the UK, only one currency,
the pound sterling, will be involved. If, however, a
UK resident buys a good which has been produced
abroad and imported into the UK, currency exchange
must take place. This is because the UK resident will
use sterling to buy the product in the shop but the
foreign factors of production will require payment in
their own currencies. If, for example, a UK consumer
purchases a television set which has been produced
in China he or she will use pounds sterling, because
this is the currency which is used as the medium of
exchange in the UK. In China, however, the pound
sterling cannot be used to settle debt because the
yuan is the medium of exchange. This means that
those who worked in the Chinese television factory
will not accept the pound in payment of their wages.
They will insist that their wages are paid in yuan.

Foreign exchange market in New York

At some stage in the transaction, currency exchange
must take place and pounds must be exchanged for
yuan. The exchange of one currency for another
takes place in the foreign exchange market.

Nominal exchange rates

The nominal value of the exchange rate is simply the
price of one currency in terms of another, so that
for example we might quote the price of the pound
sterling in terms of the yuan, or the price of the
US dollar in terms of the yen. The prices of foreign
currencies are usually quoted daily in the national
newspapers. Table 6.5 gives a few examples of the
exchange rate of the yuan against other selected
currencies. Changes in the nominal exchange rate

Currency	Exchange rate in yuan
US dollar	6.82653
euro	10.2200
UK pound	11.2098
Hong Kong dollar	0.880845
Japanese yen	0.0754076
Mauritius rupee	0.224941
Pakistan rupee	0.0820484
Saudi riyal	1.82041
Thai baht	0.204327
Trinidad/Tobago dollar	1.08444

Table 6.5 *Currency exchange rates against the yuan, 20 October 2009*

Source: x-rates.com

of one country's currency with that of another will affect the transaction price of goods and services bought and sold between these two countries. Because one country's currency is expressed in terms of that of one other country, nominal exchange rates are bilateral rates.

Trade weighted exchange rates

As explained, changes in the nominal exchange rate of one country's currency with that of another will alter the price of goods and services traded between these two countries. In the global economy, however, most countries trade with lots of other countries. A country's nominal exchange rate may be falling against the currency of some of its trading partners and rising against those of others. In 2009, for example, the UK pound depreciated against all other major currencies such as the euro, the yen and the Swiss franc compared to the same period in 2008. It was much more volatile in relation to the US dollar, ending the year at almost the same rate as the previous year.

A far more useful measure of exchange rate changes is arrived at through the **trade weighted exchange rate**. This is a measurement in index form of changes in the value of a country's currency against a basket of other currencies. These are weighted according to the relative importance in trading terms for the country in question of each of the currencies in the basket. If, for example, the UK undertakes three times as much trade with the US as with Japan, the US dollar will be given three times as much weight in the calculation of the index as the Japanese yen. Since the currencies of more than two countries are involved in the calculation of a trade weighted index, this is known as a multilateral exchange rate.

The real effective exchange rate

As stated earlier, changes in a country's exchange rate will affect the transaction prices of goods and services which that country imports and exports. These transaction prices are not only affected by changes in the exchange rate; they are also affected by differences in inflation rates between trading countries. As a result, changes in the real value or real effective exchange rate are calculated. This adjusts changes in exchange rates to take into account relative rates of inflation. For example, if a country's exchange rate is depreciating, as was the case for the UK in 2009, this means that exported goods from this country have now become cheaper in foreign markets. This is because a given amount of that country's currency can now be purchased using less of the importing country's currency. Effectively the impact of the declining exchange rate is that the price of the good has fallen in the foreign market. It may be, however, that the exporting country has been suffering from inflation at a higher rate than the inflation rate in the overseas market. As a result, in real terms its export prices could actually be increasing. Whether the exported goods are actually cheaper in the importing country depends upon the exchange rate change, together with the effects of any price changes in both of the trading countries. The real effective exchange rate takes price changes as well as exchange rate changes into account. It is the most accurate way of measuring changes in the competitiveness of an economy's goods and services in global markets.

The determination of exchange rates

The buying and selling of foreign exchange takes place on the foreign exchange market. Importers of goods into the UK will use pounds sterling to buy the currency of the country from which they are purchasing the goods. This act provides a supply of pounds on to the foreign exchange market. Similarly, those who have bought products from the UK will be using their own currencies to purchase pounds – this action creates a demand for pounds.

The foreign exchange market does not exist in a single location but is made up of banks and other financial intermediaries that buy and sell foreign currency on behalf of their private and business customers. There is a continuous flow of currency through the market on a particular day. The price of the currency or exchange rate is determined by the relative strength of the supply and demand for the currency.

So far we have considered the supply and demand for pounds which arises from the export and import of goods into the UK. There are, however, other sources of the demand for and supply of pounds on the foreign exchange market.

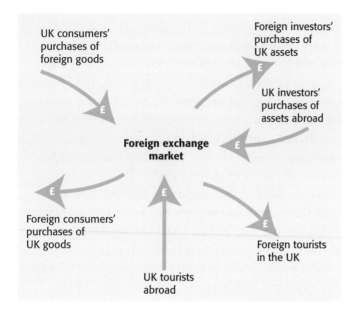

Figure 6.5 *Currency flows on to the UK foreign exchange market*

Figure 6.5 shows the flows of currency on to the market. These are indicative of the structure of the balance of payments (see Chapter 4) and are generated through trade in both goods and services and in addition, short- and long-term capital flows that move between economies in search of the highest returns.

The determination of the equilibrium exchange rate in a free market

In a free market, the value of the exchange rate is determined solely by the forces of supply and demand. Figure 6.6 shows the supply and demand for pounds on the foreign exchange market. For simplicity we will illustrate this only with reference to the relationship between the pound and the US dollar.

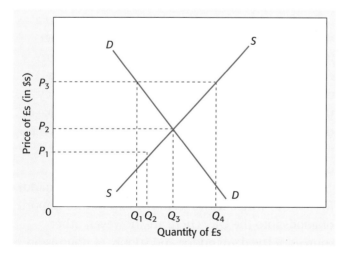

Figure 6.6 *Exchange rate determination in a free market*

In this diagram we see that the demand for pounds slopes down from left to right. This is because when the price of the pound in terms of dollars is high at P_3, then British goods and services are expensive to US consumers – they have to pay lots of dollars to gain pounds. As a result, the demand for British goods and services will be very low in the US and this means that few pounds are demanded on the foreign exchange market. As the value of the pound falls against the dollar, however, US consumers can gain more pounds for their dollars and so more pounds are demanded on the foreign exchange market. The supply curve of pounds is shown to be upward sloping from left to right. This is because when the pound is very low against the dollar, for example, P_1, then US goods are very expensive in the UK. Few UK consumers will buy US goods and, as a result, few pounds will be supplied to the foreign exchange market. As the value of the pound against the dollar rises, US goods become more affordable to the UK consumers and more pounds are supplied to the market.

Now imagine that the price of the pound on the foreign exchange market is at P_3. Here the pound is overvalued because UK exporters have difficulty selling in the US market. Their goods are too expensive. The demand for pounds is very low but, because US goods are so cheap in the UK, British consumers are buying lots of US goods and services and supplying lots of pounds to the market. As we can see, at this exchange rate there is an excess of pounds on the market. Whenever there is an excess supply in a free market, market forces will result in a fall in price. The exchange rate of the pound will fall to an equilibrium rate at P_2 where supply equates to demand.

SELF-ASSESSMENT TASK 6.7

With reference to Figure 6.6, explain what would happen to the value of the pound if the rate was at P_1.

Causes of changes in the equilibrium exchange rate

Any change in supply or demand for a currency will cause a depreciation or appreciation in the exchange rate.

For illustration we will now consider the market for US dollars in terms of all other currencies.

A depreciation in the exchange rate

A **depreciation** in an exchange rate can occur, as shown in Figure 6.7. Here there has been a fall in the demand for the dollar. This is represented by a shift of the demand curve to the left and could be caused, for example, by the following:

- **A reduction in the number of US goods and services sold abroad**. Importers of US goods and services are demanding fewer dollars to settle accounts with US firms. This could be caused, for example, by an increase in the price of US goods and services due to inflation or a longer-term decline in the quality of US goods and services.
- **A reduction in the number of international investors who wish to place their funds in the US economy**. This might be because interest rates in the US are lower than in other economies and, as a result, give a poorer return to investors.

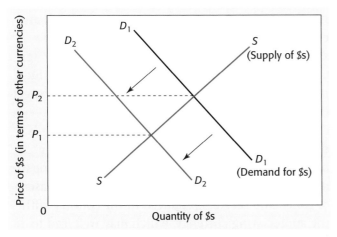

Figure 6.7 *A depreciation in the dollar exchange rate*

An appreciation in the exchange rate

An **appreciation** in the exchange rate can occur as shown in Figure 6.8. Here there has been a decrease in the supply of the dollar. This is represented by a shift in the supply curve to the left and could be caused, for example, by the following:

- **A decrease in the number of foreign goods and services imported into the US**. US importers are using dollars to purchase foreign currency on the foreign exchange market. They

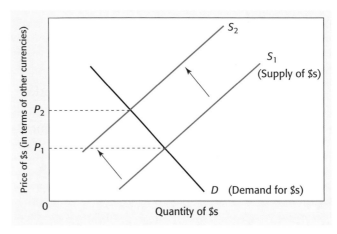

Figure 6.8 *An appreciation in the dollar exchange rate*

provide a supply of dollars on to the market. The fall in the number of foreign goods purchased in the US could be caused by a rise in the price of foreign goods and services relative to those produced in the US, or perhaps there has been a decline in the quality of foreign goods and services.

- **A decrease in the number of US investors who want to place their funds in foreign economies**. Again, if interest rates fall abroad, then US investors will want to place their funds in US banks rather than abroad. They will now choose not to exchange their dollars for foreign currencies and the supply of dollars on the foreign exchange market will decrease.

SELF-ASSESSMENT TASK 6.8

Consider the impact of the following changes upon the value of the dollar. Provide a sketch for each change.

a A rise in interest rates in the US.
b A substantial current account deficit on the US balance of payments.

Effects of changing exchange rates on the economy

As stated earlier, if there is a change in the value of a country's currency against that of others it will change the transaction price of any goods and services which that country buys or sells in international markets.

The effects will be as follows:

- A fall or depreciation in the value of the exchange rate will mean that the price of imports into the country will rise and the price of the country's exports will fall.
- A rise or appreciation in the country's currency will mean the opposite, that is the price of imported goods will fall and the price of the country's exports will rise.

The impact of a depreciation in the exchange rate

As we have seen above, a balance of payments deficit will cause a depreciation in a country's currency, which will mean that import prices will rise. This will have a number of consequences. Domestic manufacturers who sell in the home market will find that their goods are now more competitive compared to imported manufactures that have now become relatively more expensive. They may find that there is an increase in demand for their products and they will try to expand production to meet this demand. There will be an increase in the demand for the factors of production, including labour. The impact of this will depend upon the level of employment in the economy. If there is a lot of spare capacity in the economy with lots of labour unemployed we would expect unemployment to fall. As full employment is approached, however, labour becomes increasingly scarce and, as a result, we would expect labour to ask for higher wages. Because they are facing increased demand, manufacturers will be prepared to pay the higher wages and pass this on to the consumer in the form of higher prices.

The extent to which cost increases can be passed on to consumers depends upon the price elasticity of demand for domestic manufactured goods. The higher this is for domestically produced manufactured goods, the less domestic manufacturers will be able to raise prices. Nevertheless, we would expect some inflationary pressure because of increases in the demand for domestically produced goods when an economy's currency depreciates. Inflationary pressure will also arise from the supply side of production when a currency depreciates. This is because any imported raw materials will become more expensive when the exchange rate falls. If there are no domestic supplies of the raw material, then manufacturers have no alternative but to pay the increased price if they wish to respond to the increase in domestic sales. Again they will try to pass the increase in cost on to the consumer, so prices will tend to rise.

A depreciation of a country's exchange rate will also mean that its export prices will fall. This will mean that there will be an increase in the demand for that country's products in foreign markets. This, in turn, could be inflationary because exporting firms will be competing with other firms who are producing in a buoyant domestic market.

Despite the inflationary pressure we would expect the depreciation of the exchange rate to lead to a fall in imports and a rise in exports which could mean that the balance of payments deficit is replaced by a balance of payments surplus.

The impact of an appreciation in the exchange rate

When a country experiences a balance of payments surplus we have seen that this will cause a rise in that country's exchange rate. This will have a number of consequences. Import prices will fall and export prices will rise. Domestic consumers will switch to imported goods and services while foreign consumers will turn to their own country's products in preference to imports. As a result we would expect the volume of imports to rise and the volume of exports to fall. The extent of the volume change is determined by the price elasticity of demand for both imports and exports. There will be a decline in demand from both domestic and foreign purchasers of goods and services produced in the country with the appreciating currency, which may well lead to unemployment as producers face declining sales both at home and abroad.

The appreciation of the currency should have sufficient impact upon import and export spending that the balance of payments surplus is replaced by a balance of payments deficit.

Figure 6.9 shows how the UK pound's exchange rates against the euro (€) and the US dollar have fluctuated from October 2008 to October 2009. The greater volatility has been against the dollar. The UK's principal trading partners though are fellow EU member states which to some extent reduces the impact on the UK economy.

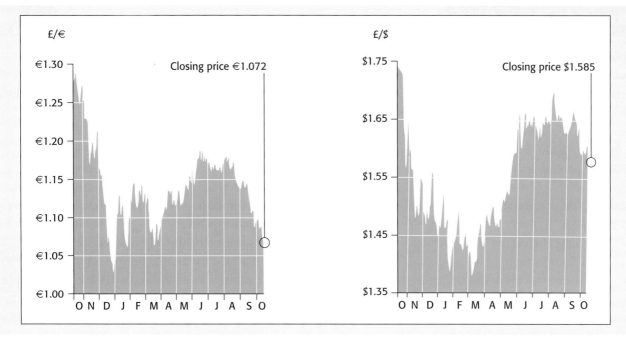

Figure 6.9 *Sterling exchange rates, October 2008–October 2009*

Source: Bloomberg

SELF-ASSESSMENT TASK 6.9

Study the information in Figure 6.9 and then answer the following questions.

1 Has the pound depreciated or appreciated against the euro and the US dollar over the period shown? Justify your answers with evidence from Figure 6.9.
2 Explain the likely effects of the exchange rate changes shown on **(a)** exporters **(b)** importers.

Exchange rate systems

In deciding upon their exchange rate policy, governments can choose between a variety of approaches. They can decide to have a floating exchange rate system. This means that the rate of exchange of a currency is decided purely by the flows of demand and supply of that currency on to the foreign exchange market. An alternative approach is for the government to intervene in the foreign exchange market either directly or indirectly to influence the value of the currency in some way. Managed exchange rate systems come in a variety

of forms. The degree of intervention can vary quite considerably. A government may choose to have a **managed float**. This describes an exchange rate policy in which the value of the currency is broadly decided by market forces but the government takes action to influence the rate of change of the currency's value. If the exchange rate is depreciating for example, the government might take action to slow down the rate of fall.

Fixed and **pegged exchange rate systems** involve far more intervention. The term describes a system in which the government declares a central value for its currency and then intervenes in the foreign exchange market to maintain this value. There are several ways in which this system might work. Sometimes, for example, the value of the currency is held at a constant rate. In other systems the rate is allowed to vary within a narrow band with upper and lower limits. Sometimes the currency is pegged against one other major currency, such as the US dollar; sometimes it is pegged against a 'basket of currencies'. We need to consider in more detail how each of these systems operates, and then consider the advantages and disadvantages of each.

SELF-ASSESSMENT TASK 6.10

Calculate the impact of the exchange rate changes below upon transaction prices in the following cases. Assume that the nominal exchange rate of pound sterling to US dollars is £1 = $1.5. A cashmere sweater made in the UK and which sold for £200 would cost a US importer $300. Similarly, a US car which sold for $12 000 would cost a UK importer £8000.

1 Assume that the nominal exchange rate changes to £1 = $2.0.

a Calculate the cost of the cashmere sweater to the US importer.

b Calculate the cost of the US car to the UK importer.

c What would you expect to happen to the volume of UK exports of cashmere sweaters and imports of US cars as a result of the new exchange rate?

2 Assume that the nominal exchange rate now changes to £1 = $1.0.

a Recalculate the cost of the cashmere sweater to the US importer.

b Recalculate the cost of the car to the UK importer.

c What would you expect to happen to the volume of UK exports of cashmere sweaters and imports of US cars as a result of the new exchange rate?

d As the exchange rate has changed it has changed the transaction prices of the trade in cashmere sweaters in the UK and the US. As a result, we will expect the volumes of imports and exports to change. Explain what further information would be required to assess the impact of these changes in sales upon total spending on exports and imports.

Floating exchange rate systems

When the value of a currency depreciates or appreciates purely as a result of market forces, that is changes in demand and/or the supply of a currency, then the exchange rate is said to be freely floating. Under this system the exchange rate is determined purely by market forces. The major advantage of this is that since the government has no exchange rate target it is free to pursue other policy objectives, such as full employment. This means that where freely floating exchange rates are adopted there is considerable independence in economic policy making.

This can be explained as follows. If a country suffers inflation at a higher rate than its competitors in world trade, then the likely outcome is that this country's goods and services become uncompetitive in world markets. Domestic consumers will turn to lower-priced imports, and consumers in overseas markets will purchase their goods and services from low inflation countries. This is likely to lead to a deficit on the current account of the country's balance of payments. As we have seen, this leads to a fall in the exchange rate of that country's currency as an excess supply of the currency occurs in the foreign exchange market. A fall in the exchange rate will restore competitiveness of the economy's goods and services, because domestic consumers will now find

that they have to pay more to obtain imports. Foreign consumers will also now find that they have to give up less of their own currency to buy the exports of the country with the depreciating currency. The subsequent fall in imports and rise in exports should correct the balance of payments deficit.

This adjustment process does depend upon certain assumptions. These include the responsiveness of consumers to the price changes that result from the depreciating currency. In addition we have seen that one of the consequences of a declining currency is that inflationary pressures are created in the economy. This means that, as the currency depreciates to offset the inflation which has made the country's goods and services uncompetitive, it may well create further inflationary pressures within the economy. This will mean that the goods and services remain uncompetitive and the cycle goes on. The inflationary pressure can become so bad that there is a complete loss of confidence in the currency in both the domestic and in foreign exchange markets. Nevertheless, as explained, it is usually expected that given sufficient time it is likely that demand for exports and imports is sufficiently price elastic to ensure that the deficit is removed, despite the inflationary pressures that are created. This tendency for deficits (and surpluses) in the balance of payments to be removed through changes in the exchange rate with no need for government action is known as an automatic adjustment mechanism.

Despite the advantages of the self-regulating nature of floating exchange rates, most governments tend to favour some degree of intervention in foreign exchange markets. This is because of a number of serious disadvantages which freely floating regimes bring. These can be summarised as follows:

- Exchange rate fluctuations discourage trade. When contracts are signed to finance international trade in goods and services entrepreneurs will assess the usual risks when considering whether a venture will result in profits being earned. They will consider their costs and revenue and this will allow them to estimate profit. In a floating exchange rate regime an extra risk is added to the transaction. A sudden fluctuation in the exchange rate might upset their calculations and wipe out estimated profit. It could, of course, result in severe losses if revenue falls below costs. There are several ways in which the risk of losses through currency fluctuation can be minimised, but the uncertainty which surrounds trade in floating exchange rate regimes remains a serious disadvantage of such a system.
- It is suggested that the fact that a floating exchange rate system has a self-regulating mechanism to deal with balance of payments deficits means that governments do not face any pressure to exercise financial discipline in their policies. As we have seen, any inflation which results from lax economic policy making is offset by a decline in the exchange rate. It is clear from the above analysis, however, that the decline in the exchange rate can itself cause prices to rise. As a result, it is claimed that floating exchange rates can be inflationary.

The disadvantages of floating exchange rates have encouraged governments to seek ways of intervening in the foreign exchange market to manage exchange rate change in order to provide stability and a favourable environment for growth in trade.

Managed exchange rate systems

If governments are to manage their exchange rates, they need to intervene in the foreign exchange market. They can intervene directly by buying and selling currencies in order to offset upward or downward pressure on the exchange rate. This means that governments must have access to a large quantity of reserves of foreign exchange sufficient to influence the price in the market. They can also intervene indirectly through variations in the rate of interest. If, for example, there is downward pressure on the exchange rate because there is an excess supply of the currency on the foreign exchange market, a rise in domestic interest rates will attract inflows of capital in search of good returns. This will create an increase in the demand for the currency and offset the downward pressure. This means that the rate of interest is used as a tool to maintain the exchange rate.

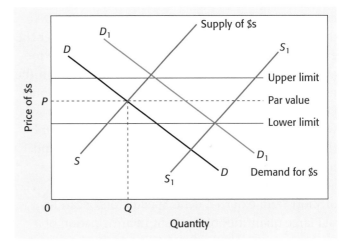

Figure 6.10   *A managed exchange rate system*

Figure 6.10 shows the principles of a managed exchange rate system, whereby the currency has a par value of $0P$, with an upper and a lower limit. If there is an increase in the supply of dollars, for example due to an increase in imports, then the supply curve shifts to S_1. This will reduce the value of the dollar in a free market to below its agreed lower limit. To maintain the currency at its lower limit, the demand for dollars has to shift to the right, an action requiring the use of foreign exchange reserves by the government. If it wishes to return the dollar to its par value, then even greater reserves are needed to bring it back to $0P$. This is fine in theory but in practice can involve a massive drain on the foreign exchange reserves held by a country.

The South East Asia currency crisis of the mid-1990s

In 1996 South East Asia was hit by a currency crisis which provides a vivid example of the difficulties associated with a managed exchange rate regime. At this time most of the countries had exchange rates pegged to the value of the US dollar – the USA provided the main market for the goods and services produced and exported from here. These countries, which included Thailand, Indonesia, South Korea and Malaysia, found that pegging their rate against the US dollar would ensure that their goods and services would not lose competitiveness in the US market because of an exchange rate appreciation. This was seen as the key to export-led growth.

The crisis started in Thailand. The Thai currency unit, the baht, was rigidly fixed to a basket of currencies which was dominated (85%) by the US dollar. In 1995 the dollar began to rise and, under the exchange rate regime in operation, the baht rose too as the Thai economic policy makers intervened in the market to maintain the managed rate with the dollar. Unfortunately, the rate of inflation in Thailand was higher than the rate of inflation in the US and this resulted in a decline in Thai exports. Thailand had for some years accumulated large current account deficits and, as a result, large quantities of short-term external debt. Speculators began to sell large quantities of the baht in anticipation of a devaluation. The Thai authorities tried to maintain the value of the baht but as their reserves became exhausted they bowed to the inevitable and allowed the baht to float down. Between December 1996 and January 1998 the baht declined in value by 52.02%.

The exchange rate speculation then spread to other economies in South East Asia. The Malaysian ringgit fell by 45.98% over the same period and Indonesia's rupiah by 74.48%. South Korea was one of the most successful of the 'tiger economies'. In fact, in 1997 it was the eleventh largest economy in world. Nevertheless, its currency (the won) fell by 54.2% and this resulted in the IMF lending the South Korean government a total of $57 billion, its largest ever rescue package. The fallout even spread to Japan with the yen falling to an eight-year low against the US dollar.

The currency speculation then spread to other regions. In August 1998 and at the beginning of 1999 crises occurred in Russia and then Brazil. The Russian government had maintained a managed exchange rate between the rouble and the dollar, but, as the speculators turned their attention to the rouble, the Russian authorities were forced to abandon their support for the rouble and it declined in value by 50% in ten days. Brazil's currency, the real, depreciated by 22% in two days.

The world economy was on the point of collapse, but complete disaster was averted because the central banks of the US and Europe took action to restore confidence in world financial markets. In addition, the health of the US economy ensured that the threatened economies of South East Asia could restore their economies through sales of exports to US consumers.

SPECIMEN EXAM QUESTIONS

The following questions have been set in a recent CIE examination paper.

1 a Explain the difference between cost-push and demand-pull inflation. [8]

b Discuss whether a country experiencing inflation will always have a balance of payments problem. [12]

[20 marks]

(October/November 2006)

SUMMARY

In this core section it has been shown that:

- All types of economy are concerned about problems of inflation, balance of payments disequilibrium and fluctuations in their exchange rates.
- These problems have particular relevance and significance for developing economies.
- Inflation is caused by monetary, cost and demand factors.
- If unchecked, inflation affects the domestic and external well-being of a country.
- Disequilibrium in the balance of payments of an economy is caused by a high propensity to import, a lack of confidence in an economy and an expansion in the domestic economy of a country.
- This disequilibrium can have an adverse effect on the domestic economy and lead to a fall in the foreign exchange rate compared with major currencies.
- There are three main types of exchange rate – nominal, real and trade weighted.
- Exchange rates are crudely determined by the demand and supply of a foreign currency in international markets – under certain circumstances, the change in exchange rates may not occur or is managed between certain specified limits.
- Exchange rates can depreciate or appreciate as a consequence of changes in demand or supply for a currency.
- Changing exchange rates affect import and export spending and the balance of payments of a country.

6 Macroeconomic problems
Supplement

On completion of this supplement section you should know:

- the difference between economic growth and economic development
- how economies can be classified in terms of indicators of their comparative development
- how economists measure the many characteristics of developing economies
- the difference between actual and potential growth
- what factors cause economies to grow
- why economic growth can have certain costs as well as benefits
- how to define unemployment and the problems of its measurement
- the main causes and consequences of unemployment
- the relationship between the internal and external value of money
- the relationship between the balance of payments and inflation
- the relationship and trade-offs between inflation, unemployment and the balance of payments.

Economic growth and development

Economic growth

Economic growth occurs when an economy achieves an increase in its national income, measured by Gross National Product (GNP), in excess of its rate of population growth. This will lead to an increase in GNP per capita. For many years it was assumed that the existence of poverty in many of the world's poorer economies could be eradicated if these countries managed to sustain economic growth over a period of time. As a result economic growth was seen as synonymous with economic development. If economies grew they would also experience development. It was assumed that increased availability of goods and services in an economy would lead to a 'trickle down' effect which would have an impact upon all, including the poorer members of society, in terms of jobs and other economic benefits. In reality, however, despite the fact that in recent years many developing countries have achieved quite high growth rates, it has been observed that, although economic growth has resulted in benefits for poorer members of society in some countries, in others the levels of living for the mass of the population have remained unchanged. In

some cases this level may even have deteriorated. As a result, a wider perception of economic development is now accepted which is related to, but distinct from, economic growth. In other words, economic development is the process of improving people's economic well-being and quality of life. Economic growth is the actual annual percentage change in output.

Economic development

In its *World Development Report* of 1991 the World Bank offered the following view of development:

> 'The challenge of development ... is to improve the quality of life. Especially in the world's poor countries, a better quality of life generally calls for higher incomes – but it involves much more. It encompasses as ends in themselves better education, higher standards of health and nutrition, less poverty, a cleaner environment, more equality of opportunity, greater individual freedom, and a richer cultural life.'

This statement remains true. Although it acknowledges that economic growth is important, it makes it clear that higher income in itself is not sufficient to ensure that there is a rise in the

Read the feature below and then answer the questions that follow.

Asia's emerging economies are leading the way out of recession

The emerging economies of Asia, notably China, Indonesia, South Korea and Singapore, are important exporters of goods and services to developed economies. At a time of global recession there was a strongly held view that they could not themselves revive until customers in the rich world revived.

According to the IMF's Word Economic Outlook (April 2009), the euro area and the UK will continue to experience negative growth in 2009 whilst in 2010, the projected growth rate will be less than 0.5%. Growth in the US is forecast to be a little more at 0.8%.

In contrast, for the second quarter of 2009, four emerging Asian economies have reported annualised growth rates that average more than 10%. Even Japan seems to be recovering at a faster rate than its Western peers. Overall in 2009, emerging Asia is forecast to grow by around 5%, at a time when the G7 economies could contract by 3.5% (see Figure 6.11).

So what have been the causes of this recovery from recession at a time when developed economies are struggling? Various reasons can be given. These include:

- Manufacturing is very important in Asian economies, particularly cars and electronics. Output will spurt ahead at the first signs of recovery.
- The region's decline in 2008 was exacerbated by the freezing of global trade finance. This is now flowing again.
- Significantly, domestic spending has bounced back because the fiscal boost given to their economies was bigger and worked faster than in the West. Excluding India, this was due to healthier government finances. Asia's emerging consumer spending power has more than offset the drop in spending in the US and the euro area.

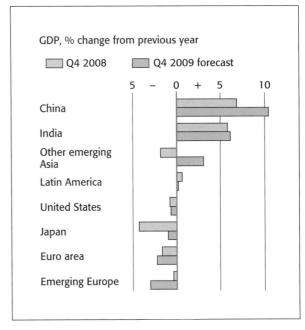

Figure 6.11 *Asia's emerging economies, 2008–2009*

Source: JPMorgan

Car manufacturing is very important to Asian economies

There is though a warning that this growth may not be sustained unless exchange rates rise. At present they are clearly undervalued. A rise in the Asian exchange rates against the dollar and the euro will reduce export growth but will stimulate domestic demand and real spending power. This is the real key to future sustained economic growth.

Source: The Economist, *15 August 2009 (adapted)*

1 Use economic analysis to explain how:
 a Asian economies benefit from a 'fiscal boost'
 b European and US economies benefit from a switch in consumer spending from imports to domestically produced goods.

2 Discuss why forecasts of economic growth may be unreliable.

quality of life for the citizens of a country. This is a much broader view of development than one confined purely to increases in GNP. It is one that provides a different focus for those responsible for development policy planning, and moves away from measures designed purely to increase and maintain an economic growth target. Todaro states that development must be seen as a multidimensional process:

> 'Development … must represent the whole gamut of change by which an entire social system, tuned to the diverse basic needs and desires of individuals and social groups within that system, moves away from a condition of life widely perceived as unsatisfactory toward a situation or condition of life regarded as materially and spiritually better'.
>
> (M. P. Todaro, *Economic Development*, 1995)

Indicators of comparative development

Classification according to levels of income

The simplest way in which economies can be classified is according to the value of their Gross Domestic Product (GDP) per capita. This is used by the World Bank which classifies every economy as low income, middle income (subdivided into lower and upper middle), or high income. Low-income and middle-income economies are sometimes known as **developing economies**. Classifying economies in this way is convenient, but as we have seen, the level

of development of a country goes beyond relative levels of income. It can also be misleading if it is assumed that all countries classed as 'developing' are at the same stage of development. In fact, economies grouped together in terms of income may well be at completely different stages of development. Nevertheless, categorising economies according to their levels of income provides a simple and measurable way of grouping economies. It is also a convenient way of identifying those economies in need of help and assistance from aid providers.

Low income	US$ 905 or less
Middle income	US$ 906 to US$ 3595 (lower middle)
	US$ 3 596 to US$ 11 115 (upper middle)
High income	US$ 11 116 or above

Table 6.6 *Classification of economies, GDP per head, 2009*

The thresholds between the categories are updated each year to account for international rates of inflation. As a result the thresholds are constant in real terms over time.

Classification according to levels of indebtedness

Sometimes it is useful to classify developing economies according to the degree of their indebtedness. These categories are: severely (or highly) indebted, moderately indebted and less indebted. The categorisation depends upon a number of measures of international indebtedness, the most important of which is the proportion of GNP which is devoted to servicing the debt. The fact that such a categorisation is used is a reflection of the extent to which international indebtedness is an obstacle to economic development.

Characteristics of developing economies

The term 'developing economy' is used to describe a great variety of different countries and there are many differences between them, so in some ways it is wrong to think of them as a distinct group with the same characteristics. Very often the differences which exist between them are related to the geographical area in which the countries are located. This also means that developing countries located in the same region are usually affected by the same types of problem. The problems of developing countries in sub-Saharan Africa may, for example, be quite distinct from those of developing countries in Asia. In this sense there is no such thing as a 'typical developing economy', and policies to foster economic development may need to be country-specific. The policies that are appropriate for one may not be appropriate for all.

Nevertheless, for some purposes it is necessary to treat developing countries as a group and it is useful to identify their shared characteristics. Very often the characteristics that they share generate similar problems that they all have to face. The following is a brief description of the shared characteristics of developing economies. Recognising the differences between developing countries while identifying the characteristics that they have in common can be characterised as 'unity in diversity'.

Economic structure

Economic activity can be placed in the following sectors:

1 **Primary sector** This includes agriculture and the extractive industries, such as oil extraction and coal mining.
2 **Secondary sector** This is all manufacturing industries and the construction sector.
3 **Tertiary sector** This is also known as the service sector.

Developing countries typically have a high dependency upon the primary sector. In those

economies classified as low-income economies, agriculture invariably contributed between 30% and 60% of output in the 1990s. This high dependency on agricultural output makes developing countries vulnerable to the forces of nature. In those economies in which agricultural output is mainly for subsistence a drought can swiftly lead to famine. In those developing economies that are dependent upon agricultural products for their exports the drought can wipe out their foreign currency earnings. In contrast to this, in high-income economies the average figure for agricultural production was only 5% or less of GDP.

Table 6.7 gives a few selected indicators of development for the World Bank's broad classification of economies. Excluding debt, there is a clear relationship between GDP per head and the other variables that are shown in this table.

	Low income	Lower middle income	Upper middle income	Higher income
GDP per head US$	578	1887	6987	37566
Life expectancy:				
Male	56	67	67	76
Female	58	71	74	82
Adult literacy rate %	61	89	93	99
Births attended by skilled health staff	41	69	94	99
Extended debt as % GDP	30	102	55	196

Table 6.7 *Indicators of development for groups of countries in 2007*

Source: World Bank Development Report, *2009*

Population growth and population structure

In 2008, around 85% of the world's population lived in developing economies. The poorest of these

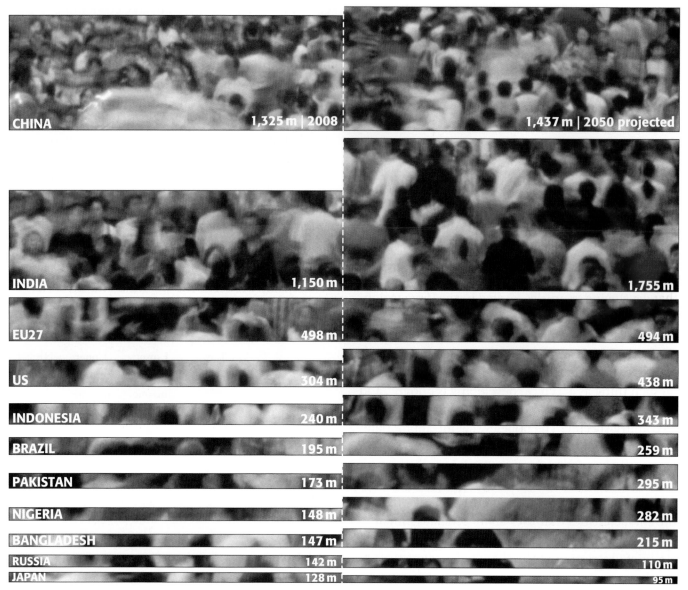

Figure 6.12 *Forecast populations in 2050 for selected countries*
Source: Daily Telegraph, *14 September 2009*

countries such as Bangladesh, India and Pakistan had the highest rates of population growth. Moreover these high rates seem likely to persist. Figure 6.12 shows the projected populations of selected developed and developing economies in 2050.

Many observers suggest that the theories of Malthus can be applied to the current population problems of the developing countries. Writing as long ago as 1798 the Reverend Thomas Malthus offered a quite pessimistic view of population growth. The essence of his view was that a country's population had a tendency to grow in geometric progression over time. However, food supplies had a tendency to increase only in arithmetic progression:

- population grows in geometric progression 1, 2, 4, 8, 16, 32, 64 …
- food supplies grow in arithmetic progression 1, 2, 3, 4, 5, 6, 7 …

This was because the quantity of land was in relatively fixed supply (the fixed factor), and, as increasing quantities of ever-more readily available labour (the variable factor) were added in production, diminishing returns would set in. The tendency over time therefore was that population increases would outstrip increases in food supplies. This would cause a number of 'checks' to population growth so that the population would fall to a level sustainable by the available food supplies. These checks included famines brought on by the overpopulation, diseases and epidemics caused by malnourishment, and wars as countries, increasingly desperate to feed their growing populations, fight over dwindling resources.

This Malthusian view of population growth can be challenged on a number of grounds. The main weakness is that it fails to recognise the impact of changes in technology upon food production and distribution. Malthus could not have been aware of the huge changes that have occurred in agricultural production, such as mechanisation, the application of more effective fertilisers and insecticides and the introduction of new high yield seeds such as the 'miracle' strains of rice introduced in Japan, Taiwan and South Korea. These changes mean that food supplies have increased to a level capable of supporting a much higher level of world population.

Nevertheless, malnourishment and famine remain depressing features of many developing countries. However, these problems are more likely to be caused by a wider range of factors than an overall Malthusian analysis would suggest. These include factors such as the uneven distribution of resources in the world, poor management of agricultural sectors, vulnerability to sudden shocks, such as floods and drought, and an inability to respond to these. As we shall see, the crippling impact of international debt in developing countries also creates conditions in which human miseries, including hunger and famines, can flourish.

Figure 6.13 shows average fertility rates for broad geographical groups of countries from 2005 to 2010 (projected). In Europe especially, the populations of some countries are falling due to low fertility rates. A typical example is Italy. In contrast, in the UK, the population is increasing due to continuing immigration and relatively high fertility rates amongst immigrant women. Elsewhere, notably in Africa, fertility rates are generally high and around twice the level of those in America and the Caribbean.

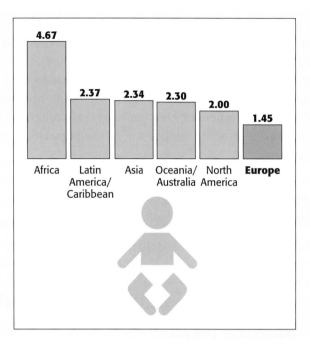

Figure 6.13 *Fertility rates (children per woman 2005–2010)*
Source: Daily Telegraph, *14 September 2009*

The fact that developing countries have much higher fertility rates than the developed economies not only leads to greater increases in their total populations but all the attendant problems which this brings. It also has an impact upon the population structure of these countries. It means that when the age composition of developing countries is considered it is seen that they tend to have a large number of very young people. This creates a high proportion of dependent, non-productive members of the population. They are said to have very high **dependency ratios**. This means that a proportionally small working population has to produce enough goods and services to sustain not only themselves but also a large number of young people who are economically dependent upon them. This will give rise to conditions of poverty and in addition creates pressure to force the young into the workforce. There is also the problem of child labour. It is estimated that over 100 million children now live or work on the streets.

Developed countries also tend to have problems with the age structure of their populations. Here the problem is different because the birth rate is so low and below the rate required to replace the present population. The result is that the population is actually ageing. In the European Union it is estimated that by 2050 two-thirds of the population will be over 65 and therefore considered 'not economically active'. Again, dependency ratios are high and this brings problems, but this time because of the high number of old people who are reliant upon the productive proportion of the population for support.

Developing economies also have problems of ageing populations. The cause tends to be more one that people are living longer rather than birth rates falling. In India, for example, it is estimated that one-fifth of the population will be 60 years and over by 2050. This compares with around 8.5% in 2009. Pakistan is also confronted with an ageing population as indicated in Self-assessment task 6.12.

SELF-ASSESSMENT TASK 6.12

Read the feature below and then answer the questions that follow.

Pakistan's ageing population – the challenge for health care

Pakistan's population was estimated to be 173 million in 2008; by 2050 it is forecast to grow by a further 70%. This is not the only problem Pakistan has to face up to – the proportion of the population aged 65 years and over is increasing because life expectancy is increasing. This is currently 62 years and much lower than in developed countries. At present, the elderly population is just 4% of Pakistan's total, a figure that is expected to rise to around 15% by 2050.

The rising geriatric population presents a huge challenge for health care in Pakistan. Prof. Qidwai of the Aga Khan University in Karachi has spelled out some of these challenges. His research has identified a growing need for post-retirement support for people aged 65 and over and a more preventive approach to health problems that ultimately affect the elderly.

The lack of government support for the elderly has traditionally been compensated for by strong support from within the family. Prof. Qidwai believes that this is breaking down at a fast rate much to the detriment of the elderly's health. He further maintains that what is required is for the government to take measures to ensure continued family support or to look at alternative methods if this is not possible. All of these problems place a heavy burden on the government and health care

providers; there are also very clear social issues that affect the fabric of Pakistani society.

To meet these needs and challenges, massive resources are required. Existing resources and provision are inadequate which exaggerates the problem. Prof. Qidwai believes that what is needed are innovative, cost-effecive methods to address the medical and non-medical problems of an increasingly ageing population.

1 What economic methods could be used to reduce some of Pakistan's health care problems of its ageing population?

2 As well as health care, what other problems might Pakistan face as a consequence of an ageing population?

The concept of optimum population

The concept of the optimum is useful when considering the idea of overpopulation and underpopulation. The **optimum population** is said to exist when output per head is the greatest, given existing quantities of the other factors of production and the current state of technical knowledge (see Figure 6.14). As the population grows it can make better use of the stock of the other factors of production such as land and capital. This is because increasing returns are enjoyed as the population grows. If as the population increases the output per head continues to grow we could consider the country to be underpopulated. As the population continues to grow we would expect the output per head to eventually peak and then decline as decreasing returns are experienced. At this stage the population has gone beyond the optimum and the country is considered to be overpopulated. In the real world, the situation is more dynamic and the state of technical knowledge is constantly improving. The quantity of the other factors also continuously changes so that the optimum population for a country is not a fixed entity. In addition, the criteria for assessing under- or overpopulation are purely economic and may be disputed by conservationists.

Income distribution

It is a characteristic of developing countries that income is unevenly distributed. This is partly because income-generating assets, especially

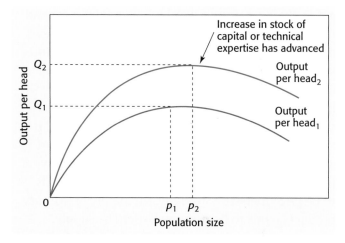

Figure 6.14 *Optimum population*

land, are owned by the few. As a result, there are great extremes of rich and poor. The 2009 World Development Report gave data on the share of the poorest 20% of the population in national income. The most extreme cases were in South America. In Bolivia, the figure was just 1.5%, in Argentina 3.1% and in Brazil, 2.9%. In Africa, the lowest figure was 3.5% in South Africa. More typical figures were in the range 5–7%. The transition of Eastern European countries from centrally planned to market economies has increased inequality as a small number of people have benefited enormously from the new opportunities that have been forthcoming. One exception is the Czech Republic which has the least uneven distribution of national income in Europe, with 10.3% accruing to the poorest 20% of the population in 2006.

Unemployment

Developing countries tend to suffer from higher levels of unemployment and underemployment than developed countries. Unemployment tends to be high because in countries with surplus populations the supply of labour tends to exceed the supply of the other factors of production. Typically, developing economies suffer from shortages in capital and entrepreneurial skills but there is also pressure on the supply of land suitable for the production process.

External trade

The foreign trade of many developing countries tends to show a great reliance upon the export of primary produce. When we consider manufactured goods as a proportion of an economy's exports, we find that, generally, most poorer developing countries depend upon primary products and developed economies depend much more upon manufactured goods and services. The significance is that those developing countries that participate in international trade become reliant upon primary exports for foreign currency earnings. This makes them vulnerable in their trading relationships because of the demand and supply conditions in the markets for primary products. The demand for primary products tends to be price inelastic. Similarly, the supply of primary products tends to be price inelastic. The supply of some products is also subject to frequent shifts depending, for example, on the size of the harvest. This means that the market for primary products is subject to frequent and severe fluctuations in price.

These fluctuations in price can destabilise the economies of developing countries. In addition, the demand for many primary products, especially foodstuffs, is income inelastic. This means that as world incomes rise there is little impact upon the demand for primary products because most of the countries with higher incomes spend on manufactured goods. Over time there is a tendency for the terms of trade of primary goods to decline compared to manufactured goods (see Chapter 4). Therefore those developing countries that are dependent upon primary products receive relatively low prices for their exports of primary products and pay relatively high prices for imports of manufactured goods. There has been a decline in the number of developing countries that are heavily reliant upon primary products as manufacturing sectors have been established.

China provides the best example. In 2006, 92% of exports were manufactured goods. Elsewhere in Asia there are heavy exporters of manufactured goods, particularly clothing and electronics. In India, the figure was 70%, 74% in Malaysia and 81% in Pakistan. In contrast, sub-Saharan African countries export very few manufactured goods and where they do, many are processed food products. In 2006, for example, manufactured exports made up only 18% of Tanzania's exports of goods, A notable exception was South Africa where manufactured goods made up 53% of merchandise exports.

Urbanisation

There are still high proportions of the populations in developing economies who live in rural areas. On average over half of the population of developing countries is classified as rural. Nevertheless developing economies show very rapid rates of rural–urban migration. High-income countries already have the majority of their populations living in urban areas. As a result, there is relatively little growth in the urban population of developed countries. The rural–urban migration in developing countries can cause extra pressure on resources in already overcrowded urban areas. There is pressure on the infrastructure, with housing, roads and schools incapable of coping with the extra demand.

Technology

The gap between developed and developing countries in terms of the application of new technology is deep and widening. This covers a wide range of applications including new production techniques, new more efficient means of communication and the electronic storage and retrieval of information. Only 5% of the world's computers are located in developing countries. Although the application of the internet to commerce will increase efficiency, especially in distribution, it will widen the technology gap for those developing countries that lack the technical skills and the infrastructure to participate effectively.

Off to the city

Government eases the rules

It was one of Mao Zedong's many big ideas, and thus far one of his most enduring. In the late 1950s, at the time of the 'great leap forward', China established its hukou, or household registration system, which required people to live and work only where they were officially permitted to. For a government intent on running its economy according to a strict central plan, it was well to have people stay where they were told. For China's hundreds of millions of rural dwellers it made leaving their village nearly as difficult as leaving the country.

Over the past 20 years China has moved steadily further from central planning, and workers have moved in huge numbers away from the nation's economically backward countryside to its far more vibrant cities. According to official estimates, China's migrant labour force now numbers somewhere around 100 million. The government expects another 46 million to come looking for jobs in the cities in the next five years as the number of surplus rural workers swells to 150 million.

In light of such numbers, China's announcement on 16 August 2001 that it plans to revamp the registration system seems a bit like closing the barn door after the horse has escaped. But if the government carries through with its plan to abolish restrictions on labour mobility, it will in fact make a huge difference to the lives of those migrants.

While that is clearly true, it has also helped avert an outcome that many of China's urban dwellers dread: an unrestrained influx into the cities of people from the countryside. While city people are glad to have enough migrants to handle the jobs they themselves do not want, they fear that too many will put unbearable strain on housing, communications and other resources. Some municipal governments have already tinkered with existing rules to admit only 'desirable' outsiders. The cities of Shenzhen and Zhuhai offer residency to those who can buy property, and Beijing grants documentation to technical workers with senior qualifications.

Apartment blocks in Shenzhen, China

Source: The Economist, *1 September 2001*

Multinational corporations and foreign direct investment

A multinational corporation (MNC) or transnational corporation is defined as a firm that operates in more than one country. In other words, it is a business with a parent company based in one country but with production or service operations in at least one other country. The largest MNCs such as the Coca-Cola Corporation, Ford, Nestlé, McDonald's, Toyota, Hilton Hotels and so on are worldwide operations, with manufacturing and retail outlets in many countries of the world.

Through their activities, MNCs provide **foreign direct investment** (FDI) to the economies in which they operate. This is investment that is necessary to produce or sell a good or service in a foreign country. FDI therefore involves capital flows between countries. It should not be confused with portfolio

253

investment which is the purchase of shares by foreign investors in businesses that are located in another country.

The activities of MNCs and the effects of foreign direct investment on the economies of recipient countries have been the subject of much debate and discussion by economists and politicians. In the Caribbean area, for example, the impact of FDI from MNCs has been substantial. It has been particularly significant in the bauxite, alumina, petroleum and natural gas industries. There has also been considerable FDI in sugar, tourism and utilities. US MNCs especially have been heavy investors in these businesses. At the same time, not all MNCs are well liked in the countries where they invest mainly because profits earned invariably go back to the home country of the MNC and in many cases, foreign rather than home labour is employed.

Table 6.8 shows the estimated FDI for the three Caribbean economies that have received the largest flows since 2003. The flows have been far from smooth. Most of the flows have come from US corporations although in the case of Jamaica, Spanish companies have expanded their investments in tourism and tourist properties.

	Jamaica	Trinidad & Tobago	Bahamas
2003	250.0	0	550
2004	0	1000	0
2005	259.7	1200	0
2006	260.0	1500	n.a.

Table 6.8 *Estimated FDI in three Caribbean economies 2003–2006 ($USm)*

Source: LOCO monitor, *2006*

External debt

A final characteristic of most developing economies is their indebtedness. Some are categorised as heavily indebted poor countries (HIPC). This means that one of two key debt ratios is exceeded. The first ratio is the relationship between the debt service ratio and the GNP. The second is the relationship between the present value of debt service to exports. If either the proportion of debt service exceeds 80% of GNP or the present value of debt service is 220% of exports, then the country is considered to be heavily indebted. If either of the two ratios exceeds 60% of the critical level, then the country is said to be moderately indebted. The presence of debt on such a scale diverts resources to debt repayment and away from spending on health and education, on infrastructure and poverty relief. Such debt provides a very real obstacle to development.

Table 6.9 shows the extent of external debt for selected developing economies in 2006. As this shows, the position is diverse. Some countries have high absolute debt yet are not classed as heavily indebted. Others, including many in central and eastern Europe, are heavily indebted and struggling to make their annual repayments. Debt remains a major obstacle to the future economic development and growth of many developing economies.

	Total debt US$m	Present value as % GNP
Argentina	122 190	68
Brazil	194 150	28
Central African Republic	1 020	53
Congo, Dem Rep	11 201	119
Croatia	37 480	93
India	153 075	15
Indonesia	130 956	45
Kazakhstan	74 148	132
Kenya	6 534	26
Pakistan	35 909	26
Russia	251 067	34
Tanzania	4 240	16
Zimbabwe	4 677	110

Table 6.9 *External debt of selected developing economies in 2006*

Source: World Development Report, *2009*

Conclusions

A well-known development economist has summarised the problems that stem from these common characteristics as follows:

'Widespread and chronic absolute poverty, high and rising levels of unemployment and underemployment, wide and growing disparities in the distribution of income, low and stagnating levels of agricultural productivity, sizeable and growing imbalances between urban and rural levels of living and economic opportunities, serious and worsening environmental decay, antiquated and inappropriate educational and health systems, severe balance of payments and international debt problems, and substantial and increasing dependence on foreign and often inappropriate technologies, institutions and value systems.'

International comparisons of living standards – a word of warning

There are many problems when interpreting data on comparative living standards between countries. This equally applies to all comparisons, even where most countries are at a similar stage of development, as well as to comparisons between countries that differ more significantly in their relative levels of development. Problems include:

- fluctuations in the exchange rate against the US dollar – large movements can affect the GNP/GDP per head measure
- measuring purchasing power, particularly in economies where prices are not well known
- no allowance is made for the size of the subsistence sector – this can be large in emerging and less developed economies
- the shadow or informal economy is not included and can often be at least 25% of GNP
- no allowance is made in GNP per head for the distribution of income
- countries with a high GNP per head may have achieved this through the serious denigration of their physical environments or through excessive expenditure on defence
- traditional measures do not take into account variables such as social justice and political freedom.

Actual and potential growth

The production possibility curve described in Chapter 1 can be used to explain the important distinction between changes in the actual output of goods and services and changes in the potential output of goods and services.

A change in the actual output of goods and services can be achieved by the better utilisation of existing factors of production. In Figure 6.15 assume the economy is currently producing at point X. This is a point well within the production frontier shown by the production possibility curve. Production at this point might be caused by a lack of aggregate demand in the economy. The movement from point X to point Y on the curve could, for example, be achieved by increasing demand through fiscal and/or monetary policy (see Chapter 7). This would lead to an increase in the output of both goods and services. In turn, it would certainly lead to an increase in Gross Domestic Product and be considered as actual economic growth. In the long run, however, further increases in output could only be achieved if the potential output of the economy was to grow. This is represented by a shift in the production possibility curve itself. In Figure 6.15 the shift of the curve from PPC_1 to PPC_2 represents a growth in the potential output or productive potential of this economy. In the long run, therefore, explanations of economic growth need to focus upon those factors which increase the potential output of an economy.

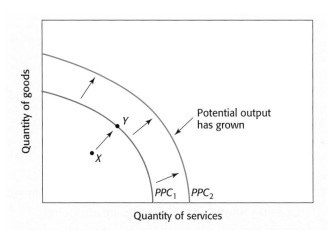

Figure 6.15 *An increase in the potential output of an economy*

Factors contributing to economic growth

The position of the production possibility curve is determined by an economy's production function (see Chapter 2). This shows the maximum output that can be produced by an economy taking into account the current factors of production and the current state of technical expertise.

In order to achieve economic growth which can be sustained it is necessary to:

- **Increase the quantity of resources at the disposal of the economy**. All of the factors of production could potentially be increased. Clearly, given the growth in population in

SELF-ASSESSMENT TASK 6.13

Study the data below and then answer the questions that follow.

Country	GNP per head PPP US$	Employed labour force (%) 2001			Life expectancy (years)	Adult literacy %
		Agric	Ind	Services		
Antigua & Barbuda	10 360	4.0	5.6	90.4	71.9	89
Bahamas	16 140	3.8	5.4	90.8	65.5	96
Barbados	15 060	4.2	7.1	88.7	72.6	99
Belize	6 510	20.2	9.6	70.2	68.4	77
Dominica	5 250	21.0	10.1	68.1	74.6	94
Grenada	7 000	13.8	7.6	78.6	64.5	96
Guyana	4 110	23.1	18.8	58.1	65.5	99
Jamaica	3 630	19.9	8.1	71.7	73.3	89
St Kitts/Nevis	11 190	14.7	7.9	77.4	72.2	98
St Lucia	5 560	20.8	9.8	69.4	73.6	90
St Vincent & the Grenadines	6 250	24.9	8.7	66.4	73.6	96
Suriname	n/a	13.0	11.7	75.4	68.9	88
Trinidad and Tobago	11 180	7.8	13.5	78.7	66.7	99

Table 6.10 *Selected indicators of development for CARICOM member states, 2004*
Sources: CARICOM, World Bank

1 On the basis of GNP per head, it might be concluded that living standards in Barbados are about four times higher than those in Jamaica. Do you agree?

2 Explain the variations in the employment structure of CARICOM economies and discuss any implications these variations might have for the economic development of the region.

developing countries it would seem that the supply of labour would grow through the natural increase in population. If there is a positive net migration the population will also grow as the number of immigrants exceeds the number of emigrants. An increase in the labour force will not create a great impact upon production possibilities, however, without an increase in the other factors. Capital goods can only be increased if investment takes place. Enterprise can be increased through training and government policies that encourage risk-taking in the economy. Land can only really be increased through new discoveries of valuable resources or in extreme cases, armed conflict. Any land gained through reclamation schemes should really be considered as a type of capital because it needs investment before it becomes available.

- **Increase the quality of resources at the disposal of the economy.** Improvements in the quality of resources will increase the productivity of the factor inputs. The quality of labour can be improved through education and training. This is known as investment in human capital. This term can also be applied to any development of the factor enterprise. The quality of capital goods is improved as technology improves. The quality of capital goods used in developing countries improves as these countries participate in international trade. The quality of land for agricultural use can be improved through the application of fertiliser and through irrigation and drainage schemes.

The main obstacle to increases in the quantity and quality of resources in developing countries is the opportunity cost of diverting resources away from their current use. Although the labour supply may be abundant it is invariably difficult to improve its quality. Many young people are deprived of education because of a shortage of schools, teachers and textbooks. Devoting more resources to education means such resources have to be diverted from some other use. In addition, many children are required to work to support family incomes. Capital goods are created through the process of investment. Because many developing countries are barely above the

subsistence level it is impossible for them to divert resources away from current consumption without creating a decline in living standards below that required for survival. The opportunity cost is too high. Very often the only way in which capital goods can be acquired in such circumstances is for the necessary resources to be provided from abroad in the form of loans or aid. As we have seen, many developing countries have acquired a large debt problem which has necessitated the transfer of funds in the form of debt repayments from themselves to the richer countries. This again diverts much needed resources away from development projects and poverty alleviation in developing countries. The provision of development aid might be the answer to the difficulties of providing sufficient funds for development.

One important factor necessary for growth is to improve the state of technical expertise utilised in the economy. The high rates of growth experienced by the developed countries in the industrial era have been sustained by the application of technological innovations to mass production. This could only be achieved through extensive research and development into new techniques of production.

Again, the concept of opportunity cost can be used to explain the problems faced by the developing countries. Research and development is expensive and has a high opportunity cost in the developing countries who can ill afford to divert scarce resources into this use. The benefits to the economy will only be experienced in the medium to long term. Today over 90% of the world's research and development expenditure takes place in developed economies. This allows them to maintain their dominance of world markets in manufactured goods even though the manufacturing is taking place in low cost economies far away from where the technological knowledge originates. In addition, the new technology developed in the richer countries has been developed to be applied to rich countries' problems. For example, rich countries tend to use capital-intensive production methods. They try to economise on the use of highly skilled and expensive labour which is in short supply in the rich countries. They also produce for the mass market, so the scale of production is large. The developing countries have large supplies of unskilled labour and often produce for much smaller markets. As we have seen, they cannot afford to divert resources to the production of capital goods which are capable of utilising the new technologies. As a result, the new technologies cannot be easily transferred from the developed countries to developing countries. The technology transfer which might be considered necessary to allow the developing countries to progress is seen as inappropriate.

Improving the quantity and quality of the components of an economy's production function, together with the level of technical expertise in an economy, will certainly result in an increase in the potential output of an economy. Changes that lead to such improvements can be considered as the sources of growth. An example might be an increase in the savings ratio in an economy. This might lead to the diversion of resources from consumption to investment in the economy and an increase in capital accumulation.

Benefits and costs of economic growth

Benefits

The main benefit of economic growth is the increase in goods and services which become available for the country's citizens to enjoy. This raises their material living standards. For developing economies, this means that more people can eat better quality food, have improved living accommodation and, maybe, own their own car. Economic growth also makes it easier to help the poor. Without any increase in output and income, the only way in which the living standards of the poor can be raised is by taking income and hence goods and services from higher income groups. Whereas if economic growth occurs at least some of the extra income can be given to the poor in the form of higher benefits, thereby enabling them to enjoy more goods and services.

A stable level of economic growth increases business' and consumers' confidence. This makes planning easier and encourages investment. Economic growth may also increase a country's international prestige and power. For example, China's rapid growth in the early 1990s increased its status not only as a major manufacturer in the global economy but also in world politics.

Costs

Economic growth may bring with it a number of costs. If the economy is operating at the full employment level there will be an opportunity cost involved in achieving economic growth. To produce more capital goods, in order to increase the country's productive capacity, some resources will have to be moved from producing consumer goods to producing capital goods. So current consumption of goods and services will have to be reduced. However, this will only be a short run cost since in the long run the increased investment will increase the output of consumer goods and services.

Economic growth may, though, bring increased stress and anxiety. A growing economy is a dynamic economy that also undergoes structural changes. Workers may have to learn new skills and may have to change their occupation and/or where they live. Some workers may find this difficult to cope with. Economic growth may also be accompanied by increased working hours and pressure to come up with new ideas and improvements. When Japan was growing rapidly in the 1980s some workers put in very long hours and students felt under considerable pressure to pass examinations. This is now the case in China, India and Pakistan.

Economic growth may also be accompanied by the depletion of natural resources and damage to the environment. Higher output may, for example, involve firms using more oil, building on greenfield sites and creating more pollution. However, this does not have to be the case. Output can be increased in ways which do not damage the environment or which at least limit the damage.

Sustainable development

Very rapid growth may be achieved but this may be at the expense of the living standards of future generations if it results from the reckless use of resources. Countries, developed and developing, are now becoming more concerned to achieve sustainable development. This occurs when output increases in a way which does not compromise the needs of future generations. Materials such as aluminium, paper and glass can be recycled. More use could be made of renewable energy resources in preference to non-renewable resources, and improvements in technology may both increase output and reduce pollution.

Cutting back on CO_2 emissions, reducing landfill and dumping less waste into rivers and the sea are all central to realising improved sustainability.

Pursuing **sustainable development** ensures that economic growth improves living standards and the quality of life not only in the present but for the future. To achieve this requires a deliberate and concerted effort to balance economic, social and environmental objectives. More specifically:

- **Economic objectives require a better use of scarce resources.** To be sustainable, growth should ensure that sufficient resources are available to invest in human capital as well as physical capital. Education and training programmes are central to this requirement (see Chapter 7).

- **Social objectives focus on the distribution of the benefits of growth.** Food, housing, health care and secondary education are essential if people's lives are to be productive. A sustainable approach involves an educational system that gives girls the same opportunities as boys, is serious about reducing fertility rates, controlling the spread of HIV/AIDS and providing for the elderly.

- **Environmental objectives require the responsible use of natural resources.** This means that mineral extraction and forest depletion especially should be done in such a way that the benefits are not just short-term. Many people in developing countries lack clean water and proper sanitation, a reason why UNICEF invests heavily in these areas.

SELF-ASSESSMENT TASK 6.14

Read the feature below and then answer the questions that follow.

Food miles – care needed for developing economies

Consumers in many European countries are becoming increasingly aware of the environmental impact of the food they buy. Food miles, the distance food travels from field to plate, is a simple way of measuring this impact. The most contentious examples are those where fruit and vegetables are freighted by air from Africa, South East Asia and parts of South America. The carbon footprint, total CO_2 emissions generated, is around 200 times greater than if that food had been transported by ship.

Kenya is a particularly good example of an economy where exports of vegetables, fruit and flowers to the European market have provided a major boost to this poor country's economy. In 2009, these horticultural products are expected to generate US$1300 million in export earnings, considerably more than tourism and telecommunications. Small farmers can earn a lot more money from export crops of green beans, sweet potato, and baby corn than they can if they grow

Kenyan horticultural producer

maize, the country's staple food crop. In turn, this income provides a reasonable level of living for extended families.

Such exports though are controversial in countries like Kenya for two reasons:

1 **Food security.** There is a view that it harms Africa as a whole if food is exported out of the continent. It is argued that the food should remain in Africa for internal consumption.

2 **The CO$_2$ emissions generated through air freighting products to Europe and the US.** There has been a very strong recommendation from the UK's Soil Association that there should be a ban on air-freighted organic produce in the UK market. This proposal has been vehemently opposed by Kenyan growers.

---

1 Describe the benefits of exports of Kenyan horticultural products to:
  a consumers in the UK
  b producers in Kenya.

2 Discuss whether a carbon tax should be placed on all imports of air-freighted food from developing countries such as Kenya.

Achieving sustainable development is by no means easy nor is it necessarily the simplest way to achieve economic growth. The cost of NOT following a sustainable strategy should never be a consideration.

Unemployment

People are unemployed when they are able and willing to work but cannot find a job. Unemployment can bring with it serious problems both for those who are unemployed and for the economy. With some people being out of work, the country's output will be below its potential level, tax revenue will be lower and more state benefits will have to be paid out. The unemployed, in addition to having lower incomes, may experience higher rates of divorce and mental and physical illness and will miss out on training and work experience. There is also increasing evidence of a link between levels of unemployment and crime.

Economists measure not only the level of unemployment but also the rate of unemployment. The level refers to the number of people who are unemployed, whereas the rate of unemployment is the number of people unemployed as a percentage of the number of people in the labour force (that is, the employed and the unemployed).

Just what constitutes **full employment** is a matter of debate. It is often considered to be achieved when unemployment falls below 4%, although this varies a lot between different economies. This may appear to be somewhat surprising as you might have expected it to be 0% unemployed. However, in practice, at any particular time some people may be experiencing a period of unemployment as they move from one job to another job.

The **natural rate of unemployment**, which can also be referred to as the non-accelerating inflation rate of unemployment (Nairu), is largely a monetarist concept. It is the level of unemployment which exists when the aggregate demand for labour equals the aggregate supply of labour at the current wage rate and so there is no upward pressure on the wage rate and the price level. The inflation rate is constant, with the actual inflation rate equalling the expected one.

Whilst monetarists argue that the natural rate of unemployment cannot be reduced, in the long run, by expansionary monetary or fiscal policy, it can change over time. The factors which do determine the natural rate of unemployment are supply-side factors. Over time the natural rate of unemployment may fall as a result of:

- an increase in the mobility of labour
- an improvement in the education and training levels of workers
- a reduction in trade union restrictive practices
- a reduction in state unemployment benefits
- a cut in income tax.

Difficulties of measuring unemployment

Most governments use two main methods to measure unemployment. One is to measure the number of people in receipt of unemployment-related benefits – this is called the claimant count. It has the advantage that it is relatively cheap and quick to calculate as it is based on information which the government collects as it pays out benefits. However, the figure obtained may not be entirely accurate. This is because it may include some people who are not really unemployed and may omit some people who are genuinely unemployed. Some of those receiving unemployment benefit may not be actively seeking employment (**voluntary unemployment**) and some may be working and so claiming benefit illegally. On the other hand, there may be a number of groups who are actively seeking employment but who do not appear in the official figures. These groups may include the elderly, those below a certain minimum age, those on government training schemes, married women looking to return to work and those who choose not to claim benefits. As this measure is based on those receiving benefits, it changes every time there is a change in the criteria for qualifying for benefit.

The other main measure involves a labour force survey using the International Labour Organisation definition of unemployment. This includes as unemployed all people of working age who, in a specified period, are without work, but who are available for work in the next two weeks and who are seeking paid employment. This measure picks up some of the groups not included in the first measure. It also has the advantage that as it is based on internationally agreed concepts and definitions, it makes international comparisons easier. However, the data are more expensive and time-consuming to collect than the unemployment benefit measure. Also as the data are based on a sample survey they are subject to sampling error and to a multitude of practical problems of data collection.

The causes of unemployment

Monetarists believe that even at the natural rate of unemployment, when the labour market is in equilibrium, some people will still be unemployed. These are the people who are not able or willing to work at the current wage rate. This equilibrium unemployment can be divided into two main categories, frictional and structural. **Frictional unemployment** is unemployment which arises when workers are between jobs. One form of frictional unemployment is search unemployment which arises when workers do not accept the first job or jobs on offer but spend some time looking for a better-paid job. Casual and **seasonal unemployment** are two other forms of frictional unemployment. Casual unemployment refers to workers who are out of work between periods of employment including, for example, actors, supply teachers and construction workers. In the case of seasonal unemployment, demand for workers fluctuates according to the time of the year. During periods of the year, people working in, for example, the tourist, hospitality, building and farming industries may be out of work.

Unemployment can also arise due to changes in the structure of the economy. Over time the pattern of demand and supply will change. Some industries will be expanding and some will be contracting. Because of the immobility of labour, workers may not move smoothly between industries, so structural unemployment may arise. Structural unemployment can take a number of forms. One is **technological unemployment**. In this case people are out of work due to the introduction of labour-saving techniques. For instance, in many EU countries a high number of banking staff have lost their jobs in recent years with the introduction of telephone and internet banking.

When the declining industries are concentrated in particular areas of the country, the unemployment is sometimes referred to as regional unemployment. Another form of **structural unemployment** is international unemployment. This is when workers lose their jobs because demand switches from their industries to more competitive foreign industries. This occurs in many developed economies when manufacturing industries move to developing countries where costs are lower.

Keynesians, however, think that, in addition to these causes of unemployment, people can be without work because of a lack of aggregate demand. This will affect the whole economy and is referred to as **cyclical unemployment** or **demand-deficient unemployment**. Figure 6.16 shows the labour market initially in equilibrium at a wage rate of *W*. Then, as a result of a fall in aggregate demand, firms reduce their output and aggregate demand for labour shifts to ADL₁. If workers resist wage cuts, demand-deficient unemployment of XQ will exist.

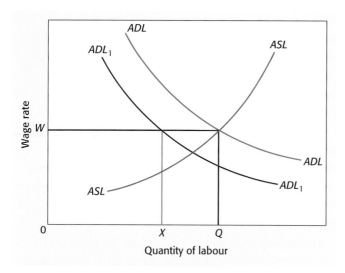

Figure 6.16 *Demand-deficient unemployment*

Even if wage rates fall, this type of unemployment may persist. This is because a cut in wages would reduce demand for goods and services, which would cause firms to cut back their output further and make more workers redundant.

Figure 6.17 shows the trend in unemployment in the UK from 1993 to 2010 when the economy was moving out of recession. In mid-2009, 2.38 million people were unemployed, an unemployment rate of 7.6%. Moreover, economists forecast that the number unemployed would rise to a peak of over 3 million in mid-2010. Of all major EU countries, the UK economy has experienced most problems of moving out of recession.

All economies have been affected by the global downturn since 2008. The ILO estimated that by the end of 2009 global unemployment would be about 220 million, a rate of around 7%. In the US, the unemployment rate in mid-2009 was higher at 8.1%, whilst in Japan it was at its highest ever since 1960 of 4.4%. At the same time, the pain of unemployment was being felt much more widely. In India, the unemployment rate was 8.2% of those employed in the organised sector – this covers just one in ten of the workforce. In China, the official rate of unemployment was 4.2%, but economists believed that the actual rate was more than double, even allowing for the

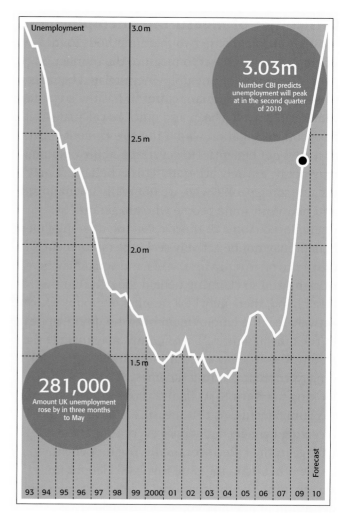

Figure 6.17 *UK unemployment, 1993–2010*
Source: Daily Telegraph, *16 July 2009*

exclusion of rural areas. Finally, in South Africa, the unemployment rate was a massive 21.9%.

The relationship between the internal and external value of money

The internal value of a country's currency and its external value are closely connected. If the value of a country's money falls as a result of a rise in its inflation rate above that of its competitors, demand for its products will fall. As a result, demand for the currency will fall as foreigners buy fewer of the country's exports, whilst the supply of the currency on the foreign exchange market will rise as more imports are purchased. The outcome will be a depreciation of the currency, depending on the strength of these effects (see Figure 6.18).

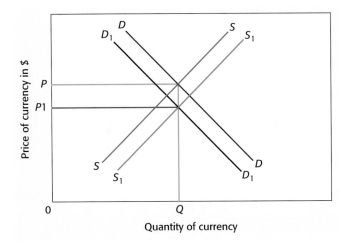

Figure 6.18 *Relationship between the demand for foreign currency and the rate of inflation in an economy*

A change in the exchange rate will, in turn, affect the internal purchasing power of a country's money. A fall in the exchange rate will raise the price of a country's imports in terms of the home currency. This will directly and indirectly reduce the value of the country's money. Each unit of currency will now buy fewer of the now more expensive finished imported products. Purchasing power may also be reduced as a result of the increase in the price of imported raw materials and the reduction in competitive pressure, driving up the prices of domestically produced products. So the internal and external value of the money tend to be directly related.

Relationship between the balance of payments and inflation

If demand for exports and imports is price elastic, a fall in the exchange rate will result in a rise in export revenue and reduced import expenditure. This will improve a country's balance of payments position. This is sometimes referred to as the Marshall–Lerner condition: namely, a fall or devaluation of the exchange rate will improve a balance of payments deficit when the combined price elasticities of demand for exports and imports are greater than one. However, if inflation rises due to the extra demand generated and the rise in the price of imported

finished products and raw materials, the balance of payments position will worsen in the longer run.

The J-curve effect is related to the Marshall–Lerner condition. In some countries, a fall in the exchange rate will actually worsen the balance of payments deficit before it starts to improve it. The reason for this is that many economies (the UK, some transitional and developing ones, for example) need to import raw materials, other supplies and components in order to produce their exports. With the fall in the exchange rate, they must pay more for such items in the short term. Hence, demand for imports is relatively inelastic, although the demand for exports is more elastic. Figure 6.19 shows a diagrammatic representation of this concept.

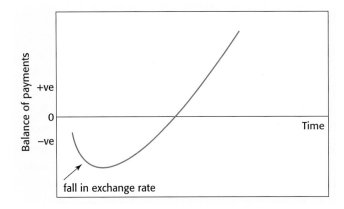

Figure 6.19 *The J-curve effect*

If a country's inflation rate rises above that of its main competitors, its price competitiveness will fall. Export revenue will decline whilst import expenditure rises and the current account balance will deteriorate.

Relationship between inflation and unemployment

Economists have devoted considerable attention to the relationship between inflation and unemployment. The most famous study on the relationship was carried out by Phillips, a New Zealand economist based at the London School of Economics. He analysed the relationship between changes in money wages (taken as an indicator of inflation) and unemployment in the UK over the period 1861–1957. He found an inverse relationship, as shown in Figure 6.20 (page 264). A fall in unemployment may cause higher inflation due to the extra aggregate demand generated and the possible upward pressure on wages.

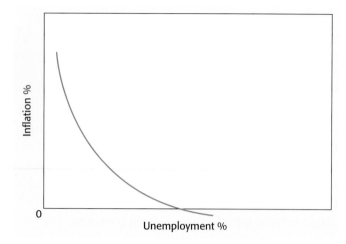

Figure 6.20 *The Phillips curve*

This traditional **Phillips curve** suggests that a government can select its optimum combination of inflation and unemployment and can trade off the two. For example, if the current unemployment rate is 8% and its inflation rate is 4%, a government may seek to lower unemployment to 5% by increasing its expenditure whilst accepting this improvement may have to be bought at the cost of higher inflation.

However, this interpretation is questioned by monetarists. They argue that whilst there may be a short run trade-off, in the long run expansionary fiscal or monetary policies will have no impact on unemployment, but will only succeed in raising the inflation rate. To support this view Milton Friedman developed the expectations-augmented Phillips curve (also known as the long run Phillips curve), as shown by the vertical line in Figure 6.21. The position of this line is determined by the natural rate of unemployment.

Figure 6.21 shows that an increase in aggregate demand does succeed in reducing unemployment from the previous 8% to 4% but creates inflation of 5% and moves the economy on to a higher short run Phillips curve. Firms expand their output and more people are attracted into the labour force as a result of the higher wages. However, when firms realise that their costs have risen and their real profits are unchanged, they will cut back on their output and some workers, recognising that real wages have not risen, will leave the labour force. Unemployment returns to 8% in

the long run but inflation of 5% has now been built into the system. Firms and workers will presume that inflation will continue at 5% when deciding on their prices and putting in their wage claims.

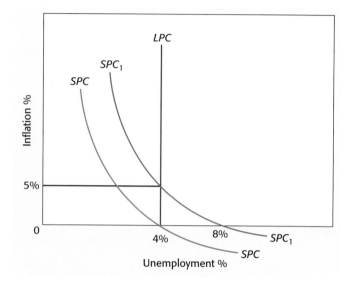

Figure 6.21 *The expectations-augmented Phillips curve*

SELF-ASSESSMENT TASK 6.15

Study the table below and then answer the questions that follow.

	USA	
	Unemployment %	**Inflation %**
1995	5.6	2.3
1996	5.4	2.2
1997	4.9	1.9
1998	4.5	1.1
1999	4.2	1.8
2000	4.0	2.4

Table 6.11 *US unemployment and inflation, 1995–2000*

Source: Tables, 5, 14 and 15, National Institute Economic Review, *No.175, January 2001, National Institute of Economic and Social Research*

1 Explain the expected relationship between changes in unemployment and inflation.
2 Analyse whether the data above support this expected relationship.

The following questions have been set in recent CIE examination papers.

1 The Chairman of a national bank stated 'It is important to rely on a range of qualitative and quantitative data to assess the economic health of a nation.' Explain what data might be employed in this assessment and discuss how useful it is likely to be.   [25]

[25 marks]

(October/November 2007)

2 The solution to unsatisfactory economic development and growth is to focus on economic theory, scientific advances, new technology and market forces.
  a Explain what is meant by economic development.   [10]
  b Discuss whether you agree with this statement.   [15]

[25 marks]

(May/June 2008)

SUMMARY

In this supplement section it has been shown that:

- There is a difference between economic growth and economic development.
- GDP/GNP per head is a simple but relevant way of classifying economies.
- Developing economies have certain common characteristics; geographical variations in the characteristics should also be recognised.
- Developing economies in general are facing many problems of population pressure.
- In general, the economic growth experienced by an economy depends on the quantity and quality of factors of production that are available.
- There are two main definitions of unemployment and ways of measuring it.
- Economists recognise various causes of unemployment.
- There is a relationship between the internal and external value of a currency and the balance of payments; the J-curve effect is often recognised.
- The Phillips Curve suggests that unemployment and inflation are inversely related.

7 Macroeconomic policies
Core

Introduction

The exchange rates of all major international currencies fluctuate on a daily basis. As seen in Chapter 6, some exchange rates are freely floating. However, many currencies are managed in the sense that they are linked to either the US dollar or the euro, the principal reserve currencies in global markets.

Euro currency

The Hong Kong dollar is an example of a currency that has a managed exchange rate traditionally pegged to the US dollar like other Asian currencies. It can fluctuate but only within a very narrow range of HK$7.75–7.85 to the US dollar. This has been a good system for Hong Kong. It has brought exchange rate stability which has been so important to its economy which is heavily dependent on international trade and related services. Fluctuations against other currencies have been more extreme. From October 2008 to October 2009, for example, the UK pound exchanged at between HK$ 10.52 and 12.64, a

variation of around 20%. The downside of stability against the US dollar has been that the Hong Kong authorities have, on occasions, had to use large reserves of currency to keep within the narrow pegged rate for its own dollar. In turn, this has caused instability and uncertainty in the domestic economy.

The move to a single currency, the euro, by 12 EU member states from 2002 has been designed to give these countries exchange rate stability. There is just one exchange rate for trade outside the eurozone whilst internal trade takes place using the common currency. Supporters of the euro believe that it has led to increased investment in the eurozone from the US, China and elsewhere in Asia and provided a stable currency regime for increased internal trade. By 2010, four more countries had joined the euro, with others expected to follow. The UK, Denmark and Sweden remain outside the eurozone but remain as member states of the EU.

Where exchange rates are managed and there is pressure to keep a currency within its permitted range, it is necessary for governments to buy and sell reserve currencies such as the US dollar or the euro. If there is persistent upward pressure, there is the added problem that currency reserves are not limitless. So, a country may not be in a position to use reserves indefinitely in this way. When this occurs, it is indicative that there is some fundamental underlying weakness – it is consistently spending more on imports of goods and services than it is generating from export revenue. To restore balance, import and export prices have to be adjusted.

Correction of the balance of payments

There are two broad policy approaches that can be used to correct an imbalance in the balance of payments where an economy has such underlying weakness. These are **expenditure switching** and **expenditure dampening** policies.

Expenditure switching policies

An expenditure switching policy is any action taken by a government which is designed to persuade purchasers of goods and services both at home and abroad to purchase more of that country's goods and services and less of the goods and services produced by others. Effectively this would include any policies designed to persuade domestic purchasers to purchase home-produced goods and services rather than imports. It would also include any policies designed to persuade foreign purchasers to buy more exports from the domestic economy. These policies are not designed to reduce the total amount of spending in a country but to redirect or 'switch' spending to a country's products rather than those produced in another country. The impact should be a fall in import expenditure and a rise in export earnings. The former will lead to a fall in the supply of a country's currency on the foreign exchange market and the latter will lead to a rise in the demand for the country's currency on the market. Both will lead to upward pressure on the exchange rate.

Expenditure switching policies include the following measures:

- tariffs
- quotas
- exchange controls
- export subsidies.

These were described in Chapter 4. Along with embargoes and voluntary export restraints, all have the disadvantage that they interfere with market forces and prevent the consumer from benefiting from the effects of specialisation and trade. Expenditure switching policies may be ineffective if the demand for imports is price inelastic or if domestically produced goods are poor quality substitutes. In addition, a government's ability to resort to expenditure switching policies is limited by its membership of the World Trade Organization

(WTO). As a result, it may be forced to resort to expenditure dampening policies.

Expenditure dampening policies

An expenditure dampening or reducing policy is any action taken by a government that is designed to reduce the total level of spending in an economy. This will have two effects. First, a reduction in spending will mean that there will be fewer purchases of imported goods and services. Secondly, domestic producers will find that their domestic market is 'dampened'. As a result, they may try to make up for the decrease in domestic sales with increases in sales abroad. The overall impact therefore should be a fall in imports and a rise in exports. Expenditure dampening policies include the following:

- **Deflationary fiscal policy** This means raising taxes and reducing government expenditure. Raising taxes will reduce disposable incomes meaning that less will be available to spend on imports. In addition, the reduced government spending will lead to a downward multiplier effect which will depress incomes further. The extent of the reduction in import spending will depend upon the **marginal propensity to import**. This measures the change in import spending as disposable incomes change. A high marginal propensity to import will mean that a fall in disposable incomes will have a great impact upon import spending, and taxes may not have to be raised by much to reduce import spending by the required amount. Alternatively, if the marginal propensity to import is low, it will require a large increase in taxes to bring about the necessary reduction in import spending.

- **Deflationary monetary policy** This means raising interest rates and reducing the money supply. In addition to attracting inflows of foreign capital that will increase the demand for the currency on the foreign exchange market, increases in the rate of interest will reduce the money supply and deflate the economy. This is because the higher interest rate will reduce the demand for loans for consumption and investment and lead to a fall in aggregate monetary demand.

A major disadvantage of a managed exchange rate system is that it creates a deflationary situation when there is downward pressure on the exchange rate as a result of a balance of payments deficit. The deflationary outcome will have the intended effect of reducing spending on imports, but it will also have the additional unintended effect of reducing spending on home-produced products. This means that unemployment will rise in the domestic economy.

The maintenance of a managed rate in times of balance of payments deficits requires exchange market intervention on a daily basis together with expenditure switching and expenditure dampening policies with their resulting negative side effects. If the problem persists, then it is clear that the deflationary pressure will cause the economy to operate at less than full capacity, with all the waste in terms of lost output that this implies. Under these circumstances there may be a case for a **devaluation** of the currency. This means that the government announces that it will now adjust or peg the exchange rate at a new lower value. This has the same effect as a depreciation of the currency. It alters the relative price of imports and exports to restore competitiveness. If the economy continues to suffer from inflation, devaluation will become increasingly frequent and the benefits of a managed exchange rate will be lost.

The long-term answer to the difficulties associated with a persistent balance of payments deficit is to improve the quantity and quality of goods and services produced in the economy. As a result governments have increasingly adopted supply-side policies to improve the underlying competitiveness of the economy so that persistent deficits do not arise (see Supplement section of this chapter). Only in this way can economies enjoy full employment and the full benefits of international trade.

A persistent balance of payments surplus can also create difficulties for an economy but under these circumstances the pressure on the government will not be so acute. This is because the government will be selling quantities of its own currency to prevent a rise in the rate. The effect is that the country's reserves of foreign exchange will be rising. Nevertheless, if an economy suffers from a persistent surplus it may choose to undertake a **revaluation** of the currency to restore long-term equilibrium to the accounts.

Finally, it is worth raising the whole question as to whether an imbalance on the balance of payments caused by a current account deficit or surplus is really a bad thing. Economists are somewhat divided on this issue. Look at the current global position. The US has had a string of deficits for many years. In 2009 this was estimated at $540 billion. To fund this, at a time of recession, the US government has done what it has always done, namely borrow money from itself. In stark contrast, China had an estimated surplus of $364 billion. China has also been feeling the wind of global recession and has continued to resist pressure to revalue its seriously undervalued exchange rate. In neither case have these countries really done what economic theory says they should have done.

Conflicts between policy objectives on inflation, the balance of payments and the exchange rate

Managing the economy is a far from an easy task. There are many reasons for this, one of which is the inherent conflict that exists when governments are confronted with policy objectives which cannot be simultaneously achieved. This inevitably means that priorities have to be made or, more likely, there has to be compromise.

Most developing (and indeed some developed) economies have persistent deficits on their balance of payments. These deficits are likely to be on trade in goods and services, other parts of the current account or the capital account. Expenditure switching and expenditure dampening policies, often used together, are the usual policy methods used to try to rectify the situation. This is particularly the case when the deficit is on the balance on goods, the balance on services or both.

Switching expenditure away from imports may reduce trading deficits and can be achieved by a fall in the exchange rate. This makes imported goods more expensive relative to those produced in the domestic economy. This is fine, but it could create a rise in the rate of inflation since domestic producers are increasing their share of the home market and are also in a better competitive position to sell what they make on the international market. In turn, after a time lag, it is likely to mean that the government

Study the information below and then answer the questions that follow.

America's economic weakness?

	Current account balance ($bn)	As % of GDP
2001	−384	3.8
2002	−461	4.7
2003	−523	5.1
2004	−624	5.8
2005	−728	6.1
2006	−788	5.9

Table 7.1 *US current account balance, 2001–2006*

On the surface, the United States has the strongest economy in the world. Investors have been happy to pour their money into the US's booming markets. As a result, the current account deficit has ballooned. In 2006 it stood at an estimated 5.9% of GDP.

The worry is that foreign investors will be concerned that the US is using their capital to finance low savings and a consumer spending boom rather than boost investment. As a result, they will start to shift their money elsewhere – the dollar should therefore fall, boost US exports and slow import growth. A weaker dollar in turn will aggravate fears of inflation and a slowdown in economic growth.

1 As well as currency depreciation, what other policies could the US use to reduce the current account deficit? What consequences might occur?

2 Discuss whether the US government should be concerned about the large negative current account balances that are occurring?

has to introduce further policies to suppress domestic demand. This is not entirely a bad thing since it will be consistent with the objective of reducing balance of payments deficits.

This is fine in theory. It is most likely to be effective in the case of economies that have a strong manufacturing sector since this sector can respond to the challenge of increased demand. Where an economy is dependent upon agricultural goods and raw materials, as with most developing economies, the effect is less clear since export demand is likely to be price inelastic. It is also likely to be effective, with a time lag, in the case of economies that have

substantial earnings from international tourism. A fall in the exchange rate say of the East Caribbean dollar will make holidays in Jamaica more attractive to US tourists in the same way as the price of a bottle of Jamaican rum will be cheaper in the US domestic market.

For some economies, where their currency is directly linked to the US dollar, there is often very little they can do to directly affect their exchange rate. As a result, they may experience balance of payments problems as a result of a weak US dollar on the global currency market.

SPECIMEN EXAM QUESTIONS

The following questions have been set in a recent CIE examination paper.

1 a Explain what is meant by a current account deficit.   [8]
b Discuss the effectiveness and desirability of imposing tariffs to correct a current account deficit.   [12]

[20 marks]

(May/June 2008)

SUMMARY

In this core section it has been shown that:

- Governments may find it necessary to use various policies to correct a balance of payments deficit or surplus.
- The use of these policies is necessary where a country has a managed exchange rate.
- Such policies can have short-term detrimental effects upon the domestic economy.
- From a longer-term standpoint, supply-side policies can enhance a country's competitiveness.

7 Macroeconomic policies
Supplement

On completion of this supplement section you should know:

- what policies are applied globally to assist the economic development of developing economies
- the objectives of macroeconomic policy
- what is meant by fiscal, monetary, exchange rate and supply-side policies
- how policies can be used to control inflation, stimulate employment and economic growth and correct balance of payments disequilibrium
- how economists assess the effectiveness of these policies
- the possible conflicts between policy objectives.

Policies towards developing economies

Before looking at macroeconomic policies in detail from the perspective of the domestic economy, it is important to establish the wider context within which developing economies have to manage their macroeconomic affairs. This introductory section builds upon the content of Chapter 4 and looks at the activities of the World Trade Organization, the International Monetary Fund and the World Bank and how these impact on developing economies.

World Trade Organization head quarters in Geneva, Switzerland

World Trade Organization

The World Trade Organization (WTO), with headquarters in Geneva, Switzerland, currently has 153 members. Vietnam was the latest country to be admitted from 2007. Significantly after 15 years of tense negotiations, the People's Republic of China became a member in 2001.

The WTO's mission is a simple one. In its own words, it 'helps trade flow smoothly, freely, fairly and predictably'. In practice, this should produce a trading system with the following characteristics:

- **Non-discrimination**   Two key principles are involved here. The first is known as the most-favoured-nation treatment. Under WTO agreements, countries cannot grant a special favour (for example a lower rate of duty or

duty free access) to one WTO member over another. In other words, all countries should be treated on an equal basis. The second principle is called national treatment. This involves treating foreigners and locals equally. Under this agreement, imported and locally produced goods should be treated equally after goods have reached the domestic market. This does not prohibit a country imposing tariffs on imported goods though it does mean that the goods then compete on the same basis thereafter. The principle also applies to services so that foreign firms, for example, trying to set up in business elsewhere should be treated in exactly the same way as domestic firms wishing to expand their operations.

- **Free trade** The most obvious way in which this can be done is by lowering trade barriers, tariff and non-tariff barriers. This will enable goods and services to flow more openly and fairly between members, providing the benefits of the gains from trade that were described in Chapter 4.

- **Predictability** The purpose of this objective is to 'bind' WTO members once they have agreed to open their markets. The rationale behind this is to provide a stable business environment whereby firms will feel secure that trade barriers will not be raised at some future date. This should create a business environment where investment is encouraged, jobs are created and consumers can enjoy the benefits of lower prices and more choice. It has particular relevance for businesses moving into emerging and developing economies where there is likely to be concerns over future political stability and economic prospects.

- **Promoting fair competition** The WTO system allows tariffs and in some circumstances, other forms of protection. Having said this, once a restriction has been imposed by a member, WTO agreements mean that thereafter there should be free and fair competition in the market. This must not be distorted by further constraints on foreign-produced goods and foreign-owned services.

- **Special provision for developing countries** From the outset, the WTO has sought to assist the development of developing countries. This has not been easy given the stances taken by the USA and EU, for example, with respect to trade in certain agricultural products. Nevertheless, the WTO has sought to give such countries time and flexibility to implement various agreements. The agreements provide special assistance and trade concessions for developing countries.

The agreements

Agreements by the WTO cover goods, services and intellectual property. They are often called the WTO's trade rules since the WTO is a rules-based system of agreements that have been negotiated by governments. The so-called Uruguay Round agreements are the basis of the current WTO system.

The Uruguay Round covered three main areas:

- **Tariff cuts** Developed country members of WTO agreed a 40% cut in their tariffs on industrial products to be phased in over a 5-year period from 1995. This agreement reduced the average tariff from 6.3% to 3.8%. They also agreed that fewer imported products should be charged at higher duty rates. This was of particular benefit to developing countries which saw the proportion of their exports faced with tariffs of 15% and above in industrialised countries fall from 9% to 5% of total products.

- **More binding tariffs** This is the term used to denote a commitment by a member to not increase tariffs above the listed rate. Developed countries increased the number of 'bound' product lines to 99%; developing countries increased their pledges to 73%. The purpose behind these agreements is to provide rather more security for traders and other investors.

- **Agriculture** Substantial progress was made to remove almost all import restrictions of a non-tariff form on agriculture products in world trade. Most of these physical restrictions were converted to tariffs, a process known as *tariffication*. At the same time, tariffs applying to products from developing countries have been progressively reduced and commitments have been received from developed countries to reduce domestic support and export subsidies for agricultural products. The Uruguay Round represents the first time that such agreement has been reached in principle.

Doha Round

This round of negotiations started in November 2001 at the Fourth Ministerial Conference in Doha, Qatar. Negotiations have been extremely contentious and agreement on many issues has not been reached.

Central to the Doha Round has been the determination of members to put the needs of developing countries at the heart of the WTO's work programme. In particular, there has been some commitment to assist the least developed countries through seeking to provide them with an increasing share of world trade as a means of assisting their economic development.

Some limited agreement has been forthcoming. Countries have agreed to phase out all export subsidies by the end of 2013 and to terminate any cotton subsidies. Other concessions to developing countries are known as the 'Everything But Arms' initiative – this is an agreement to introduce tariff-free access for goods from least developed countries for 97% of all products that are traded.

International Monetary Fund

The International Monetary Fund (IMF) was set up in 1945 at the Bretton Woods Conference to help promote the health of the world economy following the catastrophic damage caused by World War II. With headquarters in Washington DC, it currently has 184 members. Notable non-members are Cuba and North Korea.

Over the past 60 years of its operation, the IMF's purposes have remained unchanged, although its activities have evolved and developed in line with the emerging global economy. These purposes and responsibilities are:

- to promote international monetary co-operation
- to facilitate the expansion and balanced growth of international trade
- to provide exchange rate stability
- to assist in setting up a multilateral system of payments
- to make resources available to members experiencing balance of payments difficulties, provided adequate safeguards are provided.

These activities have been central to the development of global trade since a stable system of international payments and exchange rates is necessary for trade to take place between two countries. In carrying out its responsibilities, the IMF has three main functions that are known as surveillance, technical assistance and lending. The first two are in line with its mission of promoting global growth and economic stability by encouraging countries to adopt sound economic policies. The third function is used where member countries experience difficulties in financing their balance of payments.

Many IMF members have experienced severe balance of payments problems over the past 60 years. In the 21st century, it is mainly developing economies that face fundamental disequilibria on their current accounts. In such circumstances, the IMF lends money to such countries to ease their immediate positions – it is though a necessary condition for such help that recipients work closely with the IMF to avoid similar, probably more serious problems in the future.

World Bank

Like the IMF, the World Bank arose out of the Bretton Woods agreements. Unlike the IMF though, the World Bank's function is to provide financial support for internal investment projects such as building new roads, improving port infrastructure, constructing new health facilities and so on.

It is best described as the World Bank Group through the activities of its five constituent agencies. These are:

- International Bank for Reconstruction and Development (IBRD)
- International Finance Corporation (IFC)
- International Development Association (IDA)
- Multilateral Investment Guarantee Agency (MIGA)
- International Centre for Settlement of Investment Disputes (ICSID).

The IBRD and IDA provide low or no interest loans and grants to countries that do not have favourable access to international credit markets. Therefore, the focus of activities is very much on developing economies, including the emerging economies of central and eastern Europe and South East Asia. Grants are only provided to the world's poorest countries. Loans cover areas such as:

- health and education in order to enhance human development in a country – for improving sanitation and combating Aids
- agriculture and rural development – for irrigation programmes and water supply projects

- environmental protection – for reducing pollution and for ensuring that there is compliance with pollution regulations
- infrastructure – roads, railways, electricity
- governance – for anti-corruption reasons.

Like the IMF, loans tend to be linked to conditions that involve wider-reaching changes being made to the economic policies of the recipient countries.

The World Bank has its critics. It has been accused of being a US/Western European dominated agency for supporting their economic and political interests. Through its strong support for free market reforms, its policies have been criticised as being harmful to the interests of some countries, particularly where the 'shock therapy' of reform has been introduced too quickly. Notwithstanding these and other criticisms, the World Bank has had a considerable impact in assisting the world's poorest economies.

Trade and development

As we saw in Chapter 4, in terms of economic theory it is clear that participation in international trade brings benefits to participant countries in respect of economic welfare. In the early 19th century David Ricardo developed the Principle of Comparative Advantage to argue that where differences in opportunity cost ratios exist, specialisation and free trade will result in participant economies enjoying living standards beyond those achievable if they pursued a policy of self-sufficiency. Developing this idea further it can be argued that if developing countries pursue policies to encourage the growth of trade, not only will living standards rise in the present time period, but also the economy will experience an increase in the pace of its economic development. This view suggests that international trade can act as an engine for growth.

This approach offers a very positive view of the participation of developing countries in international trade. The full benefits can be summarised as follows:

- International trade improves supply conditions in developing economies since:
  - economies of scale become possible because the market is much wider

  - the increased competition encourages domestic entrepreneurs to innovate and look for new techniques of production
  - trade leads to the transfer of skills and technology from developed to developing economies
  - because international trade raises incomes, it provides the means for increased savings and investment.
- As a result, it is claimed that international trade increases the supply of capital in developing economies.
- All of the above will lead to reduced costs and more efficient production and provide a stimulus for growth.
- In addition to the impact upon the supply side of the economy, participation in international trade will impact upon demand conditions. This is because the expansion of production to cater for the export market will draw formerly unused resources into production. The result will be an expansion of spending power in the home market that will create demand for domestic output.

Although the beneficial effects of international trade upon the growth rates of developing economies have a strong theoretical basis, many economists have a far more pessimistic view. This is based upon the pattern of world trade that emerged as economies specialised. Developed economies specialised in manufactured products, while the developing countries specialised in primary products. This meant that the developing countries were at a distinct disadvantage in trading relations since the prices of primary products have declined relative to the prices of manufactured products over time. This is for two reasons:

- First, the income elasticity of demand for primary products is low so that as world incomes have risen, there has been little extra demand for primary products and demand has shifted to manufactured goods.
- Secondly, producers of manufactured goods in developed economies have an element of monopoly power which they have used to maintain high prices.

In addition, the effects of trade have been quite limited in their impact upon the internal economies of developing countries for the following reasons:

- Usually the production of primary products took place on plantations and mines that were foreign owned so that profits were remitted abroad. Profits were seldom re-invested in the host country.
- The techniques of production adopted in the plantations and mines were often inappropriate in terms of the resource endowments of the developing country. As discussed earlier, developing economies have abundant labour but usually capital-intensive methods were used. This typically had to be imported from abroad, as did the skilled labour, and had negative effects upon the balance of payments position of developing economies.

Unsurprisingly, given these features of trading relationships between developing and developed economies many have questioned the value of policies designed to generate export-led growth in developing economies. Trading patterns are seen as essentially exploitative. As a result, many developing economies turned to import substitution policies. They tried to prevent imports of manufactured goods from developed countries in order to develop their own manufacturing industries. The overall trend is that developing countries are now generally less dependent upon exports of primary products than they once were. The total number of developing countries in which the export of primary products makes up 80% or more of total exports is now falling. Those countries that remain overly dependent upon primary products, with all the attendant problems that this dependency brings, tend to be concentrated in Africa. Emerging countries in other regions tend to have more balanced exports, with increasing emphasis on manufactured consumer goods.

The case of China is in many respects exceptional in its scale and impact. The consistently high rates of growth recorded over many years have come largely from export-led growth derived from the sale of manufactured goods to more developed high cost economies such as the USA, Canada, Australia and the EU. Chinese exports have also figured prominently in the imports of poorer countries in the Caribbean and parts of Africa. It is a model of growth that is also being followed by other Asian economies such as Malaysia, Thailand and Indonesia.

Development thinking is now inclined to accept that there is no single policy which is appropriate for all countries at all times. There is a recognition that sweeping policies are often incomplete and development issues are often quite complex. Policies that were appropriate and successful in generating development in some countries at some times are not necessarily appropriate in all countries at all times. In any given country, progress depends on a wide range of factors, the relative importance of which shifts over time. Sustainable development has many objectives of which raising per capita incomes is only one among many. Although governments matter in the development process, there is no simple set of rules which tell governments what to do and which apply in which circumstances.

Objectives of macroeconomic policy

Governments share the same main objectives of macroeconomic policy regardless of whether they are developed, emerging or developing economies. However, at any particular time, they may have different priorities. In seeking to achieve these macroeconomic objectives, governments can use a range of policies, although each of these policies has its limitations. There can also be conflicts between policy objectives.

The main government macroeconomic policy objectives are:

- full employment
- low and stable inflation
- equilibrium in the balance of payments position
- sustainable economic growth
- avoidance of exchange rate fluctuations.

Few economists would argue with these objectives. There is though considerable debate as to which macroeconomic policies should be used to achieve these objectives. As introduced in Chapter 5, various schools of economic thought persist as to what is the best way to deal with, for example unemployment, rising inflation, a current account deficit, sluggish economic growth and so on. Figure 7.1 summarises the two main approaches.

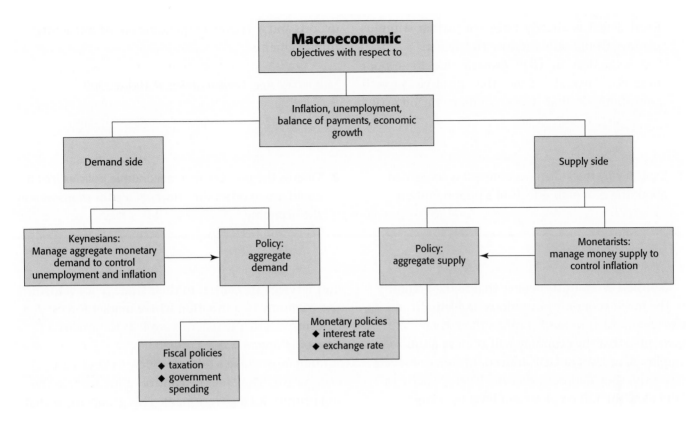

Figure 7.1 *Macroeconomic issues and policies*

Read the feature below and answer the questions that follow.

Poor monsoon to hit growth

India's growth rate will take a hit of 0.5% to 1% if the current shortfall in the monsoon continues. This was the view of Mr Jyotivardhan Jaipuria, head of research at DSP Merill Lynch. Indian GDP growth for 2009 was expected to be around 7% but if the shortfall in the monsoon continues, the output of the agricultural sector is likely to fall by at least 2%. This would inevitably mean higher food prices.

Agriculture is very important in the Indian economy and is responsible for generating an estimated 18% of GDP. If there is a decrease in output many farmers would be in trouble, prompting calls for the government to offer a stimulus package. The problem for the economy is that the

Parched farmland in India

fiscal deficit is already huge – a further stimulus package would only increase the deficit.

A reduction in GDP growth due to a poor monsoon would offset the positive growth contributions that have come from increased exports and government spending on infrastructure improvements.

Source: The Age, *London edition, 8 August 2009 (adapted)*

1 Explain why the Indian government is concerned about the economic effects of a poor monsoon.

2 Discuss the possible macroeconomic policies that it could use to offset the effects of a poor monsoon on the economy.

Keynsian economists believe that market failure in the macroeconomy is a serious problem. In particular, if left to market forces there is no guarantee that the economy will achieve a full employment level of GDP. Indeed, in times of severe recession, they maintain that the level of GDP can fall below the full employment level by a large amount and for long periods of time.

Keynsians maintain that government intervention is needed to improve the workings of the market. So, if there is high unemployment, they argue that the government should engage in deficit financing to raise the level of spending in the economy. The role of government is to assess the appropriate amount of spending to inject into the economy and to act accordingly. For most Keynsians the avoidance of high unemployment is seen as a key priority.

Keynsian principles for managing the macroeconomy were very much to the fore in many economies, the UK especially, up to around the mid-1970s. Today, many Keynsian principles persist as the world's economies struggle out of the worst recession since the 1930s. The use of fiscal policies involving an increase in aggregate demand through tax cuts and increased government spending will be discussed below and in Self-assessment task 7.5 on how the US is trying to address its unemployment problems (see page 285).

The new classical economists take the view that markets usually work efficiently. In their view, government intervention is not required apart from ensuring that laws, regulations and institutions are in place to allow market forces to operate in an appropriate way. Deregulation and reducing government involvement in the provision of goods and services are central to their strategy for returning the economy to a situation where market forces determine how the macro as well as the micro economy operates.

Monetarists take a different view to Keynsian economists. They see the control of inflation as the top priority for a government. This group argue that the prime macroeconomic function of government is to control the money supply. By controlling the money supply, inflation can be controlled. They also maintain that the attempts to reduce unemployment by increasing government spending will have the negative long-term effect of raising inflation. They believe that economies are in the main stable, unless disturbed by erratic changes in the growth of the money supply.

The Great Debate in Economics has been one of Keynsian versus Monetarist views on how the economy should be managed. Although Keynsian views are much more to the fore than a generation ago, empirical experience has shown that the most successful economies have applied macroeconomic policies that encompass both types of approach.

Introduction to fiscal and monetary policies

Figure 7.2 shows a broad representation of the means by which governments are able to manage their economies. Traditionally, fiscal policy and monetary policy have been used in virtually all types of economy to manage aggregate demand in order to achieve the government's macroeconomic objectives. This is still the case, although particularly in developed economies and increasingly in developing

| Problem | Short-term policy | | Difficulties |
	Monetary	Fiscal	
↓ Unemployment	↓ rate of interest ↑ MS	↓ indirect taxes ↑ government spending	Higher inflation in short-term. Could increase national debt.
	→ Shift to right of AD		
↓ Rate of inflation	↑ rate of interest ↓ MS	↑ direct taxes ↓ government spending	Increased unemployment and lower output. Unpopular with voters.
	→ Shift to left of AD		
Current account deficit on balance of payments	↑ rate of interest (depreciate exchange rate)	↑ taxation	Effectiveness depends on price elasticity of demand for imports and exports.
	→ Shift to left of AD		

Key: , ↓ – decrease, ↑ – increase, → – leading to

Figure 7.2 *Monetary and fiscal policy options*

economies, **supply-side policies** have been used to meet longer-term objectives such as sustained economic growth.

Fiscal policy is the way in which governments manage aggregate demand by making changes to taxation and their own expenditure. This is the traditional Keynesian approach and like monetary policy, has been widely practised in all types of economy. Like monetary policy, fiscal policy is used to 'fine tune' the economy from a short-term perspective.

Monetary policy refers to any measures that are used by the government to bring about changes in the supply of money or interest rates. (Some economists would also include policies that change the exchange rate.) Increasingly though, experience has shown that the control of interest rates rather than the money supply is the most effective way of regulating aggregate demand. This is now the main policy that is used by central banks and governments for the short-term management of the economy in most types of economy.

Monetary policy and fiscal policy do not operate in isolation – they work together in affecting aggregate demand at any one time, although one may well have rather more importance than the other. (This is a very valid reason for considering both topics in this section.)

The effects of monetary and fiscal policies on aggregate demand are shown in Figure 7.2. This figure also indicates the reasons why these policies are applied and some of the difficulties that might arise. As shown, using monetary and fiscal policies are by no means straightforward and the outcomes are by no means guaranteed as will be explained later.

Fiscal policy

Managing the economy is a complex task. The annual budget, which is the most important statement of fiscal poicy, is eagerly awaited and attracts much media attention as the overall outcome is a very clear indicator of the state of the economy. In this statement, the Finance Minister outlines the government's spending and taxation plans for the year ahead. The direction taken in the budget should give a clear indication of the government's macroeconomic priorities.

In principle, there are three types of budget:

- **Budget deficit** In this situation, projected government spending exceeds projected revenue from the many forms of taxation. This is where the government sees the need to reflate the economy by increasing aggregate demand. Normally this is in response to a situation where there is a need to expand the economy in order to create more jobs and income.

- **Budget surplus** In contrast, this describes a budget where government revenue from taxation exceeds the projected expenditure by the government on social protection, health care, education, transport and so on. Here the government has identified a need to deflate the economy by cutting back aggregate demand. This is normally in response to a situation where the rate of inflation in the economy is higher than the government feels to be appropriate. It could also be in response to a deteriorating deficit on the balance of trade.

- **Balanced budget** As its name suggests, this is a neutral situation where projected revenue and government spending are equal. Within the budget though there is likely to be some re-allocation of taxation and expenditure.

As seen in the different types of budget, a government can deliberately alter tax rates and levels of government spending to influence economic activity. This is referred to as discretionary fiscal policy and can be used to influence aggregate demand. If a government wants to raise aggregate demand it will increase its spending or cut tax rates. Keynesians favour raising government spending because they believe this will have a bigger multiplier effect (see Chapter 5). This is because the rise in government spending, especially if it is on welfare payments, is most likely to benefit the poor who have a high marginal propensity to consume (mpc). In contrast, a cut in tax rates may benefit mostly the rich who tend to have a low mpc.

A government can also allow automatic stabilisers to influence economic activity. These are forms of government spending and taxation which change, without any deliberate government action, to offset fluctuations in GDP. For example, during a recession government spending on unemployment benefits automatically rises because there are more unemployed people. Tax revenue from income tax and indirect taxes will in contrast fall automatically as incomes and expenditure decline. Figure 7.3 shows how tax revenue and government expenditure automatically change as GDP changes.

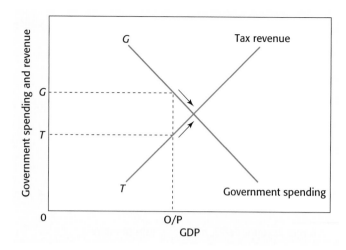

Figure 7.3 *The automatic stabilisation process*

Fiscal policy may also be employed to affect aggregate supply by changing incentives facing firms and individuals. In recent years, governments throughout the world have increasingly been using fiscal policy in this way to improve the competitiveness of their economies.

For fiscal policy to be effective it is important that the government can accurately estimate the impact that changes in government spending and taxation will have on the economy. To do this they have to have a good idea of the value of the multiplier and an awareness of the possible side-effects of policy measures. If a government underestimates the value of the multiplier, it may inject too much extra spending and thereby generate inflation and balance of payments problems. Fiscal policy instruments may also have undesirable side effects. For example, a government may raise more tax in order to reduce aggregate demand. However, this may also have disincentive effects and so reduce aggregate supply (see Chapter 5). This is true of progressive taxation such as with income tax where rates increase as the level of earnings increases. Indirect taxes such as sales taxes and excise duties are regressive since they have to be paid at the same rate irrespective of income.

Some instruments of fiscal policy also suffer from significant time lags. Whilst changes in indirect taxes are relatively easy to effect, alterations in direct taxes and government spending take longer to implement and to work their way through the economy.

It can be difficult to raise taxation and lower government spending because of the political unpopularity of such measures and because of, in the case of government spending, the long-term nature of some forms of government spending.

For example, once a decision has been announced that the pay of government employees will be increased it would be difficult to reverse it and will commit the government to higher spending for some time.

SELF-ASSESSMENT TASK 7.3

Read the feature below and answer the questions that follow.

Barbados PM delivers long-awaited budget

After postponing his budget statement on two occasions, Prime Minister Owen Arthur has delivered news that will bring some relief to low and middle income earners.

The Prime Minister has also proposed a major initiative to reduce energy costs in a plan that could save BD$65 million to $90 million.

The main features of the Economic and Financial Statement are:

- an increase in the National Insurance Scheme contributory pensions
- personal allowance for low income earners to increase from BD$20 000 to BD$22 500.
- marginal tax rate to fall from 37.5% to 35%.

With respect to energy saving measures:

- import duty on energy-saving systems to be waived; 5% tax on fluorescent light bulbs and fittings to be introduced

- taxi owners and operators of vehicles used for tourism must purchase diesel powered vehicles with an engine capacity of 1600 cc or more in order to be exempt from import duty
- a flat rate excise tax of 20% to be levied on energy-efficient vehicles, including those using alternative energy sources
- financial incentives for farmers growing fuel cane and significantly
- an increase in the import tax on goods from outside the Caribbean region from 3% to 6%. Food and special health care products to be taxed at former rate.

Source: Caribbean Net News, *19 January 2006 (adapted)*

1 Explain why these measures appear to be constituent parts of an overall deficit budget.

2 What objectives appear to underpin this budget?

Monetary policy

Monetary policies are usually implemented by the Central Bank of the country or area. In recent years, in a number of countries, changes in interest rates have been the main policy used to control inflation and, more recently, to influence economic activity.

An increase in the rate of interest, for example, will tend to reduce aggregate demand. This is because saving will be encouraged, borrowing discouraged and the spending power of households, who are borrowers, will be reduced. This downward pressure on spending is likely to reduce inflationary pressure but it may have an adverse effect on the balance of payments. This is because a higher rate of interest will attract hot money flows into the country which will raise the value of the currency and cause export prices to rise and import prices to fall.

It has been found difficult to control the money supply. In the past, governments have sought to limit the growth of a range of money supply measures, without great success.

The use of interest rates is not without problems. As with some fiscal policy instruments, there is a time lag between changing interest rates and the change taking effect. Some economists have estimated that it can take as long as 18 months for interest rate changes to fully work their way through the economy.

Interest rates are a powerful instrument but they are also a blunt and uncertain one. When the rate of interest is changed all households and firms are likely to be affected. Some are more likely to cope with such a change. For example, a rise in the rate of interest may hit the poor more than the rich as they are more likely to be net borrowers. Firms and households may also not respond in the way the government expects. If the economy is entering a recession, lowering interest rates may not persuade households and firms to spend more if they are worried about their job prospects and future markets.

With increasing mobility of financial capital, it can be difficult for a country to operate an interest rate that is significantly different from its competitors. If, for example, the country reduces its interest rates to a level noticeably lower than that in its competitor countries, hot money may flow out of the country.

Exchange rate policy

Exchange rate policy covers government decisions on whether to influence the value of its currency, whether to operate a fixed, managed or floating exchange rate and whether to link its exchange rate to that of other countries (see Chapter 6 Core).

A government can influence the value of its currency by changing its interest rate and/or buying and selling its own currency. Raising the value of the currency will increase its purchasing power and put downward pressure on inflation. However, it may also harm its balance of payments position and reduce economic activity. In contrast, reducing the value of the currency may increase employment and growth, help the balance of payments position but increase inflationary pressure.

Operating a floating exchange rate allows market forces to determine the value of its currency but may create some uncertainty. A fixed exchange rate removes uncertainty but to maintain it, a government may have to introduce policies which harm its other macroeconomic objectives. For example, if there is downward pressure on the exchange rate, the government may raise taxes to discourage spending and thereby reduce expenditure on imports. Such a measure may lower economic growth and increase unemployment.

In deciding on its exchange rate policy a government may face a number of restrictions. In the case of the eurozone, members have agreed to a common currency and a single exchange rate. In other cases they may have adopted another country's currency. This is true of some Latin American and African countries that have adopted the US dollar for all external transactions.

If a country is operating an independent exchange rate policy and decides to have a fixed exchange rate, it can be difficult to decide on the rate. It should be at the long run equilibrium level but this is hard to assess. If the government, for example, over-estimates the value it may run out of resources in seeking to maintain it or may have to raise interest rates to an unacceptable level. If it operates a floating exchange rate, speculation may result in significant fluctuations in its value. Changing an exchange rate to achieve a macroeconomic objective may not always work because its effects can be offset by other factors. For example, lowering the exchange rate to improve the balance of payments position will not work if demand for exports and imports is interest inelastic or if the quality of the country's products falls.

Read the feature below and then answer the questions that follow.

Land of the rising yen

For much of the 20th century Japan's growth has been driven by exports; consumption has remained stable at about 55% of GDP since 1980. It can be argued that there has been a fixation with a weak yen which keeps export prices cheap and import prices uncompetitive. Stacking up positive current account balances has been the norm.

This fixation, it is believed, has come at a high price – much needed capital, and with it, purchasing power goes abroad. So much so in fact that Japan is ready to scrap some of its long-held economic traditions.

The reason can be illustrated by looking at the case of automobiles. When these are manufactured in Japan and sold on the domestic market, this gives a boost to Japanese car dealers, insurance brokers and motor vehicle repairers. But when the vehicles are shipped abroad, they do not make the same meaningful contribution to the Japanese economy. This is because income earned by exporting is offset by the capital that Japanese manufacturers invest in the US. Replacing external demand with domestic demand would cause the yen to appreciate.

Honda car assembly production line in Guangzhan, China

Keeping the yen weak is costly to the Japanese economy. Japan has been hit hard by the global financial crisis. Some economists are of the view that this time, exports will not save Japan. The yen cannot be undervalued forever because it is costing the domestic economy dear.

Source: International Herald Tribune, *8–9 August 2009 (adapted)*

1 Explain how exchange rate policy has been used to:
  a increase demand for exports
  b suppress demand for imports.

2 Discuss the arguments for and against the use of exchange rate policy in this situation.

Supply-side policies

These are policies designed to increase aggregate supply by improving the workings of product and factor markets in an economy. Typical supply-side policies are increasing incentives to work, education and training, trade union reform, privatisation and deregulation.

More people may be encouraged to enter the labour force by cutting income tax and welfare benefits. This will increase a person's incentive from work and reduce the return from not working.

Improving education and training will raise workers' productivity and increase their flexibility and mobility. Trade union reform may also increase workers' flexibility and mobility and cut down on the number of days lost through strikes.

Many countries in recent years have adopted privatisation programmes in the belief that firms operate more efficiently under private ownership (see Chapter 3 Supplement). Some have also deregulated a number of their industries by removing barriers to entry.

Supply-side policies have become very popular in recent years and there is evidence that reforms have increased the responsiveness of labour markets and reduced unemployment. However, the effectiveness of some labour market reforms and some of the other measures is more uncertain. For example, cutting income tax may encourage some people to work fewer hours if they are currently content with their earnings; lowering welfare benefits will not succeed in reducing unemployment if there are no jobs available. Privatisation may also not result in an increase in efficiency if the privatised industries act as a monopoly and do not take into account external costs and benefits.

Supply-side policies tend to be long-term and uncertain in their measurable outcome as they require structural changes to be made to increase aggregate supply in the economy. They therefore have little relevance from the point of view of short-term economic management.

Monetary policy, fiscal policy and unemployment

If an economy has high unemployment, or if there is a substantial risk of unemployment increasing, the obvious monetary policy response is to cut interest rates. The response to this action is that:

- firms may increase investment as the cost of borrowing has fallen
- consumers may save less and spend more as the return from holding money in commercial banks has been reduced
- consumers may also decide to borrow more money for financing large purchases such as a new house or car
- the exchange rate may depreciate leading to a rise in exports.

Reflationary fiscal policy can also be used to reduce unemployment. Various possibilities include:

- a reduction in indirect or direct taxation to increase people's purchasing power and disposable income
- a cut in the profits tax on firms in order to stimulate new investment
- an increase in government spending, in particular current spending.

Taken together these responses are designed to increase the level of aggregate demand. The extent of any of these changes will depend on the size of the multiplier and many other factors such the extent of the changes, the response from consumers and firms and the general level of confidence in the economy. Figure 7.4 shows the effect of the increase in aggregate demand which shifts from AD to AD_1 and real GDP increases from Y to Y_1. Provided the economy is operating on the horizontal part of its long run AS curve, the price level will remain at P. The difficulty, as Figure 7.4 indicates, is that the increase in aggregate demand might fuel inflation – if this happens, the shift in AD_1 will cross the $LRAS$ curve at some point on its vertical section, indicating that the full employment level of real GDP has been reached at that time.

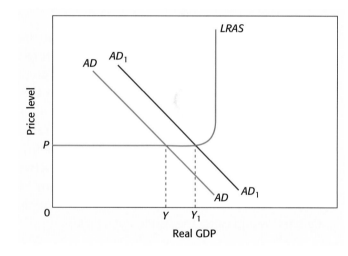

Figure 7.4 *An increase in aggregate demand*

Monetary policy, fiscal policy and inflation

In theory, monetary policy and fiscal policy can be used to control a problem of inflation through lowering aggregate demand. In practice, monetary policy is now more widely applied for this purpose, in particular through a rise in the rate of interest. This should reduce inflationary pressures as:

- borrowing will become more expensive. Firms may cut back on their investment plans and individuals may defer large-scale purchases as their real cost has increased.

Read the feature below and then answer the questions that follow.

Job losses in US hit 2.6 million for 2008

US employers shed 2.6 million jobs in 2008, the worst year since 1945. Further substantial losses are predicted for the rapidly deteriorating economy. The unemployment rate jumped to 7.2%, with more than 11 million Americans unemployed at the start of 2009. In 2008, manufacturing lost 800 000 jobs and construction shed 630 000 jobs. The remaining jobs were largely lost in the services sector.

A leading economist, Nariman Behravesh at IHS Global Insight commented that 'the US economy is in a free fall...unless something is done and done quickly to turn the economy around, we're looking at an awful situation later in 2009'.

This bad news put further pressure on President Obama and Congress to act quickly on a stimulus package that mixed tax cuts and public spending. Critics have argued that even with such a package, unemployment will rise.

The problem faced by the US economy is a lack of demand and poor business confidence. Measures are needed to strengthen consumer demand and to encourage banks to make more credit available in order to revive consumer spending.

Source: International Herald Tribune, *10–11 January, 2009 (adapted)*

Unemployed US workers protest

1 Explain what types of macroeconomic policy are being suggested to enhance the economic prospects of the US economy in 2009.

2 Discuss how the US government might assess the effectiveness of these policies in reducing unemployment.

- savings will be increased. At the same time, those people with bank loans will have to pay more for the money they have borrowed, reducing disposable income.
- firms begin to shed labour, putting pressure on wage demands to be reduced.

- 'hot money' will flow into the economy; the increased demand for a domestic currency will cause the exchange rate to rise which in turn will raise the price of exports. This loss of price competitiveness is likely to lead to a reduction in earnings from visible exports.

Deflationary fiscal policies may also be used to reduce aggregate demand. Such policies involve:

- raising direct taxation in order to cut back on the disposable income of consumers or increasing indirect taxes on products such as alcohol, tobacco, petrol and purchase taxes so as to reduce spending power
- cutting back on various forms of government spending – this is a direct means of reducing aggregate demand.

Figure 7.5 shows how reducing aggregate demand can achieve the objective of reducing inflation. As aggregate demand falls from AD to AD_1, as a consequence of one or more of the means described above, the price level falls from P to P_1. The level

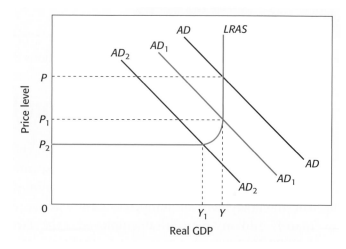

Figure 7.5   *A reduction in aggregate demand*

of real GDP remains unchanged at Y. The reality of reducing aggregate demand is that the final effect

SELF-ASSESSMENT TASK 7.6

Read the feature below and then answer the questions that follow.

Beijing moves to curb consumer price increases

Beijing has issued price control measures for certain consumer products. These measures include a freeze on prices it controls.

The measures strongly indicate that the Chinese government is giving top priority to combating inflation, which is currently running at an annual rate of 6.5%, an 11-year high brought about by soaring food prices.

The prices that will be frozen at least until the end of 2007 include transport, water, electricity, fuel and land. Some economists believed that these new price controls would ease pressure on the central bank to raise interest rates.

Other prices though will continue to rise due to the demand for goods exceeding supply. Shortages

of pork and cooking oil especially have led to price increases. Fresh food prices are also rising.

Supermarket in Beijing

1   Discuss the advantages and disadvantages of price controls as a means of combating inflationary pressures in an economy.

2   How else might the Chinese government control inflation?

of any measure is uncertain. So, it could be that aggregate demand is reduced too much resulting in real GDP falling below Y. This is shown when aggregate demand falls from AD to AD_2, the cost being more unemployment. The skill in managing the economy in this situation is to control aggregate demand so that it is at the full employment level.

Monetary policy, fiscal policy and the balance of payments

Fiscal policy measures can be effective where an economy is experiencing a deficit on the current account of its balance of payments. (The most likely reason for the deficit is that imports of visible goods exceed the exports of such goods.) Two main ways are possible:

- Expenditure dampening measures that aim to reduce total expenditure by consumers and firms on imported goods (see Core section of this chapter). A rise in income tax, for example, will reduce disposable income, leaving less income for consumers to spend on imported as well as home-produced goods. A cut in government spending, particularly where this involves imported goods, could also be used.

- Measures that result in domestic consumers substituting home-produced goods for imported goods. An obvious way to achieve this is by imposing a tariff or increasing the tariff levied on imported goods. Such a measure works more effectively where quality home-produced substitutes are readily available. A second measure could be to provide subsidies for home producers – this would reduce the price of domestically produced goods relative to similar imported products.

Monetary policy is unlikely to be used in this context. It may even worsen a current account deficit since a rise in interest rates could lead to an increase in the value of a currency, making imported goods even cheaper.

Overall the potential for using fiscal policy to correct a balance of payments problem is short term. For most economies, supply-side weaknesses underpin adverse balance of payments situations. The only long-term policy therefore is for a deliberate and concerted effort to use supply-side policies to improve competitiveness.

The potency of monetary policy and fiscal policy

There is little argument that monetary and fiscal policies are powerful tools that are available for the effective management of the economy. If proof were needed, it comes in the extent to which they have been used and remain in use in all types of economy, developed or developing, where there is some form of market function in operation. Over time, they have had different levels of importance and influence.

In the UK, for example, successive governments have taken the view that monetary policy is the best means of controlling aggregate demand, avoiding the 'boom–bust' cycle experienced when fiscal policy was the dominant means of economic management. In Caribbean economies, fiscal policies arguably have a greater role to play in managing the economy, mainly because of the nature of these economies due to their stage of economic development (see Self-assessment task 7.3, page 281).

For any country though, the short-term management of the economy invariably involves the use of both fiscal and monetary policies in order to regulate aggregate demand. The role of government is therefore one of deciding which policies will best allow it to meet its stated objectives, and to take such decisions within the much broader context of its underlying political ideology. Managing the economy therefore cannot be entirely set apart from political reality. It is though necessary to appreciate that as policy tools, their effectiveness is limited. Some limitations are summarised in Table 7.2.

A more general problem facing any government is that of a lack of up-to-date, accurate information on the present state of the economy and forecasts of future prospects. This is particularly acute in many developing economies where the quality of statistical information available to the government is not what it is in most developed economies. Although the quality has much improved in recent years through

Monetary policy	Fiscal policy
• A rise in interest rates is likely to cause new unemployment.	• It can take a long time to implement major changes to the tax structure in an economy.
• A rise in interest rates will benefit savers at the expense of borrowers. The converse applies when interest rates fall.	• There are long time lags in making changes to most types of government spending.
• Changes in interest rates will only be effective if businesses and consumers match the government's confidence in future economic prospects.	• Increases in some forms of direct taxation can have a disincentive effect on working and on the investment plans of firms.
• 'Hot money' flows are likely to be influenced by interest rates.	• Some fiscal measures have side effects. For example, an increase in sales taxes to reduce inflation will increase the cost of living.

Table 7.2 *Limitations of monetary policy and fiscal policy*

the efforts of the World Bank and regional trade blocs such as CARICOM, it remains an obstacle to more effective economic management. A further obstacle that affects all economies is that of uncertainty brought about by external stocks to the global economy. Events such as the Asian financial crisis of the mid-1990s, the aftermath of 9/11, conflicts in the Middle East and the collapse of US financial institutions have had profound effects on all economies. Events like these could not possibly have been forecast.

Conflicts between policy objectives

If we look back at Figure 7.2 (page 279), we can see that the final column indicates that economies are likely to experience problems when applying fiscal and monetary policies. This final section will explain some of these conflicts.

The most common conflict that has faced most developed economies is that between inflation and unemployment. (Their relationship was shown earlier in Figures 6.20 and 6.21 on page 264.) The problem is that when governments use policies to increase aggregate demand, and hence the level of employment, this invariably leads in time to an increase in the rate of inflation. This

has been particularly true with attempts to push unemployment below the natural rate. In turn, there is likely to be an increase in the growth rate. The reverse of this relationship also holds true. How this conflict is addressed largely boils down to which of the three objectives has priority. For the last 20 years or so, the control of inflation has been the more pressing objective – governments have been prepared to tolerate a modest rise in the unemployment rate if this has meant an inflation rate of less than 4% or 5%. It has also meant that growth has had to be sacrificed in order to keep inflation under control.

The above conflicts can also affect the exchange rate. Again, for a developed economy, there may be a conflict when the central bank (or Monetary Policy Committee in the case of the UK) sets the interest rate. If there is inflationary pressure, then the accepted reaction is to raise the interest rate. Such a move will not only increase unemployment; there will also be a knock-on effect on the balance of payments position and the exchange rate. A rise in the interest rate is likely to lead to an appreciation in the exchange rate. This makes imported goods cheaper, more difficult to sell exports and so worsen the current account position. On the other hand, 'hot' FDI may well be attracted by the higher interest rates.

There are particular conflicts within the eurozone, the term used to describe those EU member states which have joined the single currency (see Chapter 4). They have also been required to accept a common interest rate. This so-called 'one size fits all' approach has not been welcomed by all since it is based on the flawed assumption that all members' economies have the same economic problems. For example, if the main members wish to reflate their economies, then the European Central Bank (ECB) will reduce its interest rate. This would also apply to countries with an inflation problem, so accelerating the rate of inflation. This has applied in the cases of Ireland, Greece, Portugal and Spain.

Eurozone members also have to accept a common exchange rate since all operate the single currency, the euro. This has caused problems for some countries with trading deficits – they have been prohibited from taking charge of their own exchange rate in order to reduce their trading deficits. Consequently, their goods are not as competitive as they might be if their currency had been allowed to depreciate.

Conflicts such as those referred to above might be reduced through other policy instruments. A good example is the case of a central bank increasing the rate of interest to control inflation and using supply-side policies to make labour market reforms in order to promote economic growth. Aggregate supply can be increased through more resources being expended on education, training, apprenticeships, trade union reform and so on. If successful, these policies will assist the economy to operate at full capacity, resulting in increased economic growth.

The macroeconomic conflicts also apply to developing and emerging economies. We must though acknowledge that their priorities are often different to those of developed economies. For some such as China and India, increasing and sustaining a high rate of economic growth is paramount; for others, it may be a case of reducing a public debt problem, in which case austere fiscal policies and supply-side reforms will be necessary. For most developing economies in the Caribbean, South America and elsewhere, their priority has had to be one of reducing the effects of public and private debt on their economies. With firm, decisive policies, as advocated by the IMF, this economic weakness has to be addressed before they can achieve their true economic potential.

SPECIMEN EXAM QUESTIONS

The following questions have been set in recent CIE examination papers.

1 Analyse why the aims of government policy might conflict with each other and discuss which of the aims ought to be given priority. [25]

(October/November 2007)

2 In some countries the rate of unemployment has remained low for several years.
  a Explain what causes unemployment [12]
  b Discuss whether the reduction of unemployment should always be the main aim of government policy. [13]
  [25 marks]

(October/November 2008)

SUMMARY

In this supplement section it has been shown that:

- Policies of trade and aid to assist developing economies are carried out by individual governments and various international organisations.
- Governments manage their macroeconomies using fiscal, monetary, exchange rate and supply-side policies.
- These policies aim to achieve particular objectives with respect to inflation, employment, the balance of payments, the exchange rate and economic growth.
- Conflicts inevitably arise since it is most unlikely that all objectives can be achieved simultaneously.

8 Preparing for examinations

On completion of this chapter you should know:

- about the various skills and abilities that are assessed in the CIE examinations
- how to plan your preparation for examinations in an effective way
- how to feel confident in tackling CIE examination questions and knowing what examiners expect when marking your script
- why some students do not succeed or perform to their true ability in written examinations.

Introduction

The assessment processes in CIE Economics are designed to test your skills and abilities to:

- recall, select and use economic theories, principles, concepts and methods
- identify and analyse economic problems and formulate solutions
- interpret and analyse economic data and draw logical conclusions
- analyse economic problems by using the models and concepts introduced in the course
- develop structured and reasoned expositions on economic theory and policy.

The evidence on which this assessment of your skills and abilities in each chapter is based comes from your performance in two written examination papers at AS Level and A Level (see Introduction to the book for more details).

If you approach the assessment in a positive and meaningful way, then you should achieve the grade you are expecting, consistent with the time and effort you have devoted to your CIE Economics studies. For some students though, for all sorts of reasons, the final grade may be a disappointment.

So, what should you do to be successful? There is no magic formula but if you do the following, you will give yourself every chance of success:

- Read the Core (AS Level) and Supplement (A Level) sections in this book and feel confident that you have understood the main subject content.
- Complete all or most of the self-assessment tasks.

- Where possible, understand how the various problems, concepts, theories and policies might be applied to developing economies as well as to developed economies.
- Know what to expect and how best to tackle the examination papers.
- Make sure to use the additional information that is provided on the accompanying Student's CD.

The seeds for success therefore are sown long before you enter the examination room. The key thing is to be prepared. It is worth remembering: 'If you fail to prepare, you are preparing to fail'. Why not put this on your wall? But if you do, remember to practise what it says.

Adapted from an original drawing by Emily Bamford

A few hints on how to study

As an AS Level CIE student, study is something you do from the first day of your course. This involves the gradual accumulation of the knowledge and skills that constitute the subject you are studying. You should also see the regular review or revision of such knowledge and skills as part of this process. (This is where the self-assessment tasks in this book are a great help.) Revision therefore is not something that is only confined to the last week or so before an examination. So: 'make study a habit; make revision a habit'.

Managing your time in an effective way is crucial. There should be regular periods in the week when you have spare blocks of time that you can devote to studying Economics. Even if it is only 30 minutes, if this is spent effectively, it will be of value to you. You should also try to have set places where you can study, ideally free from distractions such as loud music, talking, television noise and so on. This may not be easy but try to have set times and places for your study and stick to a routine.

A second important aspect of time management is *planning*. All students should try to do this by thinking ahead. This is particularly important where, as in the CIE examinations, you are taking the examinations on a staged basis. (Papers 1 and 2 are usually taken at the end of the first year of study.) Time is therefore limited between the start of teaching and when you have to take your first examinations.

Here are a few simple suggestions that might help:

- Read through your class notes on a daily basis; follow this up by reading the relevant topic in this book.
- Make a weekly plan of what you have done; at the end of each week, go over the reading again and see if you can do the self-assessment tasks that are incorporated into the topic.
- When you have completed a topic, see if you can answer the examination questions at the end of each section – ideally without referring to your notes or to the book.

Think and plan ahead. Find out when you might have to do a 'mock' examination and, above all, make sure you know when the actual examination will be taking place.

All of these simple things should help you feel relaxed and confident when you take the examinations. So, remember: 'If you fail to prepare, you are preparing to fail'.

Adapted from an original drawing by Emily Bamford

A few hints on how to study effectively

Each of us has a preferred study environment where we can work in an effective and efficient way. For some it may be at home; for others it may be in a school or public library where the distractions going on around us can at least be shut off for an hour or two. The best time for study may also vary – much will depend upon your family circumstances and how you can arrange to study in relation to these and other commitments on your time.

Whatever the best time, the following advice should help you.

- Put yourself in a position where you can concentrate on your work. This is most unlikely to happen if your favourite television programme is on in the same room. The attention span of most people is 40–60 minutes. After such a period, have a drink and a rest, maybe do something else before studying for a further period.
- When reading, make notes on what you have read and incorporate these into your class notes

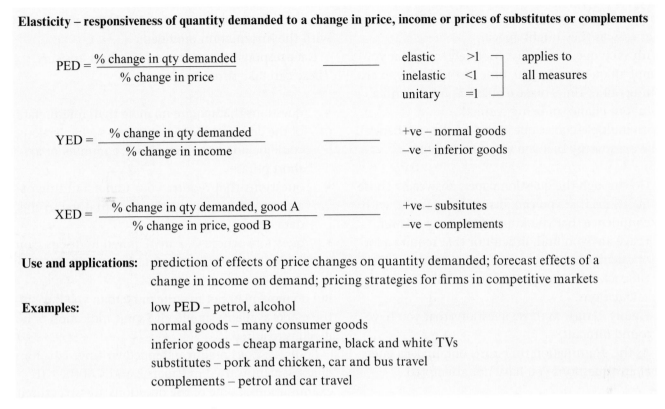

Elasticity – responsiveness of quantity demanded to a change in price, income or prices of substitutes or complements

$$PED = \frac{\% \text{ change in qty demanded}}{\% \text{ change in price}}$$

elastic   >1 ⎤ applies to
inelastic <1 ⎬ all measures
unitary   =1 ⎦

$$YED = \frac{\% \text{ change in qty demanded}}{\% \text{ change in income}}$$

+ve – normal goods
–ve – inferior goods

$$XED = \frac{\% \text{ change in qty demanded, good A}}{\% \text{ change in price, good B}}$$

+ve – subsitutes
–ve – complements

Use and applications: prediction of effects of price changes on quantity demanded; forecast effects of a change in income on demand; pricing strategies for firms in competitive markets

Examples: low PED – petrol, alcohol
normal goods – many consumer goods
inferior goods – cheap margarine, black and white TVs
substitutes – pork and chicken, car and bus travel
complements – petrol and car travel

Figure 8.1 *Example of a revision card*

on a particular topic. You will also find it useful to do the self-assessment tasks in this book and work through sample CIE examination questions on a topic. Writing and working in this way greatly enhances your understanding of a topic. Do not just read material on its own – the problem with this approach to study is that you will very quickly forget what you have read. The big advantage also of making notes is that they will be there for future revision when you need them.

- Once you have completed the study of a particular topic, condense your notes and write them on a revision card, which you will find invaluable for use shortly before examinations. An example of such notes is shown in Figure 8.1.

So, it is not so much how long you study but how effective you are in your studying. Make sure you use your time in such a way that you feel in control of your own learning experience.

Examination questions

Types of question

There are three main types of question in the CIE Economics examinations. These are:

- multiple-choice questions
- data-response questions
- essay questions, including structured questions.

All questions draw upon the subject content of each section of the curriculum content at AS Level and at A Level.

Let us look at each type in turn, as various skills are being examined in each of these forms of question.

Multiple-choice questions are used to assess the extent to which you understand the full subject content of the syllabus. Typically, they take the form of a 'stem' followed by four possible answers. You are required to identify which of these so-called 'keys' is the correct answer. In most questions, one key is clearly wrong, two are temptingly correct whilst one is the correct answer. So, beware! These questions are not as easy as they might appear.

With such questions, it is absolutely vital that you attempt all questions in the time available. If you are running out of time, make a guess. You have still a one in four chance of being correct!

With multiple-choice questions, practice is essential. Below is a strategy that you may find helpful.

- Go through the question paper, answering those questions that you can answer quickly and with confidence that you know the correct answer.
- Leave any you find difficult or that require a lot of calculations.
- Go back and attempt those questions requiring calculations.
- Finally, return to those questions that you have found difficult.
- As the examination time runs out, make a guess at any questions you have not attempted.

If you take a 'mock' examination, find out all the correct answers – be sure you know how and why you got the right answer or why the answer you selected was wrong. It is very important that you do this so that you can prepare better for the real examination.

Data-response questions are more varied. At AS Level, this type of question draws upon a relatively short, simple set of economic data with some text. For A Level, the questions are derived from more varied stimulus material, e.g. graphs, diagrams, reports or from text which may also contain data. The data-handling skills you need to feel confident when answering such questions are those contained in the Introduction.

When you come across a data-response question for the first time:

- look at the title as it may give some clues about its content
- read any table or column headings and see if you know what they mean
- see if you can pick out the main patterns in the data using the 'eye-balling' technique referred to in the Introduction
- pick out any notable features of a chart or diagram
- see if you can recognise the economic concept or concepts contained in the data.

Once you have done this you should feel comfortable with the information provided.

Data-response questions require short answers. These can take three forms:

- questions that require no more than interpretation of the data provided – answers to such questions could be no more than a word, a number or a short phrase
- questions that require your understanding of an economic concept that is contained in the data
- questions where you are required to discuss some aspect or theme in the data.

But do remember not to write more than you have to – the marks available should give some indication of how much is required.

Essay questions require extended writing. This form of assessment is used in Papers 2 and 4 of the CIE examinations. Some of the questions are 'structured', i.e. they consist of a number of parts, usually two. Others, especially at A Level, take the form of a single task. You are expected to spend a total of around 50 minutes writing your essay questions.

General advice on how to write in an effective way is given in the Introduction – why not go back and refresh yourself on the main points?

The wording of questions

A lot of care, thought and attention goes into the final production of all CIE examination papers. So, when you sit an examination, it is important to appreciate that the questions which are on the examination paper have been set by an examiner who requires you to answer these questions. Put another way, examination papers never contain questions such as:

Write all you know about…

or

Write as much as you can remember about…

Unfortunately, students don't always appreciate this point!

All examination questions contain two very important instructions:

- **Directive words** indicate what form the answer should take. For example, it could be in the form of a description, a discussion, an explanation or merely a statement. These words are there for a purpose, namely that they have been used by the examiners to say what they are looking for (in skill terms when you answer a particular question).

- **Content words** are much more diverse in nature since they cover the whole of the subject area of the syllabus. Their aim is to make clear what is the focus of the question and what examiners require you to write about.

Table 8.1 (page 296) shows a list of key directive words which are most likely to occur in CIE Economics examination questions. You should study these carefully and understand what each means. You will then appreciate that a question which asks:

'Define price elasticity of demand'
is not the same as
'Explain what is meant by price elasticity of demand
is not the same as
'Discuss the relevance of price elasticity of demand in business'.

A simple method for interpreting essay questions

The following question was set in the October/November 2008 9708/02 examination:

a Explain the market failure which arises from the characteristics of public goods. [8]
b Discuss whether the use of cost–benefit analysis helps to improve economic decision making. [12]

The subject content comes from the Core section of Chapter 3. The question is in two parts. You need to spend about 20 minutes on part **a** and about 30 minutes on part **b**…not the reverse. This is important.

Part **a** has 'explain' as the directive word. This is widely used in Economics examinations and indicates that your answer should contain reasons. The subject content is 'the characteristics of public goods'. Having briefly described these characteristics, you must then explain why market failure could arise. In other words, you need to explain why the characteristics of public goods may not always be

applicable. A good approach is to include some typical examples in your answer.

Part **b** is more challenging. This is indicated by the directive word 'discuss'. This is flagging up that you need to put two sides of the argument in your answer. (Remember the two-handed economist! On the one hand… on the other hand…) In terms of content, the question is inviting you to say why cost–benefit analysis can 'improve economic decision making' and why in some cases, it does not 'improve economic decision making'. Again a few examples that are known to you will enhance the quality of your answer.

How to impress CIE economics examiners

Let us start with a few typical comments that CIE examiners often write on some of the examination answers they read:

- 'Does not answer the question'
- 'Too vague'
- 'Misses point of question'
- 'No application'
- 'Descriptive. No analysis of issues'
- 'No discussion'
- 'Ignores second aspect of question'

These comments clearly indicate that the candidates have not done what was expected from them. So, the first way to impress any examiner reading your examination scripts is:

- **Answer the question** In other words, produce an answer as directed by the question. The information above, in particular the simple method for interpreting examination questions, should help you to write your answer in a clear, well-structured manner as directed by the question. This point cannot be emphasised too much!

There are various other ways in which you might impress an examiner. For example:

- **Diagrams** These are very important and a relevant means of economic explanation. Many of the topics you come across in Economics can be illustrated by a diagram or by means of

Directive word	What it means	Where you can expect it to be used
Calculate	Work out using the information provided	
Define	Give the exact meaning	
Describe	Give a description of	
How	In what way or ways	
Identify	Give an example	
Illustrate	Give examples/diagram	
Outline	Describe without detail	
State	Make clear	Usually in the early parts of data-response questions, short answer, multiple-choice questions and some structured essay questions.
Summarise	Give main points, without detail	
What	State clearly	
Which	Give a clear example/ state what	
Analyse	Set out the main points	
Apply	Use in a specific way	
Compare	Give similarities and differences	
Explain	Give clear reasons or make clear	In the later parts of data-response questions and in the early parts of essay questions.
Account for	Give reasons for	
Consider	Give your thoughts about	
Assess	Show how important something is	
Comment upon	Give your reasoned opinions on	
Criticise	Give an opinion, but support it with evidence	
Discuss	Give the important arguments, for and against	In the final part of data-response questions and in essay questions.
Evaluate	Discuss the importance of, making some attempt to weight your opinions	

Table 8.1 *Key directive words*

an explanation supported by a diagram. You have only to glance at the topics in this book to see this. So, a relevant, correctly drawn diagram, used effectively and referred to in your answer, will impress an examiner reading your examination script. An example of good technique is shown in Figure 8.2.

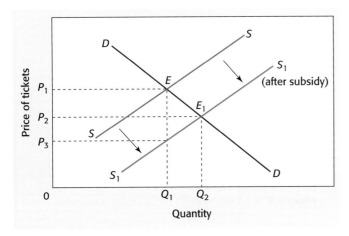

Figure 8.2 *The effects of a subsidy on the price of tickets*

The diagram shows how the price of tickets to watch cricket will be affected by the introduction of a subsidy. As this diagram indicates, the subsidy will lead to an increase in supply, shifting the supply curve downwards and to the right. The price which spectators will have to pay falls from P_1 to P_2 – it does not fall to P_3, as part of the subsidy (that shown between P_3 and P_2) will be retained by the ground owners to offset the higher costs incurred as a result of the increase in the number of spectators.

- **Current issues and problems**   One of the reasons for studying Economics is to help you understand some of the things that are taking place around you. So, when you get the opportunity to demonstrate your knowledge, do so! For example, if you are answering a question on the negative externalities associated with environmental pollution, you might refer to a local example which is known to you or something you have seen in a newspaper or magazine. Most of the topics in the syllabus can be supported by additional up-to-date material that is not always found in textbooks.

- **Refer to things you have read.**   It follows that there are instances where it would give more meaning to your answer if you referred to some material by name, e.g. an article, an example from a textbook or the views of a particular economist.

Common mistakes made in CIE Economics examinations

In addition to a failure to answer the question, the other main mistakes made by candidates are:

- a failure to allocate writing time in an appropriate way
- confusion over similar terms
- meaningless, wrongly drawn diagrams or diagrams which add nothing to an answer.

Let us conclude this section by looking at each in turn.

- Figure 8 in the introduction showed the time allowed for each of the examination papers. You must make sure you allocate your writing time in the examination in a meaningful way. Roughly speaking, allocate your writing time in direct proportion to the marks available for each question.
  - Do not exceed the time you have allocated for each question.
  - If you cannot do a particular question, leave it and move on to the next one. (You can always return to it later on in the examination if time permits.) You will only get marks for the questions you answer – your script, though, will always be marked out of the total marks allocated.
- A second problem in Economics examinations is that, on occasions, candidates sometimes confuse terms which are similar (in terms of content) or which have similar names (but mean something different).

Table 8.2 contains a few common examples. Watch out also that you express formulae correctly – in particular elasticity formulae.

Topic	Often confused with
elastic demand	inelastic demand
allocative efficiency	productive efficiency
prices	costs
merit goods	public goods
direct taxation	indirect taxation
external costs/benefits	social costs/benefits
real income	nominal income
rate of interest	exchange rates
fiscal policy measures	monetary policy measures
aggregate demand	aggregate supply
balance of trade	balance of payments
income	wealth
monopoly	monopolistic competition

Table 8.2 *Common errors over terms and topics in the CIE Economics syllabus*

Finally, a common mistake which candidates often make is in the way in which they use diagrams in their answers. Common errors are:

- labelling axes incorrectly or not labelling them at all
- making diagrams too small
- drawing lines and curves incorrectly, usually through being wrongly sloping
- failure to use a diagram in an answer when asked for one to be included
- including a diagram when one is not needed and where it does not enhance an answer at all.

SELF-ASSESSMENT TASK 8.1

Below are examples of badly drawn diagrams. How many improvements can you make?

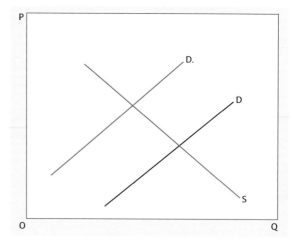

Figure 8.3 *A reduction in the quantity demanded for a good*

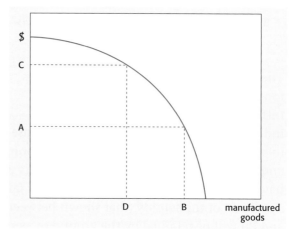

Figure 8.4 *A PPC showing how the output of one good changes*

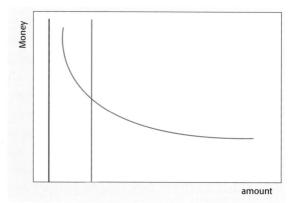

Figure 8.5 *Figure showing an increase in the money supply*

SUMMARY

In this concluding section it has been shown that:

- It is very important for you to be well organised and to be able to plan ahead if you are to succeed in CIE Economics.
- Candidates who underperform in examinations have usually not been adequately briefed on the type and style of question.
- Revision should be an ongoing process, not just a last-minute activity you carry out just before a written examination.
- A lack of time and an inability to understand the relevance of directive words are the most common causes of underperformance.
- CIE examinations contain three forms of examination questions.

Glossary

The CIE 9708 syllabus contains examples of economic concepts and terms. These are divided into those included at the Core (AS level) and Supplement (A Level) stages. Concepts and terms introduced at the Core stage may also be included in examinations at the supplement stage.

These examples have been provided by CIE to assist teachers in the effective delivery of the syllabus. We have added others. When they first occur, terms have been reproduced in bold, blue type in the text.

This glossary provides an alphabetical listing of the most important concepts and terms – in particular it includes those which are most likely to be used in CIE examination questions and data response material. For the convenience of students, this glossary is divided into Core and Supplement sections.

Core stage – economic concepts and terms

absolute advantage – used in the context of international trade to represent a situation where, for a given set of resources, one country can produce more of a particular good than another country.

ad valorem tax – a tax which is charged as a given proportion of the price.

Adam Smith – Scottish economist who laid down the foundations of market economics.

adverse selection – where information failure in (say) the health insurance market results in unsuitable people obtaining insurance.

aggregate demand – the total spending on goods and services in the economy.

aggregate supply – the total output of any economy.

anticipated inflation – that which might be expected.

appreciation – an increase in the value of a currency as measured by the amount of another foreign currency it can buy.

average product – total product divided by the number of workers employed.

balance of payments – a record or overall statement of a country's economic transactions with the rest of the world, usually over a year.

balance of trade – the difference between the exports of goods and services and imports of goods and services (visibles).

barter – when people exchange goods and services without using money.

base date – the period or year whose data is identified as 100 in the construction of an index number.

birth rate – the number of live births per 1000 population per year.

capital – one of the factors of production; a man-made aid to production, such as industrial machinery, factories and roads.

capital account – part of the balance of payments showing transfers of financial assets between a country and the rest of the world.

capital consumption – the amount of capital required to replace that which is worn out on an annual basis.

change in demand – the outcome of a change in those factors which can be explained by a shift in the demand curve. Not to be confused with a change in quantity demanded.

change in quantity demanded – this term is used to show the outcome of a movement along a demand curve, that is to show the change in quantity demanded when price changes.

cheque – a written order made by a customer to a bank to pay money.

choice – underpins the concept that resources are scarce so choices have to be made by consumers, firms and governments.

coincidence of wants – where there is a need for two parties to be willing to trade; relevant to money as a medium of exchange.

command economy – one in which decisions on resource allocation are taken by a central body.

consumption – total spending by consumers over a period of time.

comparative advantage – used in the context of international trade to explain why trade can be beneficial even if one country has an absolute advantage in production but where the opportunity costs of production vary compared with another country.

complementary goods – those that are consumed together.

concentration ratio – the proportion of the market in the hands of a given number of firms.

consumer surplus – the difference between the value a consumer places on units consumed and the payment needed to actually make a purchase of a commodity.

contestable market – one where there is ease of entry for new firms.

cost–benefit analysis – a technique for assessing the desirability of a particular project, taking into account all of the respective costs and benefits.

cost of living – the cost of a range of goods and services that are necessary for normal existence.

cost-push inflation – a situation where inflation is caused by an increase in particular prices or wage rates.

costs – the value of inputs into the production process.

cross elasticity of demand – a numerical measure of the responsiveness of demand for one product following a change in price of a related product.

current account – within the balance of payments, a record of the trade in goods and services, investment income and current transfers.

customs union – free trade between member states and a common external tariff on imports.

death rate – the number of deaths per 1000 population per year.

demand – the quantity of goods or services that consumers want to buy at different prices.

demand curve – a representation of the relationship between quantity demanded and price.

demand-pull inflation – where inflation is caused by an increase in aggregate demand such as an increase in government spending or a reduction in the overall level of taxation in the economy.

demand schedule – the data from which a demand curve is drawn.

demerit goods – any good that has negative externalities associated with it, such as passive smoking or the excessive consumption of junk food.

dependency ratio – the proportion of the population that is not productive.

depreciation – a decrease in the value of a currency as measured by the amount of another foreign currency it can buy.

devaluation – an explicit decrease in the value of a currency.

developing economy – one in which there is not a high income per head.

disequilibrium – a market situation where supply and demand are not equal.

division of labour – workers specialise in one job within an overall production process.

dumping – selling goods in an overseas market at below their cost of production.

economic goods – those having a cost in terms of resources used.

economic growth – an increase in the productive potential in an economy.

economic integration – the processes, e.g. trade agreements, whereby individual economies get together to form a single unit.

economic problem – scarce resources in relation to unlimited wants; choices have to be made.

economic union – where member states agree to common economic policies and, sometimes, a common currency.

effective demand – demand that is supported by the ability to pay.

elastic – where the estimated elasticity value is greater than 1.

elasticity – a measure of responsiveness to change.

elasticity of demand – the responsiveness of the quantity demanded or of demand to a change in one of the determinants.

elasticity of supply – the responsiveness of the quantity supplied or of supply to a change in one of the determinants.

enterprise – the factor of production that refers to the willingness to take risks.

entrepreneur – an individual who is willing to take risks in the production of goods or services.

equilibrium – a situation where there is no tendency for change given current circumstances.

equilibrium price – the price where demand and supply are equal; where the market clears.

equilibrium quantity – the amount traded at the equilibrium price.

excise duties – taxes on specific products, often to restrict consumption.

expenditure dampening policies – fiscal or monetary policies that are designed to restrict aggregate demand.

expenditure switching policies – fiscal and monetary policies that are designed to reduce domestic expenditure on imports and transfer such demand to domestically produced goods.

exports – goods and services sold to another country.

external benefits – benefits that accrue to a third party.

external costs – costs that are borne by a third party.

externality – action that results in external benefits or external costs.

factor endowment – the range of resources available in an economy.

factors of production – anything that is useful in the production of goods and services.

factor mobility – the ease with which factors of production can be moved around.

financial account – that part of the balance of payments that records overseas investment.

floating exchange rate – one that is determined in the market by the forces of demand and supply.

foreign direct investment – provided by companies outside of their own national market.

foreign exchange rate – the price of currency in terms of a recognised global currency, for example $US or euro.

free goods – those with no price and which can be enjoyed by all.

free rider – someone who has no incentive to pay for the use of a public good.

free trade area – where member states agree to remove any restrictions on trade among themselves.

globalisation – the processes by which the world's economies are becoming increasingly dependent upon each other.

hyperinflation – an exceptionally high rate of inflation which results in people losing confidence in money as a medium of change.

imports – any goods and services purchased from another country.

income elasticity of demand – a numerical measure of the responsiveness of demand following a change in income.

inelastic – a situation where the estimated elasticity of demand value is between 0 and 1.

infant industry argument – the case for protecting new firms in a developing economy.

inferior good – one whose demand falls as income increases.

inflation – a persistent increase in the level of prices in an economy.

information failure – where people do not have full information.

interest – a payment that has to be made in order to obtain money or a reward for parting with money.

investment – the creation of capital goods or of adding to the stock of productive assets in an economy.

J-curve – the short term response from the current account of the balance of payments due to a sharp fall in the exchange rate.

joint demand – when two items are consumed together.

joint supply – when two items are produced together.

labour – the human resources available in an economy; one of the factors of production.

labour force – the number of people available for work.

labour force participation rate – the labour force as a proportion of the total population.

labour force survey – a quarterly government survey of employment and unemployment.

land – the factor of production that consists of the natural resources in an economy.

law of demand – when price falls, the quantity demanded will increase (and vice versa).

law of supply – when price increases, the quantity supplied will increase (and vice versa).

liquidity – the extent to which a firm or bank has an adequate supply of assets that can be turned into cash.

macroeconomics – economic concepts and theories that apply to the economy as a whole.

marginal propensity to import – the proportion of an increase in income that is spent on imports.

market – where buyers and sellers get together to trade.

market demand – the total amount required by consumers.

market economy – one in which most decisions are taken through market forces.

market failure – where the market mechanism does not give an efficient allocation of resources.

Marshall-Lerner condition – for an exchange rate devaluation to be successful, the sum of the price elasticities of demand for exports and imports must be greater than one.

market mechanism – where decisions on price and quantity are made on the basis of demand and supply

measure of value – the way in which money that is accumulated can be measured.

medium of exchange – a function of money that is the basis on which transactions take place.

menu costs – additional costs incurred by a business as a consequence of inflation.

merit goods – those goods and services that have positive externalities.

microeconomics – economic concepts and theories that apply to particular parts of an economy such as consumers and firms.

migration – the movement of people from one country to another for work purposes.

monetary inflation – inflation caused by excessive increases in the money supply.

moral hazard – the risk of taking advice from someone who is better informed.

multilateral trade – trade between a number of countries.

multinational corporation – a firm which operates in differnet countries.

national income – total income for the economy as a whole.

needs – goods and services that are preferred.

negative externality – a situation which occurs when there are external costs associated with the production, or consumption of a good or service.

nominal value – value in money terms.

non-excludable – a characteristic of public goods whereby it is not possible to restrict the consumption of a good or service.

non-rival – a characteristic of public goods whereby all consumers should be able to enjoy a particular good or service as they are not in competition with each other.

normal good – one where the quantity demanded increases as income increases.

normative economics – issues that involve making a value judgement.

opportunity cost – the cost expressed in terms of the best alternative that is foregone.

other things being equal – where a single change can be isolated, all other factors remaining the same.

paternalism – an attitude that favours laws and policies over the individual's preferences.

pegged exchange rate – one where the exchange rate is kept between an upper and lower limit.

perfectly elastic – all that is produced is sold at a given price.

perfectly inelastic – where a change in price has no effect on the quantity demanded.

planned economy – the same as command economy.

positive economics – those aspects that can be checked against particular criteria or evidence to see whether they are proven.

positive externality – an activity that generates external benefits.

price elasticity of demand – a numerical measure of the responsiveness of the quantity demanded to a change in price of a particular good or service.

price elasticity of supply – a numerical measure of the responsiveness of the quantity supplied to a change in price of a particular good or service.

price mechanism – the means of allocating resources in a market economy.

primary sector – production of agriculture, mining, fishing and forestry.

private benefits – those that directly accrue to an individual.

private costs – those that are directly incurred by an individual.

private goods – any that are consumed by someone and not available to anyone else.

production – the act of making goods and services.

production frontier – a representation of all products that can be produced with given resources.

production possibility curve – a representation of the maximum level of output that an economy can achieve when using the existing resources to the full.

product transformation curve – as production possibility curve.

productivity – for labour, output per person employed.

progressive tax – a tax that takes a higher proportion from high income earners rather than from low income earners.

protectionist policies – policies that are used to protect an economy from foreign competition.

public goods – those that are non-excludable and non-rival and for which it is usually difficult to charge a direct price.

Quantity Theory of Money – the theory that links inflation in an economy to changes in the money supply.

quasi-public goods – goods that display some but not all of the characteristics of public goods.

quota – a physical restriction on imports.

ration – limit the quantity available for consumption.

reallocation of resources – where resources are changed due to a change in demand.

real value – where an adjustment has been made for inflation.

regulation – rules and laws that apply to firms.

resources – inputs available for the production of goods and services.

Retail Prices Index (RPI) – a measure of inflation used in the UK to calculate price changes on a wide range of goods and services.

revaluation – a deliberate increase in the value of a currency relative to that of others.

risk – the possibility that events may not turn out as expected.

scale of preference – the order in which needs are ranked.

scarcity – a situation in which wants and needs are in excess of the resources available.

secondary sector – manufacturing.

shadow price – one that is applied where there is no recognised market price.

shoe leather costs – a cost of inflation when consumers spend time and money trying to find the best prices.

social costs – the total costs of a particular action.

specialisation – the process by which firms, individuals and economies concentrate on producing those goods and services for which they have an advantage.

specific tax – an indirect tax that is fixed per unit.

standard deferred payment – the basis on which money can be used for future payments.

stocks – unsold items stored for future sale.

store of wealth – how money can be held over time before being used.

subsidy – a payment made to producers to reduce the market price of a good or service.

substitute goods – possible alternatives for consumers.

supply – goods and services produced.

supply conditions – those factors that determine supply.

supply curve – a representation of the relationship between price and the quantity supplied.

supply schedule – the data from which the supply curve is drawn.

tariff – a tax that is imposed on imports.

taxes – payments made to the government and levied on income or the consumption of goods and services.

terms of trade – a numerical measure of the relationship between export prices and import prices.

tertiary sector – production of services.

Tiger economies – the term given to the emerging economies in South East Asia.

total revenue – price multiplied by the quantity sold.

trade creation – where high cost domestic production is replaced by more efficiently produced imports from within a customs union.

trade diversion – where trade with a low cost country outside a customs union is replaced by higher cost products supplied from within.

trading possibility curve – a representation of what trade is possible for given terms of trade.

trade weighted exchange rate – for a given currency, this is calculated using weights that are directly proportional to other countries' shares in trade.

unanticipated inflation – that which has not been forecast.

unemployment – where those willing and able to work are not able to find a job.

unitary elasticity – where the estimated value is 1.

unit of account – the function of money as a measure.

urbanisation – an increasing proportion of the population lives in large towns and cities.

value judgement – conclusions that are based mainly on opinions rather than facts.

wants – needs that are not necessarily realised.

weights – values given to (say) goods in a price index to take into account their relative importance.

Supplement stage – economic concepts and terms

abnormal profit – that which is earned above normal profit.

accelerator – a model that links changes in investment to changes in output.

active balances – the amount of money held by households or firms for possible future use.

aggregate expenditure – the total amount spent at different levels of income in the economy.

allocative efficiency – where price is equal to marginal cost.

automatic stabilisers – fiscal policies that operate to reduce fluctuations in aggregate demand without needing to make adjustments.

autonomous investment – that which is made independently from output.

average propensity to consume/save – the proportion of income that is consumed/saved.

balanced budget – one where government spending and receipts from taxation are equal.

barriers to entry/exit – any restrictions that prevent new firms from entering/leaving an industry.

broad money – a measure of the money supply that includes interest-bearing deposits held in financial institutions.

budget – an annual statement in which the government outlines plans for its spending and tax revenue.

budget line – a representation of the maximum amount of two goods that can be bought with a consumer's income.

capital-output ratio – a measure of the amount of capital used to produce a given amount of output.

cartel – a group of firms that deliberately collude to restrict output or fix prices for their own benefit.

circular flow of income – a simple model of the process by which income flows around an economy.

closed economy – one which does not trade with other economies.

closed shop – employment is restricted to workers belonging to a particular trade union.

collective bargaining – when employers and trade unions get together to negotiate wages and conditions of employment.

credit multiplier – the process by which banks can make more loans than deposits available.

cyclical unemployment – that which results from a downturn in the economy.

deadweight loss – the welfare loss to consumers when there is market failure.

decreasing returns – where the ratio of inputs to outputs falls as the scale of production increases.

deflationary gap – where there is a negative difference between the level of demand and that needed to achieve full employment.

demand-deficient unemployment – that caused by a lack of aggregate demand.

derived demand – where the demand for a good or service depends on the use that can be made from it.

diminishing marginal utility – where marginal utility falls as more of a product is consumed.

diminishing returns – where the output of an additional unit of input results in a fall in the marginal product.

diseconomies of scale – where long run average costs increase as the scale of output increases.

dissaving – where households are obliged to withdraw savings from a bank in order to support current consumption expenditure.

distribution of income – the way in which total income is shared amongst different groups.

economic efficiency – where scarce resources are used in the most effective way to produce maximum output.

economic rent – payment made to a factor of production above that which is necessary to keep it in its current use.

economies of scale – the benefits derived from falling long run average costs as the scale of output expands.

economies of scope – the benefits accruing to a firm as a consequence of it developing activities that are closely related to its core business.

equimarginal principle – a firm will produce most efficiently when the marginal valuation of returns from all of its factors of production are equal.

external economies of scale – the benefits to all firms as an industry grows and develops; those not directly controlled by a firm.

firm – any business that hires factors of production in order to sell goods and services.

fiscal policy – the use of taxation and government spending to manage the level of aggregate demand.

fixed costs – those that are independent of output in the short run.

frictional unemployment – that which is temporary and which arises where people change jobs.

full employment – the level of employment corresponding to where all who wish to work have found jobs, excluding frictional unemployment.

government failure – where in seeking to correct a market failure, the government creates further distortions in the market.

Gross Domestic Product (GDP) – a measure of total output produced by activities located in a country.

GDP deflator – a price index used to find the real value of output.

Gross National Product (GNP) – a measure of total output that takes into account the net income of residents from activities carried out abroad as well as in the home economy.

horizontal integration – a merger or take-over where firms are in the same type of activity.

idle balances – assets that are temporarily held in the form of cash as the current returns are too low.

immobility of labour – where the smooth flow of labour is inhibited for geographical or occupational reasons.

increasing returns – where a firm's output increases at a proportionally faster rate than inputs.

induced investment – that made in response to changes in output.

income effect – that part of a change in quantity demanded arising from a price change that is attributed to a change in real income.

income tax – a direct tax that is levied on earned and unearned income.

industry – a collection of firms in a particular activity.

injections – additions to the circular flow of income.

integration – the processes by which individual economies agree to form a single organisation.

internal economies of scale – the benefits arising within a firm as a result of an increase in the scale of output.

Keynesian (approach) – based on the ideas of John Maynard Keynes, the approach to managing the economy whereby government intervention should be used in situations where the market mechanism fails to produce the best allocation of resources.

leakages – a withdrawal from the circular flow of income.

liquidity preference – A Keynesian concept that explains why people demand money.

liquidity trap – a situation where interest rates cannot be reduced any more in order to stimulate an upturn in economic activity.

loanable funds theory – a theory which states that the rate of interest is determined where the demand for investment funds is equal to the supply of savings.

long run – the time period when a firm is able to alter all of its factors of production.

managed float – where a central bank buys and sells foreign exchange to keep the exchange rate at a given value.

marginal cost – the addition to total cost when one more unit of output is produced.

marginal product – the increase in output arising from the use of one additional unit of a factor of production.

marginal propensity to consume/save – a measure of the increase in consumption/saving in relation to an increase in income.

marginal revenue – the addition to total revenue arising from the sale of one more unit.

marginal revenue product – the addition to total revenue due to the employment of one more worker.

marginal utility – the utility derived from the consumption of one additional unit of a good or service.

mobility of labour – the ease with which labour can switch occupations or move around in the economy.

Monetarist (approach) – a school of economic thought that believes that the control of the money supply is essential for economic stability.

monetary policy – the use of interest rates or direct control of the money supply as a means for managing the economy.

money supply – the total amount of money in an economy.

monopolistic competition – a market structure where there are many firms, differentiated products and few barriers to entry.

monopoly – a market structure with technically one firm and high barriers to entry that keep out potential competitors.

monopsony – a market situation where there is only one buyer.

multiplier – a numerical estimate of a change in spending in relation to the final change in expenditure.

narrow money – rates and coins in circulation, cash held in banks and balances made by commercial banks at a central bank.

natural monopoly – a market where average costs are lowest with one provider and where duplication is wasteful.

natural rate of unemployment – that which would prevail with a constant rate of inflation.

net advantages – monetary and non-monetary factors that can affect the supply of labour.

Net Domestic Product (NDP) – Gross Domestic Product minus capital consumption.

Net National Product (NNP) – Gross National Product minus capital consumption.

net property income from abroad – the net receipts from rent, dividends, interest and retained profits received from abroad.

non-pecuniary advantages – non-monetary factors that can affect the supply of labour.

non-price competition – when firms compete through branding, advertising and customer service rather than by price.

normal profit – a cost of production that represents the level of profit that is just sufficient for a firm to keep operating in a particular industry.

occupational mobility – the extent to which someone trained in a skill which is no longer in demand is able to obtain another job.

oligopoly – a market structure with a few large firms and high barriers to entry.

open economy – one which is involved in trade with other economies.

optimum allocation of resources – where resources are allocated in the best possible way.

optimum population – the size of population that is consistent with the highest level of output per head.

paradox of thrift – where people start to save a larger proportion of their incomes, the result of which is a fall in aggregate demand that will eventually produce a fall in the level of saving.

pecuniary advantage – a monetary factor that can affect the supply of labour.

perfect competition – an ideal market structure that has many buyers and sellers, identical products and no barriers to entry.

Phillips curve – this shows the relationship between the rate of inflation and the unemployment rate in an economy over a period of time.

poverty trap – where someone may be worse off in employment compared to living on means-tested benefits.

precautionary motive – a reason for holding money for unexpected or unforeseen reasons.

price agreements – a feature of oligopoly when firms get together to fix prices.

price competition – when firms use market prices as the basis for competition.

price discrimination – a feature of monopoly whereby the market is segmented so that different prices are charged to different customers.

price leadership – a feature of oligopoly whereby one firm sets or varies the market price and other firms follow.

privatisation – the sale of publicly owned businesses to the private sector.

production function – this shows the maximum possible output from a given set of inputs.

productive efficiency – this occurs when a firm is producing at the lowest point of its average cost curve.

profit – the difference between total revenue and total costs.

profit maximisation – the normal objective of firms that is achieved where marginal cost is equal to marginal revenue.

progressive taxation – one where the rate rises more than proportionately with the rise in income.

regressive taxation – one where the ratio of taxation to income falls as income increases.

sales maximisation – an objective of firms whereby the aim is to maximise the volume of sales.

sales revenue maximisation – an objective of firms that involves maximising total revenue.

satisficing profits – a behavioural objective of firms that aims to achieve a level of profits acceptable to owners or shareholders.

saving – the difference between income and consumption.

seasonal unemployment – that which only occurs at certain times of year.

short run – the time period when a firm is unable to alter all except one factor input.

speculative motive – a reason for holding money with a view to making future gains.

structural unemployment – that caused as a result of the changing structure of economic activity.

substitution effect – that part of a change in quantity demanded arising from a price change that is attributed to the change in relative prices.

supernormal profit – same as abnormal profit.

supply-side policies – any policy that affects the total output of an economy.

sustainable development – the extent to which the interests of future generations are being safeguarded without compromising the well-being of the present generation.

technical economies of scale – the benefits of falling long run average costs that arise out of the increased efficiency of applying technology in a firm.

technological unemployment – that caused by the increased use of technological equipment to replace labour.

total currency flow – the total flow of liquid monetary assets in the economy.

total product – the total output of a firm.

trade union – an organisation that represents labour in the collective bargaining process.

transactions motive – the reason why there is a demand for money for the day-to-day buying of goods and services.

transfer earnings – the amount that is earned by a factor of production in its best alternative use.

utility – the satisfaction received from consumption.

variable costs – those directly related to the level of output.

vertical integration – where a firm combines two or more stages of production that are normally carried out by separate firms.

voluntary unemployment – that where workers agree to be made redundant.

wage differentials – variations in the wages paid within and between occupations.

withdrawals – leakages from the circular flow of income.

Index

Acknowledgements

The author and publishers are grateful for the permissions granted to reproduce materials in either the original or adapted form. While every effort has been made, it has not always been possible to identify the sources of all the materials used, or to trace all copyright holders. If any omissions are brought to our notice, we will be happy to include the appropriate acknowledgements on reprinting.

pp 3, 143, 253, © The Economist Newspaper Limited, London (2009, 1997, 2001); p 20 Copyright Guardian News & Media Ltd, 1997; p 24 The Caribbean Times, 2006; p 80 adapted from VOA News; p 141 Business Daily News Desk, Nairobi, 2009; p 151 © International Railway Journal; p 163 Letters used by permission of Robert Gibber, Tate & Lyle and Helen Bletcher; pp 167, 184 © The Times, July 2008, August 2009/NI Syndication; p 172 map © Maplecroft 2010; pp 194, 219 The Financial Times, 2000; p 203 © The Economic Observer

Examinations questions throughout are reproduced by permission of the University of Cambridge Local Examinations Syndicate:
page 9, Q2: adapted from 9708/02, May/June 2008, question 1 (a–i);
page 68, Q1: 9708/02, Oct/Nov 2007, question 2;
page 119, Q1: 9708/04, Oct/Nov 2008, question 3;
page 119, Q2: 9708/04, May/June 2009, question 4;
page 138, Q1: 9708/02, Oct/Nov 2007, question 3;
page 138, Q2: 9708/02, Oct/Nov 2008, question 3;
page 158, Q1: 9708/04, May/June 2008, question 4;
page 177: 9708/02, Oct/Nov 2008, question 4;
page 220, Q1: 9708/04, Oct/Nov 2007, question 4;
page 220, Q2: 9708/04, May/June 2008, question 6;
page 242: 9708/02, Oct/Nov 2006, question 4;
page 265, Q1: 9708/04, Oct/Nov 2007, question 5;
page 265, Q2: 9708/04, May/June 2008, question 5;
page 271: 9708/02, May/June 2008, question 4;
page 289, Q1: 9708/04, Oct/Nov 2007, question 7;
page 289, Q2: 9708/04, Oct/Nov 2008, question 6;
page 295: 9708/02, Oct/Nov 2008, question 3.

Questions from OCR Advanced Level GCE Economics, F581, June 2009 used by permission of OCR

Cover image: Johnny Stockshooter/Alamy

The publishers are grateful to the following for permission to reproduce copyright photographs and material:

p.16 Darren Marshall/Alamy; p.20 Ron Yeu/Alamy; p.24 Eye Ubiquitous/Rex Features; p.26 imagebroker/Alamy; p.27 Nevade Weir/Corbis; p.28 AFP/Getty Images; p.30 scuba bartek/istockphoto; p.33 Bishop Asare/Corbis; p.39 Ricardo Azoury/istockphoto; pp.43, 52 Courtesy of Dell Inc; p.46 Keith Bedford/Corbis; p.47 J B Reed/Bloomberg/Getty Images; p.53 Crispin Hughes/Panos; p.56 Rex Features; p.58 Ryan Pyle/Corbis; p.62 Greg Baker/AP/PA Photos; p.65 Cristiano Burmester/Alamy; p.67 Ed Wray/AP/PA Photos; p.71 Rob Wilkinson/Alamy; p.74 Ron Giling/Specialist Stock/Still Pictures; p.76 Aflo Foto/Alamy; p.80 67photo/ Alamy; p.82 AFP/Getty Images; p.90 AFP/Getty Images; p.92 Paul C Pet/Corbis; p.95 Naiyyer/Shutterstock; p.96 AMR Nabil/AP/PA Photos; p101 Take Stock Photography/ Shutterstock; p.104 AFP/Getty Images; p.105 Li Wa/ Shutterstock; p.107 Mark Henley/Photolibrary; p.109 Blue Eyes Photography Ltd/Alamy; p.116 Adam Berry/LANDOV/ PA Photos; p.118 Charles Polidano/Touch The Skies/Alamy; p.125 Natalie Behring/Panos; p.124 Tata Motors; p.127 Image State Media Partners Ltd/Impact Photos/Alamy; p.129 Crossrail; p131 Mark Boulton/Alamy; p.134 Mike Finn-Kelcey/Corbis; p.141 Keith Erskine/Photolibrary; p.144 Jochen Tack/Alamy; p.146 Natalie Fobes/Corbis; p.148 AFP/Getty Images; p.152 Robert Harding Picture Library/Alamy; p.154 Eva-Lotta Jansson/Water Aid; p.163 Associated British Foods/PR Shots; p.167 Jeremy Horner/ Corbis; p.177 Peter Frischmuth/argus/Specialist Stock/ Still Pictures; p.181 Warwick Page/Panos; p.183 Shehzad Noorandi/Majority World/Specialist Stock/Still Pictures; p.184 Doug Pearson/Photolibrary; p193 Azure Republic Photography/Alamy; p.195 Ron Giling/Lineair/Specialist Stock/Still Pictures; p.204 East Images/Shutterstock; p.205(l) Topham Picturepoint/Topfoto; p.205(r) Brooks Kraft/Corbis; p.208 JTB Photo/Photolibrary; p.213 Peter Adams Photography/Alamy; p.219 Katsumi Kasahara/AP/PA Photos; p225 Tom Taylor/Alamy; p.234 AFP/Getty Images; p.245 Seokyong Lee/Bloomberg/Getty Images; p.249 Bob Krist/Corbis; p.250 John Cole/Science Photo Library; p.253 Luis Castaneda Inc/Getty Images; p.259 AFP/Getty Images; p.267 PixAchi/Shutterstock; p.272 imagebroker/Alamy; p277 Jitendra Prakash/Corbis; p.283 Aurora Photos/Alamy; p.285 Scott Olson/Getty Images; p.286 MARK/Corbis.

314